Introduction to infant development

Oxford: Oxford
University Press, 2002

8506465

Introduction to
Infant development

EDITED BY

Alan Slater
University of Exeter

Michael Lewis
University of Medicine and Dentistry of New Jersey

OXFORD
UNIVERSITY PRESS

OXFORD
UNIVERSITY PRESS

Great Clarendon Street, Oxford OX2 6DP

Oxford University Press is a department of the University of Oxford.
It furthers the University's objective of excellence in research, scholarship,
and education by publishing worldwide in

Oxford New York

Auckland Bangkok Bogotá Beunos Aires Cape Town Chennai
Dar es Salaam Delhi Hong Kong Istanbul Karachi Kolkata
Kuala Lumpur Madrid Melbourne Mexico City Mumbai Nairobi
São Paulo Shanghai Singapore Taipei Tokyo Toronto

with associated companies in Berlin Ibadan

Oxford is a registered trade mark of Oxford University Press
in the UK and in certain other countries

Published in the United States
by Oxford University Press Inc., New York

A catalogue record for this book is available from the British Library

Library of Congress Cataloging in Publication Data
(Data applied for)

ISBN 0 19 850646 5

Typeset by SNP Best-set Typesetter Ltd., Hong Kong
by RefineCatch Limited, Bungay, Suffolk
Printed in Great Britain
on acid-free paper by
Biddles Ltd., Guildford, Surrey

To Theresa, Adam and Sam, for inspiration and memories (AS)
To Suzanne, whose intelligence and support makes all things possible (ML)

Preface

Infancy is the time of life during which enormous changes take place—the helpless newborn seems almost a different creature from the active, inquisitive 2 year old. Although accounts of infant development date back many centuries, the scientific study of infancy really began in the 1960s when ways of investigating early development were found, and it is true to say that the study of infant development is a truly modern science.

Our aim in producing this textbook is to offer a representative, comprehensive, and completely up to date, 'state-of-the-art' account of infant development. We appreciated that this needed to be an edited book rather than one written by the two editors, as one can be an expert in a couple of fields of study, but not all! By making it an edited book that fulfilled our aims of a comprehensive textbook we first decided the areas that needed covering, specified in some detail the topics for each chapter, and then invited the world's leading experts to write the chapters. Our invitations were received with enthusiasm, and we have been extremely gratified at the ways in which our authors have responded to our suggestions. The danger of uneven writing levels, and lack of integration of the chapters was dealt with in two ways. First, we gave clear and extensive instructions to our authors as to content and level, and of course carefully edited the chapters. Second, we had a science writer, Ian Hocking, go through each chapter carefully to ensure that the book reads well and coherently as a whole.

The book is organized into five parts, each concerned with different aspects of development and each containing two or more chapters. Here are brief comments on each part.

Part 1: History and methods. In order to see how our current knowledge of infancy has developed the student needs to be aware of the history of infancy research, and of the several methods that have been developed since the 1960s to explore development in preverbal infants. These are described in Chapters 1 and 2.

Part 2: The foundations of development. The development of the infant has a starting point, and in Chapter 3 we have an account of the biological and psychological development from conception to birth. In order to act upon, learn about, and communicate with the world the infant has to have functioning motor (action) and sensory systems. We know that many important motor and sensory developments take place in the womb, and Chapters 4 and 5 continue the story of their development after birth.

Part 3: Cognitive development. Cognition refers to our ability to reason and to make sense of the world, and the study of cognitive development is a major area of research. In Chapter 6 we have an overview of major theories of infant cognitive development, followed in Chapter 7 by an account of infants' ability to categorize objects and people—without the ability to categorize the world would be an impossibly complex place. In Chapter 8 infants' growing understanding of objects and space is discussed, and Chapter 9 describes the beginnings of language development. What has become clear is that an understanding of speech begins in the womb, and by the time infants produce their first word, about a year from birth, they have a detailed understanding of speech sounds and words—the young infant may be preverbal, but he/she is definitely not prelingual!

We end this section on a sad and tragic note. Peter Jusczyk, whose contribution to our understanding of speech perception in infancy has been unequalled, passed away on 23 August 2001.

Part 4: Social and emotional development. The infant is born to develop into a social creature engaging in social interactions and communications with others. One of the most important social stimuli for infants (and adults!) is the human face, and Chapter 10 gives an account of how infants perceive faces. If we observe newborn infants we see a rather narrow range of emotional behaviour—they display pleasure, distress, and interest. By 3 years of age these same children display a wide range of emotions. Development take place within the social network that surrounds the infants, and the story of social and emotional development is discussed in Chapters 11 and 12. All humans and even non-human primates play. Chapter 13 describes the changing nature and purpose of play throughout infancy.

A major theme throughout Part 4 is that social development can only be understood in relation to developments in children's verbal and cognitive abilities. This theme is emphasized in Chapter 14: young infants communicate by acts such as crying, but the cry of the newborn is certainly not an *intentional* communication; by the end of the first year the infant is able to communicate intentions through symbolic gestures and words, and can read the intentions of others through their social signals.

Part 5: Early interventions and social policy implications. Not all infants are born into an ideal world, able to fulfil their potentials. This sad fact alerts us to many social concerns—how can we (parents, communities, and governments) improve the life course of children in adverse circumstances or at risk for developmental delay? These important issues are discussed in Chapters 15 and 16. These chapters are written from an American perspective, as it is in the United States that we have the most detailed and comprehensive research on these topics, but the findings and implications are applicable to any community and country that has disadvantaged infants and children.

The text is designed for a broad range of readers, and in particular those with little previous exposure to psychology. The comprehensive coverage and emphasis on core topics on infant development make it an appropriate text for introductory students. We owe enormous thanks to our authors, and to Oxford University Press who have encouraged us from the start, and have been patient with the delays. We extend our grateful thanks to Tracey Sharp, who was the transatlantic messenger between the editors and collated the chapters, as well as Ruth Gitlen, whose unfailing editorial eye helps keep us honest. The order of editors was determined by random means.

September 2001   A.S. and M.L.

Contents

Part 3   Cognitive development

Part 4   Social and emotional development

Contributors

Bendersky, Margaret
Institute for the Study of Child Development, University of Medicine and
  Dentistry of New Jersey, Robert Wood Johnson Medical School, USA

Bornstein, Marc H.
Child and Family Research, National Institute of Child Health and Human
  Development, Suite 8030, 6705 Rockledge Drive, Bethesda MD 20892-
  7971, USA

Bower, Tom G. R.
School of Human Development, University of Texas at Dallas

Brady, Anne E.
Eliot-Pearson Department of Child Development, Tufts University, Medford,
  MA, USA

Cotton, Janice N.
Civitan International Research Center, University of Alabama at
  Birmingham, USA

Fernald, Anne
Department of Psychology, Stanford University, USA

Field, Tiffany
Touch Research Institutes, University of Miami, Florida, USA

Goldfield, Eugene C.
Children's Hospital, Department of Psychiatry, Boston, MA, USA

Hepper Peter G.
Wellcome Trust Fetal Behaviour Research Centre, School of Psychology,
  Queen's University of Belfast, Belfast, BT7 1NN, UK

Hernandez Reif, Maria
Touch Research Institutes, University of Miami, Florida, USA

Jacobs, Francine H.
Eliot-Pearson Department of Child Development, Tufts University, Medford,
  MA, USA

Jaswal, Vikram K.
Department of Psychology, Stanford University, USA

Jusczyk, Peter W.
Johns Hopkins University, Baltimore, USA

Katz, Jill C.
Bank Street College, New York, USA

Landesman Ramey, Sharon
Civitan International Research Center, University of Alabama at
    Birmingham, USA

Langlois, Judith H.
Department of Psychology, The University of Texas at Austin, Texas, USA

Lerner, Richard M.
Eliot-Pearson Department of Child Development, Tufts University, Medford,
    MA, USA

Lewis, Michael
Institute for the Study of Child Development, University of Medicine and
    Dentistry of New Jersey, Robert Wood Johnson Medical School, USA

Quinn, Paul C.
Department of Psychology, Washington & Jefferson College, USA

Ramey, Craig T.
Civitan International Research Center, University of Alabama at
    Birmingham, USA

Ramsey, Jennifer L.
Department of Psychology, The University of Texas at Austin, Texas, USA

Slater, Alan
School of Psychology, University of Exeter, Devon, UK

Sternberg, Robert J.
Department of Psychology, Yale University, USA

Sullivan, Margaret W.
Institute for the Study of Child Development, University of Medicine and
    Dentistry of New Jersey, Robert Wood Johnson Medical School, USA

Tamis-LeMonda, Catherine S.
New York University, 239 Greene St., 5th floor, New York, New York
    10003, USA

Wolff, Peter H.
Children's Hospital, Department of Psychiatry, Boston, MA, USA

Part 1

History and methods

1

A brief history of infancy research

MICHAEL LEWIS and ALAN SLATER

Our earliest memories

There are two interesting and apparently simple questions to which everyone will have an answer. The questions are 'What is the earliest thing you are sure you can remember?' and 'How old were you?' If you ask a group of people these questions, perhaps a class of students, you find that the age of the earliest memory is about 3 years 4 months, and that there are some interesting trends—the age of earliest memory increases over birth order (first borns have the earliest memories), females have earlier ones than males, and, curiously, it is earlier for Caucasian than Asian children (Mullen, 1994).

Here is one of the earliest memories recounted by the great infant and child psychologist, Jean Piaget:

. . . one of my earliest memories would date . . . from my second year. I can still see, most clearly, the following scene. I was sitting in my pram (stroller), which my nurse was pushing in the Champs Elyséc, when a man tried to kidnap me. I was held in by the strap fastened round me while my nurse bravely tried to stand between me and the thief. She received various scratches, and I can still see them vaguely on her face. Then a crowd gathered, a policeman with a short cloak and a white baton came up and the man took to his heels. I can still see the whole scene, and can even place it near the tube station (cited in Sants & Barnes, 1985).

Notice the vividness and clarity of this dramatic incident. The remarkable thing about it is that it never happened! Piaget believed this until he was about 15 at which time the truth was told to him—his nurse had simply made up the story, for which she received a reward (a watch) and the gratitude of his parents—and much later she confessed! It turns out that many early (and later) memories bear only a slight resemblance to the truth—memory plays tricks and often what we *think* we remember is actually an inaccurate recollection of something which (as in Piaget's case) may never have happened.

These considerations tell us two things. One is that it is pointless to study infant development by asking adults and children to think back to their infancy, because we can't remember it! The other is that when people do give accounts of early memories we can't trust them as they may not be a true record of what happened. Neither can we trust parents' reports of their infant's development. For example, mothers will give very unreliable accounts of developments which, at the time, were of great importance—'When did your baby first take solid foods?'—'When did he/she first start to walk?'

Baby diaries

From what has been said so far it is clear that in order to begin to study infant development we cannot rely on memory, whether this is our own early memories, or others' memories of their infant's development. The first scientific attempts to record infant development are known as *baby diaries* (or sometimes *baby biographies*) in which those who are close to the infant (mother, father, or guardian) make detailed written observations of aspects of the child's development from birth to 2 or 3 years of age.

These diaries are notable for at least two main reasons: (1) they give us an insight into child rearing practices and theories at different ages, and (2) they give insights into important aspects of infant development. Here we will give accounts taken from four baby diaries to illustrate these themes.

The seventeenth century—King Louis XIII of France

In 1601 Louis the dauphin (the oldest son of the king of France) was born to King Henri IV of France, and his physician, Dr Jean Héroard began a lengthy journal, which continued until Héroard's death in 1628. Louis became King Louis XIII in 1609 and died in 1643. During infancy Héroard recorded Louis' play with peers, temper tantrums, nightmares, the beginnings of language development, and discipline. Louis was not weaned until he was 2 (being breastfed by wetnurses) and for the first 9 months he was swaddled—that is, his body was tightly wrapped—in the belief that this would make his limbs strong. Henri IV wrote to Louis' governess insisting that he be whipped regularly:

I command you to whip him every time that he is willful or naughty, knowing by my own experience that nothing else did me so much good. (Wallace *et al.*, 1994, p. 4).

Fortunately, Louis managed to make it to 2 years old before he received his first whipping, and presumably the 9-year-old King was able to tell them to stop! It is worth noting that Dr Héroard was against this practice and recommended that we teach children 'rather by the way of gentleness and patience than by harshness'.

In these short extracts we have an example of child rearing practices (early swaddling) and of 'folk theories' of development—kindness or harshness. We will comment on the first of these in the next few extracts, and on the second a little later.

The eighteenth century—Dietrich Tiedemann

The German philosopher Dietrich Tiedemann kept a diary of his son's development following his birth in 1781. While this record is detailed, and it is often referred to as the first *scientific* diary, we will focus only on one set of observations. Like the future Louis X111 180 years earlier, this child was swaddled in order to prevent free movement of the limbs, and Tiedemann recorded of his 19-day-old son that:

If now for short periods his hands were released from their swathings, he beat and scratched himself painfully . . . (Wallace *et al.*, 1994, p. 5).

Fortunately for the infant a fairly short period without being swaddled reduced the number of such 'self-beatings'. The practice of swaddling infants, which has been around for thousands of years, was intended to strengthen the limbs by preventing too much wasteful and uncoordinated movement, but as we have seen, when released from their wrappings infants are liable to harm themselves unintentionally. Why might this be the case? One clue came from a study by Melzack and Scott (1957). They reared puppies in an environment intended to remove any unpleasant experiences—there were no hard edges, no steps and if they fell over they experienced no harm. A very interesting effect was observed when the puppies were exposed to a noxious stimulus in the form of a lighted candle. What happened then was that the puppies, who were naturally curious, put their noses in the flame, yelped, and gave other signs of distress, *but they didn't take their noses out of the flame!*

As we now understand it, what was happening was this. The puppies, just like the infants Louis and Tiedemann's son, have learned that their movements—in the infants' case muscle movements of the arms—have no negative consequences, and the longer your environment tells you this, the more ingrained the learning. When you then find out that your own movements *can* lead to painful consequences, it takes a while to unlearn old habits. We know that this is a general principle throughout development. For example, when infants first begin to crawl, about 9 months of age, they have a tendency to fall down stairs and get into dangerous situations, simply because they don't know the possible consequences of their actions (Campos *et al.*, 2000).

The nineteenth century—Charles Darwin

Charles Darwin (1809–82) is widely regarded as the greatest naturalist of the nineteenth century, and his powers of observation were sharpened by his 5 years (from December 1831 to October 1836) round the world voyage on the *HMS Beagle*. Not long after his return he married his cousin Emma (on 29

January 1839), and their first child, William Erasmus Darwin (nicknamed Doddy) was born on 27 December 1839. Shortly afterwards Darwin began a diary record to detail his son's early development, but this account was not published until 1877, by which time he and Emma had had another nine children, five boys and four girls: thus Darwin was able to compare his eldest child with his others. We will give three extracts from this account in order to illustrate some of the strengths and weaknesses of such biographies:

Seeing With respect to vision,—his eyes were fixed on a candle as early as the 9th day, and up to the 45th day nothing else seemed thus to fix them; but on the 49th day his attention was attracted by a brightly coloured tassel . . .

Hearing Although so sensitive to sound in a general way, he was not able even when 124 days old easily to recognize whence a sound proceeded, so as to direct his eyes to the source

Moral sense (When 2 years and 7½ months) I met him coming out of the dining room with his eyes unnaturally bright, and an odd unnatural or affected manner, so that I went into the room to see who was there, and found that he had been taking pounded sugar, which he had been told not to do. As he had never been in any way punished, his odd manner certainly was not due to fear and I suppose it was pleasurable excitement struggling with conscience. . . . *As this child was educated solely by working on his good feelings, he soon became as truthful, open, and tender, as anyone could desire.* (italics added)

Despite the fact that Darwin was one of the finest observers of natural behaviour who has ever lived, we now know that his account of the development of vision and hearing is wrong. As is described in Chapter 5 we know from careful experimentation that, although vision at birth is poor it is sufficient for the infant to begin learning about the visual world: for instance, within hours from birth infants show some preference to look at their mother's face when hers is shown paired with that of a female stranger. We also know that newborn infants can localize sounds at birth, an ability that Darwin was unable to detect in his son, even at 124 days (4 months).

Darwin assumed that children brought up in the absence of physical punishment will display less antisocial behaviour in later life. We can compare this view with those of King Henri IV and Dr Jean Héroard, mentioned earlier. Henri IV, in demanding that his son Louis be whipped regularly, was expressing the belief embodied in the expression 'Spare the rod and spoil the child'—the belief that the failure to use harsh physical punishment carries with it the possibility, if not the certainty, that the child will grow up to be disobedient, and his/her very soul may be at risk. This belief has been prevalent in views of child rearing. Here is part of a letter from Susanna Wesley (a woman of strong religious beliefs) to her son John Wesley (the founder of the religious movement known as Methodism) about how to rear children, written in 1872:

Let him have nothing he cries for; absolutely nothing, great or small; else you undo your own work . . . make him do as he is bid, if you whip him ten times running to effect it. Let none persuade you it is cruelty to do this; it is cruelty not to do it. Break his will now, and his soul will live, and he will probably bless you to all eternity (cited in Sants & Barnes, 1985, p. 24).

Charles Darwin and Jean Héroard were of the opposite persuasion, perhaps captured in the expression 'like begets like'—that children should be reared with gentleness and patience and the absence of physical punishment. It turns out (from the findings from many years of research) that Darwin and Héroard were right: that is, the use of punishment is not a good way of changing behaviour, and children disciplined with the use of physical punishment are more likely to misbehave and become aggressive. Here is an extract from the famous poem 'If a child lives' by Dorothy Lawe Holt, which expresses this view—the complete poem can be found at http://www.oswego.org/staff/sbernreu/PoemChildLives.html

> If a child lives with criticism she learns to condemn
> If a child lives with hostility he learns to fight
> > BUT
> If a child lives with approval she learns to like herself
> If a child lives with acceptance and friendship he learns to find love in the world

The twentieth century—Jean Piaget

We have already referred to Piaget and an account of his views on infant development is given in Chapter 6. Piaget (1896–1980) was born in the town of Neuchâtel and his first publication—an account of an albino sparrow—appeared when he was aged 11. This short paper marked the beginnings of a brilliant scientific career, during which he published over sixty books and several hundred articles, most of them on child development.

He began his exploration of infant development by making very detailed records of the development of his own three children, Jacqueline, Lucienne, and Laurent. But Piaget was not content simply with observing his infants' development. He would note an interesting behaviour and then, in order to understand it better, he varied the task to note any changes in the infant's response. This technique, which is a combination of observation and loosely structured experimentation, is known as the *clinical method*. Here is a brief extract (Piaget, 1954, pp. 177–178) to illustrate the procedure—Piaget observed his son Laurent (aged 6 months 22 days) when reaching for objects:

Laurent tries to grasp a box of matches. When he is at the point of reaching it I place it on a book; he immediately withdraws his hand, then grasps the book itself. He remains puzzled until the box slides and thanks to this accident he dissociates it from its support.

Piaget's reasonable interpretation of this observation is that when one object is on top of, and hence touching, another object, his infant did not realize that there were two objects. In fact, it was not until he was 10 months old that Laurent

immediately grasps matchboxes, erasers, etc., placed on a notebook or my hand; he therefore readily dissociates the object from the support (p. 178).

Piaget's observations and experiments enabled him to develop a theoretical account of the development of reasoning and thinking that is still influential, and he was one of the first to begin systematic experimentation of infants' development.

Coming of age: towards the present day

In the last 50 years there have been enormous advances in our understanding of infant development. In the past, theories and speculations about infants had come from those who had strong views but no evidence, and from the many baby biographies that really began the systematic study of infant development. There are some drawbacks to baby biographies. For example, the biographers may have biases that lead them to note anecdotes supporting their own theories, so that their observations may be unsystematic and biased. However, there are many strengths of such accounts: (1) the biographer can give a detailed account of subtle changes in behaviour because of his/her intimate knowledge of the child, and (2) the observations can lead to the production of theories of child development, which can then be given a more systematic (often experimental) test.

The proper understanding of infants awaited the development of research methods that could reveal the nature of the perceptual, cognitive, and social abilities of creatures who, by definition, are unable to speak. Many of these research methods are described in detail in Chapter 2, so we will give just a few illustrations here, from investigators who told us that the worlds of infants could be explored and that it revealed a fascinating world of change and development.

The first studies: social development

The scientific interest in infancy can be traced from several important events that all occurred around the 1950s and 1960s. To begin with, the psychoanalytic tradition started by Sigmund Freud extended into research with children, even very young ones. Wolf's work with infants raised without their mothers in hospitals and orphanages gave rise to the ideas of 'hospitalism' and 'anaclitic depression,' both of which describe infant's depression brought about by the absence of their mothers (Wolf & Wolff, 1947). A bit later, John Bowlby, a British psychoanalyst, working for the World Health Organization, wrote a 1951 monograph, which continued the psychoanalytic tradition, now called object relation theory, and said that the mother was the most important person in the infant's life and that her absence constituted a significant loss for her infant. At the same time, there were any number of other scientists working with infants who believed that the effects of the loss of the mother were due to the general loss of all positive stimulation, and that if it was supplied by others, would not lead to failure to thrive (see Leon Yarrow's 1961 excellent review of this work). The argument continued in the 1960s with the classic, but now out of print work by Sally Provence and Rose Lipton (1962) on orphans in institutions and which concluded that the loss of the mother mainly affected infant's development because there were not enough consistent caregivers to satisfy the social and emotional needs of the infant.

This argument in regard to the social and emotional needs of the infant led to a series of volumes published under the editorship of another English psychologist, Brian Foss, who edited four excellent volumes on infants' social and emotional development. Among these reports is the work of the American Psychologist, Harry Harlow and his wife, Margaret, who published widely on non-human primates (1965). Harlow's work gave an important boost to the argument that biological forces dictated the importance of the mother (not father) in the infant's life. Harlow's work, as reviewed in Chapter 12, involved isolating infant macaques monkeys and letting them live alone, away from other infants and their mothers. Harlow found and reported on the same phenomenon that Wolf had observed in hospitalized infants, namely that when separated from their mothers, these monkeys failed to thrive. Indeed, when they were raised alone, they showed severe problems in their social and emotional development. They failed to mate properly when they were sexually mature and when they did give birth, these 'motherless mothers' were abusive and uncaring, often killing their infants. From this, Harlow argued that mothers are biologically important for their infant's development.

There were several problems with these studies, the most important of which was that the infants were not only raised without their mothers, they were raised in social isolation. Alone in a cage, they could not see other monkeys nor make physical contact with them. Were the results of Harlow's studies the result of not being with their mothers or, as has been claimed, being without proper stimulation? As it turns out for the most part, raising these infants with other infants without mothers at all takes care of the problem. Even Harlow thought that the peer system was equal to that of the mother (Harlow, 1969). As for the mothering of the motherless mothers, it also turns out that with the birth of each new infant, these mothers got better and better at raising their young. This suggests that these mothers, raised without mothers, could do the job if they got some experience.

In the study of infant social development, Michael Lewis, in Chapter 12, has argued that this controversy can be handled by considering the infant as being born into a social network and that the child's evolutionary task is to adapt to that larger network, which includes mothers, fathers, siblings, and peers. If there is only the mother present, then her absence is highly destructive to the infant's development, but if there are others present, then the infant has the ability to adapt (Lewis & Feiring, 1979).

As you can see, this argument anticipated the contemporary arguments on the risks of infant day care; a risk that an important US Government study has now shown to be misguided. The results are in and they show that if infants receive good infant care, they thrive as well as mother reared infants! (National Institute of Child Health and Human Development—NICHD—report, 1997).

This work of the 1950s and 1960s has relevance for our own times and represents, long before the work on perceptual and cognitive development, that the study of infants was well on its way.

The next studies: attentional and cognitive development

William James (often regarded as the father of modern psychology) in his book *Principles of Psychology* (1890) talked about two different kinds of attention, one passive and one active. In passive attention, the infant is drawn toward an object or sound because the stimulus pulls the child; for example, a loud noise automatically causes the child to hear the sound and to jump with startle. It was the other kind of attention, the active one, which was of more interest for him and has mostly occupied the work of others since his classical work.

Active attention involves the infant's interests and association and the child attends because of these associations. An infant will look longer at the face of his mother than a stranger because the mother is associated with the infant's care and the satisfaction of his or her needs. It is this type of attention that has been the chief concern of infant researchers, although as you can see in Chapter 5 by Alan Slater, Tiffany Field, and Maria Hernandez-Reif, infants' sensory capacities also have been studied by using attentional processes.

While Darwin, at the turn of the twentieth century, observed infants and while there were early studies of infants' social behaviour, the study of infants' perceptual and learning ability was not studied. This is also because of William James' belief that infants, and certainly newborns, could not see or hear and could not learn; in fact, he called the infant's world a 'blooming, buzzing confusion.'

This state of affairs lasted until the late 1950s, early 1960s when Robert Fantz (1958) conducted a series of studies using a very simple technique. He presented infants with two pictures—one, an all grey pattern and one, a striped pattern. Looking at the infant's face from a peek hole, he could see the reflection on the infant's pupil, and could tell which picture the infant was looking at. Fantz found that infants preferred to look at the more complex picture, whether it was on the left or right side. This told him that the infant could see *and* that she preferred to look at the more complex picture. These findings excited the research community and they quickly realized that the infant had many perceptual capacities: that they could see, hear, smell, and that they had preferences. It also indicated that many of these capacities were present at birth and did not have to be learned. That they were inborn and innate meant that part of Piaget's theory about the role of learning was wrong and needed to be revised.

Tom Bower (the author of Chapter 8) was one of the first to demonstrate that training and conditioning procedures could be used with young infants in order to explore their visual worlds. In an early experiment (1966) he trained (conditioned) infants to turn their heads whenever they saw a cube of a particular size—whenever they turned their heads when the cube was there a hidden experimenter suddenly appeared and 'peek-a-booed' at the infant (she smiled and nodded, tickled the baby's tummy, and then disappeared from view). Once the babies were conditioned they were shown either the same cube at a different distance, or a larger cube that was farther away. Would the babies recognize the same size cube despite the change of distance? It turned out that they did—they turned their heads when this cube was shown (expecting the reinforcing adult), but not when the different-sized cube was shown. This was an experiment into what is called *size constancy*—appreciating that an object is the same size despite changes to its distance from the infant. Size constancy has even been shown in newborn infants (see Chapter 5) and variations on this conditioning procedure are much used in exploring infant development.

At about the same time Fantz was publishing his studies, researchers were studying other attentional processes. Lewis *et al.* (1963) and Kagan and Lewis (1965) were exploring attentional processes, investigating whether the child was looking at visual information, and studying their physiological responses. Changes in heart rate—how many heart beats per minute—was shown to be related to looking. Infants who looked intently at a picture slowed their heart rates. From these studies of looking patterns and physiological responses researchers were now able to study infant ability (Lewis *et al.*, 1966a,b). The use of heart rate also allowed for the study of the infant's auditory processing, as infants do not reliably turn their heads while listening.

The Russian, Sokolov (1963), a student of Pavlov's work, was interested in one particular aspect of attention. He wanted to know what would happen if you looked at the same picture over and over again and what would happen if you changed the picture. He found that for adults, seeing the same picture led to increasing boredom and, therefore, a decrease in looking at the picture.

However, when the picture was changed, adults renewed their interest and again looked a lot. This procedure was used by Lewis *et al.* (1969), and led to a published monograph about infant attention. He found, as had Fantz (1964), that as infants got older, they showed faster loss of interest (habituate faster) than younger infants. He also showed that infants who were born with birth difficulties showed slower habituation than normal infants and finally, and most interestingly, he found that the speed of habituation in infancy was related to their later IQ as pre-school children. This last was particularly important as infant IQ tests were not very good at predicting subsequent IQ. These findings and more, using different techniques and measures, were explored by a large number of early infant researchers, including Robert McCall, Leslie Cohen, and Jeffrey Fagan. Of even more interest was that the understanding that rate of habituation and recovery could be used as measures of other infant abilities allowed such researchers as Tom Bower to study important cognitive capacities.

The last studies: emotional development

The emotional development of infants was the last area of infant studies to receive much attention. By 1983 when Lewis and Michalson published the first volume on emotional development, they reported between 1933 and 1979 that on average only 7% of the pages of the leading textbooks were devoted to emotional development. Since the mid-1980s, the research on emotional development has blossomed, although there were earlier works that led the field (Lewis & Rosenblum, 1974, *The origins of fear*, for example). In 1979, the Social Science Research Council of the United States started a discussion group called SAD, which stood for Social Affective Development, the result of which was published in a book on the measurement of emotion (Izard, 1982).

In fact, it was the ability to measure emotion that led to its burgeoning development. Charles Darwin is often considered to be the leader of the study of emotions, since in 1872 he published a book called *The expression of emotions in man and animals*. In it, he described emotions as sets of action patterns that had significance because these behaviours were adaptive. For example, anger was an action pattern of facial and bodily behaviours designed to overcome an obstacle to a desired goal. Darwin also described two classes of emotions, those that emerged early, which were for him the primary emotions and those that required the development of cognitions, which he called the self-conscious emotions. His descriptions of the action patterns was further developed by Sylvia Tomkins (1962, 1963), in a set of books that led directly to elaborate measurement systems developed by Paul Ekman (Ekman & Friesen, 1978), and Cal Izard (1983). These measurement systems, utilizing the movements of the facial muscles, notably those around the eyes and mouth, gave researchers a way to measure reliably such emotions as fear, anger, sadness, joy, and disgust (see Lewis, Chapter 11). Having a measurement system that everyone would agree on led to the growth of the research on emotions, allowing the direct measurement of their expressions rather than relying on self-report, a procedure impossible in infants!

Children's emotions and moods (Lewis & Michalson, 1983) was the first to articulate a theory about emotional development. In it, the two classes of emotion that Darwin discussed, the primary emotions and the self-conscious emotions, were linked in a developmental model, which showed for the first time, the interface between the emotions and their development, and their dependency upon the growth of cognitive skills, most notably the development of the self as a cognitive representation. This research was an outgrowth of earlier research that Lewis conducted, which was on the development of consciousness. Borrowing the idea of self-recognition in minors from Gordon Gallup's (1977) work with chimpanzees, Lewis and his colleagues developed techniques for measuring self-recognition which they argued was really a measure of consciousness or the idea that 'that's *me*, in the mirror.' By applying rouge to the infant's nose and standing (or sitting) them in front of the mirror, they found that somewhere between 15 and 24 months, infants can recognize themselves by touching their noses, not the mirror image (Lewis & Brooks-Gunn, 1979). This ability, along with the growth of personal pronouns, such as 'me' or 'mine' and the onset of pretend play, represent the origins of consciousness.

It was the onset of consciousness that allowed for the development of the self-conscious emotions, notably embarrassment, pride, shame, and guilt, most of these emerging by 3 years of age. Thus, the work of Darwin and his observation of his son's own development of moral sense at the age of 3, was confirmed 100 years later by using the research teachings developed during this time period. Chapter 11 on emotional development describes this development in some detail.

Key issues in infancy research

A number of key issues have dominated research into infant development and you will encounter these as you read the chapters of the book. Here we describe three related issues: the nature–nurture debate; stability versus change; are infants active or passive in their development?

The nature–nurture debate

We are all a product of the interaction of two broad factors: *nature* (our inheritance or genetic factors), and *nurture* (environmental influences or our upbringing). It is important to note that without both factors no development could occur! For example, it has been argued that humans are genetically predisposed to acquire language, but which language we acquire is determined by the language(s) we hear and learn (Chapter 9). We will see many examples of the nature–nurture issue in this book: Do infants have to learn to see (Chapter 5)? Is motor development caused by maturation (a term that means development, which reflects genetic influences and not environmental ones) or is it influenced by the environment (Chapter 4)? Are infants born with an innate knowledge of the human face (Chapter 10)? The nature–nurture issue arises in all aspects of development, even the development of the fetus (Chapter 3).

Stability versus change

Infancy can be characterized by its rapid change—the 2 year old is so very different from the newborn baby in almost every characteristic. Change is an important part of development. Piaget argued for an orderly sequence of change; all infants go through the same sequence of stages. In some sense then, human infants develop in the same manner.

The question of stability and change is one of the most discussed topics in development. The question has to do with whether differences between infants remain the same—are stable—or do differences between infants change. Is the infant who first sits up the same infant who first walks? Does the infant who shows more fear of strangers at 8 months remain the same infant who is fearful of new situations when she is 2 years old?

This question continues to be asked, as it has important social policy issues. For example, some believe that what an infant is like in the first 2 or 3 years will tell us what she/he will be like when they are an adult. Because they believe in stability, they feel that the more they do for the infant, the better will be the adult. Social policy is designed to make the first years the best as possible and so the most money should be spent early, as later it is too late. Such a view fits well with the psychoanalytic view except Freud argued that the first 6 years were important, while John Bowlby (1969) and Mary Ainsworth and colleagues (1978) have argued that it is the first year where the infant forms its attachment to the mother that is the most important. Their concept is what Lewis (1997) in his book, *Altering fate: Why the past does not predict the future*, calls the inoculation theory. When you inoculate the baby against diseases, it is forever safe from them. So, too, it is with the early relationship with the mother. A good mother–infant relationship or attachment forever protects the infant. On the other hand, psychoanalysis also believed that people could change; that is, the purpose of therapy was to allow us to separate out the early bad experiences from the future.

The view of change, rather than stability, is an optimistic one for if infants have a bad childhood, they are not doomed, but can change. The research that follows children over long periods of time is called *longitudinal research*.

Most of the longitudinal studies that have been done show only a little stability over age. In fact, as the distance between ages increases, the stability decreases. The idea of stability rests on the notion that forms and functions, once developed, cannot be easily changed by the environment in which the child lives. The idea of change rests on the notion that environments have profound effects on children and that if the environment changes, so, too, does the child. An environment approach is often contrasted with the more biological view, as it is often assumed that if it is biological, it is fixed. The most recent brain research, however, now sees the brain as continuously changed with the creation of new cells. Gerry Edelman, a Nobel laureate, has argued for something he calls 'Neural Darwinism,' which meant for him that neurons are connected, grown, and are maintained as a function of the kind of intellectual activities the infant is engaged in. Increasingly, then, the idea of change as a function of the environment rather than stability seems to characterize best many of the infant's capacities.

Is the infant passive or active in development?

What has become clear is that the infant and the child are active in shaping their own development. That is, they are not simply dependent on others and moulded in any direction that parents and environmental influences dictate, but actively involved in learning and making sense of their worlds. Their development of consciousness, this idea of me, facilitates this growth and change. Perhaps, this is nowhere better illustrated than in the examples of the terrible two's—the time where infancy ends. Up until the age of 2, infants generally do what their caregivers tell them to do. However, somewhere around 2, infants start to say 'no' to their mothers. This negativism is a pain for their parents who don't understand why this is happening. We know, however, that the infant has now started to develop a sense of itself; he/she is no longer just part of the mother or father, but is now a separate self with his/her own needs and wants. What appears to be a problem turns out to be an important marker in the infant's development.

Overview

A comprehensive picture of infant development is emerging as researchers use a variety of observational and experimental procedures to explore different aspects of development. The systematic study of infant development began with the early baby biographies or diaries, and the experimental study of development really began with Piaget's observations and experiments. In the last half of the twentieth century more and more techniques have been developed to help us understand how infants sense, feel, and know, and it is these to which we turn next.

2 Basic methods in infant research

MARGARET BENDERSKY[1] and MARGARET W. SULLIVAN

How do researchers figure out what non-verbal infants know and feel?

In just 3 years, infants change from totally dependent creatures to active children who understand much about their immediate social and physical world. Developmental science seeks to understand what infants know and feel, when and how they develop these capacities, and the processes of change. Because infants cannot tell us what they know and feel directly, researchers must devise ways to discover these answers. As you will know from Chapter 1, although infant research goes back several centuries, many of the techniques used to study infants were developed in the last half of the twentieth century. The tremendous increase in the amount and breadth of infant research occurring during this period was made possible, in part, by improvements in technology. Better recording equipment, electronic control and automation of stimulation, more accurate, automated measurement, and of course, the computer revolution, put new and more sophisticated tools into the hands of scientists. They have developed them into a wide range of innovative techniques for answering questions about how and why infants behave the way they do. This chapter surveys some of these methods and describes how they have been applied to questions about infant behaviour.

Even if you have limited experience with infants, you probably have many questions about how infants change from helpless, naive creatures to 'real' people. They are likely to be some of the same ones that researchers have asked over the years. Questions such as:

- Do very young infants see and hear the things we do?
- Can you tell how smart an infant is?
- What do infants learn and remember?
- How do infants learn to interact with others?
- How do infants react to stressful events?

---

[1] The authors are listed alphabetically. Each contributed equally to this chapter

- How do infants express emotion?
- Are infants born with different personalities?
- When and how do infants develop a sense of themselves as individuals?

Each of these and many related questions have been posed by those interested in understanding how infants develop. The answers to these questions are not at all simple or obvious. As you will see from the chapters in this book, many continue to generate active research and sometimes controversial findings.

The methods of study that researchers choose will depend, in part, on the particular question of interest. Researchers may choose to observe the everyday, spontaneous behaviour of infants, interfering as little as possible with the setting and participants. This form of observation, which is found in the baby diaries described in Chapter 1, is called **naturalistic observation** and is analogous to observations of animals in the wild made by ethologists. Researchers may choose to measure the progress infants are making toward attaining specific milestones. They then may compare an infant's progress to the average age when developmental milestones are reached based on large representative samples of infants using **standardized developmental tests**, questionnaires, or scales developed for this purpose. Or, they may use **experimental designs** developed to observe infant behaviours under controlled conditions that the researcher manipulates. There are two basic forms of experimental methods. In one, researchers randomly assign infants to conditions that differ from each other in one critical way. The research question is answered by comparing infants in these conditions, known as **experimental and control conditions**. For example, to study how a mother's presence affects her infant's response to strangers, infants are randomly assigned either to have their mothers present (experimental) or not (control) when a stranger approaches. The two groups differ in just one way: the critical condition in this example is mother's presence. Specific behaviours shown by the two groups of infants then are compared. Systematic differences can be attributed to whether or not the mother was there when the stranger approached.

In the other common experimental method, groups of infants are identified for study based on some characteristic of interest and the responses of this target group are compared with a similar group without the characteristic. For example, infants born prematurely would be compared with full-term infants under the same controlled conditions.

Whatever their approach, researchers always try to obtain information that is accurate and that can be replicated reliably. Reliability, validity, and generalizability of findings are three standards that mark good research methods. **Reliability** refers to whether the same behaviours will be observed if the study is repeated. Usually this is addressed by having a second observer record the same behaviour. Do two observers agree, for example, that a baby played with a particular toy for the same amount of time? Seem simple? Consider this case:

The baby pauses for 2 seconds and then resumes play. Is this counted as one continuous play period or two? Researchers make their decisions based on the questions they are asking, and determining whether such fine distinctions can be coded reliably. The observations are considered to be reliable only if the inter-rater agreement is high, usually at least 80%. The observations also must be **valid** or relevant to the research question posed. To insure validity, researchers often will use behaviours shown to be relevant in previous work. Or, alternatively, they may figure out several ways to measure the same underlying behaviour. For example, (1) beginning to cry when a stranger approaches, (2) looking at mother anxiously, and (3) avoiding the stranger, are all behaviours that should measure stranger wariness—fearful behaviour that infants often display after about 7 months of age. Finally, the best studies generate knowledge about infant behaviour that can be extended beyond the specific context of the study. That is, the new finding explains behaviour under many conditions or for infants in general, not the particular groups of infants who were studied. This is called **generalizability of findings.** As we describe techniques researchers have used to obtain answers to some of the questions listed, keep in mind that each has met acceptable standards of reliability, validity, and generalizability.

Many of the techniques we will describe are experimental designs as these have been some of the most innovative methods and have led to important findings as well as new theories of infant development. We have organized the research questions into major areas of psychological functioning such as sensory capacity, mental abilities, and social–emotional behaviour, although some questions fall into more than one area.

Sensory capacities

Sensation is the basis for taking in the world. Most of us have the full range of senses: seeing, hearing, feeling, tasting, touching. Unlike many other mammalian species, most of our senses are functional at birth, although some refinement occurs as a result of the development of the nervous system and exposure to environmental stimulation. It is important to find out if newborns have the basic sensory capacities and are developing properly, because if not, their further mental (cognitive) and emotional development may be compromised. Some methods can detect responses to stimuli presented in one or more sensory domains to even very young infants.

Do young infants see and hear the things we do?

Tracking

One of the earliest signs that an infant can see and hear is tracking behaviour. Normally, newborns will turn their eyes and heads in the direction of an interesting sound or sight, especially the human voice and face. Many assessments of newborns and infants observe tracking to determine the infant's early visual integrity. Similarly, newborns, as well as older infants, show reactions to sounds that are made from objects out of view. A startle is a normal reaction to an unexpected loud noise. A reduction in movement and head turning indicate the ability to hear softer sounds.

Tracking ability often is examined using a standardized instrument called the **Neonatal Behavioural Assessment Scale** (NBAS; Brazelton, 1984). The examiner attempts to elicit the best performance by bringing the infants through a careful progression of states designed to arouse and then calm them. The NBAS has six orientation items to measure the infant's attention and tracking of inanimate stimuli and the examiner's voice and face. A failure to orient to any of these stimuli indicates that a newborn may have a serious vision or hearing problem.

Habituation

Experimental methods also have been used to examine an infant's ability to see and hear. One of the most often used is based on the principle of **habituation**. This and related procedures rely on the observation that infants prefer to pay attention to novel sights and sounds rather than familiar ones. This has been used in assessment by presenting the same stimulus repeatedly (familiarization) to see if the infant stops paying attention to it. Then a novel stimulus is introduced. If the infant has habituated to the familiarized stimulus, the novel stimulus will re-engage the infant's attention (Sokolov, 1963; Lewis, 1971). This procedure can easily be used to test sensory abilities by varying specific characteristics of the familiar and novel stimuli, for example, the shape of a visual stimulus, or different speech sounds. In an early study Barrera and Maurer (1981), for example, showed that 3-month-old infants can discriminate between smiling and frowning expressions by using one expression as the familiar and the other as the novel stimulus in an habituation procedure.

High amplitude sucking

It is a bit more difficult to find a reliable measure of an infant's attention to sound. One response that has been used extensively is called high amplitude sucking. Young infants can control the rate as well as the pressure at which they suck, and will suck even if they are not obtaining food, as on a pacifier or dummy. Researchers have capitalized on this voluntary response system. Infants are given a non-nutritive nipple to suck that is connected to a pressure transducer. When the sucking pressure reaches a predetermined level a stimulus will go on. This has been used in habituation procedures designed to determine if infants can tell the difference between two sounds. A sound is turned on when the infant sucks sufficiently strongly. Once the sucking pressure declines and remains below that level, it can be assumed that the infant has habituated to the redundant stimulus. When a new sound is introduced, researchers know that the infant is able to tell the two sounds apart if he or she starts sucking strongly again. For example, if we were interested in knowing if infants can distinguish between two similar speech segments, one ('Hello, Baby!') would be used as the familiarization stimulus and the other ('Hi, Sweetie!') as the novel. If the infant habituated to 'Hello, Baby!', and then increased sucking pressure when the 'Hi, Sweetie!' was presented, it indicates that he or she can distinguish these two samples of maternal speech. The procedure would be presented to infants of different ages and with different characteristics to determine whether and at what age they were capable of hearing the distinction (see Chapter 9 for a detailed account of speech perception in infancy).

Preference paradigms

The preference paradigm is based on an infant's tendency to attend to the more complex of two novel visual stimuli. In preferential looking procedures, the infant is shown two targets side by side (see Figure 2.1). An observer who cannot see the stimulus makes a judgement about which target the infant is looking at. This procedure has been used to study visual acuity in very young infants. The infant is presented with one stimulus that contains black vertical stripes that have specific widths corresponding to a level of visual acuity, and another target that is a uniform grey. If infants can distinguish the stripes, they

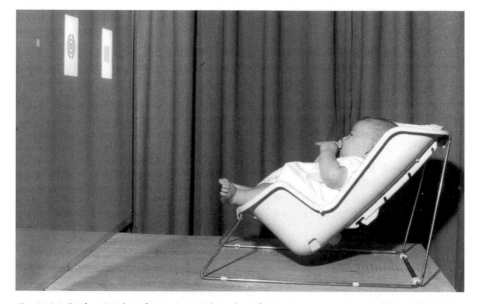

Figure 2.1 In the visual preference procedure the infant is shown two targets side by side and an unseen observer records which the baby looks at.

will prefer to look at that more complex target. If not, both targets will look grey, and there will be no preference over a series of trials (Teller, 1979).

Conditioned head turning

The conditioned head turning technique is used to assess hearing thresholds in young infants (see Kuhl, 1985, for a review). In this procedure a sound is presented through a speaker away from the infant's gaze. If the infant turns toward the sound, an animated toy beside the speaker is activated to reward the head turn response, as in Figure 2.2. The volume of the sound is varied systematically and an estimate of the hearing threshold is obtained by comparing head turns toward the speaker in the presence versus the absence of the sound. This procedure can also be used to find if infants can detect a change in sounds, e.g., from one rhyming sound to another (Hayes *et al.*, 2000).

Cognition and learning

Sensory capacities have to do with an infant's ability to take in the stimulation afforded by the world, while cognition has to do with how the infant makes sense of those sensations. Cognition is therefore about what infants learn, think, remember, and know. There are many methods used to measure cognition and learning, including standardized instruments and ingenious experimental procedures.

Can you tell how smart an infant is?

Standardized assessment

The **Bayley Scales of Infant Development** (BSID; Bayley, 1993) have the longest history of use in infant assessment and are the most widely used of contemporary tools in assessing the general cognitive level of infants. The BSID presents test items arranged in a developmental sequence. The child's responses to these tasks determines his or her developmental level. The BSID has a set of items tapping mental capacity that is summarized by the Mental Development Index (MDI), and a motor skill set summarized by the Psychomotor Development Index (PDI). These scores are like IQ scores, where 100 designates average performance for age, with a range of 50–150. It is these norms for the MDI and PDI that make this assessment instrument so popular. The most recent revision (BSID-II) has test items appropriate for ages 1–42 months. Although several items are observational (e.g., 'vocalizes four different vowel-consonant combinations'), the majority have specified administration procedures and often require standard materials. Examples include determining if the infant turns to the sound of a bell, how many cubes

Figure 2.2 An infant performing in the Conditioned Headturn Procedure. The top picture was taken when the reinforcer (a bouncing toy) was not activated, and the bottom picture when it was.

can be stacked, and if all pegs can be put in a board within a certain amount of time.

MDI scores are often used by investigators to provide information about developmental level or as a measure of the effects of intervention. For example, the BSID has been used to assess the general impact of prenatal drug exposure on cognitive development, as well as the effects of early intervention programmes (Lewis & Sullivan, 1994; Alessandri *et al.*, 1998).

Rate of habituation

Standardized instruments such as the BSID have not been found to predict later outcomes from early infancy very well. Other methods, designed to tap basic cognitive processes, such as learning and memory, may do a better job. One such method is based on how quickly an infant habituates. The rate of habituation is an indication of brain integrity and fundamental cognitive competence. For example, Lewis (1969) showed that older infants needed less looking time to habituate to repeated trials of a visual display than younger infants over the age range 3–24 months. Furthermore, infants who had medical complications in the newborn period, continued to need relatively long looking times through 12 months of age. Rate of habituation is thought to reflect the fundamental cognitive processes of sensing, perceiving, and remembering.

What do infants learn and remember?

Infants at very young ages learn and remember a lot more than we typically realize. Habituation and conditioning procedures often are used to explore this question. Infants learn early in life that certain events in the environment are associated with their behaviour. Researchers can study this in two ways. They use classical conditioning methods to study how infants learn associations between environmental signals or cues. They use contingency (operant) learning methods to study how infants learn that their actions have consequences. Learning procedures have particular appeal for researchers. Unlike habituation, which essentially measures passive behaviour (i.e., not looking at or attending to something), learning procedures inform researchers how infants act on what they know.

Classical conditioning

Even very young infants learn signals or environmental cues that are related to events important to them. For example, in the first weeks of life they learn the many auditory, olfactory, and sensory cues that predict being fed (Rovee-Collier, 1986). This form of learning is called classical conditioning. Studies of this type of conditioning are based on the principle that repeated pairings of one stimulus with another allow the infant to learn that one event predicts the occurrence of the other. Because the sound of mother's voice, and the smell of her milk are associated with her touch and being fed, infants learn not only to nurse efficiently but also that the world is a predictable place. Researchers know that the infant has learned an association when they respond to the previously novel cue. For example, newborn infants will turn toward the breast and begin rooting when the cheek is stroked (the rooting reflex). Noirot and Algeria (1983) preceded the touch of the infant's cheek by the taped sound of their mother's voice. After several pairings of voice and touch, newborns anticipated the touch. Cued by mothers' voices alone they began to root! Classical conditioning methods such as these show the types of stimulus information the youngest infants learn, how rapidly they learn, and how long they remember (Fitzgerald & Brackbill, 1976; Ivkovich *et al.*, 1999).

Expectancy violation

After the newborn period, a more complex procedure can be used to assess infants' abilities to predict events in the world. Because young infants will readily watch and track moving objects, their visual and facial responses when an object deviates from a path are good ways to infer what infants expected to happen. Increased looking, search behaviour, and sometimes a wide-eyed, surprised expression (Charlesworth, 1969), allow researchers to infer that an infant's understanding of a visual event has been violated. These procedures have been used extensively in studying young infants' understanding of the physical world because they require only visual tracking and no other motor responses. Infants typically watch an event, for example, an object appearing in different locations successively. The same action sequence is then repeated several times so that infants can learn to predict the object's location. On the test trial, the object's appearance in the expected location is delayed. Monitoring of eye movements allows researchers to observe whether infants anticipated the next location, indicating that they have understood that there is a sequence and are able to predict the object's next appearance (Haith *et al.*, 1988).

Contingency or operant learning

A major developmental task is understanding that certain behaviours have consequences. Infants use many responses to explore, or operate on the environment, including vocalizing, touching, kicking, pulling, banging, etc. The relation between such behaviours (called operants) and the consequences they produce is called a **contingency**. Operant behaviour will increase when it is followed by a rewarding consequence. Contingency methods assess whether infants' behaviours increase and decrease systematically, indicating learning of the relation between behaviour and the rewarding consequence. For example, infants were taught to pull a ribbon to see a colour slide of a happy baby and hear children singing (Bendersky *et al.*, 1995). The infants were placed in the apparatus shown in Figure 2.3. The spontaneous level of pulling was recorded but was not rewarded in any way (**baseline**). During the next phase

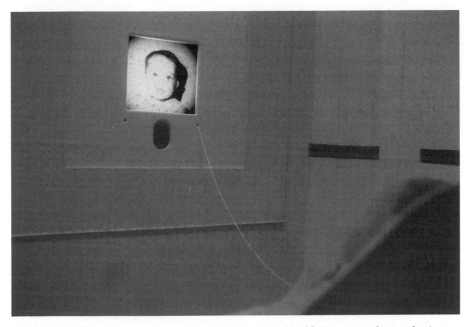

Figure 2.3 An infant in a contingency learning apparatus. A ribbon connected to an elastic wrist band worn by the infant triggers a slide to appear, accompanied by pleasant music.

(**contingency**), pulls were followed immediately by 3 seconds of the slides and music. For many infants from about 8 weeks on, this contingency results in increased pulling as the infant learns that arm action turns on an interesting event. In the next 2-minute phase pulling no longer turned on the pleasant stimulus. This period of non-reward is called **extinction** because it ultimately leads to reduction of the learned response. However, infants by this time may have some expectation that their pulling results in reward. Not only does it take time to learn to suppress a previously learned response, but several studies have shown that infants initially respond somewhat more during extinction (Alessandri *et al.*, 1990; Sullivan *et al.*, 1992). Increased response during this phase may reflect mild frustration. Imagine your own behaviour when money inserted into a soda machine does not result in the expected outcome. The absence of the soda may cause you to press rapidly a number of the selection buttons and then the coin return before you become angry. So, it was with the infants, who fortunately in this experiment were treated to another phase of contingency. With the return of the reward they settled back to their previous level of responding. Through procedures such as this researchers can focus on what is learned, how long it takes infants to 'make the connection', whether certain groups of infants learn more rapidly than others, as well as what motivates infants to respond.

Imitation

Imitation is another way that infants learn how to act in the world. It is more common after about 6 months, although some have reported imitation of certain facial actions in newborns (Meltzoff & Moore, 1977, 1983; Field *et al.*, 1982). Researchers are interested in what behaviours infants will imitate (e.g., facial actions, sounds, or gestures) and who (or what) they will imitate at a given age. Facial expressions, familiar and novel gestures, and actions on objects, such as talking on the telephone have been modelled by live or televised people, and even objects. Imitation shows what infants regard as interesting or important behaviour, as well as their ability to perceive and process similarities between their own actions and those of others.

Several different target actions may be used in an imitation study to see if infants might be more likely to copy some actions than others. For example, facial movements seem to be easier to imitate than manual gestures because infants lack the necessary fine motor skills for gestures, and some facial movements seem to be more readily matched than others. Mouth opening and tongue protrusion are the most frequently copied facial movements by newborns. To study imitation, a model typically displays a target action following a baseline period. The baseline is used to determine how often infants perform the modelled action spontaneously, that is *before* they ever see the model do it. After seeing the model, the infant has the opportunity to reproduce the target action. If the behaviour occurred more frequently after exposure to the model then the infant imitated it. For example, Lewis and Sullivan (1985) studied young infants' ability to imitate several different models performing such familiar actions as head turning and hand waving. There was a baseline period during which no model was present. Then they examined how well infants imitated each of the target actions in response to the different models. They found that young infants were likely to become active when anything moved, but their actions did not match the modelled ones up to 6 months of age, the endpoint of the study.

In studies of delayed imitation, several days or weeks may pass between an infant's initial exposure to a novel modelled action and a test (Meltzoff, 1988; Bauer & Hertsgaard, 1993). For example, infants observe a model using a banana like a hammer during a play session. During the test, a banana is present among other toys and researchers observe if the infant uses it as a hammer. The focus of these studies is to see how long infants are able to remember the novel action, and the level of prompting needed to recall the behaviour. Imitation has also been used to study the development of early communicative gestures (e.g., waving bye-bye, pointing) and vocalizations (Masur-Frank & Ritz, 1983; Poulson *et al.*, 1991).

Memory

Both habituation and conditioning procedures are used to study memory. Using habituation to study memory is very straightforward. A particular stimulus is repeatedly shown to an infant, and then is presented again on the memory test after a delay as brief as several minutes or as long as several days. The response on the memory test lets infants answer the question 'Have you seen this before?'. If the infant pays a lot of attention to the old repeatedly presented stimulus, effectively treating it as 'novel', then researchers infer that infants do not recognize that they have seen it before. The amount of time between the habituation and memory trials is varied to see how long infants of different ages remember. In just such an experiment researchers found that $3\frac{1}{2}$ month-old infants could remember a familiar stimulus for at least 24 hours (Martin, 1975).

When memory is tested using contingency learning procedures, the time between initial learning of the contingency and the memory test is varied (Rovee-Collier, 1999). For example, infants learn to jiggle colourful mobiles hung above their cribs by means of a ribbon attached to one ankle (Figure 2.4). Different infants are then tested after days or weeks with either a dissimilar mobile (a large colourful butterfly chime or a mobile composed of different coloured and shaped objects) or an identical one to see if they will attempt to jiggle it (Grecco *et al.*, 1990). The research shows that infants initially remember exact details about the mobile for at least a few days because they will only activate an identical one during the memory test. After 4 days, although the specific mobile appears to be forgotten, infants still remember that mobiles are for jiggling. For 2 weeks or longer after original learning, they will activate any mobile hung above their crib!

Social–emotional behaviour

How do infants learn to interact with others?

Most studies of early social behaviour focus on mother–infant interaction. This makes good sense because up until the infant is about 6 months of age, most social contact takes place face-to-face during play or caregiving with a primary or limited set of caregivers. The importance of the early relationship between mother and infant is a cornerstone of developmental theory (see Chapter 12). The focus of mother–infant interaction research has grown from what the mother does to the infant, to how she responds to the infant's cues, to what both members of the pair (dyad) are doing together (Lewis & Goldberg, 1969; Beckwith, 1971; Lewis, 1978; Kochanska, 1997; Kochanska & Murray, 2000). However, the procedures used to measure these interactive behaviours have remained fairly constant.

Many studies of mother–infant interaction are observations in naturalistic settings such as the home or in settings designed to be home-like, such as a laboratory playroom. Typically the mother and infant are observed while playing

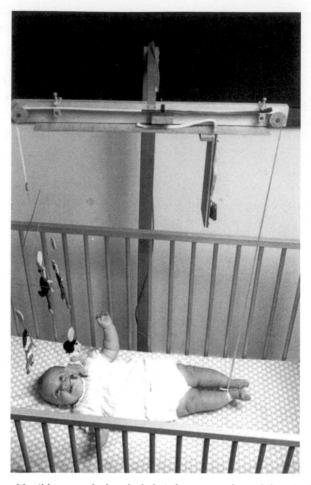

Figure 2.4 The ankle ribbon attached to the baby's foot causes the mobile to jiggle about when she kicks her leg. Photo by Rachel Cooper.

or during feeding. The interaction is coded as it occurs, or is videotaped and later coded for a variety of mother and infant behaviours of interest. Coding schemes vary depending on the focus of the study. Often a list of specific behaviours is used. For example, several studies have used a list developed by Lewis and Lee-Painter (1974), in which the occurrence of 13 maternal and infant behaviours is noted every 10 seconds (Lewis & Coates, 1980; Greene *et al.*, 1983; Bendersky & Lewis, 1986). An additional aspect of the interaction that is often of interest is the sequence, i.e., was the behaviour an initiation or a response to behaviour of the other member of the dyad? More complex methods of analysing response patterns, such as conditional probability, and sequential analysis also are used (Lewis & Freedle, 1973; Lester, Hoffman & Brazelton, 1985; Bakeman & Gottman, 1989). Another common approach is to have observers rate the dyad on more global categories of behaviour, for example maternal warmth (Ainsworth *et al.*, 1974; Greenberg & Crnic, 1988; Isabella, 1993). Once a sample of mother–infant behaviour is obtained, researchers can compare the infants to see if different interactive patterns are related to the child's development.

Several more structured procedures have become fruitful methods for studying particular aspects of mother–infant interaction. These procedures examine how infants react when their mother's usual pattern of responding changes.

Still-face procedure

Think of a mother playing with her young infant. Mothers usually assume an animated style, coaxing the baby to interact by using exaggerated facial and verbal expressions. At very early ages infants come to expect this sort of reciprocal social behaviour from their mothers. The still-face procedure was designed to see how infants react when this expectation is violated (Tronick *et al.*, 1978). The mother is seated facing her infant who is in an infant seat. She is asked first to play with her infant briefly as she normally would at home, and then to assume an expressionless, unresponsive facial expression. After a few minutes of this 'still-face' period, she is told to resume face-to-face play. Both mother and infant are videotaped and observers code vocalizations, facial expressions, direction of gaze, and head and body position of the two participants. Typically, when the mother assumes the unresponsive still-face the infant attempts to get her to respond by smiling and talking. When these behaviours that usually engage the mother fail, the infant withdraws and turns away. Turning away is one way for young infants to regulate their emotional arousal. Typically, infants quickly resume play when their mothers re-engage following the still-face period. This procedure is used to explore normal parent–infant interaction, as well as deviations due to high-risk conditions affecting the infant, such as being exposed prenatally to drugs of abuse, or conditions affecting the mother, such as depression (Field, 1984; Bendersky & Lewis, 1998).

Desynchronized interaction

The still-face procedure violates the infant's normal expectation about social contingencies with its mother. Several other ingenious experiments have 'uncoupled' infant and maternal behaviour to examine the importance of the contingent quality of maternal interactions (Murray & Trevarthan, 1985; Cohn & Tronick, 1987; Bigelow *et al.*, 1996). In one such study (Bigelow, 1998), mothers responded to their infants via closed circuit video for a brief period. This allowed the infants to 'interact' with their mothers shown on 'live' TV. The mothers' behaviour was taped during this period. The baby then viewed the taped mother on the monitor but maternal behaviour was no longer tied to what the infant did—the two were 'out of sync'. This procedure elegantly controls the level and distribution of maternal stimulation. As the infant views its own mother, the stimulation is exactly the same in both phases. However, the responsivity or contingent quality of the social interaction for the infant has been lost. Studies tend to agree that infants detect this disruption in maternal contingency rather quickly and become upset.

Attachment

Strange situation

Sometime after 6 months, most infants develop a strong emotional attachment to the primary caregiver, usually their mother. One of the most influential procedures used to study the development, the quality, and outcomes related to this first emotional relationship is the 'the Strange Situation' (SS; Ainsworth *et al.*, 1978). The SS shows that, although the infant is able to move freely about the environment, the mother serves as a 'secure' base that the infant will seek when stressed (Bowlby, 1973, 1982). The procedure is comprised of eight increasingly stressful episodes in which a stranger interacts with the infant in the mother's presence and alone. The most stressful episode is when the infant is left entirely alone (separation). The reunion episode that follows assesses the calming effect of the mother's return. The infant's behaviour during the separation and reunion allows researchers to classify the maternal–child relationship into one of three major attachment types. During reunion, infants who easily calm while showing little resistance to being comforted are called securely attached. About 65% of middle class infants fall into this category. This type (B) is considered the ideal form of emotional attachment at 1 year of age. In contrast, insecurely attached infants may be avoidant (A) or ambivalent (C). The type A infant does not seek to contact mother upon her return, and may not have become severely distressed at her leaving. The type C infant seeks contact but remains upset throughout the reunion episode (Ainsworth *et al.*, 1978). Sometimes an additional classification (D, disorganized) or subcategories have been used (Main & Solomon, 1990; Schneider-Rosen, 1990; Braungart & Stifter, 1991). These classifications are frequently used as the basis of grouping infants whose subsequent or earlier behaviour is examined in relation to attachment classifications. Most researchers agree that attachment is related to both maternal and infant factors. Major issues in the latest studies are determining the process through which attachment develops, the relative contribution of specific maternal and infant behaviours to the classification, and the stability over time of the attachment classification (Lewis & Feiring, 1989; DeWolf & Ijzendoorn, 1997).

Social referencing

Social referencing procedures are designed to present the infant with a potentially distressing or ambiguous situation in which mother is available. This allows researchers to study if and how infants use maternal behaviour and signals to regulate their emotions or guide their responses. Social referencing occurs when the infant attends and then behaves in a manner consistent with mother's message in the ambiguous situation. The approach of a stranger, originally designed to study fearfulness, has been adapted to study social referencing because it mimics a common dilemma in the lives of infants: should the infant accept the stranger as a friend or not? In these studies, when the stranger enters the room, mother greets and interacts with the stranger in one of three ways. She responds either positively, negatively, or not at all. Subsequently, the stranger interacts with the infant offering a toy in some studies, or picking the child up in others. At about 1 year of age, the infant will respond positively to a stranger when mother's reaction to the stranger is positive (Feinman, 1982; Feinman & Lewis, 1983; Feiring *et al.*, 1984; Walden & Baxter, 1989). The results for negative reactions are more mixed. It also is not yet clear if infants pick up cues simply from observation of the mother–stranger interaction or require more direct social/emotional cues from mother to accept the stranger's overtures (Saarni *et al.*, 1998).

Other studies have used potentially frightening situations to study whether infants use maternal cues to guide their behaviour. The Visual Cliff, originally designed to study depth perception, was adapted to study infants' monitoring of maternal facial expressions (Sorce *et al.*, 1985). Infants were placed on a raised glass surface in which the visual pattern beneath the glass made it appear that there was a deep drop-off in the surface just ahead. Their mothers, positioned on the opposite side, tried to coax the infants across the 'chasm'. Infants were more likely to cross the cliff when mothers looked happy, and less likely to cross when mothers looked fearful (Feinman *et al.*, 1992). The Noisy Toy procedure (Klinnert, 1984) uses a variety of novel, familiar, and somewhat unusual toys likely to elicit mixed or negative reactions from infants (for example, a robot). In one experiment, mothers are told to remain neutral or to show either positive or neutral vocal or facial responses to each toy. At 1 year of age, only maternal vocal cues influenced the infants' responses (Mumme *et al.*, 1996).

How do infants react to stressful events?

There are two ways that all people, including infants, react to stress. Our behaviour changes, and we have internal, bodily changes as well. Researchers examine both stress response systems to understand how infants react to stress.

Behavioural stress reactivity

We usually react to stressful situations by changes in behaviour. For example, you might clench your fists and grimace when the dentist performs a painful procedure. While adults may be able to mask their stress levels and not show too much outward reaction, infants usually cannot. Infants will show different levels of distress in response to a painful event, such as inoculation, and also will calm down at different rates. Typically, infants are videotaped during the inoculations until they are completely calm. The intensity of crying and fretting, as well as facial expressions, are coded from the tapes (Lewis & Ramsay, 1995a). Of interest is that the initial reaction and the return to calm do not necessarily go together. Intensely negative reactions, as well as difficulty calming in stressful situations have widespread implications for social interactions and learning (Lewis & Ramsay, 1999).

Physiological responses

Think of how you feel when you are in the middle of a big exam and time is running out, or while in your car, you suddenly hear the brakes of the car behind you screeching just before it hits your rear bumper. Your body will react to these kinds of stressful situations, first with a rush of adrenaline, the 'fight or flight' hormone, that makes your heart pound and your hands sweat. About half an hour later you are still in an agitated state because the level of another more long-acting stress hormone, cortisol, has risen. Production of stress hormones and heart rate changes are other ways to study infant reactions to stress.

Cortisol is a hormone released by the adrenal glands in response to stress. It is easily extracted from saliva and has become a popular measure of the physiological stress response due to ease of collection from subjects of all ages. Cortisol typically has been collected during painful medical procedures such as circumcision (Gunnar, 1986, 1989) and inoculation (Lewis & Thomas, 1990; Lewis & Ramsay, 1995a,b). A baseline level is obtained prior to and a post-stimulation level obtained following the procedure. The post-stimulation sample is usually obtained about 20 minutes after the painful procedure because that is when the cortisol reaction is at its peak. The mouths of infants are swabbed with cotton pads to absorb saliva that is then squeezed into test tubes and assayed for cortisol. Both baseline levels and the change from base to post-stimulation (reactivity) are used in analyses. Cortisol measures have been associated with behavioural inhibition (Kagan et al., 1987; Nachmias et al., 1996; Schmidt et al., 1997), other temperamental qualities (Rothbart, 1981; Gunnar et al., 1997), insecure attachment (Spangler & Grossman, 1993; Hertsgaard et al., 1995), and emotion regulation (Stansbury & Gunnar, 1994).

Heart rate changes

Heart rate and variability of heart rate are other measures of emotional response that are relatively easily measured. The variation in heart rate due to breathing, called *vagal tone*, is related to control by the brain of cardiac acceleration and deceleration in response to arousal. It is considered more reflective of brain activity than other measures of heart rate change (Fox & Porges, 1985) and has been used frequently as a measure of physiological self-regulatory capacity (Porges, 1985, 1996; Porges & Droussard-Roosevelt, 1997; Bornstein & Suess, 2000). In order to measure heart rate, a small number of sensors are placed on the infant's chest and a count of the heart rate is obtained. These data are processed to obtain the desired cardiac baseline and reactivity measures. Some studies have been interested in resting measures (e.g., Fox & Porges, 1985; Fox, 1989), and others have examined changes in response to stimulation (e.g., Fox, 1989; Bornstein & Suess, 2000). Both resting and reactivity measures have been shown to relate to and predict cognitive and social–emotional competence (Fox & Lewis, 1983; Fox & Porges, 1985; Kagan *et al.*, 1987; Richards, 1987; Porges *et al.*, 1996).

Relation between measures

Behavioural responses and physiological reaction to the same event are not necessarily related. Lewis *et al.* (1993) for example, found that infants fell into four groups in their reactions to inoculation: (1) 'cry babies' had low physiological reactions, but took a long time to quiet; (2) 'stoics' had high physiological reactions, but quieted quickly; (3) 'high reactors' had both strong physiological reactions and took a long time to calm; (4) and finally, 'low reactors' had neither strong physiological nor behavioural responses. These findings suggest that behavioural and physiological stress reactions have different meanings, and are likely to relate to development in different ways.

How do infants express emotion?

Infants express emotion by crying and vocalizing, by their body posture, and by their facial expressions. Parents no doubt make use of all of these cues in attempting to figure out what their infants are feeling.

Facial expressions

However, and as we will see in Chapter 11, researchers have been particularly interested in facial expressions as a way of understanding how emotions are organized early in life and develop. Infants make a variety of facial expressions that can be scored by observing the muscle movements in the brow, eye/cheek, and mouth regions of the face (Oster, 1978; Izard, 1995). Movements in each of these three regions are scored from videotape and the combination of particular movement patterns is used to identify the particular emotion expressed. For example, pretend for a moment that you are surprised. How did your face change? Probably, you raised and arched your brows, your eyes widened and your jaw dropped—the typical surprised expression. Now, pretend to express anger and notice the contrast. Your brows are now lowered and drawn together; your eyes narrowed, and your mouth, if open, was wide and squared, and if closed, your lips and teeth were strongly compressed, chin drawn up. All of the basic emotions that adults express (e.g., enjoyment, surprise, anger, fear, sadness, and disgust) can be distinguished by these or similar distinctive patterns of facial movements in infants and are observable from the opening weeks of life. However, infants do not always make the facial expressions that adults expect in a given situation and they may show several different emotions in rapid succession. These observations have triggered a lively debate on the meaning of the various expressions, particularly the negative ones. Researchers have developed situations designed to produce such emotions as disgust (tasting of sour and bitter solutions—Steiner, 1979; Rosenstein & Oster, 1988) and anger (arm restraint—Stenberg & Campos, 1990; inability to activate pleasant sights and sounds—Lewis *et al.*, 1990). Some of the newest, and potentially groundbreaking work in measuring emotional expression has been the addition of physiological measures such as heart rate, cortisol, and electroencephalograms (EEG) to the study of facial expression to see how both relate to emotion in infants.

Are infants born with different personalities?

Most of us would agree that adults have different personalities. Some people are easily excited, while others are easy-going; some seem to be eternal optimists, while others seem to see only the dark side of a situation. Perhaps you know what type of personality you have. The key is that people seem to behave in similar ways no matter what the circumstances. Thus, personality is thought of as a 'trait', or an unchanging characteristic. Are we born that way, or do our environments contribute to the development of our personalities? The term *personality* is generally reserved for adults. In infants and children, the concept most closely related to personality is *temperament*. Definitions vary, but there is general agreement that temperamental differences appear relatively early in life and seem independent of social experience, cognitive ability, or learning; they later interact with family and other environmental experience; are relatively enduring, and contribute to behaviour across a variety of situations (Kochanska, 1993; Rothbart & Bates, 1998). The intensity of emotions, thresholds to react to environmental stimuli, and the ease with which an infant calms down, are important emotional and self-regulation components of temperament (Bates, 2000). It is easy to understand how powerful a contributor temperament is to developing social interactions. Difficult temperament, i.e., low threshold to react, intense negative reactions, poor adaptability to new situations, and difficulty calming, presents a particular challenge to caregivers.

Parent reports

The most widely used method of measuring temperament in infancy is standardized parent questionnaires. The starting point for most of these is the nine dimensions of temperament derived from extensive parent interviews done as part of the New York Longitudinal Study (Thomas *et al.*, 1963). These are: (1) activity level, (2) rhythmicity (regularity), (3) approach/withdrawal, (4) adaptability, (5) intensity of reaction, (6) attention span/persistence, (7) distractability, (8) quality of mood, and (9) threshold of responsiveness. These dimensions are used to characterize infants as difficult, easy, or slow-to-warm-up. Several questionnaires have been derived from these dimensions (Infant Characteristics Questionnaire, ICQ—Bates *et al.*, 1979; Infant Temperament Questionnaire, ITQ—Carey, 1970; Carey & McDevitt, 1978). The Infant Behavior Questionnaire (IBQ—Rothbart, 1981; Rothbart & Derryberry, 1981), also designed for infants under 1 year of age, measures six dimensions of temperament: activity level, soothability, fear, distress to limitations, smiling/laughter, and duration of orientation. This instrument has a broader conceptual base than the others and is widely used. Rothbart (1981) used not only the Thomas *et al.* (1963) perspective, but also those of perceptual-cognitive, neurophysiological, genetic, interactional, and adult temperament work. There are temperament questionnaires for older infants as well (Toddler Temperament Scale—Fullard *et al.*, 1984; Toddler Behavior Assessment Questionnaire—Goldsmith, 1996).

These questionnaires have similar formats. The parent is asked to rate how much a statement about a child's behaviour applies to her child. For example, 'Before falling asleep at night during the last week, how often did the baby show no fussing or crying?' (choices range from never to always, IBQ), or 'The infant is fussy on waking up and going to sleep' (almost never to almost always, ITQ). There are large numbers of questions worded in different ways on these instruments that ask about the same underlying temperament dimension across various situations in order to obtain a reliable report from the parent.

Despite the popularity of parent reports of temperament, these instruments tend to have relatively poor validity, test–retest and inter-rater reliability (Bornstein *et al.*, 1986). Moreover, responses reflect what the mother *thinks* about the infant's temperament, which is not necessarily objective (Sameroff *et al.*, 1982). However, several researchers have pointed out that how the mother perceives her infant's temperament may be as important to mother–child interactions and social development as a more objective measure (Bates, 1983; Bornstein *et al.*, 1986).

Observational methods

Observational procedures have been devised for certain aspects of temperament, especially behavioural inhibition. In general, researchers study reactions to unfamiliar stimuli. Brightly coloured toys, tape recordings of voices, and unpleasant odours have been used in young infants; interactions with unfamiliar adults, being shown frightening toys, and being encouraged to participate in novel activities have been used in the second year of life (Garcia-Coll *et al.*, 1984; Calkins *et al.*, 1996; Ramsay & Lewis, 1999). These procedures indicate to what extent infants exhibit the temperamental quality of being withdrawn and inhibited.

When and how do infants develop a sense of themselves as individuals?

Infants acquire a good deal of knowledge about objects and about others during the first 2 years of life. Infants' ability to know and think about themselves also develops between 1 and 2 years (Bertenthal & Fischer, 1978; Lewis & Brooks-Gunn, 1979; Lewis, 1992). Its appearance has important implications for social–emotional behaviour, as well as motivation and personality development (Lewis, 1998). In a classic series of studies using mirrors, videotaped playback, and photographs, Lewis and Brooks-Gunn (1979) established that visual recognition of the self emerges by 18 months. The most widely known of their procedures is the Mirror Rouge Task. Infants are first placed before a mirror and the infants' responses are recorded. Next, the mother surreptitiously puts a dot of rouge on her child's nose. After a short interval the infant is placed again in front of the mirror. Infants who look in the mirror and then touch their noses, or indicate that there is something different about it, are classified as showing self-directed behaviour. Self-directed behaviour never occurs before 15 months of age and increases dramatically between 18 and 24 months, with virtually all 24 month olds showing this behaviour.

Recent studies in the area of self-recognition are beginning to focus on its antecedents and consequences. For example, infants who were classified as showing self-recognition in the Mirror Rouge Task were more likely to show embarrassment (Lewis *et al.*, 1989). Embarrassment is elicited by procedures that call the children's attention to the fact that they are being observed by others, such as being pointed to, being paid elaborate compliments, or being asked to behave in an unusual way while watched by others. It has been shown that greater physiological reactivity to stress and less soothability in infants is related to earlier self-recognition (Lewis & Ramsay, 1997). These findings suggests that self-recognition is related to other aspects of the child's social and emotional life.

Conclusions

This overview has described how researchers go about answering questions about infant development. Many of the methods described will no doubt continue to be used, refined, and revised as we learn more about how infants become 'real people'. In addition, new procedures based on advances in technology will be developed, as new questions challenge the next generation of researchers to find ways of understanding why and how infants behave the way they do.

Part 2

The foundations of development

3 Prenatal development

PETER G. HEPPER

Introduction

The prenatal period is one of the most fascinating, yet least well understood, stages of our development. Its end is marked by a beginning; the birth of a newborn baby. In most societies the newborn is given an age of zero, as if to imply that nothing of importance has occurred before this. But as I shall demonstrate the prenatal period is vital for our development.

The prenatal period encompasses the most rapid phase of development of our lives, beginning as a single cell and ending as a newborn baby emerges into the world. For many years this period was viewed as simply one of growth and maturation, a time during which the body and organs were formed—in this context the term **maturation** refers to those aspects of development that are primarily under genetic control. Thus, development during this time was considered as proceeding largely under genetic control and immune to external influences. However, as technology advanced and scientists have become more sophisticated in examining the fetus, it has become apparent that development during this time is far from a simple question of genetically determined growth. Environmental agents may adversely affect the development of the fetus; moreover, the environment may determine the functional capacity of the organs of the body. The actions and reactions of the baby will shape its own development.

The following chapter provides an introduction to prenatal development. It examines the physical development of the individual before birth and explores the impact of the environment on development. It discusses the behaviour of the fetus, and demonstrates that the fetus is not merely a passive passenger during the prenatal period but is an active manager of its own development.

Key issues

Three key related issues have dominated discussion of the prenatal period.

First, is the *nature/nurture debate*. How much is development during this period determined by genes and how much by the environment? Traditionally, the prenatal period has been viewed as largely under the control of genes that direct the physical growth of the individual. However, environmental influences contribute more to development than previously thought. Development during this period is an interaction between genes and environment.

Second, is development *continuous or discontinuous*? For many years the event of birth was considered a new beginning, ignoring events before as having little meaning for future development. However, this view is now changing. As progress has been made in understanding the abilities of the newborn the question 'When do newborn abilities begin?' has been raised. It is logically possible, although unlikely, that at the moment of birth the behavioural, sensory, and learning abilities of the newborn are suddenly switched on. More plausible is that these abilities have their origins in the prenatal period, implying a continuity of development across the birth period.

Third, as studies have begun to unravel the behavioural abilities of the fetus, the question of what is the *function of fetal behaviour* has been raised. Why does the fetus exhibit the behaviour and reactions that it does? Are these a by-product of its maturation or do they serve a function?

These issues will be discussed as the prenatal development of the fetus is described.

Physical development

The prenatal period, beginning at conception and ending at birth, is divided into three stages: (1) the conceptual or germinal period; (2) the embryonic period; and (3) the fetal period (Moore, 1988).

The germinal period

The **germinal period** begins with the fertilization of the egg by the sperm and concludes with the establishment of the pregnancy, approximately 2 weeks later. During ovulation a mature egg is released from the ovary and enters the fallopian tube (the passage that connects the ovaries to the womb). Sperm travel up the tube to meet the egg and fertilization takes place in the fallopian tube. The fertilized egg (the **zygote**, a single cell) now begins to divide. The first division to produce two cells takes place 24–36 hours after fertilization. The cells divide, first to form a ball of cells (the **morulla**) and then, with the formation of a cavity within the morulla, the **blastocyst**. The cells, while dividing, travel down the fallopian tube and enter the womb where the blastocyst implants itself into the wall of the uterus (5–6 days after fertilization). During the next 5–7 days the blastocyst establishes a primitive **placenta** and circulation, thus ensuring the supply of nutrients and oxygen essential for development.

Two weeks after fertilization and following implantation the pregnancy is established. As well as developing a placenta the blastocyst must also ensure that pregnancy continues, and so it secretes hormones: first, to prevent menstruation and thus stop the shedding of the uterine lining and consequent loss of the pregnancy, and, second, to prevent the mother's immune system from attacking the embryo and fetus.

The embryonic period

The **embryonic period** begins during the middle of the second week and concludes at the end of the eighth week, at which time the physical appearance of the embryo is clearly human (see Figure 3.1). It is during this time that all the major organs of the body begin to form. It is a time of specialization where cells divide and differentiate to form specific organs, e.g., the heart and lungs. One of the mysteries of development is how cells 'know' to become a heart or lung cell given they are all identical at the start of the differentiation process. The local environment of surrounding cells and chemical messages is undoubtedly important but exactly how one cell becomes a toenail, another a hair, is unknown. During this period the individual is called an **embryo**. The heart, although only two chambered, begins to 'beat' and blood is circulated around the embryo by the end of the third week. This enables the removal of waste and the acquisition of nutrients. As all the body's organs begin to form during this period it is considered the most critical stage of prenatal development.

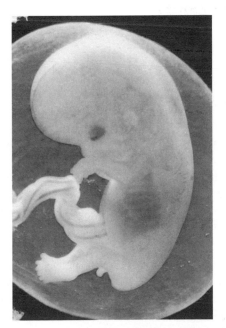

Figure 3.1 The fetus around 9 weeks (from Nilsson, 1977).

The fetal period

The **fetal period** follows from the end of the embryonic period, beginning at 9 weeks and ending with the onset of labour and birth of the baby. The individual is referred to as a **fetus** during this period. The period is marked by the continued development and differentiation of structures that emerged during the embryonic period. Basic structures that were laid down in the embryonic period are refined and grow to their final form. Very few new structures appear. Particularly noticeable is the rapid rate of growth during the third and fourth month, with the fetus growing from about 1 inch at 8 weeks to 5–6 inches at 16 weeks. It is during this period that the origins of motor, sensory, and learning behaviour are to be found (see below).

Principles that guide development

Three major principles seem to guide development.

1. Development proceeds in a *cephalocaudal* direction (from head to foot). That is, at any specific time structures nearer the head are more developed than those near the toes.

2. Development proceeds from the *basic to the more specialized*. Thus, organs do not initially appear as a miniature version of their final form but first develop their basic characteristics, and detail is added as development proceeds. For example, the heart is initially a two-chambered structure and its final four-chambered form develops later.

3. Development proceeds *in order of importance*. Thus, it begins with the 'more important organs' for survival and the less important ones develop later. Thus, the brain and heart are among the first organs to develop, perhaps reflecting their importance.

Brain development

The brain begins its development at 18 days after fertilization and is one of the slowest organs to develop, with development continuing for many years after birth (Caviness *et al.*, 1996). The relative proportion of brain in comparison with the body decreases as development proceeds; the brain comprises some 25% of body weight in the 9-week fetus, 10% in the newborn and only 2% in the adult.

The brain develops from a layer of cells on the embryonic disc, the neural plate (see Figure 3.2). This plate folds to form the neural tube, which closes, beginning in the middle and progressing to each end (Moore, 1988). Neural tube defects, e.g., spina bifida or anencephaly (literally meaning 'without a brain'), arise as a result of the failure of the neural tube to close properly. The neural tube has closed by fourth week and the walls begin to thicken (Moore,

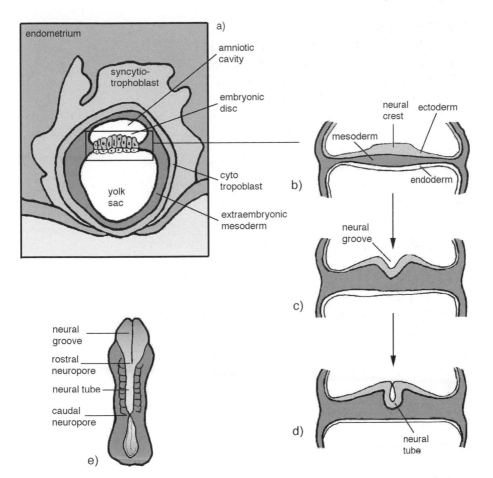

Figure 3.2 Formation of the neural tube (adapted from Moore, 1988). (a) Approximately 9 days. The blastocyst has nearly fully implanted itself into the endometrium. The embryonic disc forms between the primary yolk sac and amniotic cavity. The individual develops from the cells of the embryonic disc. Initially formed as a layer of two cells thick, the embryonic disc undergoes a process of *gastrulation*. This begins at the end of the first week and continues to the third week by which time three layers of cells the primary germ layers are formed: the ectoderm, mesoderm, and endoderm. (b) At about 16–18 days, cells in the ectoderm thicken to form the neural plate, (c) a groove appears in the neural plate at about 18 days, and (d) begins to close over forming the neural tube. The walls of the neural tube will thicken and form the neuroepithelium from which all the cells of the brain, neurones, glia develop. (e) View of the embryo and closure of the neural tube in embryo at about 22 days. Closure of the tube begins in the middle and moves to each end. The neural tube is fully closed by the end of the fourth week. Failure to close properly may lead to conditions of spina bifida.

1988). The walls of the neural tube contain progenitor cells that will give rise to the neurones and glia cells of the brain.

The development of the brain may be considered at two levels. First is the gross level, which concerns how the neural tube develops to form the main

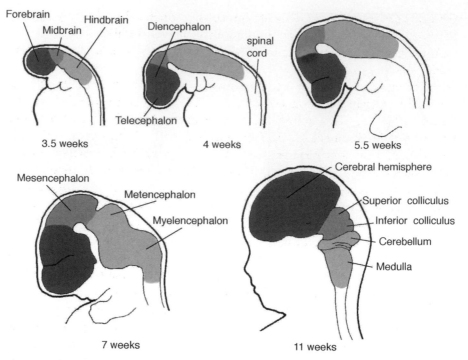

Figure 3.3 Development of the brain (adapted from Carlson, 1994). The brain begins its development following the closure of the neural tube. The rostral end, destined to become the brain enlarges to form three swellings: the forebrain, the midbrain, and the hindbrain. During the fourth week the forebrain further subdivides into the diencephalon and telencephalon. Towards the end of the fourth week the hindbrain divides into the metencephalon and myelencephalon. By the fifth week this 5-part structure of the brain is clearly visible. Although much more complexity is added as the brain develops this basic 5-part organization remains throughout the rest of life. By the 11th week the telencephalon has greatly developed and covered the diencephalon to form the cerebral hemispheres. Although initially smooth in appearance, future development will see a massive increase in the surface area of the cerebral hemispheres, which become folded and assume their adult-like appearance with many grooves (sulci) and convolutions (gyri).

structures of the brain: the hindbrain, midbrain, and forebrain. Second, at the micro level, we can examine how the complex organization of cells within the brain is achieved.

At the gross level (see Figure 3.3) the hindbrain, the midbrain, and the forebrain are formed during the fourth week as one end of the neural tube expands to form three primary vesicles (Moore, 1988). The forebrain then subdivides during the fifth week into the **telencephalon** and **diencephalon**. The telencephalon gives rise to the **neocortex** (cerebral cortices). The hindbrain and brainstem develop first, followed by the midbrain and later the cerebral cortices, the development of which continues after birth. This probably reflects the need for basic biological functions, controlled by the hindbrain and forebrain, to be operational at birth, e.g., breathing and digestion. The cerebral cortices involved in mental processing (often called the grey matter) develop later, a process that continues well into postnatal life.

At the micro level, all the neurones that we will ever have, have been generated by the end of the second trimester (Caviness *et al.*, 1996). Cells are produced at an extremely rapid rate between the 10th and 26th week. At its peak some 250 000 cells are produced a minute. The adult brain contains an estimated 100 billion cells. Initially, there is massive overproduction of cells and part of the development of the brain includes natural cell death. Although mainly occurring after birth this cell death (pruning) is a key element of the developmental process removing neurones that have not made connections or have made inappropriate connections. It is estimated that up to 50–70% of brain cells initially produced are pruned in the postnatal period. While development is often seen as an additive process, the development of the brain involves cell death as a central element in its growth (Oppenheim, 1991).

The cellular development of the brain comprises three main stages. The first, **proliferation**, the production of nerve cells, is completed by the end of the second trimester. Second is the **migration** of cells. Cells are formed from progenitor cells in the wall of the neural tube and move from there to their final location. Other cells, the radial glia cells, are produced alongside the neurones and these cells serve as guides forming pathways along which the nerve cells migrate to their final position (Rakic, 1972). Migration takes place between the fourth and ninth month of gestation. The third and final stage involves both **myelinization** and **synaptogenesis**. Myelinization is the process whereby the nerve cell is insulated from other cells by the development of a fatty sheath, myelin, around it. This greatly enhances the transmission of nerve impulses along the nerve. Synaptogenesis is the process by which nerve cells communicate with each other or with end organs, e.g., muscles, to enable the transmission of neural impulses across the brain and from the brain to other organs and vice versa. These latter processes continue for some time after birth.

The development of the brain is a highly complex process in which the timing of events is crucial to ensure that development proceeds normally (Goodman & Shatz, 1993). Numerous factors control the organization of neural development with it being largely under genetic control. While some of the genes involved are now known (e.g., des Portes *et al.*, 1998) our understanding of the processes that enable the progenitor cells in the neural tube to form the most highly complex organ in our body—the brain—are poorly understood.

Environmental influences on development

Prenatal physical development appears to proceed largely under instruction and direction from the individual's genes. However, this does not mean that it is immune to external influences that may alter the course of development.

Environmental factors may influence the individual's ontogenesis[1] and indeed may be crucial for establishing the functional capabilities of the various organs of the body.

Teratogens

The clearest example of environmental influence is presented by those substances that exert an adverse influence on development, called **teratogens**. Initially, it was thought that while developing within the womb the fetus was safe from external influences that could harm its development. However, it is now appreciated that the developing individual is at risk while in the womb from environmental influences. The study of adverse consequences of exposure to environmental agents is termed *teratology* and the agents that cause such abnormalities are called *teratogens*. It should be noted that teratogenic effects are not only caused by substances *extra* to the embryonic or fetal environment, e.g., alcohol through maternal drinking, but also *deficiencies* of substances, e.g., vitamin and other dietary deficiencies such as malnutrition, which may also lead to adverse development, as discussed below.

The first agent to be identified as a teratogen was rubella (the medical term for German measles) when it was noticed that children born to women who had German measles during their pregnancy often suffered eye anomalies (Gregg, 1942). However, it wasn't until the thalidomide tragedy in the 1950s and 1960s that it was finally accepted that environmental agents could severely affect the individual's development. Thalidomide was a supposedly safe tranquillizer/sedative that was taken by mothers during pregnancy and resulted in, most noticeably, the birth of children with severe arm or leg abnormalities (Lenz & Knapp, 1962).

The effects of teratogens may range from spontaneous abortion of the fetus, major and minor structural defects, growth retardation through to developmental retardation and behavioural disorders. While some effects are readily apparent at birth, e.g., the major structural anomalies resulting from exposure to thalidomide, others, e.g., behavioural anomalies arising from exposure to alcohol, may not become apparent until later life.

One crucial factor determining the impact of any teratogen is the time of exposure. Generally speaking, exposure during the embryonic period, i.e., the period of *organogenesis* (when the major organs of the body begin to form), results in major impairments and malformations, while exposure during the fetal period (from about 9 weeks from conception) results in growth impairments and delay. Many organs have specific periods, often just 2–3 days, during which they are especially susceptible, and exposure to teratogens at this

---

[1] The term *ontogenesis* refers to the development of the individual from conception to death. *Ontogenetic adaptations* refer to adaptations to specific periods of life, so that the fetus adapts to life in the womb, the newborn infant to life in the outside world, and so on. Ontogenesis can also refer to the development and adaptation of specific aspects or parts of the individual.

time will have major effects on their formation, whereas outside of these times the effects will be more limited. For example, a crucial period of development of the arms is between 27 and 30 days and exposure to thalidomide at this time resulted in malformation of the arms. Outside of these times the severity of effect on the arms was reduced or non-existent.

Many substances have been identified as having harmful effects on the fetus (see Table 3.1). The length of the period during which the brain is developing makes it particularly vulnerable to the effects of teratogenic agents. Substances may result in abnormalities in brain development in the absence of major physical structural abnormalities. These effects are much more difficult to detect as they may only become apparent years after birth.

Many teratogens are freely taken by mothers, e.g., alcohol and cigarette smoking. Exposure to large amounts of alcohol may result in fetal alcohol syndrome, the symptoms of which include a small head, an abnormal facial appearance, growth retardation, learning disabilities, and behavioural disorders (Abel, 1989). At lower doses the individual may manifest fetal alcohol effects, where facial appearance may be normal but learning and behavioural problems are present in later life (Abel, 1989). Alcohol exhibits what is called a *dose-dependent effect*, the greater the exposure the greater the effect on the fetus. It appears that even small amounts of alcohol may exert an effect on the developing individual (Little, 1999).

Teratogenic effects are not simply the result of environmental exposure. In many cases the effect(s) is a result of an interaction between the individual's genes and the environmental agent. For example, not all women who drink the same amount of alcohol during pregnancy will have babies with identical syndromes. Some will be more affected than others, dependent on the interaction between the environment and the individual's genes.

Fetal origins hypothesis

Postnatal health may be influenced by prenatal factors, a phenomenon that is known as the 'fetal origins hypothesis' (Barker, 1992; Nathanielsz, 1999). This hypothesis argues that the environment experienced during the individual's prenatal life programmes the functional capacity of the individual's organs and this has a subsequent effect on the individual's health.

When the fetus experiences a poor nutritional environment it develops its body functions to cope with this. The environment experienced prenatally is the one that it expects to continue experiencing and hence its body develops to cope with this. A basic principle of development is that in times of deprivation the body saves the most important organ, the brain. Thus, when the fetus experiences poor nutritional status, resources are redistributed to ensure that the brain is adequately supplied, but as a consequence other areas of the body are deprived. Growth-retarded babies may thus have a normal head circumference but a small abdominal circumference. Redistributing resources away from organs in the body to spare the brain influences the development

Table 3.1 Teratogens and some of their main effects. Duration and timing of exposure play a key role in determining the extent of any effect.

Drugs	Prescription	Thalidomide (sedative)	Arm and leg malformation
		Warfarin (anticoagulant)	Mental retardation, microcephaly (abnormally small head)
		Trimethadione (anticonvulsant)	Developmental delay, 'V'-shaped eyebrows, cleft lip and/or palate
		Tetracycline (antibiotic)	Tooth malformations
	Substances of abuse	Heroin	fetal/newborn addiction, slower growth
		Cocaine	Growth retardation possible long-term behavioural effects
		Solvents	Microcephaly
	Social drugs	Alcohol	Fetal alcohol syndrome, fetal alcohol effects
		Smoking	Spontaneous abortion, growth retardation
		Caffeine	High doses induce abnormalities in animals. Few human studies.
Disease		Rubella	Cataracts, deafness, heart defects
		Herpes simplex	Microcephaly, micro-ophthalmia (abnormally small or absent eyes, associated with blindness)
		Varicella (chicken pox)	Muscle atrophy, mental retardation
Radiation			Cell death, chromosome injury, mental and growth retardation. Depends on dose and timing of exposure
Maternal		Altered metabolism (e.g., diabetes)	Increased birth weight, increased risk of congenital abnormalities
		Stress/anxiety	Evidence pointing to effects on birthweight, behavioural development

of these organs, e.g., the liver. Decreased body size in babies is associated with increased cholesterol levels when they become adults. Fetuses experiencing poor nutrition may save the brain by diverting resources from the liver, the major organ in the abdomen and the organ responsible for regulating cholesterol levels. These low birth weight babies, when born, experience a normal nutritional status but one for which their organs are not programmed and cannot deal with, hence the increase in cholesterol levels when they become adults.

A number of functions may be programmed in the womb, including blood pressure, insulin response to glucose, and cholesterol metabolism. In situations of poor nutrition, these may be programmed incorrectly and lead, possibly, to subsequent health problems. While the extent of prenatal programming is debated, evidence suggests poor prenatal conditions have long-term effects (Nathanielsz, 1999). The prenatal environment may thus determine the functional capacity of various organs for the rest of life.

Behaviour of the fetus

The behaviour of the human fetus has aroused much speculation, but scientific study has only come in recent years (Hepper, 1994). Views of the behaviour of the fetus have ranged from the fetus as a miniature human with all its abilities, to the fetus as an unresponsive passive organism. As science has examined the prenatal period a picture of an active fetus is emerging: a fetus that exists in an environment of stimulation and reacts to it. The following sections shall review evidence pertaining to fetal movement, fetal sensory abilities, and fetal learning.

Fetal movements

The advent of ultrasound technology (see Figure 3.4) has provided clinicians and scientists with a window through which to watch the behaviour of the fetus.

Mothers feel their fetus move from about 18 to 20 weeks gestation (a time known as the 'quickening'), although there is much individual variation in the maternal perception of movements (Neldam, 1986). Using ultrasound, however, fetal movements are observed to emerge much earlier, at 8 weeks gestation (Prechtl, 1988). These movements appear slow and originate in nerve impulses from the spinal cord, and may result in passive movements of the arms and legs. Over the next few weeks a variety of different movements emerge (see Table 3.2) and by 20 weeks gestation most of the movements the fetus will produce are now present in its behavioural repertoire (Prechtl, 1988).

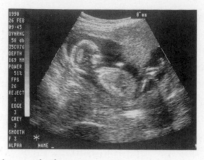

Figure 3.4   An ultrasound scan of a fetus.

Table 3.2 The gestational age at which behaviours are first observed in the fetus (from de Vries *et al.*, 1985).

Behaviour	Gestational age (weeks)
Just discernible movement	7
Startle	8
General movement	8
Hiccup	9
Isolated arm movement	9
Isolated leg movement	9
Isolated head retroflexion*	9
Isolated head rotation	9–10
Isolated head anteflexion*	10
Fetal breathing movements	10
Arm twitch	10
Leg twitch	10
Hand-face contact	10
Stretch	10
Rotation of fetus	10
Jaw movement	10–11
Yawn	11
Finger movement	12
Sucking and swallowing	12
Clonic movement arm or leg*	13
Rooting	14
Eye movements	16

* Retroflexion = head bends backwards; anteflexion = head bends downwards; clonic = short spasmodic movements.

Behavioural states in the fetus

The fetus remains active throughout its time in the womb but as it develops its movements become concentrated into periods of activity and periods of inactivity (James *et al.*, 1995). Towards the end of pregnancy, behavioural states have been observed in the fetus (Nijhuis *et al.*, 1982). Behavioural states are defined as recognizable and well defined associations of variables, which are stable over time and with clear transitions between each. Four behavioural states have been identified in the fetus (Nijhuis *et al.*, 1982) based on the observation of behavioural states in the newborn (Prechtl, 1974). Behavioural states are observed from 36 weeks of gestational age (Nijhuis *et al.*, 1982) and it has been argued that their emergence represents a greater degree of integration within the various parts of the central nervous system. The four states that have been defined, using the variables of heart rate pattern, the presence or absence of eye movements, and the presence or absence of body movements, are as follows.

- *State 1F: 'Quiet sleep'.* The fetus exhibits occasional startles, no eye movements, and a stable fetal heart rate. This state increases in occurrence from about 15% at 36 weeks of gestation, 32% at 38 weeks to 38% at full term.
- *State 2F: 'Active sleep'.* This state is characterized by frequent and periodic gross body movements. Eye movements are present and the fetal heart rate shows frequent accelerations in association with movement. This is the most commonly occurring state, being observed about 42–48% of the time in the fetus.
- *State 3F: 'Quiet awake'.* No gross body movements are observed, eye movements are present, and the fetal heart rate shows no accelerations and has a wider oscillation bandwidth than state 1F. This is a rare state to observe as it occurs only briefly. In fact its occurrence is usually represented by number of occurrences rather than as a percentage of time.
- *State 4F: 'Active awake'.* In this state the fetus exhibits continual activity, eye movements are present and the fetal heart rate is unstable and tachycardia (increased pulse rate) is present. This state occurs about 6–7% of the time between 36 and 38 weeks of gestation increasing to 9% just before birth, about 40 weeks of gestation.

Fetal senses

All the senses adults have operate to some degree in the fetus (with the possible exception of vision, see below). However, in order to operate a requirement is that stimulation penetrates the womb to be received by the fetus's sensory receptors. As we shall see the fetal environment is one of the ever-changing stimuli that the fetus can detect and respond to.

Hearing

The fetus responds to sound from 22 to 24 weeks exhibiting a change in its movement (Shahidullah & Hepper, 1993). The fetus's response is influenced by the frequency, intensity, and duration of the sound presented (Hepper & Shahidullah, 1994a). For example, louder intensities elicit a greater response. The fetus's hearing begins in the low frequency part (250 Hz, 500 Hz) of the adult hearing range (20–20 000 Hz) and as it develops the range of frequencies it responds to increases (Hepper & Shahidullah, 1994b). As well as simply responding to sounds the fetus is able to discriminate between different sounds, e.g., spoken words 'BABI' and 'BIBA' (Lecanuet *et al.*, 1987).

The environment of the fetus is quite noisy. Sounds from the mother's heartbeat, blood flow, and digestive system will permeate the fetal environment (Querleu *et al.*, 1988). All the sounds you or I hear will also penetrate the mother's womb and stimulate the fetus's hearing. However, sounds from the external environment will be attenuated by the mother's skin and other tissues. High pitched sounds over 2000 Hz will be attenuated as much as 40 decibels (Querleu *et al.*, 1989) and thus will probably not be experienced by the fetus. To make them audible to the fetus would need a sound level that would damage the hearing of the mother! Interestingly, there is little attenuation at about 125–250 Hz, the fundamental frequency of the human voice. Thus, the mother talking and other speech sounds in the environment will be readily heard by the fetus.

Chemosensation

The senses of smell and taste are difficult to separate *in utero* as the amniotic fluid bathes both receptor types and may stimulate both sensory systems. For this reason the fetal responses to smell and taste are usually considered under the same heading, chemosensation.

Researchers have found that the fetus is able to discriminate between sweet and noxious substances added to the amniotic fluid. Fetuses increase their swallowing when a sweet substance (sugar) is added to the amniotic fluid but decrease it when a noxious, but harmless, substance (iodinated poppy seed) is added by injection (De Snoo, 1937; Liley, 1972). Newborns show a preference for the odour of their mother compared with that of another female (Macfarlane, 1975; Porter, 1991) and orient to their own amniotic fluid (Schaal *et al.*, 1991), further suggesting *in utero* experience of odours/tastes.

The fetus swallows amniotic fluid from about 12 weeks gestation so substances that diffuse into the fluid, e.g., from the mother's diet, will be experienced by the fetus (Schaal *et al.*, 1995). Moreover, as the mother's diet changes so will the stimulation received by the fetus.

Somatosensory stimuli

Pain

The question of whether the fetus feels pain is at the centre of many scientific and political debates. Answers to this question are made more difficult by the fact that pain is a subjective phenomenon and can be difficult to examine. Pain responses have been observed in the premature infant from about 24–26 weeks (Anand & Hickey, 1987), and neural pathways for pain are formed at about 26 weeks of gestation (Anand & Hickey, 1987; Fitzgerald, 1993). Behavioural reactions to possibly painful stimuli have been observed in the fetus, e.g., if the fetus is touched by the needle during amniocentesis (a test for chromosome abnormalities in the fetus) or during fetal scalp blood sampling (to assess fetal status during labour) (Ron *et al.*, 1976; Hill *et al.*, 1979). Biochemical stress responses have been observed to needle punctures during blood transfusions from 23 weeks gestation (Giannakoulopoulos *et al.*, 1994). These, however, are all indirect measures of pain experience and there is still a debate as to whether the fetus feels pain (Derbyshire & Furedi, 1996; Glover & Fisk, 1996; Lloyd-Thomas & Fitzgerald, 1996; Szawarski, 1996).

Temperature

Anecdotal reports suggest that mothers feel more fetal movements as they take a hot bath. However, in the normal course of pregnancy the mother regulates and maintains the temperature of her womb and there will be little variation for the fetus to experience.

Touch

Touch is the first sense of the fetus to develop at about 8 weeks. If the fetus's lips or cheeks are touched at 8–9 weeks the fetus responds by moving its head away from the touch (Hooker, 1952). Later in pregnancy this response changes and during the second trimester the fetus now moves towards the touch. By 14 weeks gestation most of the body, excluding the back and top of the head, is responsive to touch. The fetus's arms will make contact with its face from about 13 weeks gestation (de Vries *et al.*, 1985) providing a source of stimulation. For twins, and other multiple pregnancies, there will be much tactile stimulation from other womb partners.

Vision

Vision is the least likely sense to be stimulated during the normal course of pregnancy (Hepper, 1992). At best the fetus may experience some general change in illumination. When tested under experimental conditions the fetus exhibits a change in heart rate (Peleg & Goldman, 1980) or movement

(Polishuk *et al.*, 1975) when a bright light is flashed on its abdomen from about 26 weeks gestation demonstrating that the visual system is operating to a certain extent.

Fetal learning

The ability of the fetus to learn is perhaps the most fascinating of all fetal abilities, because learning is often seen as the pinnacle of adult achievement. The ability to learn also has implications for the functioning of other abilities, e.g., it requires a sensory system able to detect and discriminate stimuli and a memory system able to store information.

Habituation

The presentation of a loud discrete sound initially elicits a large reaction (change in heart rate or movement) in the fetus but as this sound is repeated the fetus's response wanes and eventually disappears (Hepper & Leader, 1996)—this waning of response is termed *habituation*. The fetus habituates to auditory stimuli from about 22 to 24 weeks of gestation (Leader *et al.*, 1984). Female fetuses have been observed to habituate faster at any particular gestational age compared with male fetuses and may indicate that female fetuses are developmentally more advanced than male fetuses (Hepper & Leader, 1996).

Exposure learning

Most studies examining fetal learning have studied whether the newborn responds differently to sounds it has been exposed to before birth compared with sounds it has not been exposed to (Hepper, 1996).

Mother's voice

Newborns prefer their mother's voice to that of an unfamiliar female's voice (DeCasper & Fifer, 1980; DeCasper & Spence, 1986). Some very elegant experiments were performed to reveal this remarkable ability. These studies used the newborns' ability to suck, as described in Chapter 2. Newborns sucked on a dummy in the absence of any stimulation to establish a baseline sucking rate. Once this was established the newborn was given two choices: if it sucked faster than the baseline it received the sound of its mother's voice through headphones, whereas if it sucked slower it received the voice of an unfamiliar female. Newborns sucked faster to hear their mother's voice. If the contingencies were reversed and sucking slower led to hearing the mother's voice, newborns sucked slower. What is clear is that this ability to recognize the mother's voice is acquired before birth (Fifer & Moon, 1989).

Music

Newborns prefer music they have heard prenatally compared with that which they have never heard. Interestingly, this preference can be observed at 36 weeks gestation but not 30 weeks gestation, which may indicate that learning of familiar sounds or tunes occurs after 30 weeks (Hepper, 1991).

Functions of behaviour

The fetus exhibits a complex and varied behavioural repertoire. The question that is now raised is why? Why does the fetus exhibit these behaviours? There are a number of possible reasons.

Practising for life outside the womb

One key role for prenatal behaviour is to practise behaviours that will be essential for survival after birth, fetal breathing movements are an example of this. Fetal breathing movements are observed from 9 to 10 weeks gestation (de Vries *et al.*, 1985). Although there is no air in the womb these movements, motion of the diaphragm and rib cage, would result in breathing after birth and hence are termed fetal breathing movements. At 30 weeks of gestation fetal breathing movements occur at about 30% of the time (Patrick *et al.*, 1980). Later in pregnancy, fetal breathing movements increase during periods of fetal activity. Practising before birth ensures the neural pathways responsible for breathing are fully mature thus ensuring a fully operational system when required, at the moment of birth.

Ontogenetic adaptations

While the current zeitgeist in fetal behaviour research emphasizes the continuity of development, it should not be forgotten that the embryo and fetus exist in a very different environment from that to be experienced after birth. It may thus be expected that the fetus would exhibit behaviour designed to ensure its survival *in utero*. Such behaviours are termed ontogenetic adaptations (Oppenheim, 1981, 1984)—that is, adaptations to its life in the womb. While the concept of ontogenetic adaptations is well accepted, fetal adaptations to life *in utero* have been little studied. Some reflexes may be important for the process of birth and labour. An example of these is the kicking movements that appear near the end of pregnancy. These reposition the head of the fetus so that it is in position ('vertex presentation') for safe delivery.

Recognition of mother

The learning abilities of the fetus may be crucial for its survival and development in the first weeks after birth by enabling it to recognize its mother and begin the process of attachment and exploration. Many studies have demonstrated the ability of the newborn infant to recognize its mother by auditory and odour cues (DeCasper & Fifer, 1980; Fifer & Moon, 1989; Porter & Winberg, 1999), an ability acquired prenatally. The mother is a crucial figure for the newborn's survival. In terms of recognizing items in its environment the newborn is a *tabula rasa* (blank slate) and has to learn what objects are in its environment as it develops. It makes good sense to provide one object, and a very important one at that, which the individual may recognize at birth. Prenatal learning may serve to ensure that the newborn recognizes its mother at birth.

Breast feeding

Prenatal learning may also be important for the establishment of breast feeding. The same processes that flavour the mother's breast milk also flavour the amniotic fluid (Mennella & Beauchamp, 1991). The fetus may learn about the flavour of the amniotic fluid while in the womb and when placed to the breast for the first time it recognizes a familiar flavour and sucks readily. Successful breast feeding is crucial for the newborn's survival and prenatal learning may ensure the successful establishment of breast feeding (Hepper, 1996).

Developing physical form and developing the brain

The behaviour of the fetus is important for shaping the development of its body. The movements of the fetus are important for its structural development. The formation of the body's joints and the development of muscle tone all rely on the fetus moving its limbs during development. Joints do not form properly when their movement are restricted (Drachman & Coulombre, 1962; Drachman & Sokoloff, 1966; Moessinger, 1988). The behaviour of the fetus may also influence the long-term development of the brain. Sensory experiences may shape the development of its sensory system. It is well established that visual experience after birth shapes the development of the visual system (Blakemore & Cooper, 1970; Hirsch & Spinelli, 1970), as we shall see in Chapter 5. For those senses active and stimulated before birth, e.g., audition, stimulation may influence the development of these sensory systems. The potential for experiential factors to influence the development of the brain is great.

Birth and labour

For most of pregnancy the aim of mother and baby is to keep the baby within the uterus until sufficiently mature to survive outside. Once this time is reached, however, the fetus can leave its uterine environment for life in the postnatal world.

Preparation for birth

The activity of the uterine muscles are inhibited during pregnancy by the hormone progesterone (the hormone found in the ovaries that helps to maintain pregnancy). However, the muscles of the uterus are not completely inactive. During pregnancy mothers often feel a tightening of the uterus at regular intervals, known as *Braxton Hicks contractions*. These contractions are 'painless' but play an important part in preparing the uterus for delivery by developing its muscle tone. These are different from the contractions that are felt during labour, which are shorter in duration and occur every few minutes, increasing in frequency as labour progresses.

As the time of birth approaches the fetus's brain signals for more production of new chemicals, e.g., adrenocorticotrophin (ACTH) and cortisol. These chemicals act to convert progesterone to oestrogen. Oestrogen, in contrast to progesterone, promotes muscle activity in the uterus. The inhibitory control exercised over the muscles from the beginning of pregnancy is removed and mothers may feel a 'tightening' in their uterus and may experience contractions in the days prior to delivery.

These changes also stimulate the breast to prepare for the production of milk—a process finished off when the baby begins to suck.

Labour and birth

Birth and labour involve a constant interaction between the baby and mother. For example, as the fetus's head presses against the cervix, this stimulates the mother's pituitary gland to release oxytocin. This in turn stimulates the muscles of the uterus to contract, forcing the fetus's head into the cervix and continuing the cycle of contraction. Moreover, oxytocin also stimulates the release of prostaglandins, which increase the strength of uterine muscle contractions. This process continually escalates during labour, contractions becoming more forceful, and eventually resulting in the birth of the baby.

Exactly what determines the onset of labour is unknown; but, somehow the fetus 'knows' when it is ready to be born and it initiates a series of processes that culminate in its birth.

The actual birth process is divided into three stages. The first stage, usually the longest, begins with uterine contractions, each maybe lasting up to a minute, occurring every 15–20 minutes. As this stage progresses the contractions become more frequent and more intense. These contractions enable the mother's cervix to expand and stretch and enable the baby to move from the womb to the birth canal. At the end of the first stage the cervix has dilated to about 9 cm. The length of this stage generally decreases after the mother's first baby, but there is huge variability between individual mothers in the duration of this stage of pregnancy. In first pregnancies this may last between 8 and 24 hours.

Once the baby's head passes through the cervix and into the birth canal the second stage of pregnancy has begun. Mothers bear down at the time of contractions in an effort to push the baby from their body. It culminates when the baby is born, free from the birth canal attached to the mother by the umbilical cord and placenta.

The final stage of birth is the afterbirth and here contractions expel the placenta.

Survival after birth

Two important changes need to take place after birth as a result of the umbilical cord being cut and the baby having to survive on its own. First, the baby must now breathe for him or herself. The previous 25 weeks spent practising breathing movements now reap benefits as the baby starts breathing and obtaining oxygen through its own actions. The second adaptation involves a change from the fetal pattern of blood circulation to the adult pattern of circulation. This is triggered by the fact the baby now oxygenates its blood from the lungs and not the placenta. Perhaps the most important change is the closure of the foramen ovale, which prevents the blood, now deoxygenated blood, flowing from the right atrium to left atrium of the heart. These changes in blood flow occur over the first few days and weeks after birth (Moore, 1988).

Reflexes

The newborn baby's motor repertoire consists mainly of reflexes, which are involuntary movements elicited in response to stimulation, e.g., touch, light, change in position (see Table 3.3). These motor behaviours are controlled by neural structures below the level of the cortex. These reflexes are present at birth and disappear in the months after birth (Illingworth, 1983).

The normal exhibition and disappearance of these reflexes is an important indicator of the functioning and integrity of the baby's brain. Reflexes that persist beyond the time when they usually disappear, or for example are weaker than normal, may be indicative of underlying neural impairment such as cerebral palsy.

Reflexes are important for the survival of the newborn infant and also serve as the basic building blocks on which future motor development in based. Some reflexes are essential for survival, e.g., breathing, swallowing. To enable breast feeding the newborn infant has a rooting and sucking reflex. Touch on the side of the mouth or cheek stimulates the newborn to turn towards the touch, to locate the nipple. Once located another reflex initiated by stimula-

Table 3.3 Some of the reflexes of the baby describing their name, a description of the reflex, and their developmental time course of appearance and disappearance.

Reflex	Description	Development
Rooting	Touch the side of the mouth or cheek and the baby turns towards touch	Birth to 4–5 months
Sucking	Touch the mouth or lips and the baby begins to such	Birth to 4–6 months
Grasping	When the baby's palms are touched the baby grasps the object	Birth to 4 months
Moro	In response to a sudden loud sound or 'dropping' the baby suddenly the baby startles, throws its head back and arms and legs stretch out and then rapidly brings them back to the centre of the body	Birth to 4–6 months
Babinski	Stroke the bottom of the foot and the toes fan out and then curl	Birth to 9–12 months
Swimming	When the baby is placed in water it holds its breath and makes swimming movements with arms and legs	Birth to 4–6 months
Stepping	If the baby is held above a surface and its feet allowed to touch the surface it begins to show walking movements	Birth to 3–4 months
Labyrinthine	When the baby is placed on its back it extends its arms and legs or when placed on its stomach it flexes its arms and legs	Birth to 4 months

tion on the mouth or lips, sucking, enables the newborn to grasp the nipple and stimulate it to produce milk and thus obtain nutrients essential for growth. Rooting and sucking disappear at about 4–6 months to be replaced by voluntary eating behaviour. Some reflexes remain throughout life, e.g., blinking, yawning. In the normal course of events reflexes disappear or are incorporated into more voluntary gross and fine motor movements—for example, the grasping reflex of the infant.

Newborn senses

As has been discussed, all of the individual's senses are functional to a certain extent *in utero* and the arrival into the world makes little difference in the individual's abilities, but rather marks a difference in the quality of sensation the individual is exposed to. The biggest change will be in the visual stimuli experienced by the baby. Other than a diffuse orange glow the visual system of the fetus will be unstimulated during pregnancy, yet once born the newborn is exposed to the same visual stimuli as adults. However, of all the senses the visual sense is least well developed. The newborn has poor visual *accommodation* and an underdeveloped pupillary reflex. Visual accommodation is the process whereby small muscles attached to the lens change the shape of the lens thus bringing objects at different distances from the eye into focus. The newborn infant has limited visual accommodation with its focus being restricted to objects about 7–20 inches away from its eye—an excellent distance for viewing the mother's face, however, when feeding. The *pupillary reflex* controls the amount of light entering the eye and after birth this ability is poor, further inhibiting the ability of the baby to focus. Both processes rapidly develop and, along with the development of other crucial processes for accurate vision, eye movements, tracking, scanning, enable the infant's vision to improve with age.

The senses of audition, chemosensation, and various somatosensory senses have been operating since before birth and continue their development after birth to provide the baby with information about its new environment.

Conclusions

The prenatal period is a crucial period of development in our lives. The potential exists for severe disruption to the normal developmental process from environmental agents. However, for the vast majority of pregnancies the environment exerts a positive effect shaping the individual's development. The fetus during this time is an active participant in its development. Its behaviour is important for normal development within the womb and for its life in the postnatal world.

Motor development in infancy

EUGENE C. GOLDFIELD and PETER H. WOLFF

Overview by Alan Slater

One of the most obvious signs of development in infancy is the baby achieving the various **motor milestones**. Parents are very proud of these acquisitions and they are a focus of parental conversations about their infants—'Jimmy can sit now', 'Jennifer has just started to crawl', 'Michael can walk without help', 'Ellie loves to climb up stairs'. The development of motor skills has very important implications for other aspects of development. The ability to *act* on the world affects all other aspects of development, and each new accomplishment brings with it an increasing degree of independence. For example, when infants begin to crawl they become independently mobile and one of the major transitions in early development begins. These changes affect emotional and social development, communication, appreciation of heights, and an understanding of distance and space.

Table 4.1 charts the sequence of development of various motor milestones during infancy. As we will see, at birth the infant has an impressive range of well-developed motor skills, which include sucking, looking, grasping, breathing, crying—skills that are vital for survival. However, the general impression of the newborn is one of uncoordinated inability and general weakness. Movements of the limbs appear jerky and uncoordinated, and it takes a few weeks before infants can lift their head from a prone position. The muscles are clearly unable to support the baby's weight in order to allow such basic activities as sitting, rolling over, or standing. By the end of infancy, about 18 months, all this has changed. The toddler can, walk, run, climb, communicate in speech and gesture, and use the two hands in complex co-ordinated actions.

The questions that a theory of motor development needs to explain include the following: Do the early motor activities prepare the way for the more complex voluntary activities that follow, and if so, how do they do it? How do new motor patterns (such as pointing, running, speaking, tool use) develop as they appear to be qualitatively different (i.e., of a different type) from earlier patterns? As we shall see, the answers to these questions are complex.

Table 1 The Development of Motor Skills in Infancy

Age	Gross Motor Skills	Fine Motor Skills
1–3 mo	Stepping reflex, lifts head, sits with support	Grasps object if placed in hand, sucks, control of eye movements, the first smile.
2–4 mo	When prone lifts head and uses arms for support	Grasps cube when placed near hand
5–8 mo	Sits without support	Reaches for and grasps object, using one hand
5–10 mo	Stands with support, and pulls self to stand	Points at object of interest, grasps with thumb and finger ('pincer grip).
5–11 mo	Crawls	Grasps spoon, gradually learns to direct food to mouth!
10–14 mo	Stands alone, and walks alone	Puts objects into small containers, builds 'tower' of cubes. Produces first meaningful word.
13–18 mo	Walks backwards and sideways, runs, climbs, walks up stairs	Holds crayon with fingers, scribbles energetically
18–30 mo	Runs easily, jumps, skips, rides and steers tricycle, walks on tiptoe	Vocabulary and articulation increases rapidly, picks up small objects (e.g., candy)

When you look at Table 4.1, two things will become apparent. First is that the different motor milestones emerge in a regular sequence—sitting with support, sitting unaided, crawling, standing, walking, and climbing appear almost always in this order. The second is that there is a considerable age range in which individual infants achieve each skill—e.g., some infants crawl at 5 months while others are as late as 11 months. These two aspects of motor development give separate support to two major theories of motor development that are discussed here—*Maturational theories*, and *Systems theory*.

Introduction

Shortly after birth, healthy full-term infants already have at their disposal a rich repertoire of spontaneous and elicited motor patterns that define the 'baseline' with which human infants start extrauterine life. For example, infants typically alternate between periods of sleep and waking in a cycle that corresponds closely with their feeding schedules. Depending on their behavioural state (i.e., whether they are soundly asleep, drowsy, awake, or crying) their breathing movements are organized in several distinct patterns (Prechtl & O'Brien, 1982). Some of these are the following:

- They have at their disposal a number of distinct crying patterns with which to alert the immediate social environment that they are either hungry or in pain (Wolff, 1987).
- When they are given a rubber nipple that delivers no milk, they will almost immediately after birth engage in *non-nutritive* sucking patterns that are organized in a stable rhythmic alternation of rapid bursts and pauses. However, as soon as the nipple delivers milk, they immediately switch to a pattern of *nutritive* sucking that is organized as a continuous stream of slower sucks. In order to take a feeding without gagging, newborn infants are able to form a vacuum inside the mouth, to move the tongue from the back to the front of the mouth to strip the nipple, and to shut off the airways with each swallow so that the milk does not go into their lungs.
- While awake and alert, they turn their head and eyes in the direction of a sound when a moving target crosses their visual field, and they will track the target with both eyes.

Even at birth, they will react almost automatically to appropriate stimulation with stimulus-specific (and relatively fixed) motor reflexes that tell the paediatricians whether infants are neurologically intact and performing in an appropriate way for their age. Thus, when their cheek is gently stroked with a finger, waking infants will turn their head to the side of stimulation and open their mouth as if they were preparing to receive the nipple (the 'rooting reflex'). On the other hand, when their knee tendon is tapped briskly with a rubber hammer, they respond with a sudden single kick ('*knee jerk*' or *patellar reflex*). When they are held in an upright position so that the soles of their feet touch a firm surface, they will retract and extend their legs in an alternating pattern (the *stepping reflex*) that resembles mature walking movements, but in fact differs qualitatively from the latter.

Because the number of such reflexes exhibited by the infant is very large (see, for example, Swaiman & Ashwal, 1999, for a detailed inventory), some investigators have proposed that reflexes are the basic building blocks from which more complex voluntary motor actions are constructed during development. However, neonatal motor reflexes are neither as automatic nor as primitive as their name implies. In its own specific way, each of these deceptively simple motor patterns depends critically on the infant's behavioural state at the moment when the reflex is elicited, as well as on internal organic variables such as pain or hunger, and on the immediate environment. We are likely to take it for granted that infants will only track a moving target or turn their head to the source of a sound when they are awake and alert. Yet, the same 'context dependence' holds for all reflexes (Prechtl & O'Brien, 1982), and more generally for all patterns of motor co-ordination (Wolff, 1987). For example, the knee jerk is active in deep sleep and during awake–alert periods, but cannot be elicited when infants are fussy or crying. The grasp reflex (actually a traction or pulling response) is absent in deep sleep, active in light sleep, and weak when infants are alert. It is much easier to elicit a crisp 'rooting reflex' when infants are hungry than after a meal. Such a context-dependence persists throughout the life cycle, but it is expressed most clearly and studied most easily during early infancy.

In sum, humans, like all other animal species, are equipped at birth with a rich repertoire of co-ordinated motor patterns that insure their survival after birth and prepare them to make contact with the physical and social environment. Particularly during early infancy, the expression of these motor patterns is exquisitely sensitive to changes in behavioural state.

This 'remarkable competence' of the newborn should not, however, mislead us into the belief that everything in the way of motor development that will emerge over the course of the next 2 years is already present in a primitive form at birth. Nor should it mislead us to believe that all that is required over the next 2 years (or beyond) is to stabilize, trim down, and combine these already existing movement patterns in various ways under the influence of reinforcement and experience. Any even partially adequate theory of early motor development must instead be able to account for the means by which qualitatively new patterns of motor behaviour emerge that cannot be reduced to their antecedent components.

By 1 year, infants stay awake and alert for long periods during the daytime and usually sleep through the night, having adapted their sleep–waking cycle to the cultural norm of their parents and siblings. They may still take feedings from the breast or bottle, but can also drink from a cup—a task that requires a new co-ordination between mouthing and swallowing movements.

By the age of 2, infants have acquired the necessary patterns of co-ordination and mechanisms of postural maintenance so they can not only stand without support but also walk in the typical bipedal ('two-legged') gait, even if their walking is still rocky. They have learned to approximate culturally appropriate speech sounds that require complex articulatory movements of the tongue, jaw, mouth, and larynx, and that are entirely different from the patterns of motor control required for crying. By now they can also use their hands to manipulate nearby objects, and can co-ordinate the activities of the two hands so that one hand stabilizes the object while the other explores its features (Bruner, 1971; Bushnell & Boudreau, 1993).

The great advances in skilled motor behaviour implied by our comparison of the neonate and the 2-year-old infant identify core problems that must be addressed by any theoretical account of early motor development. How, for example, does a competent but naïve newborn acquire the ability to walk with support, communicate in speech and gesture, manipulate objects, and co-ordinate the use of the two hands in complex combinations?

What happens to the reflex-like movement patterns of the newborn? Some neonatal motor patterns such as breathing and swallowing that are essential for survival will persist relatively unchanged throughout the life cycle. Others (discussed later) serve a particular function during a limited period of the life cycle and apparently disappear from the repertory once they are no longer needed (*ontogenetic adaptations*, Oppenheim, 1981—the term ontogenetic refers to changes that occur throughout an individual's life, and see Chapter 3 for an account of such adaptations for life in the womb). However, in the human case, it is often impossible to prove decisively that these ontogenetic adaptations have actually vanished. On the contrary, some investigators, as well as clinical neurologists, long assumed that they were only inhibited during development and can therefore resurface in their original form in adults after severe brain damage.

Some of the motor patterns already observed in the neonate are probably stabilized and facilitated by usage and practice, and may become elementary building blocks for the elaboration of new motor skills, although it is again difficult to prove that there is in fact a direct causal link. Of greatest interest for a coherent theory of early motor development are those qualitatively *new* patterns of co-ordinated motor skills that we find in the 2 year old, for example, speaking sentences and using tools.

What a theory of motor development needs to do

The task for any general theory of motor development in infancy is therefore to disentangle the complex causal and functional relationships between the motor repertoire of the newborn and the differentiated motor skills of the 2-

year-old infant. Such a theory must address important questions like the following: Do primitive motor patterns (reflexes) prepare for the acquisitions of complex and apparently voluntary motor skills? If yes, how do they? If not, what happens to them after they 'disappear'? How do qualitatively new forms and functions of co-ordinated motor action emerge from antecedent motor patterns with which they share neither form nor function? In other words, what do we mean when we speak about emergence, spontaneous pattern formation, and self-organization?

In the following sections, we present some dramatic examples from the empirical and experimental literature in animals and humans that will, we hope, illustrate how various theories of motor development have addressed such general questions. We have included studies on the motor behaviour of animals because it is often impossible to answer the basic questions decisively without introducing invasive experimental procedures that can never (and should never) be used in humans. We will not try to present a comprehensive inventory of all the important developmental changes in skilled motor behaviour that have been reported (see, for example, Bertenthal & Clifton, 1998 for a detailed inventory).

Although it is probably impossible to exclude all biases, we have tried to avoid 'taking sides' so that readers can decide for themselves which of the alternative solutions is most plausible in any particular example.

Theories of motor development

Maturational theories

Maturation is the term used to refer to those aspects of development that are genetically predetermined and will develop (or unfold) independently of experience. Maturational theories are therefore examples of the nature side of the nature–nurture issue. With respect to motor development maturational theories assume that motor development will simply occur as the muscles and the brain areas that control motor activity develop. Several lines of evidence have been used by such theoreticians, and we will begin by commenting on physiological studies.

During the early twentieth century students of human motor development were strongly influenced by physiological animal experiments. Sherrington (1906/1947), for example, carried out detailed experiments in cats to analyse how reflexes mediated at the level of the spinal cord ('spinal reflexes') influence co-ordinated motor behaviour. Unlike other investigators who treated reflexes as discrete entities linked to one another in linear chains, Sherrington emphasized the *integrative* functions of the central nervous system. In other words, he assumed that in the intact organism, reflexes always function as

Figure 4.1 Crawling and reaching.

Figure 4.2 Standing with support.

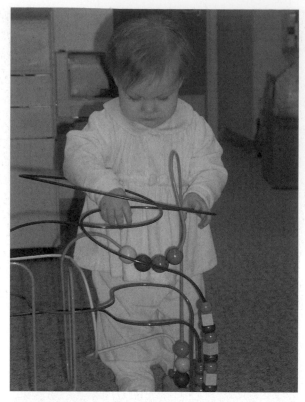

Figure 4.3 Standing unsupported.

Figure 4.4 Pointing.

Figure 4.5 Grasping and manipulating.

Figure 4.6 Feeding.

mutually interdependent units while the central nervous system as a whole orchestrates their interactions. His investigations indicated that reflexes can never be observed in 'pure culture' or studied as discrete units in the intact animal, because any single reflex always influences, and is at the same time influenced by, the activity of other reflexes. The formulation is reminiscent of our earlier examples indicating that neonatal motor patterns are constantly modified by fluctuations in the infant's behavioural state.

Starting from a somewhat different perspective, embryologists such as Coghill and Preyer investigated the influence of central nervous system maturation on the development of motor behaviour. Coghill (1929) carefully recorded developmental changes over time in the swimming and crawling patterns of the salamander *Amblystoma*. These observations led him to the general conclusion that motor development always progresses from global or total body movements to discrete motions of individual limbs that can then act as independent units.

Figure 4.7 The 18 month old can walk, climb, and run.

Later investigators have taken that principle one step further, concluding, on the basis of studies in mammalian species, that motor development proceeds both by a progressive differentiation from global to discrete movements *and* by the progressive integration of discrete movements into co-ordinated wholes.

Gesell and Ames (1940) pursued the same question of how maturation shapes motor development by observing the motor development of human infants *longitudinally* (following the same infants over a period of time) from the newborn period until the age of 9 years. After summarizing the findings on hundreds of hours of cinema films, they concluded that human locomotion progresses from the global to the specific, from head to foot along the length of the body, and from central to peripheral segments of the limbs along a lateral axis. Specifically, they reported that during early infancy, the arms and legs act as 'whole units' whose movements are directed from the shoulder and pelvic girdles. As the elbow, wrist, knee, and ankle joints become more mobile, controlled movements become independent of trunk movements, and limb flexion gains ascendancy over limb extension. Their most far-reaching conclusions were that motor development proceeds in an invariant sequence controlled by a maturational timetable in the central nervous system, that each animal species has its own timetable, and that experience has little, if any, effect on motor development.

Even today, Gesell and Ames (1940) empirical descriptions remain an important point of departure for focused experimental studies. However, their principles of motor development have been largely dismissed. For one thing, they fail to account for individual differences in motor development. For another, they imply that the entire developmental sequence is invariant and predetermined. Therefore, their formulations left no room for the remarkable plasticity of the developing nervous system or for the emergence of motor skills with novel characteristics, such as symbolic gestures, e.g., pointing. Finally, the formulations were based on the assumption that maturation *explains* motor development. Yet, the term maturation simply re-describes the well-known phenomenon that the motor repertory of older children is more differentiated than that of younger children.

McGraw (1945) refined Gesell and Ames (1940) hypothesis on the relation between brain maturation and motor development, by positing that focused training has a different effect on motor functions controlled by subcortical reflexes such as the stepping response, than on motor functions under cortical control such as crawling or walking. First, she plotted the developmental trajectories of swimming movements in newborn infants when they were supported in water, when they were creeping and crawling on a firm surface, and when they were reaching for objects. Many longitudinal observations on 82 healthy infants led her to formulate the hypothesis that bipedal locomotion (the way adult humans walk) develops in four major steps: (1) during the first phase, subcortical ('lower brain') reflexes largely control limb movements; (2)

as the subcortical reflexes are inhibited by higher cortical mechanisms during the first 4 months, the controlling function of the subcortical reflexes diminishes and/or eventually disappears; (3) between 4 and 8 months, motor development involving the co-ordination of discrete muscle groups under cortical control, takes precedence; and (4) finally, between 8 and 14 months, all subcortical and cortical components are integrated to give rise to the mature walking pattern.

As a next step, McGraw tested the hypothesis that massed practice has a relatively greater effect on cortically than subcortically mediated motor patterns. To do so, she compared rates of motor development between sets of twins when only one member of each pair received enriched motor training. Gesell and Thompson had earlier been unable to demonstrate any measurable effects of practice in similar twin-pair comparisons. By contrast, McGraw showed that the extensive additional practice of locomotor skills and reaching behaviour significantly accelerates the development of motor skills that are presumably under cortical control, whereas such training has no effect on subcortical motor reflexes, such as withdrawal from pain stimulation. Therefore, her studies challenged the notion that motor development proceeds in an invariant and fixed progression and is exclusively controlled by central nervous system maturation.

Neurophysiological studies

The neurophysiological experiments performed by Grillner and others (reviewed in Grillner *et al.*, 1999) can, for purposes of this discussion, be viewed as direct experimental extensions of McGraw's observations on human infants. Shik and others (1966) had earlier advanced the hypothesis that in vertebrate animals with an intact spinal cord, the different component movements of a co-ordinated gait (quadripedal for four-legged animals) are controlled by neural mechanisms at different levels of the central nervous system. To test the hypothesis, they compared the quadripedal gait of normal cats with that of cats whose spinal cords had been cut at the upper end (cervical, or neck level). When the spinal cord was sectioned, thus eliminating all cortical influences, the cat was no longer able to modulate the motor pattern in keeping with environmental changes. Nevertheless, the 'spinal cat' could perform the quadripedal gait in a well co-ordinated manner. On the basis of their comparisons, the investigators concluded that basic *patterns* of locomotion (rather than isolated movements) are organized at the spinal level by means of flexible 'central pattern generators' (CPG). In the intact animal, the activity of the CPGs is constantly modulated by descending cerebral pathways, permitting the animal to modify its gait according to environmental requirements.

Forssberg *et al.* (1992) extended these studies to two-legged (bipedal) human infants and children, using non-invasive electrophysiological techniques. They examined how the development of descending cortical excitations (i.e., higher brain activity) might modify the bipedal gait of the young infant, presumably by modulating the functions of spinal CPGs. According to their findings, infants were able to kick their legs in an alternating bipedal pattern during the early months, but because they could not maintain their balance and posture, they could not translate the bipedal leg movements into walking. Between 6 and 12 months, infants began to make patterned movements of the lower limbs that closely resembled the bipedal gait of the adult. On the basis of these and similar experimental observations, the investigators proposed the following sequence of developmental events: (1) initially, the only function of descending neural impulses from brainstem systems is to turn the activities of the spinal CPGs on and off—during this period, the shape of the alternating limb movements is controlled exclusively by CPGs; (2) as neural impulses from higher cortical regions mature and take over the control of the infant's equilibrium, the infant is enabled to keep its balance and to stand or walk; (3) finally, the cooperation among neuromotor systems at all levels of organization makes it possible for the older infants to walk in a mature gait with their feet planted firmly on the ground.

Challenging the maturational hypothesis

In recent years, a number of investigators have challenged the notion that regardless of the details of the underlying mechanisms, the development of motor skills is exclusively determined by developmental changes in the central nervous system. For example, it has long been known that the gait patterns of primates differ substantially from those of other mammals and that the centre of gravity of the animal is much further back in primates than in other animals. Kimura *et al.* (1979) combined these observations and experimentally tested the relation between gait and centre of gravity. They did so by adding weights to the hindquarters of dogs so that their centre of gravity would be shifted backwards, and were able to demonstrate that under these experimental conditions domestic dogs adopted a monkey-like gait. When taken in isolation, the experiment may seem trivial. However, it clearly demonstrates the principle that, even in normal organisms, variables that are not controlled by the central nervous system, such as the distributions of body weight (centre of gravity) and the overall configuration of the body plan, contribute in major ways to gait pattern of different animal species. The same general conclusion follows from many other experiments to the effect that a large array of non-neurological variables can have a profound influence on the co-ordination of motor skills (Hildebrand, 1985). In other words, such studies show that locomotion, reaching and other complex motor skills are never under the exclusive control of the nervous system, but instead depend on the interactive cooperation between central nervous system factors, non-neurological variables, and environmental circumstances, all of which also change significantly during development.

From such considerations it follows that theories of motor development that assign an exclusive or primary role to the activities of the central nervous system are probably not sufficient to account for the development of even such apparently simple motor skills as sucking, vocalization, gait, and posture. However, once one takes into account the nearly infinite number of non-neurological factors that might contribute to the early development of motor skills, it might seem that studies of motor development are intractable to empirical investigation. Yet, recent advances in the study of motor co-ordination suggest that the task is by no means impossible, even if it becomes more difficult.

In the last two decades, a number of very different approaches have been proposed that set as their goal to investigate how the many subsystems and changeable environmental conditions can cooperate to induce coherent and repeatable patterns of motor co-ordination. These approaches are sometimes grouped under the concept of a 'systems perspective'.

Systems theories

The maturational hypothesis, when stated in its extreme form, implies that the pathways by which infants acquire new motor skills are anticipated in some unspecified, genetically predetermined, maturational plan before the infant ever engages in motor action. In other words, it implies that the development (maturation) of *structures* (such as muscles and the brain centres that are involved in motor activities) always pre-dates the development of *functions* (novel behaviours such as reaching, crawling, walking, running). Therefore, it leaves no room for the possibility that novel forms and functions are discovered during the action-in-progress, or that functions may actually lead to the creation of novel structures.

As one alternative to the unidirectional model of development from structure to function, the concept of *probabilistic epigenesis* turns the problem around and focuses on the reciprocal interdependence of biological, experiential, and environmental factors in the development of behaviour (Gottlieb, 1991).

A couple of definitions are in order here! The term *epigenesis* refers to the belief that more complex structures develop from simpler ones by interactions between the organism and the environment, and the combined term *probabilistic epigenesis* is based on the key assumption that there is always a bidirectional or reciprocal (two-way or back-and-forth) relation between structure and function (or behaviour). In other words, the term implies that function determines structure, just as structure determines function.

By contrast, *predetermined epigenesis* assumes that structural maturation determines function, but function has no effect on structure; the function itself is predetermined and fixed by the development of structure. The significant advance of this systems theory approach is the assumption that function or experience not only maintains and facilitates the activation of existing motor patterns, but that function may also *induce* novel behavioural forms.

Developmental scientists working within such a theoretical framework have carried out an extensive series of studies in various fields that demonstrate that the relationship between antecedent and consequent patterns of behavioural co-ordination often is fundamentally *non-linear* (Hall & Williams, 1983). By non-linear we mean that under some of the organism's initial conditions (behavioural state, other states), a given stimulus can sometimes precipitate a major reorganization of function, even though the nature of the stimulus has nothing to do with the form in which the new behaviour is manifested. For example, when the infant is already fussy, even a mild pain stimulus can provoke vigorous crying, whereas when the same stimulus is presented while the infant is in regular sleep, it will provoke only minor withdrawal. Here, the pain stimulus triggers a major change in state, but has no direct causal link to that state. In other words, the organism's internal state that fluctuates from moment to moment determines how it will respond to environmental events at any given moment, and the relation between input and output may vary dramatically depending on the organism's internal state at the moment. We will see in Chapter 5 that various stimuli can be presented to reduce the experience of pain, even in newborn infants.

In 1921, Kuo developed a technique for observing the behaviour of chick embryos before they hatch (Kuo, 1976). He applied the technique to compare the pecking movements of chicks before they hatch and again after they had broken out of their shell. Although the two sets of movements had the same name, their patterns of co-ordination differed qualitatively when compared in detail. On the basis of such observations, he concluded that there was no causal continuity between the pecking movements before and after hatching. Further, he concluded that the major changes in the chick's initial state as well as in the environment had precipitated a reorganization of the same motor components into a qualitatively different pattern of motor co-ordination. In other words, his observations suggest that just because two motor patterns are given the same name (e.g., *pecking movements* in the chick, *stepping movements* and *unsupported walking* in the human infant) does not mean that they are causally related.

Oppenheim followed up Kuo's observations and hypothesis experimentally and was able to show just how discontinuous the relation between apparently similar motor patterns can be (for a detailed review, see Oppenheim, 1981). Also working with chicks, he demonstrated that the pecking movements before hatching were well-suited to release the chick from its shell, whereas the pecking movements after hatching were well-suited for picking up grains but would be useless for breaking out of the shell. Despite surface appearances, there were therefore major changes in both *form* (the type of pecking) and *function* (the purpose of pecking). He took one additional step by examining the underlying neural structures ('spinal reflexes') that presumably controlled pre-hatching and post-hatching pecking movements. These neuroanatomical studies showed that the neural structures associated with the pre-hatching movements degenerated soon after hatching, and new neural structures emerged as the hatched chick foraged for food.

While chicks are not humans, experiments such as these may have profound implications for the study of motor development in general. For one thing, they highlight radical discontinuities in the development of motor coordination. For another, they illustrate how an external trigger (hatching) can induce qualitatively new patterns of motor behaviour without itself being reflected in the later patterns that emerge.

Behavioural studies on human infants indicate that they too, exhibit similar *ontogenetic adaptations*—behaviour patterns that represent adaptations for only a specific period of overall development, although the examples are less dramatic and more difficult to pin down (Oppenheim, 1981). For example, the healthy fetus begins to kick intermittently at about 20 weeks of age (conceptual age) while they are still in the mother's womb where such kicking can have no conceivable adaptive function (Brandt, 1986). Although not by design, such kicking movements nevertheless serve a vital and sometimes life-saving function by reorienting the head towards the end of pregnancy into an optimal position for a safe delivery. At the same time, they may prevent the legs from becoming frozen ('ankylosed') in a flexed position in the cramped quarters of the womb. Until now, however, there is no persuasive evidence that intrauterine kicking movements are causally related to the development of mature walking.

All of the described examples could, in principle, be interpreted as expressions of the simple unfolding of a genetic 'master plan'. The inherent difficulty with the notion of such a plan is that it could, in principle, explain anything and everything that happened during development. But, if everything is already explained by this plan, there is no further need to investigate developmental processes! In our view, the detailed behavioural observations and experiments on ontogenetic adaptations described above are more consistent with the hypothesis that much of development proceeds in a series of discontinuous steps; and that qualitatively new patterns of co-ordinated action emerge spontaneously by a process of 'self-organization'. Let us look more closely at the notion of self-organization in development.

Timing, self-organization, and the flexible organization of motor control

The detailed animal experiments conducted in the early part of the twentieth century by C. H. Waddington (1971) provide strong arguments against the proposition that motor behaviour is controlled by a series of pre-programmed central nervous system commands that assemble already existing units (reflexes) into larger configurations. His arguments were largely based on the concept of 'heterochrony', or the widespread phenomenon that any complex organism is made up of many subsystems (bones, muscles, brain, different brain regions), and that each subsystem develops according to its own timetable. Waddington was able to show that such differences in the developmental timing of individual subsystems are themselves an efficient mechanism for the induction of novel structures and behavioural forms. Moreover, minor changes in the rate of development of any one subsystem can under some conditions actually induce the emergence of new species during evolution (Gould, 1992). From such conclusions, we can extrapolate with some confidence that differential growth rates across motor subsystems and other biological variables may also serve as important engines of developmental change and the induction of new patterns of motor co-ordination.

Starting from a somewhat different perspective, Paul Weiss (1939) carried out experiments in which he amputated the forelimbs of the salamander, reversed the direction in which the limbs pointed, and then reconnected them. Once the deplanted limbs were reconnected and had re-established neuronal connections with the spinal cord, they made perfectly well co-ordinated crawling movements. However, the sequence of muscle contractions in the reversed forelimbs that had originally propelled the salamander forward now tended to move it backward, while the normal hind legs still tried to move the salamander forward; and despite long practice, the four legs did not adapt to this abnormal situation. Weiss concluded that some 'higher integrative' function within the spinal cord orchestrates the timing of individual muscle contractions and generates 'normal' walking movement even when these movements serve no adaptive purpose.

Along similar lines, von Holst (1937/1973) observed that when the spinal cord of bony fish is experimentally severed from the brain, the fish's dorsal and lateral fins oscillated spontaneously and rhythmically at different base frequencies. However, each fin maintained its own frequency only as long as it was acting in isolation. When the dorsal and lateral fins were beating concurrently, their respective frequencies were spontaneously modified in one of several ways. Sometimes, the oscillations of one fin speeded up while those of the other one slowed down until they were 'coupled' or beating at a common frequency that differed from the basic frequencies of either fin. At other times, the two fins competed for dominance, and intermittently switched back and forth between the faster and slower frequency, thereby generating a temporal pattern that was much more complex than the one-to-one synchronization when they were beating in unison.

On the basis of such observations von Holst hypothesized that the spinal cord is equipped with oscillators that control the beat of different fins each at their own base frequency. Further, he concluded that under specified initial conditions, the repetitive movements of the isolated two kinds of fins will couple spontaneously, thereby integrating previously isolated or separate movements into a coherent motor patterns that may have either simple or complex temporal characteristics. The various temporal patterns in which subsystems may couple under different initial conditions (e.g., the base frequencies of either fin) may therefore identify a fundamental mechanism for the spontaneous induction of novel motor patterns. However, such coupling and co-ordination can only occur while the component systems are concurrently active. In other words, action-in-progress, rather than central nervous system instructions, is probably one important source for the spontaneous self-organization of novel motor patterns.

Going from animal experiments to humans, a German paediatrician by the name of Albrecht Peiper (1963) applied von Holst's hypotheses to study the rhythmic behaviour of newborn infants. Specifically, when he examined how the base frequencies of rhythmic breathing and rhythmic sucking interact, he found that the frequency of sucking tends to dominate by 'attracting' the basic frequencies of rhythmic breathing to its own frequency.

Technical advances in the measurement of motor behaviour patterns since Peiper reported his findings have made it possible to study such coupling phenomena in greater detail. For example, when the hand-reared infants of Nubian goats take their feeding from an artificial nipple the rates of their nutritive sucking are tightly coupled with the rates at which they wag their tails. As their sucking rate slows down toward the end of a feeding, the rate of tail wagging decreases in tandem. Other investigators, using more refined experimental tools have replicated Peiper's finding that the rhythmic patterns of non-nutritive sucking have a measurable influence on the rhythm of breathing movements, but breathing movements also influence the rhythm and rate of non-nutritive sucking. Such experimental observations foreshadowed the application of a 'dynamical systems perspective' to the phenomena of spontaneous pattern formation and self-organization in humans (Goldfield *et al.*, 1999a,b).

The dynamics of human motor development

Over the past two decades a number of investigators have begun to explore the possible uses of a special branch of mathematics, called non-linear dynamics or dynamical systems theory, as a means for investigating the conditions under which motor action either self-organizes or is decomposed into its component processes so as to prepare the way for the induction of novel motor skills (Thelen & Smith, 1994; Goldfield, 1995; Kelso, 1995). Dynamical systems theory concerns systems that are inherently unpredictable because of the complex interaction of different factors. An example of a dynamical system is the weather. Certain factors influence the chance of rain, snow, wind, and temperature for a given city, but because each of these factors are not known fully, it is likewise difficult to predict the weather fully.

To proceed with empirical studies into infant motor development, researchers incorporated a fundamental observation by the Russian physiologist Bernstein (1967). Bernstein noted that co-ordinated motor action would be impossible in principle unless some abstract mechanism obliged all possible combinations among the many individual muscles and joints to act in combinations, so that they could be assembled and disassembled freely, depending on the task to be performed (Holt, 1998; Turvey, 1990).

Locomotion

Starting with Bernstein's premise, Thelen and her colleagues reopened Gesell's basic question about 'maturational' factors in human locomotion and prehensile grasping. However, they now applied a dynamical systems perspective to explore what might be the inherent mechanisms that constrained the degrees of freedom in the infant to make walking possible (see Thelen, 1989; Thelen & Smith, 1994). Among the biological and environmental factors they examined that might reduce the degrees of freedom were: the relative weight of the leg muscles in air and in water; the energy expended by infants when displacing their legs; the effect of standing on a stable surface or keeping up with a moving treadmill; and the effect on patterns of walking when the left and right tracks of a split treadmill moved at different speeds.

They reported that the preferred configuration of the cooperating muscles needed for walking changed as these biological factors developed, or as the environmental conditions were experimentally altered. Their results again underscored the important contribution made by extra-neurological variables, both within the organisms and in the environment, to the development of co-ordinated motor action.

Posture and reaching

Equilibrium reactions are responses to loss of balance when the body's base of support is disturbed by a push, pull, or tilt. Righting reactions, in turn, serve to maintain the body's alignment to gravity and to keep the various body parts in alignment with respect to each other. Bernstein (1967), Goldfield (1995), and Reed (1988) have advanced the hypothesis that all actions, including apparently stereotypic movements (i.e., reflexes) are embedded in a basic orienting system that insures that the body, and especially the head, will be maintained in a stable posture with respect to the environment. Various experimental studies have now demonstrated that maintenance of posture is one major constraint that makes co-ordinated action possible by limiting the degrees of freedom.

For example, infants must be able to maintain the head in a stable posture in space in order to move their arm and hand efficiently when reaching for an object (Bertenthal & von Hofsten, 1998). Successful reaching for an object, in turn, involves a great deal more than just directing the arm toward an object and then grasping it, and requires in addition that the trunk and head are kept in a stable posture with respect to the object. Thelen and Spencer (1998), for example, have reported that during its early stages the infant's reaching efforts are poorly controlled and highly variable. Over time, the variability of reaching diminishes substantially, but as the infant begins to move its arms with greater speed, the rapid movements tend to destabilize the position of the head and trunk. As a result, reaching again becomes clumsy and often misses its target. However, once the infant is able to modify the speed of its arm movements without displacing the head, its reaching movements re-stabilize and remain accurate even if the infant varies its speed of arm movements.

In sum, these experiments and many others like them, converge on the conclusion that the development of co-ordinated motor actions, including independent walking and accurate reaching are always the outcome of a complex interplay between central nervous system processes, physical and physiological variables, and relevant environmental contingencies—they are a dynamic system. Therefore, the acquisition of new motor skills cannot be reduced to any unidirectional causal relationships between brain maturation or brain function and behaviour.

The role of experience and learning

The role of learning and experience will be discussed in detail in other chapters of this volume with respect to other aspects of infant development. Here we will limit the discussion to some possible influences of experience on early motor co-ordination. Some of our earlier examples already implied that the acquisition of new motor skills rarely proceeds along a simple forward path, and that *regressions* ('decomposition', 'uncoupling', and an increase of variability) are as essential a feature of normal development as *progressions*. For example, regression may be manifested as a decomposition of established motor patterns so that the component units can be reassembled in new combinations during the action in progress, and some of these new patterns may prove to be 'better' solutions to the motor task in question (Goldfield, 1995; Thelen, 1989).

As Piaget (1952) pointed out and demonstrated many years ago, infants discover new solutions to old problems and become aware of new problems as they encounter unexpected obstacles to a familiar goal. To test this conjecture, Piaget for example presented children with objects that produced 'interesting' and unexpected results. As the children repeatedly applied a familiar routine to reproduce the interesting result, their sensorimotor patterns changed step by step until they suddenly discovered a new means for reproducing the interesting result. At the same time, their success exposed them to new challenges that motivated further explorations. A series of observations of 'inventions' il-lustrates this emergence of new means. Piaget, who famously smoked a pipe, initially presents his daughter Lucienne with a matchbox, places a chain inside it, then closes the box, leaving a small opening. Lucienne explores the box by turning it over, and pokes her finger into the opening. These are her two familiar ways of acting on the box. Then, she looks intently at the opening, and several times in succession opens and shuts her mouth, wider and wider, and retrieves the chain. Here, Piaget argues is the birth of a new means for solving the problem based upon earlier sensorimotor experience. But now, the means is 'represented' by mouth opening before being enacted by the hands. Soon, the solution becomes internalized to thought.

The acquisition of new motor skills

While Piaget's example remains a classic of careful observation and 'rich' interpretation in the context of a theory, the mechanisms by which self-correction during repetition leads to the discovery of new motor skills remain largely a matter of speculation. However, two major methodological innovations have been proposed to address this question in the last decade.

The first of these elaborates on methods of observation introduced by Piaget (1952) and Eleanor Gibson (1988). The experimenter deliberately varies the learning environments in order to tease out how infants discover new solutions (Adolph, 1997). Such experiments have confirmed Piaget's hypothesis that infants are most likely to learn from the challenges that arise when the environment is filled with obstacles, with alternative pathways and with novel situations. The development of motor co-ordination facilitates such discoveries considerably. For example, once the infant can crawl, she can also explore what is behind a barrier when the caregiver is not present. Once the infant is able to walk without support, the horizon of its novel environments expands rapidly. She can explore what is hidden inside a cavity, and how to surmount physical obstacles.

Computer simulations offer a more abstract strategy for investigating the effects of experience on the acquisition of new motor skills. For example, Bullock and Grossberg (1988) have modelled how infants might learn to control their arm movements, by first specifying a target position where the arm should move, and then specifying by a separate command at what speed the arm movement should be. The computer simulation assumes that new motor patterns are constructed by a continuous updating by sensory feedback ('self-correction') of differences between present arm position and the target position. Until now, robots that are programmed according to similar learning strategies have been only moderately successful in learning how to control arm movements. It remains to be seen whether the *neural network* approach will be more informative than experimental studies of living children in clarifying how experience shapes the acquisition of new motor skills.

Recapitulation

In the preceding pages, we have selected observational and experimental studies that raise fundamental questions about behavioural development in general. These questions include: (1) the nature of brain–behaviour relationship; (2) the relative balance between simple linear and complex non-linear (dynamical) brain–behaviour relationships during development; (3) the balance between hierarchic (central) and heterarchic (peripheral) control mechanisms in motor development; and (4) the processes by which anatomical, biological, metabolic, psychological, and environmental determinants cooperate to make behavioural development possible.

As yet, we have no definitive answers to any of these questions. However, as new tools become available for measuring brain activity, they may bring new insights about the relation between brain function and motor behaviour. As we come to understand better the relevance of sophisticated mathematical tools for investigating the behaviour of young infants, we may also be able to pin down more concretely what is meant by spontaneous pattern formation, self-organization of co-ordinated motor patterns, and the induction of novel motor skills. Yet, careful observation and experiments with human infants in their natural habitats will probably remain our most important tools for making new discoveries in this complex field.

5 The development of the senses

ALAN SLATER, TIFFANY FIELD, and
MARIA HERNANDEZ-REIF

Theories, questions, and methods

In order to start making sense of the world the infant has to perceive it, and for this reason the study of perceptual development is one of the major research areas in infancy research. Two main questions have interested investigators: (1) What can infants perceive at and before birth, and (2) How do these abilities change over the first few months from birth, and what is the role of maturation and learning in their development? These questions have been seen to be important for several reasons. One, as we have already noted, is because without functioning sensory and perceptual systems the infant would be unable to make contact with the world. Another relates to the age-old nature–nurture issue: Do infants have to learn to perceive, or do they perceive in an adult-like fashion soon after birth?

Perhaps because the young infant appears to be so helpless, early theories emphasized an *empiricist* view of perceptual development, that infants perceive very poorly and that experience is vital for the development of the senses. The opposing *nativist* view would hold that perceptual development continues according to a timetable set out by an individual's genes. We noted in Chapter 1 that Charles Darwin suggested that hearing and vision were not really functional until a few weeks from birth. The famous developmental psychologist Jean Piaget (whose views are discussed in more detail in Chapter 6), writing about vision, claimed that 'perception of light exists from birth, and reflexes to light (such as pupil constriction to bright light, blinking), but all the rest (perception of forms, sizes, positions, distances, prominence, etc.) is acquired through the combination of reflex activity with higher activities' (Piaget, 1953, p. 62).

For Piaget (and perhaps for Darwin) experience was all, and the newborn baby could hardly be said to perceive anything. However, the last 40 years of research have shown that Piaget and Darwin were wrong—while experience is of great importance, infants display considerable perceptual competence at a surprisingly early age, and as we will describe here even the newborn baby perceives an organized and structured world.

Relation to earlier chapters

If you have read the earlier chapters you will know that each of them makes reference to the senses. In Chapter 2 it was noted that all of the senses (with the exception of vision) are functioning in the fetus, so that birth represents a time of change, but not a beginning. As infants cannot tell us what they perceive, studies of infant perception need procedures that do not rely on language. Advances in research techniques now allow investigators to make use of a variety of responses that help us to investigate babies' perceptual worlds. These include looking, sucking, startle responses, head turning and tracking, changes in facial expression, and physiological indices such as changes of heart and respiration rate, and changes of brain electrical activity. These measures are described in Chapters 2 and 3. However, in order to avoid the reader constantly shifting between chapters, we will make this chapter as 'self-contained' as possible, but refer the reader to other chapters where these are relevant.

Chapter overview

All of the senses provide important information and in this chapter we will review our current understanding in this order: touch (which includes touch discrimination, temperature, and pain); taste; smell; hearing; vision; posture and balance; and cross-modal integration (a modality is an individual 'sense domain', such as touch or vision). A focus of the chapter will be the sensory capacities of the newborn baby—at birth the infant enters a new world, one that he or she will experience for the rest of their life.

Touch

Touch sensitivity

The sense of touch is the first to develop *in utero*, and the sensory cortex is the most developed at birth. In evolution, virtually every animal's sense of touch is the first to develop. Touch begins to develop at about 8 weeks from conception and as early as 3 months the fetus will turn towards a tactile stimulus, much like a rooting reflex (see Chapter 3). A newborn baby can discriminate between fine brush hairs of different diameters, and will respond to electrical stimuli and puffs of air that are even difficult for adults to discriminate (Jacklin *et al.*, 1981). Recent research into touch sensitivity suggests that even newborns are able to discriminate between stimuli using their hands and mouths. In this research the stimuli were nipples that differed in texture, being either smooth or 'nubby'. When newborns were given these nipples in an alternating fashion, they sucked less to the nubby than the smooth, suggesting

that they perceived the difference between the two textures (Hernandez-Reif
et al., 2000).

Temperature

A related sense is the sense of temperature. This was recently investigated in
newborn infants by Hernandez-Reif *et al.* (2001). In their experiment, they
presented newborn infants with tiny tubes of either warm or cold water. In
contrast to the earlier study with nipples, the newborns explored the tubes
by mouth and in an active way. Over trials they habituated to one temperature
and then recovered their attention when the other temperature was
presented.

Pain

Still a third type of touch sense is the sense of pain. Neural pathways for
pain are present by about 26 weeks from conception, and there is no doubt
that the newborn infant feels pain; the most painful stimuli make contact
with the skin, and painful stimuli elicit a significant stress response from newborn infants. Pain has been measured in infants by changes in facial expressions, and also by physiological measures such as heart rate. One way of
inducing pain in the newborn infant is by a heel-stick procedure— this is a
routine blood test to check for any abnormalities. This is clearly a painful
stimulus in that it typically produces facial grimacing, heart rate changes, and
crying.

In adults pain can often be alleviated by touching—this is why we rub a
bumped 'funny bone' or 'crazy bone'. There is a physiological reason for
this—the tactile receptors that experience the touch transmit information
quicker than pain receptors, so the brain gets the rubbing or tactile information before the pain message, and the first message blocks out the second! In
infants it turns out that the stress from a painful heel-stick can be alleviated by
a variety of stimuli, which include sucking, white noise (noise that is 'random',
like that on a TV screen with no signal), the sounds of the maternal heart beat,
a sucrose solution to suck, and the presentation of odours such as milk and
lavender (Field & Goldson, 1984; Blass & Shah, 1995; Kawakami *et al.*,
1997). Thus, tactile stimuli, sounds, and odours all act to alleviate the stress
responses caused by pain.

Although the sense of pain is well developed even in the newborn infant
there is evidence that this sense develops with age: Wolf (1996) found that
older infants gave more stress responses to a heel-stick than younger ones. But
it is certainly not the case, as some have claimed, that newborn infants don't
feel pain.

Taste

In Chapter 3 we saw that even the fetus discriminates between sweet and noxious substances, and the sense of taste is well developed in the newborn infant, perhaps because of the significant experience with taste *in utero*. The amniotic fluid contains all the different tastes, including sweet, sour, salt, and bitter, and thus provides the newborn with significant prenatal experience. The newborn (like the fetus) will show a preference for sweet solutions by sucking more vigorously (Crook, 1978). In several studies newborn infants have been observed making distinct facial expressions when they tasted different sweet, sour, and bitter solutions, and these facial expressions were very similar to the expressions of adults who tasted the same solutions—typically, a smile occurs in response to sweet substances, puckered lips to sour, and disgust expressions to bitter (e.g., Rosenstein & Oster, 1997). Figure 5.1 shows an infant's reaction to sweet and to sour solutions.

Despite the newborn infant's fine sensitivity to different tastes there is still a lot to learn (preferences for hot, spicy foods take years to acquire!). At birth, the infant has food preferences and dislikes that affect their food intake. But even in the first few days and weeks from birth infants develop preferences for tastes to which they are exposed, and by about 3 months they become more active and accepting of new tastes (the introduction of solid foods usually comes around this time, or a little later). Early infancy is the time of development that the psychoanalyst Sigmund Freud called the 'oral stage'—for the first year from birth the infant sucks just about any suckable object, which, fortunately, often includes food. The young infant will often watch other

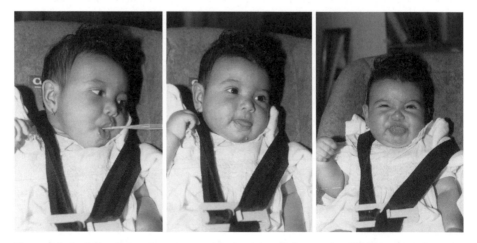

Figure 5.1 An infant being given a sweet solution (a), and the reaction (b). The response to a sour solution (c).

people feeding with great interest and in the first year a range of foods will come to form the basis of the infant's diet. Thereafter, new foods will be less readily accepted and in older infants and children the taste for new foods will depend on exposure and also cognitive factors, but the development of food phobias—the hatred of certain foods—does not usually appear until after 2 years of age (Harris, 1997).

During infancy there is a gradual shift in the importance of internal (*intrinsic*) and external (*extrinsic*) factors in food preferences and intake. Early infancy is intrinsically hunger-driven (the baby cries to be fed when hungry), and this is gradually replaced by extrinsic factors—parental and cultural conventions on meal times and appropriate foods for certain times of day (Harris, 1997).

Smell

From about 9 or 10 weeks from conception the fetus breathes—that is, inhales and exhales amniotic fluid. This gives the fetus a range of experiences with odours and the sense of smell is well developed by birth. In much the same way that they show preferences for tastes newborns show by their faces that they have very clear odour preferences and aversions. Steiner (1979) spearheaded research into odour preferences by presenting newborns with fruit odours that elicited positive facial expressions and fishy/rotten egg odours that elicited disgust expressions. Several studies have demonstrated highly developed odour perception in newborn infants—they will turn their heads towards a pleasant smell and away from an unpleasant one, and will show discrimination between subtle smells as measured by habituation procedures (e.g., Engen & Lipsitt, 1965). In the latter studies the infants are presented with one odour (such as anise oil) on a cotton bud under the nose. This produces changes to respiration rates, which soon habituate (respiration rates return to normal). When a new odour (such as asefatida) is then presented the respiration changes occur again, which is a clear indication that the infants discriminate between the odours.

A much more sophisticated olfactory discrimination is that between the mother's breast pads and those of an unfamiliar nursing mother, and even newborns will show a preference for their mother's breast pad (Cernack & Porter, 1985). To some extent, the chemical profile of breast secretions overlaps with that of amniotic fluid, which may help to explain infants rapidly learning their mother's unique scent.

In a recent study in the second author's laboratory we added lavender to the bath oil of newborn infants. The infants who received the lavender (a pleasant smell) spent more time in deep sleep and less time fussing than those who did not. In a similar manner, newborns showed more relaxed behaviour when they were given lavender odour than when given the smell of rosemary (Fernandez-Ajhar *et al.*, 2001)—aromatherapy works, even with newborn infants.

Hearing—sound, voices and speech

Once again, auditory perception begins in the womb. As was noted in Chapter 3 the fetus responds to sounds as early as 22–24 weeks, and although the womb is a noisy place it is a good conductor of sounds so that external sounds will penetrate the womb and stimulate the fetus's auditory system. Sounds that carry particularly well are those of the human voice—to paraphrase a well-known developmental psychologist, Annette Karmiloff-Smith—'When two heavily pregnant mothers-to-be are talking there are four people listening to the conversation'.

Basic auditory abilities—hearing and localizing sounds

The newborn infant's ability to hear low frequency sounds—particularly those in the range of speech—is close to that of adults, although it is possible that sensitivity to higher pitched sounds undergoes development during infancy (Bremner, 1994). It is also clear that newborn infants can localize sounds. This was first suggested by Wertheimer (1961) who reported that his newborn daughter, only 10 minutes old, would turn her head in the direction of a click (from a toy cricket) that was sounded either to her left or right ear. This finding was confirmed by Muir in several publications (e.g., Muir *et al.*, 1999). In their experiments newborn infants were tested in complete darkness (to avoid visual distractions) and they presented a rhythmic, rattle sound for a few seconds to one ear at a time, over several trials, and on 88% of these trials the babies turned their heads in the direction of the sound.

Auditory preferences at birth

In a classic study (described in more detail in Chapter 3) newborns were given the opportunity to hear either their mother's voice, or a female stranger's voice (the stranger was another newborn baby's mother). They could select which voice they heard by varying the way they sucked on a pacifier (DeCasper & Fifer, 1980), and they preferred to listen to their mother's voice. What is clear is that this preference for the mother's voice develops before birth. This was demonstrated by DeCasper and Spence (1986) who conducted a study in which one group of pregnant women read the Dr Seuss story *The cat in the hat* to their unborn babies, and another group read a version in which the words 'cat' and 'hat' were replaced by 'dog' and 'fog'. Soon after birth the newborns showed a preference for the version of the story they had been read *in utero.*

Perception of speech

The mother's voice is perhaps the most intense acoustic signal that is found in the amniotic environment of the fetus, and the fetus and newborn infant both show heart rate deceleration (a sign of interest and attention) in response to speech sounds (Fifer & Moon, 1994). It is therefore perhaps not surprising to find that babies prefer to listen to their mother's voice when they are born. What is more remarkable is that newborn infants (only 2 days old) appear to prefer their native language.[1] In a study by Moon *et al.* (1993) newborns whose mothers were monolingual speakers of either Spanish or English were tested on audio recordings of female strangers speaking either Spanish or English. They used the sucking procedure so that the babies could control the presentation of the language they heard, and they found that the babies sucked longer to hear their native language in preference to the foreign language, suggesting that sensitivity to certain aspects of language is developing in the womb.

Even the spoken expressions of emotion are most preferred in the newborn's native language to which they have been exposed *in utero* (Mastropieri & Turkewicz, 1999). In this study newborn infants were presented with a range of emotional speech expressions—happy, sad, angry, and neutral—in both their native language and a foreign language. What they found was that the newborns were more likely to open their eyes to happy speech patterns than to the other emotions. More interestingly, an increase in eye opening was observed only when the infants listened to happy speech sounds when spoken by speakers of the native language—infants born to Spanish-speaking mothers showed more eye-opening in response to the presentation of a happy vocal expression in Spanish and newborns of English-speaking mothers showed more eye-opening to the happy expression in English.

If you were to read accounts of language development written as recently as 20 or 30 years ago you would likely read that language begins at about 1 year of age—the time that babies utter their first meaningful word—and that language devices are 'switched on' around that time, perhaps because of some internal biological and genetically determined time clock. Recent research, some of which we have described, indicates that this is far from the truth—that speech and language perception begins even in the womb. By the time of birth

---

[1] In fact, English is what is called a *stress-timed* language in that individual syllables within words are either stressed or unstressed, so that the word 'language' for instance has the stress on the first syllable 'lan', whereas Spanish is *unstressed* in that each syllable of a word is given equal emphasis. It is likely that young infants distinguish languages on this basis rather than knowing more detailed information about their native language. A more detailed discussion of this topic is given in Chapter 9.

the newborn baby has learned enough about his/her mother's voice to recognize and prefer it to strangers' voices, and has even learned enough about the
pitch, intonation, and rhythm of their native language to prefer it to foreign
languages.

The infant is born with the capacity to discriminate between all the speech
sounds used in all the world's languages, but by the end of the first year something remarkable has happened—babies around the world have lost some of
this ability and have become exquisitely attuned to their native languages—in
Janet Werker's (1989) expression they have become 'native listeners'. One of
the world's leading authorities on infant speech perception, Peter Jusczyk,
gives the fascinating account of the development of speech perception
throughout infancy in Chapter 9.

Visual perception

All of the senses provide important information, but it is clear that humans
have evolved to rely heavily on vision at all ages—in adults it has been estimated that more than half of the brain deals in some way with the processing
of visual information (Sereno *et al.*, 1995). This alerts us to the fact that what
appears effortless—seeing—is actually extraordinarily complex. In this section we will discuss the development of visual abilities in infants—from basic
issues to do with how well the infant sees the world through an understanding
of the complex visual worlds of people and objects.

Basic visual abilities

Vision is unique among the senses in that there is no opportunity for it to be
used prior to birth. Although the fetus might be presented with enough visual
input to discriminate light from dark, a proper visual world, of shapes, people, and objects, awaits its arrival into the outside world. It is, then, no surprise to find that vision is perhaps the least developed of the senses at birth.
One simple way of getting at the ability to discriminate detail (known as *visual
acuity*) is to use the visual preference method (described in Chapter 2) in
which pairs of stimuli are shown to the babies. If they look longer at ('prefer')
one of the two we have clear evidence of visual discrimination. The infant is
shown a pattern of black-and-white stripes alongside a grey patch, and the
smallest stripe width that is looked at in preference to the grey gives an estimate of acuity. (This is the equivalent, for infant testing, of the acuity estimates an optician or optometrist obtains by getting patients to read smaller
and smaller letters from an eye chart.) Measured in this way acuity in the newborn baby is some 10–30 times poorer than that of adults (in Chapter 10 there
is a picture of a face as it might look to a newborn).

A newborn's level of acuity, curiously, is about the same as that of an adult cat—so that if newborns could move about they probably wouldn't bump into things. The cat, like the infant, does not need the fine acuity needed to read small print, and for the cat, as for the infant, movement and change in the visual world are particularly attention-getting. Infant acuity reaches adult levels some time after about 6 months, but may not reach full adult acuity until about 3 years. It is worth noting, though, that the poorer acuity of the young infant does not really constitute any disadvantage—the infant sees perfectly well at near distances, which is where the things happen that are of most interest in their developing world.

Many other visual abilities are poor at birth and improve to near-adult levels by 6 months. For example, sensitivity to subtle variations in contrast shows rapid improvement in early infancy. Colour vision also improves rapidly and by a few months from birth is probably like that of adults. Other abilities that are present in weak form at birth include the ability to focus on objects at different distances (known as *visual accommodation*), and precise control over eye movements—these, too, develop rapidly in early infancy. Some other abilities are not present at birth, for example binocular vision. Binocular vision refers to the fact that we have two eyes and because they are separated by a couple of inches in space they provide slightly different images of any scene that is looked at. The brain is able to fuse these two images so that we see one, and not two scenes, and it uses the variations between the two images to provide a powerful cue to depth (this is known as *stereopsis*). This ability comes in at about 3 or 4 months.

An organized visual world

Although newborn infants' vision is much poorer than ours, their visual world is highly organized. An experiment on *size constancy* serves to illustrate this: size constancy refers to the fact that we perceive an object as being the same size despite changes to its distance, and hence changes to its retinal image size. In this experiment we (Slater *et al.*, 1990) showed newborn infants (2 days old) a single object—either a small or a large cube, which, over trials, was shown at different distances from the eyes. Figure 5.2 shows a baby being tested. On subsequent test trials the babies looked more (i.e., gave what is called a 'novelty preference') at a different-sized cube than to the same-sized one, even though the two cubes were at different distances in order to make their retinal sizes the same. This finding demonstrates that size constancy is an organizing feature of perception that is present at birth. Note that this procedure is dependent on the infants learning about the characteristics of the stimulus shown in the early 'familiarization' trials, and also on the infants subsequently preferring to look at novel stimuli on the later test trials. This procedure is therefore a variation on the habituation procedures discussed in Chapter 2.

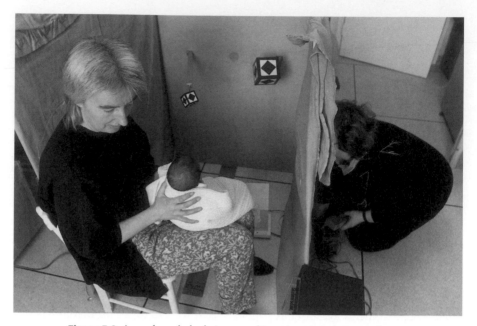

Figure 5.2 A newborn baby being tested in a size constancy experiment.

The human face is one of the most complex visual stimuli encountered by the infant: it moves; is three-dimensional; has areas of both high and low contrast; and contains features that change (when talking, when changing expression, when looking at or away from the baby), but which are in an invariant relationship (the eyes are always above the mouth, etc.). Faced with this complexity it is not surprising to find that the ability to discriminate different facial expressions, or to learn that male faces are in a different category than female faces, appears in mid to late infancy (note that an account of categorization in infancy is given in Chapter 7 by Paul Quinn).

Newborn infants have been found to look at a face-like pattern in preference to a non-face-like one, and they learn about faces from a very early age. Several groups of researchers have reported that infants as young as 12 hours from birth will spend more time looking at their mother's face when she is shown paired with a stranger's face (e.g., Bushnell, 2001; Field *et al.*, 1984; also see Figure 5.3).

While this early learning about the mother's face is impressive, perhaps the clearest evidence that faces are special for infants is the finding that newborn infants, only minutes from birth, will imitate a range of facial expressions that they see an adult produce (e.g., Reissland, 1988). Apparently, this was first discovered by one of Piaget's students (e.g., Maratos, 1998), who reported to him that if she stuck out her tongue to a young baby, the baby would respond by sticking its tongue out to her. (This goes against Piaget's views on

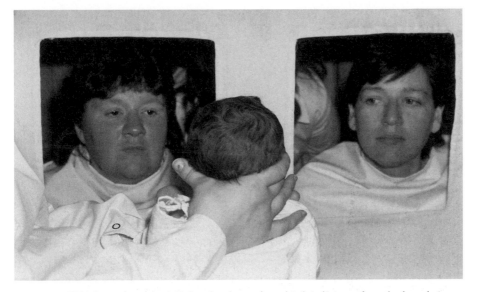

Figure 5.3 Which one is mother? Only a few hours from birth infants prefer to look at their mother's face.

imitation—according to his theory it should not appear until the second year.) Apparently, when Piaget was informed of these findings he sucked contemplatively on his pipe for a few moments, and then commented 'How rude'!

Neonatal facial imitation indicates that the baby can match what it sees to some inbuilt knowledge of its own face, and can then use this match to produce the same facial gesture (which might be tongue protrusion, mouth opening, furrowing of the brow, or other gesture), which the infant, of course, cannot see. This is clear evidence of an inborn ability and raises the question of why do infants imitate? An intriguing idea, put forward by the two researchers who have published more imitation studies than anyone else, is that babies imitate as a form of social interaction and as a way of learning about people's identity (Meltzoff & Moore, 2000).

The topic of infant face perception has probably generated more research than any other single topic, and raises questions about possible innate or inborn abilities, recognizing people, facial expressions, judgements of attractiveness, and the role of faces and people in social development. These important and intriguing issues are taken up and described in detail by Jennifer Ramsey and Judith Langlois in Chapter 10.

The infant's world of objects

At birth infants can discriminate between a variety of shapes, including people, and their visual world is structured and organized by mechanisms

Are these two objects
shaped ...   ... like this? ...   ... or like this?

Figure 5.4 Understanding occlusion.

such as size constancy, but they have a long way to go before they fully comprehend the world of objects. As we look around us most of the objects we see
are partly occluded by objects that lie in front of them—a book occludes that
part of the table it is lying on, a tree occludes part of the horizon, and so on.
Babies begin to realize that partly occluded objects are whole, or complete, behind an occluder from about 2 months of age (Figure 5.4). By about 5 or 6
months infants are beginning to understand that two objects that are touching
are two, not one. By 6 or 8 months they have learned about support and about
gravity—that an object hanging off the end of a table should fall, that ball-
bearings will travel further when rolled down a longer rather than a shorter
ramp, that cup handles will fall if not attached to the cup. They learn about
the relative importance or reliability of different types of information from experience, so that their experiences and actions on the world of objects help
shape up their understanding of physical laws. In this respect they are becoming 'budding intuitive physicists, capable of detecting, interpreting and predicting physical outcomes' (Baillargeon, 1993, p. 311).

But a proper understanding of the physical world is hard won, and even at
the end of infancy it is incomplete. In an experiment to test toddlers' understanding of solidity and support described by Hood *et al.* (2000) 2 year
olds were tested in a situation in which a ball was dropped from a height into
a box. The children knew that in the middle of the box there was a shelf,
and older children appreciated that the ball could not fall through the shelf.
The 2 year olds had different ideas, and when asked to fetch the ball they persisted in searching on the floor, below the shelf. In another experiment, also by
Bruce Hood (1995) even older children (2–4½ year olds) were given a task in
which the goal was to find a toy ball that was dropped through an opaque
tube (Figure 5.5). As is apparent from the figure if the ball is dropped into the
tube at the top right it will land in the box at the bottom left. But in this task
almost all the younger toddlers and some of the older children persisted
in searching in the box immediately beneath the dropping point—for them
gravity rules.

Figure 5.5 Gravity rules. Even when toddlers see a ball dropped into the tube they will search for it immediately below the dropping point. Picture by Bruce Hood.

Posture and balance

We have a tendency to think that we have only five senses—touch, taste, smell, hearing, and vision—but a couple of simple demonstrations convinces us otherwise: (1) stand on one leg and close your eyes, and (2) with your eyes closed touch the tip of your nose with your right hand. Note that touch, smell, taste, hearing, and seeing contributed little to these tasks, but in the first instance you didn't fall over, and in the second you touched your nose effortlessly! Your ability to do these sorts of tasks relies upon two senses—the sense of bodily posture and balance, which is controlled by the semicircular canals in the inner ear (this is known as the *vestibular system*), and feedback from the nerves throughout our bodies telling us where our body parts are (known as *kinesthetic feedback*).

These two senses begin their development in the womb (even the fetus has been known to move its hand so that it can suck its thumb!) and they are constantly developing throughout infancy and later life. Here we will give two examples, one from infant reaching, the other from the so-called 'moving room' to illustrate both their importance in infancy, and how they interact with other senses.

Infant reaching

Thelen and Spencer (1998) followed the same four infants from 3 weeks to 1 year (a **longitudinal study**) in order to explore the development of successful reaching. What they found was that this development followed a clear sequence. First, the infants acquired stable control over the head several weeks before the onset of reaching, then there was a reorganization of muscle patterns so that the infants could stabilize the head and shoulder. These developments gave the infants a stable base from which to reach, and successful reaching followed. This is an indication that infants need a stable posture before they can attain the goal of reaching successfully, and of course visually directed reaching (which first appears at about 4–5 months) needs good vision and also the kinesthetic (arm position) information to guide the hand. It is true to say that all motor developments in infancy (and indeed throughout life) are dependent on both vestibular (balance) and kinesthetic (body position) information.

The moving room

You will almost certainly have had an experience like this. You are sitting in a train in a station and there is another train on the next track. This train then starts moving, but for a moment or two you are convinced that it is your train that is moving. This impression can be so strong in some individuals that if they are standing up they will lurch forwards (or backwards, depending on the direction of the other train's movement) to compensate for the movement—that is, they make inappropriate postural controls. Infants will do this too. In early experiments by George Butterworth (1981) toddlers were tested for posture control in a 'moving room'. This was a small room placed in a larger room and this consisted simply of three walls—front and two sides—and these were on castors so that they could move independently of the floor (which didn't move). Older infants 15–34 month olds) stood up facing the front wall and then the room moved, either towards or away from the infants. The results were clear—when the room moved towards the infant, the baby fell over backwards, and if the room moved away the baby fell forwards (the floor was soft). Younger babies, from 2 months old, were tested in the moving room sitting in an infant chair, and the measure this time was movements of the head, and for all infants there were appropriate head movements when the room moved (i.e., head movements backwards when the room moved toward the infant, and forwards when it moved back).

Overview

These two examples tell us that the posture and bodily position senses are developing in the fetus, and help to guide the infant's behaviour from birth.

These senses also interact with other senses, particularly the sense of vision and motor development. With each new motor development—for instance, from sitting to crawling—infants need to readjust their posture and body senses to make the next 'step forward'.

Co-ordination between the senses

The American psychologist William James (brother of the novelist Henry James) is rightly considered to be 'the father of modern psychology'. His two-volume work *Principles of Psychology*, which appeared in 1890, set the scene for future psychological research, and in it is one of the most memorable (and much quoted) sentences that have been written about infants: 'The baby, as-sailed by eyes, ears, nose, skin and entrails at once, feels it all as one great blooming, buzzing confusion' (Vol. 1, p. 488).

This is the first expression of what is known as 'infantile synesthesia'. The term **synesthesia** means the inability to distinguish between the information coming from the different senses, and what James was claiming is that young infants are bombarded with stimulation to all the senses (which they are) and that they cannot discriminate between them—that is, they confuse the information from the different senses. A simple set of tests convinces us that James was wrong: if a pleasant substance is sucked then sucking will increase; if a light is too bright the infant will close its eyes; if a finger is placed in the baby's palm the baby will grasp it; if an unpleasant smell is presented the baby will wrinkle its nose in disgust. That is, the infant's response to sensory stimulation is highly specific and appropriate to the modality stimulated.

However, James alerted us to the importance of intersensory information, and there is no doubt that the baby's world would be very confusing if they could not integrate the information from the different senses. We will describe two experiments, both with newborn infants, which suggests that infants can indeed integrate and co-ordinate information coming from different senses, and that there are inborn, unlearned rules that guide this learning. The first study was by Morrongiello *et al.* (1998). In this study newborns were shown a toy that was accompanied by a song, and the questions asked were whether the babies could learn the sight-sound pairings, and if so under what conditions? They made use of the finding, described earlier, that even newborn infants can localize and know where a sound is coming from and they had the toy-sound coming either from the *same* place (known as spatial co-location) or from *different* places (dislocation), one to the left the other to the right. The infants learned that the sound was an attribute of a specific object only in the spatial co-location condition—that is, they needed this co-ordination before they associated the two forms of stimulation.

A rather different experiment, but with the same theme and also with sight-sound pairings and newborn babies, was carried out in the first author's laboratory (Slater *et al.*, 1999). In this we familiarized 2 day olds to two different, simple visual stimuli (these were a red vertical line and a green diagonal line) where each was accompanied by its 'own' sound. There were two different experimental conditions—in one the sound was presented for the whole time that the visual stimulus was shown, irrespective of whether the baby looked at the visual stimulus or not, and in the other the sound was presented only when the baby looked (it turned off automatically when the baby looked away, and turned on when he/she looked again). In this latter instance the presentation of each sound–sight pair was synchronized in that the baby either had both together or none at all. The results were clear—the babies only learned the sight–sound combinations when their on/off presentation was synchronized.

These two experiments tell us that even newborn infants can learn about auditory–visual events, but that this learning is guided by the same rules that apply throughout life—only associate stimuli from different modalities if there is information (such as spatial co-location and synchrony) that specifies that they genuinely belong together. We can see how these 'rules' or guides work naturally in the real world—we would only associate a voice with a person if we see their lips move, we would only associate a sound with a particular animal if it comes from the same place. In technical terms the information that specifies that information from one modality is linked with that from another is called **intersensory redundancy**, that is, the information from the two (or more) modalities provide similar, or linking information. Bahrick *et al.* (2000) suggest that redundant information is extremely important in infants and children learning the names for objects—the synchronous presentation of the word and the object it names assists the child in learning the arbitrary word–object associations.

From sensation to perception to cognition

In order to make contact with the world you have to be aware of it! This obvious statement, with which we began the chapter, tells us the senses are vitally important in order for the infant to develop. We can make a distinction between *sensation*, *perception*, and *cognition*. By sensation is meant the ability to register information. We have seen that all of the senses, other than vision, function in the fetus, and vision is clearly functioning from birth. At a slightly higher level, the term perception means acting on the sensory information in order to begin to make sense of it—so that localizing a sounding object, or visual size constancy would be considered acts of perception. At the next level up the infant (or the perceiver in general) comprehends the perceived information—to learn about people, to classify information, to make sense of the world of objects and space, to comprehend speech. All of this is known as cognition, and it is to important aspects of cognitive development that we turn to in the next chapters.

Part 3

Cognitive development

The growth of intelligence in infancy

ROBERT J. STERNBERG

Introduction

Cognition is a term relating to mental abilities—memory, thinking, problem-solving, reasoning, etc. What develops cognitively during infancy? Three major approaches have been taken to answering this question.

One of the first and most influential theorists to examine children's cognitive development was Jean Piaget, whose stages of sensorimotor development are outlined here. Other researchers study infants' cognitive development using an information-processing approach, which tends to place more emphasis on understanding the mental processes used by infants. A third way of looking at babies' cognitive growth is the psychometric approach, which relies heavily on tests to determine and predict infants' current and future cognitive abilities. The major approaches do not contradict each other, for the most part, but rather shed light on different aspects of cognitive development. Let's examine each in turn.

The Piagetian approach

Jean Piaget (1896–1980) crafted what is regarded as the most comprehensive theory of cognitive development that we have, and his ideas have influenced parents, educators, researchers, and later theorists tremendously.

Piaget (1972) believed that infants use *equilibration* to adapt to their changing environment. Equilibration involves seeking to achieve a balance between the demands of the environment and their own cognitive processes and structures. For example, if a baby calls all adult females 'mama', the baby needs to adjust her use of language to the reality of the situation—that all adult females are not her mother. Although equilibration takes place constantly, Piaget believed that cognitive development proceeded in a series of stages, each marked by the child's achievement of certain mental abilities.

The sensorimotor stage

During infancy, children develop through what Piaget referred to as the *sensorimotor stage* of cognitive development, a stage that begins at birth and lasts until roughly age 2, in which infants acquire their understanding of the world through sensory experiences and motor activities.

During the sensorimotor stage, much of the infant's progress in cognitive development is due to the development of what Piaget referred to as *circular reactions*, which are simple behaviours that give pleasure to infants and that they therefore learn to repeat. First the baby initiates an activity; next the baby learns that the activity is pleasurable; this knowledge leads to further initiation of the activity, which in turn leads to the experiencing of further pleasure. Thus, the total behaviour pattern is, in Piaget's own word, circular.

Substages of the sensorimotor stage

The sensorimotor stage is itself divided into six substages. Although each of the six substages is distinct, transitions between substages are generally fairly smooth. A baby's transitions from one substage to another usually happens rather gradually, as the baby's *schemas* (also called 'schemes'), or organized patterns of behaviour, become more complex and elaborate, until the infant has developed the ability to perform the behaviour or mental actions that characterize a new substage of development. For example, a baby may happily play with his or her toes for a few weeks, gradually developing clearer and clearer ideas about where to find the toes and what can be done with them, until one day, while uncovering the toes, the baby discovers it could also be fun to play with the slipper that has been covering his or her toes.

What can the baby do at each substage?

Substage 1: reflexes (birth to 1 month)

The first signs of sensorimotor intelligence are shown when infants exercise their reflexes, such as sucking and grasping. As they practise using their reflexes, newborns also begin to acquire some control over them. At first, infants will exhibit a reflex even if they are subjected to a stimulus that is not appropriate for the manifestation of the reflex. For example, just touching a newborn's lips with any object will often be enough to elicit a sucking reflex. Soon, though, the baby learns to seek out and eventually to find the nipple that will provide milk. Thus, infants do not just passively respond to the environment. They contribute toward actively learning about and even creating that environment.

Substage 2: primary circular reactions and acquired adaptations (1–4 months)

In the second substage, infants start to adapt and fine-tune their reflexes to fit their environments. The adaptations that infants make to their environments are acquired: they are learned through experience. Thus, the reflexes given by natural, or evolutionary, adaptations are tuned to the environment through nurture. One way infants adapt their reflexes is through what are called primary circular reactions.

Primary circular reactions are simple, repetitive acts, discovered by chance, that involve the infant's own body and that infants reproduce because of the pleasure they experience when they engage in the acts.

Let's see exactly how a primary circular reaction works. The infant is born with a sucking reflex. One day the infant discovers that he or she can suck the thumb. Most likely, the infant's thumb happened to be in his or her mouth, and the infant discovered by chance that he or she could suck it. The infant also soon discovers that this simple act can give him or her pleasure, and so the infant starts to repeat the act. Thus, sucking the thumb leads to pleasure, which leads, in turn, to more thumb sucking–a circle, or to be exact, a *primary circular reaction*. Other primary circular reactions might include kicking the legs or making various kinds of sounds.

Substage 3: secondary circular reactions (4–8 months)

By 4 months, infants can begin to manipulate objects. This ability enables them to engage in what Piaget called *secondary circular reactions*, which are simple repetitive actions, first learned by chance, that involve objects or other people and that infants reproduce because of the pleasure they experience when they engage in the acts. Notice, then, that the key difference between a primary and a secondary circular reaction is in the latter's involving objects or other people rather than the infants themselves.

An example of a secondary circular reaction might be in the shaking of a rattle. The infant is given a rattle. When the infant becomes able to manipulate it, he or she discovers the pleasure of the noise he or she can produce with the rattle. This pleasure leads to further shaking of the rattle, and so on. Another example of a secondary circular reaction would be the result of smiling at other people, vocalizing toward other people, or making a gesture toward other people. If the people react, and the infant enjoys the reaction, then the smile, vocalization, or gesture is likely to be repeated.

Substage 4: co-ordination of secondary schemes (8–12 months)

In this substage, infants begin to show clear signs of *goal-directed* behaviour: They decide on a goal, and then purposefully do what they need to in order to realize that goal. They are able to realize goals by elaborating on and co-ordinating the schemas that previously were tied to fixed contexts. For example, if babies see something they want that is at a distance from where they are, they will crawl toward the object, perhaps ignoring distractions and even pushing aside impediments along the way (such as toys or other objects that clutter the room). This seemingly simple act involves co-ordinating schemas for perceiving the existence of the object, figuring out how to get to the object, and dispensing with any obstacles that may be in the infant's path.

The co-ordinated schemas represent complex adaptations not only to objects, but also to people. If the baby's mother is holding an object the baby wants, he or she may try to grab for it. If the mother holds on tight to the object, the infant may actually grab on to the object and try to pull it away. In each case, the infant is elaborating the schema as he or she goes along, seeking to realize goals by formulating and executing a plan, and dealing with obstacles to the realization of that plan.

Substage 5: tertiary circular reactions (12–18 months)

In this substage, infants show *tertiary circular reactions*, which are slight variations of circular reactions that have been learned previously. Tertiary circular reactions enable infants to explore the results from different versions of the actions that they make. Critical to this substage is the infant's purposeful exploration and variation of what were previously stereotyped behaviour patterns. Now the infant is not merely repeating the same behaviour again and again, such as shaking a rattle or vocalizing in the presence of a parent. The infant may try shaking the rattle in different ways, in order to see what effects he or she can produce. He or she may 'speak' slightly different sounds to a parent in order to discover what effects different sounds have on the parent. The variations in behaviour, however, are still more or less at random.

Piaget referred to children in this stage as 'little scientists,' and this identification characterizes Piaget's view of the child at all subsequent ages as well. Piaget viewed the child as learning to formulate general theories and specific hypotheses about the world. Then the child conducts miniature experiments in order to test these ideas. The experiments may or may not be well designed, so they may or may not lead to proper conclusions. Piaget believed that, to a large extent, development lies in *actively* formulating better theories and hypotheses, and better experiments for testing them. The child is not merely responding to the environment that is out there: He or she is actively experimenting on it, transforming it, and even creating it in his or her attempts to understand and even master the world.

Substage 6: beginnings of thought–mental combinations (18–24 months)

In the sixth substage, children become capable of systematically representing, in their minds, events and chains of events. Trial-and-error thinking can be supplemented by deliberate plans for producing effects. The infant will no longer just shake a rattle in different ways at random, for example, but rather vary his or her behaviour systematically. The infant is becoming truly scientific in his or her way of thinking.

The infant can now use *mental combinations*; he or she can contemplate various complex groupings or mixtures of actions. What is crucial here is the word *mental*. The infant no longer actually has to *do* something to see what its effect will be. The infant can now *mentally represent* the course of action. For example, the infant can visualize what would happen if he or she took various routes across the room to reach a desired object, or what might happen if he or she tried any of several strategies to get a desired object away from a parent. With these mental combinations evolves the infant's ability to use *symbol systems*, which are abstract ways of representing ideas, things, and events.

This sixth and last substage is actually the transition to the next stage of development in Piaget's theory, because the child's functioning is no longer, strictly speaking, sensorimotor. Mental representations via various symbol systems move the child into the domain of abstract thinking, and thus beyond the here and now of strictly sensorimotor processing.

The information processing approach

The *information-processing approach* seeks to understand systematically how people (including children!), process information–what mental processes we use, how we combine these processes into strategies, and how we mentally represent information. By systematically studying information processing, psychologists have discovered that children's capabilities are not quite what Piaget believed them to be. Piaget's approach has made a valuable contribution to our understanding of infant development, but it is now known that Piaget misestimated the ages at which children are able to accomplish many kinds of information processing. Various kinds of infant information-processing abilities have been studied, including one achievement first studied by Piaget himself, and this is discussed next.

Object permanence

Piaget recognized that a major accomplishment of the sensorimotor stage is the development of the concept of *object permanence*, the awareness that an object (which can be a person or any other concrete thing) continues to exist even when it is out of sight. According to Piaget, at the beginning of the sensorimotor stage, 'out of sight' truly is 'out of mind' for infants. What the infants cannot see, they do not believe to exist.

Piaget devised a simple but ingenious paradigm for studying this notion. An infant is shown an interesting toy. Of course, the infant looks at the toy. Then the toy is covered with a cloth or a blanket. If the infant searches for the toy, then the infant must know it continues to exist. In a variation of this procedure, an object is shown to an infant, and then the object is hidden behind a screen. The question now is whether the infant continues to search for the object once it disappears, or rather, shows no searching behaviour (visual or otherwise) and acts as though the object no longer exists.

On the basis of such experiments, Piaget concluded that infants do not develop object permanence until they are fairly well along in the sensorimotor stage. In particular, they show no signs of object permanence in the first two substages. In the third substage, they will search for a partially hidden object. In the fourth substage, if an object is hidden in one place and then in another, they will search for the object only in the first hiding place, even if they saw the object moved. In the fifth substage, they will search for an object in the correct place, but only if they saw it being hidden. It is not until the sixth substage, beginning at about 18 months of age, that object permanence is fully developed and infants will correctly search for an object in its hiding place.

Piaget was probably right about the development of object permanence in the sensorimotor stage, but wrong about *what* develops *when*. The problem is that an infant's failure to search does not necessarily mean that the infant does not have object permanence. Babies may fail to search for other reasons (Ruff, 1982; Baillargeon, 1987; Harris, 1987; Baillargeon & DeVos, 1991, 1992). For example, they may not be able to perform the full sequence of actions required for them to search, such as moving something to look at what may be behind it.

Baillargeon and DeVos (1991) created an ingenious study of object permanence that circumvented some of the problems associated with young infants' lack of motor skills. The researchers let 3½-month-old infants watch a carrot slide along a track. The carrot could be either tall or short. The centre of the track was hidden by an opaque screen. Initially, infants were allowed to become accustomed to either the short carrot's or the tall carrot's disappearing behind the screen. Then they were tested.

In the test, the top middle portion of the screen was cut away, so that the infants could see part of what occurred behind the screen. The short carrot should have disappeared behind the screen, because the screen was tall enough, even in the middle, to cover the carrot in its entirety. In fact, that's exactly what happened; the short carrot disappeared completely. The tall carrot, in contrast, should *not* have totally disappeared, because the 'window' that was cut into the top middle portion of the screen would enable the infant to see the top part of the carrot. However, the whole carrot did, in fact, disappear, creating an impossible event. The researchers found that the infants looked longer at the impossible event involving the tall carrot than at the possible event involving the short carrot. The infants' attention to the impossible event suggests that the infants were aware that something was wrong with the way the tall carrot passed behind the screen. Specifically, it suggests that they knew the tall carrot was in existence, even when it was hidden. Thus, even at 3½ months (or substage 2 of Piaget's sensorimotor stage), infants presumably have developed at least some sense of object permanence.

This experiment makes a crucial point about experiments with infants, in particular, and, potentially, with children in general. It is often hard to know from research exactly what children can and cannot do at a given age, because experiments may not be designed in ways that fully expose their capabilities. Experimenters may sometimes think that their paradigms are fooling the infants, when in fact, the experimenters are really fooling themselves in the conclusions they draw! With infants, in particular, just because a child *does not* do something this does not necessarily mean the child *cannot* do it; it may mean only that, under the specific circumstances of that experiment, the child does not do it! This principle applies to object permanence, and it applies to memory as well.

Memory

The research on object permanence suggests that infants may have greater memory skills than Piaget thought, and, indeed, they do. We know that infants can remember the sounds of people's voices that they hear *in utero*. We also know that newborn babies who hear particular speech sounds *just 1 day after birth* can remember the sounds a day later (Swain *et al.*, 1993). So infants have memory skills that are quite impressive.

One programme of research by Carolyn Rovee-Collier (1987; Rovee-Collier & Fagan, 1976) has shown some of the other memory skills of infants. In one study (1987), each baby was placed in a crib beneath a complex mobile. One end of a ribbon was tied to the baby's ankle, and the other end of the ribbon was tied to the mobile. Then the researchers observed the infant kicking and making the mobile move. Two to 4 weeks later, the same group of babies was confronted again with mobiles. Each baby was placed beneath either the exact same mobile as that he or she had seen during the first session, or a different one. Even from 2½ months of age, infants started kicking to get the mobile to move if the mobile was the same one they had seen, and been tied to, before. The infants did not start to kick, however, if the mobile was a different one.

The Rovee-Collier experiments indicate that even very young babies can display impressive feats of memory. The ability to remember people, objects, and situations is very helpful to an infant in learning to adapting his or her behaviour to the requirements of these people, objects, and situations in the environment. Another useful skill in a complex environment is the ability to categorize.

Concepts and categories

Even at an early age, infants are beginning to form concepts and categories, which are needed in order to make sense of the world. For example, in one study (Bomba & Siqueland, 1983), infants of 3 and 4 months of age were shown patterns of dots that were distortions of perfect geometric figures. Some infants might see distortions of triangles, others of squares, still others of diamonds. Eventually the infants became accustomed to seeing these patterns. They were then shown a dot pattern that corresponded either to a perfect triangle, a perfect square, or a perfect diamond. Moreover, the pattern they were shown at this point either corresponded to the same basic shape as the distorted patterns they had seen earlier or did not correspond. For example, a baby who had seen a distorted triangle might now see either a perfect triangle, which corresponded to what he or she had seen before, or a different perfect shape (circle or square), which did not correspond. Infants tended to look longer at the non-corresponding pattern—which was new—thus suggesting that they had understood the prototype or category underlying the earlier figures, and were more interested in the perfect dot pattern that represented a new figure than in the one that represented the old figure. A detailed account of categorization is given in Chapter 7.

Number

Piaget overestimated ages at which children begin to be able to do things in other domains as well. For example, suppose children do not begin truly to develop symbolic representations (abstractions of various objects and ideas) until about 2 years of age, or at best in the transitional sixth substage of the sensorimotor stage, which begins at about 18 months. Then infants should not understand the idea of number, which requires making mental representations, until nearly the age of 2.

Various strands of research suggest that Piaget underestimated infants' number skills. For example, in one set of studies, Karen Wynn (1992, 1995) showed that children as young as 5 months of age seem to have a basic understanding of some number concepts. Wynn showed infants different numbers of Mickey Mouse dolls under different circumstances. For example, to illustrate the concept of '1 + 1 = 2,' an experimenter showed the babies one doll, which the experimenter then hid behind a screen. Then the baby saw a hand place another doll behind the same screen. There should now be two dolls behind the screen, and indeed, when the screen was pulled away, the baby might see two dolls. Sometimes, however, the baby would see just one doll, or sometimes three dolls, when the screen was removed, rather than two dolls. These sums (1 + 1 = 1 and 1 + 1 = 3), of course, are incorrect. Wynn did similar experiments with other arithmetic problems, such as 2 − 1 = 1 (the correct answer) or 2 − 1 = 2 (an incorrect answer). The question was whether the baby recognized that something was wrong when the answers were wrong. But how would Wynn know whether the baby sensed that something was wrong?

Wynn compared the amount of time that babies looked at the correct answers versus the amount of time they looked at the incorrect answers. She found that the babies spent more time looking at the incorrect answers. This fact suggested that they knew something was wrong—in other words, that they had at least rudimentary concepts of number.

Research based on the information-processing approach to cognitive development has shown, sometimes in contrast with Piaget's predictions, that there are several specific cognitive abilities that infants can use at very early ages. Researchers who take a psychometric approach often attempt to measure more general cognitive abilities, such as intelligence.

The psychometric approach

The *psychometric approach* seeks to understand development by focusing on measurement, particularly of individual differences. The present-day origins of this approach can be traced to the work of Sir Francis Galton.

Galton's sensorimotor approach

Sir Francis Galton (1822–1911), an Englishman, believed that the main source of individual differences in cognitive abilities, in general, and in intelligence, in particular, could be traced to differences in sensory acuity, such as the keenness of vision or hearing (Galton, 1883). Thus, Galton's notions fit well with Piaget's emphasis on the importance of sensorimotor intelligence, except that Galton believed that these differences continued to be the key to understanding intelligence throughout the lifespan. Galton devised tests of sensorimotor abilities measuring skills such as visual and auditory acuity, or how hard a person could grasp an instrument (called a dynamometer) that measured hand pressure.

Galton's work was carried over to the United States by James McKeen Cattell (1860–1944), a psychologist at Columbia, who also devised a test of sensorimotor abilities (Cattell, 1890). The test failed to predict course grades at Columbia, however, and so people started to lose interest in the Galton–Cattell approach. Another test, developed a few years later and based on a different view of intelligence, showed greater promise in predicting academic achievement.

Binet's judgmental approach

Alfred Binet (1857–1911), a psychologist in Paris, was asked to devise a test that would separate children who were genuinely mentally retarded, and thus were having difficulties in school because of lack of ability, from children who were having difficulties in school because they did not behave well. Binet and Simon (1916) disagreed with Galton's sensorimotor approach, and instead devised tests of judgement, requiring children to recognize categories into which various things belonged, or to see analogies. Binet's tests, unlike those of Galton, did succeed in predicting school performance, and the tradition of Binet became the dominant one in measuring intelligence.

Infant tests

Neither Galton's nor Binet's tests extended down to measuring intelligence in infancy, and so it was left for others to figure out how to do so. Measuring the intelligence of infants is far from a trivial task. Initially, infants do not speak, and even later in infancy, they do not write. They may not even want to pay attention to what an examiner wants them to do, regardless of what tasks are being required. Thus, special means need to be devised in order to get their attention, keep their attention, and measure their skills in a way that is *reliable* (i.e., scores are consistent from one time of measurement to another) and *valid* (i.e., scores measure what they are supposed to measure). How, then, can infant intelligence be measured?

The Gesell Scales

An early attempt to measure infant cognitive skills was made by Arnold Gesell (1934), who believed that he could derive an overall measure, which he referred to as a *Developmental Quotient* (DQ), combining more specific measures of infant motor, language, personal–social, and adaptive abilities. Gesell made up an elaborate list of behaviours that infants should show at each level of development. Although the work was influential at the time, DQ scores were not useful for predicting later IQ scores, and moreover, it was not clear just what the DQ scores were useful for. As a result, Gesell's work is today viewed as primarily of historical interest.

The Bayley Scales of Infant Development

A more modern measure, the Bayley Scales of Infant Development, was devised by Nancy Bayley (1969, 1993). There are three scales: (1) a *Mental Scale*, which measures abilities such as perception, learning, memory, and verbal communication; (2) a *Motor Scale*, which measures gross motor skills (those skills involving large muscles) and fine motor skills (those skills involving smaller muscles and the manipulation of objects by them); and (3) a *Behavior Rating Scale*, which is the examiner's assessment of the child's behaviour while the child is taking the test.

The Bayley scales are intended as a downward extension of the Stanford–Binet Intelligence Test, which is an Americanized version of Binet's tests. In actuality, the kinds of skills measured by the Bayley represent something of a cross between the kinds of behaviour thought to demonstrate judgement, theorized by Binet to measure intelligence, and demonstrations of sensory and motor skills of the kind theorized by Galton to measure intelligence. Do scores on this test, then, predict later IQ?

The answer, for the most part, is no. In fact, the prediction is quite poor (McCall *et al.*, 1973). One longitudinal study showed very large average differences, about 28.5 points, in IQ between ages 2½ and 17 years. Of course, there will be somewhat better prediction to earlier IQ, because the closer together in time the two tests are given, the higher the relationship between infant test scores and childhood IQ test scores (Bornstein & Sigman, 1986). In general, though, the inescapable conclusion of the literature is that conventional infant tests of intelligence are neither reliable nor valid as predictors of later IQ. They appear to be most useful if there is reason to believe that a child may be somehow developmentally disabled or otherwise functioning in a way that requires special testing.

Each of the three major approaches to understanding infants' cognitive development—Piaget's sensorimotor approach, the information-processing approach, and the psychometric approach—provides a useful way to look at a baby's growing mental abilities. None of the approaches we've covered seem to give us a complete picture of the way infant's cognitive skills develop, however. In fact, some of the ideas upon which these three approaches even seem to be in conflict with each other. How, then, can we ever find out what's going in babies' minds?

An integration of approaches

Although the various approaches to understanding infant development might seem to be wholly disparate, they really aren't. All of them seek an understanding of development, and particularly, of the development of intelligence. One way to spotlight some of the comparisons and contrasts among the approaches is to examine the development of intelligence testing.

Testing of intelligence

The psychometric approach to intelligence, like the Piagetian approach, has emphasized the importance of sensorimotor skills during the first 2 years of life. According to the Piagetian view and most psychometric views, there is a discontinuity in the nature of intelligence between infancy, on the one hand, and later childhood and adulthood, on the other. The idea is that, after infancy, the judgement and reasoning skills identified by Piaget and Binet become important.

Recent research, however, suggests that intelligence may be continuous, rather than discontinuous, in nature across the life span. In other words, intelligence changes in small, smooth increments rather than in sudden spurts. This research is based on the information-processing approach, but it has yielded psychometric measures of infant intelligence, and thus may be seen as integrating the two approaches. This line of research also emphasizes the importance of coping with novelty, a theme in the theory of Piaget. Thus, in a sense, it integrates all three approaches.

The research has shown that infants who prefer novelty and who have better recognition memory tend to have higher scores on intelligence tests later in childhood (Fagan & McGrath, 1981; Bornstein & Sigman, 1986; Thompson *et al.*, 1991; McCall & Carriger, 1993). Tests of infants' preference for novelty predict later IQ much better than do conventional sensorimotor tests. How do researchers determine whether a baby prefers things that are familiar or those that are new to him or her?

In a typical paradigm, infants undergo habituation, which is learning that occurs when an individual stops responding to a stimulus that has become highly familiar. You experience habituation, for example, when you get so used to hearing rock music playing in the background that you are not even aware of hearing it anymore. If an individual is presented with a change in stimulus, the individual undergoes *dishabituation*, which is an increase in responsiveness that occurs when a new stimulus is presented. For example, you might experience dishabituation if you were listening to rock music and all of a sudden it was changed to classical music. Now, suddenly, you might start to notice the music again.

Habituation and dishabituation can be measured in infancy. In a typical experiment, an infant might be shown an image of an object, such as a picture of a face. Early on, the infant pays a lot of attention to the stimulus; after a while, the infant has become habituated, and pays less attention. Now, if the image is changed, the infant will dishabituate, and start paying attention again—in this case, to the new face.

What the research has shown is that infants who are more intelligent—those who will later score at higher levels on intelligence tests—tend to habituate more quickly than do infants who will later show lower scores. Given a choice between a stimulus they have been looking at and a novel stimulus, the brighter infants will more quickly shift their attention to the new stimulus than will the less bright infants.

More intelligent infants also show better *visual-recognition memory*—the ability to recognize, after the fact, images they have seen before—and a preference for novelty. In one study (Thompson *et al.*, 1991), infants at 5 and 7 months of age were shown visual images of various kinds. Sometimes they saw images they had seen before; other times they saw new images. Those infants who spent more time looking at images that were new—that they had not seen before—would later score higher on tests of intelligence (at 1, 2, and 3 years of age).

These recent developments in the research on infant intelligence testing show that each of the three major approaches contributes an important piece of the puzzle of understanding infant cognition. The combination of the pieces, or approaches, provides a more complete understanding of babies' intelligence than we could have from any single approach, and has allowed researchers to develop reliable and valid infant tests. If an integration of approaches to infant cognition can help us develop tests, can it also contribute to assisting infants who are identified as at risk of cognitive delay?

Modification of intelligence

Attempts to improve infant intelligence have had mixed success, but there are some promising efforts (see Sternberg & Grigorenko, 1997a, for a review, and Chapter 15 on the role of early intervention). These efforts combine a variety of ideas from the Piagetian, information-processing, and psychometric approaches.

Two adoption studies show just how powerfully an infant's environment can affect his or her measured intelligence. One study was conduced by Wayne Dennis (1973) in Iran, the other by Michael Rutter (1996) in Romania. Both researchers studied children who had been placed in orphanages. Care was very poor in the orphanages studied in both countries, with children receiving little care, attention, and materials or objects to play with.

Dennis found that children placed in Iranian orphanages had low IQs. Probably because they were reared in institutions of different quality, girls had a mean IQ of about 50 and boys of about 80. Given that the average IQ is 100, these mean scores are very low. Children adopted out of an Iranian orphanage by the age of 2 had IQs that averaged 100 during later childhood; they were able to overcome the effects of early deprivation. Children adopted after the age of 2 showed normal intellectual development from that point, but never overcame the effects of early deprivation; they remained mentally retarded. These results suggest that interventions to foster cognitive development need to start early in cases of severe environmental deprivation.

Rutter's Romanian project showed increases in mean IQ from 60 to 109 for orphans who were adopted by parents in the United Kingdom before 6 months of age. These children showed complete recovery from early mental retardation. However, those who came to the United Kingdom after 6 months of age showed, on average, continuing deficits. This finding again argues for early interventions, at least in cases of severe deprivation.

Other programmes have shown success when deprivation is not as severe. Data supporting the effectiveness of interventions have been accumulating since the 1960s, when the US *Head Start* program was first launched (Chafel, 1992, and see also Chapter 15). The Head Start programme is an early education programme for children in economically deprived circumstances, which could put them at risk for problems in cognitive development. A review of 210 research reports on the effects of Head Start on children (McKey *et al.*, 1985) showed immediate gains on cognitive (as well as socio-emotional) tests for children enrolled in the programme. Although the gains of participants did not remain, relative to the gains of non-participants, over time, Head Start children were less likely to repeat grades in school or to require special education.

Many other studies have been conducted as well (e.g., Gordon *et al.*, 1977; Johnson, 1988; Ramey & Ramey, 1994). The bottom line seems to be that programmes work best when they provide scaffolding for the children, that is, they support the development of cognitive functions in children by providing a foundation for those functions (Sternberg & Grigorenko, 1997b). For example, early exposure to stimulating toys may help infants learn more quickly how to interact and control not only the toys, but their own abilities.

Cognitive intervention programmes often work in the face of adverse circumstances in the family and in the larger environment; but the programmes are often withdrawn when children reach a certain age, at which point the children are returned to their normal (and sometimes inadequate) environment. It is not surprising, therefore, that sometimes the gains are only temporary. Although some families or caregivers may not be able to provide adequate support for enhanced cognitive development in other areas, children in most circumstances typically receive support for development throughout their infancy. It is this support that enables intelligence to grow and the infant to develop.

Acknowledgements

Preparation of this chapter was supported by Grant REC-9979843 from the National Science Foundation and by a grant under the Javits Act Program (grant no. R206R00001) as administered by the Office of Educational Research and Improvement, US Department of Education. Grantees undertaking such projects are encouraged to express freely their professional judgement. This article, therefore, does not necessarily represent the position or policies of the National science Foundation or the US Department of Education, and no official endorsement should be inferred.

7 Categorization

PAUL C. QUINN

In this chapter we will focus upon an important aspect of mental development, *categorization*, which addresses a fundamental question about human knowledge: How is it stored and manipulated? Over time and with experience, members of the human species accumulate a great wealth of information about the world. An internal record of such knowledge is presumed to be compiled in long-term memory. Cognitive scientists are interested in describing how this memory is structured. Consider a system of memory storage resembling a large basket of laundry, freshly washed, and just removed from a clothing dryer. Searching for a particular item of clothing within such a basket would take time and effort because the clothing items have been thrown together in a random arrangement. Imagine instead a memory system resembling a chest of drawers in which the clothing items from the laundry basket are neatly stored with particular kinds of clothing (i.e., shirts, trousers, socks) placed in different drawers. Finding a specific article of clothing within a storage system organized by categories of clothing would be fast and easily accomplished.

Because human cognitive processes, like the recognition and retrieval of information from memory, are in most instances, also fast and easily accomplished, many cognitive scientists believe that our memory is structured according to the 'chest of drawers' model rather than the 'laundry basket' model, with information about various kinds of objects and their relations represented in particular locations within the storage system. The basic unit of organization and storage within a 'chest of drawers' type of memory system has been called a *concept* or *category representation*—terms that refer to a mental representation for similar or like entities. Concepts are believed to underlie our ability to *categorize*, that is, to respond to discriminably different entities from a common class as members of the same category. Thus, as an example, there are many varieties of dogs, but we treat them all as belonging to the same category of 'dog', despite the many perceptual differences between the different varieties.

To give students a concrete metaphor for thinking about concepts, I tell them to think about file folders. We use file folders to organize information into various meaningful groupings, and we may have mental files or category representations to hold information about various object *classes*. By developing a storage system in which information about related instances (e.g., cats) is stored in the same file, and information from related files (e.g., dogs) is nested in larger *superordinate* 'higher up' files (e.g., mammal or animal), we enable intellectual functioning to be mediated or handled by a cognitive system in which objects are related to each other through a set of interconnected concepts.

With concepts, we gain the ability to respond with familiarity to an indefinitely large number of examples from multiple categories, which will include instances never before encountered (Smith & Medin, 1981). Each day we may be presented with novel stimuli—new faces, new furry, four-legged creatures that meow, and new, shiny objects that move on rubber discs. Yet, we do not respond to these entities as if we are unfamiliar with them. Rather, we think to ourselves or even say out loud, 'This is a person. That is a cat. There is a car.' In other words, concepts allow us to respond to the novel as if it is familiar, thereby freeing finite **cognitive resources** to assist with higher-order mental activities such as problem solving and decision-making. If we did not possess concepts, then our memory would consist of a large number of unrelated instances, and intellectual development would be slow-going, because much of our experience would consist of learning to respond anew to the many novel entities encountered on a daily basis.

Concepts also help make mental life more tractable and manageable by simplifying the diversity of the natural environment. In particular, concepts reduce the inherent variation of the physical continua around us into cognitively manageable proportions, that is, a smaller number of chunks. For example, although there are 7 000 000 discriminable shades of colour, most languages collapse colour experience into a dozen or so basic categories (Bruner *et al.*, 1956). Likewise, our cognitive system parses or sorts our orientation continuum, which can be from 0° to 360°, into three basic categories: vertical, horizontal, and slanted (Quinn & Bomba, 1986). Imagine how much more complex early cognitive development would be if we had to learn to map 7 000 000 colour terms on to 7 000 000 colour experiences! And consider the cognitive load placed on the storage and search components of a memory system that represented each degree of orientation as a distinct entity. The processing of continuous information is thus simplified by concepts that represent **category-level** (i.e., summary) information, rather than **exemplar-specific** details (i.e., details about each individual instance or member of a category).

Overall, the processes of categorization, and the concepts that underlie them, permit organized storage, the capability of responding equivalently to an indefinitely large number of instances from multiple categories, and the reduction of physically continuous information into a limited number of distinct groupings. Because of the importance of concepts to mental life, and the recognition that they have to begin at some point during development, there has been interest in when and how concepts emerge.

This chapter will review what is known about the development of categorization in infants. Included in the review will be: (1) a brief account of historical views on the development of categorization; (2) a description of the methodologies that have been used to infer categorization in preverbal infants; and (3) a discussion of recent trends in infant categorization—research that centres on the kinds of category representations formed by infants, their timing of emergence during early development, and the processes by which such category representations are generated. Although category formation by infants has been studied for both visual and speech stimuli (Quinn & Eimas, 1986), the present chapter will focus on infant categorization abilities in the domain of vision, while Chapter 9 will include discussion of the categorization of speech.

Historical views briefly considered

There has been a lingering tradition in developmental psychology to consider the acquisition of concepts to be a relatively late achievement (i.e., of childhood or even early adolescence), dependent on the emergence of naming and language, the receipt of formal tuition, and the possession of logical reasoning skills. For example, Hull (1920) argued that children come to have a concept for dog by associating environmental encounters with different dogs and parental labelling of those dogs as 'dog'. The idea that verbal labels provided a means for acquiring concepts continued into the 1950s with work on *acquired equivalence*—a research programme that suggested items given the same verbal label increased in perceived similarity, whereas items given different verbal labels increased in perceived dissimilarity (e.g., Spiker, 1956; see also Waxman & Markow, 1995, for more recent work on the effect of verbal labels on concept acquisition). Another perspective, one which emerged from the anthropology literature, argued that children were taught through formal and informal means of instruction to assign objects to categories (Leach, 1964). Also contributing to the late estimate of concept emergence in humans was the classical view of concepts—the idea that concepts were represented by sets of necessary and sufficient features—and the findings that even young children, prior to the onset of logical reasoning (e.g., age 6 or the beginnings of a new stage in Piaget's theory of development—the concrete operational period), had difficulty maintaining good criteria for grouping a set of objects as members of a particular category (Vygotsky, 1962; Bruner *et al.*, 1966).

Ideas about the ontogenesis, or development, of concepts during infancy and childhood began to change as ideas about how adult concepts were represented began to evolve, particularly through the work of Eleanor Rosch and her collaborators (reviewed in Rosch, 1978). Embracing the *family resemblance* view of concepts originally formulated in the philosophy literature by Wittgenstein (1953), Rosch argued that categorization is highly determined because objects in the perceived world do not appear to human observers as unstructured sets of equally likely occurring attributes. Rather, the world is structured so that object categories are marked or characterized (like family members) by bundles of correlated attributes. For example, objects such as birds fall into one grouping because they have feathers, beaks, two legs, and an ability to chirp, whereas dogs are compiled into a separate bin because they have fur, snouts, four legs, and the ability to bark. If the Rosch view is correct, then an organism that can detect such correlations and compile them into separate representations is capable of categorization. Thus, by the Rosch view, some of the abilities involved in grouping objects into individuated categories may be present *before* the emergence of language, instruction, and logic. It therefore becomes important to examine the abilities pre-linguistic infants may have to categorize their environment, as it may be from these abilities that the complex concepts and categories of the adult will develop.

Categorization in infants

In order to study categorization in preverbal infants, researchers have utilized procedures that were initially used by investigators of an earlier era to study simple perceptual discrimination and memory abilities. These procedures capitalize on the visual selectivity of infants and the fact that infants will look at some stimuli reliably more than they will look at other stimuli. For example, if a group of infants displays a consistent preference for one stimulus over another, in the sense of looking more at the preferred stimulus, it can safely be inferred that the infants can discriminate between them on some basis.

A preference for looking at novel stimuli (or overall examining preference for novelty, which includes touching in older infants) is a reliable behaviour that extends across a variety of stimulus patterns and age groups—from newborns to 18 month olds—and has proven particularly valuable in providing a methodological inroad for understanding infant cognitive abilities. This preference is the basis for the *familiarization/novelty-preference procedure*. As can be seen in the top panel of Figure 7.1, in order to determine whether infants can discriminate between two visual patterns, infants can be familiarized with two identical copies of one of the patterns, and subsequently presented with the familiar stimulus paired with the novel stimulus. Greater looking at the novel stimulus, referred to as a preference for the novel stimulus, which cannot be attributed to an a priori preference (i.e., a 'natural' or unlearned

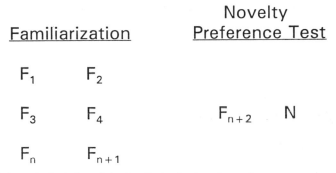

Discrimination using the Familiarization-Novelty Preference Procedure

Familiarization

Novelty
Preference Test

F   F   F   N

Categorization using the Familiarization-Novelty Preference Procedure

Familiarization

Novelty
Preference Test

F_1 F_2

F_3 F_4 F_{n+2} N

F_n F_{n+1}

Figure 7.1 Schematic depiction of the familiarization/novelty-preference procedures used to measure discrimination and categorization abilities of infants.

preference for this stimulus), implies both memory for the familiar stimulus and the ability to discriminate between it and the novel stimulus.

To study categorization in infants, it is necessary to make two modifications in the familiarization/novelty-preference procedure, and these are depicted in the bottom half of Figure 7.1. First, a number of *different* stimuli (referred to as *category exemplars*), all of which are from the *same* category, are presented during a series of familiarization trials. Second, during what is called a **novel category preference test**, infants are presented with two novel stimuli, one from the familiar category, and the other from a novel category. If infants generalize their familiarization to the novel instance from the familiar category, and display a preference for the novel instance from the novel category, then it can be inferred that the infants have on some basis grouped together or categorized the instances from the familiar category (including the novel one) and recognized that the novel instance from the novel category does not belong to this grouping (or category representation). Another way of describing infant performance is to say that the infants have formed a category representation of the exemplars presented during familiarization that *includes* the novel instance of the familiar category, but *excludes* the novel instance from the novel category.

Considerable care must be taken to insure that the infants are not responding to specific features of individual exemplars (or small sets of exemplars) when performing in a study of category formation. One way of meeting this objective is to preselect a large number of exemplars to represent each category under investigation. The exemplars should be chosen so as to approximate or match the variability of the exemplars as they appear in the natural environment. For example, if one wanted to determine whether infants would form a category representation for cats that excludes dogs and a category representation for dogs that excludes cats, then realistic, photographic exemplars of cats and dogs, representing a variety of breeds, stances, colours, and hair lengths, should be chosen (Quinn *et al.*, 1993). Black and white examples are presented in Figure 7.2. Infants in separate experimental groups could be familiarized with a subset of the cats *or* dogs, randomly selected and different for each infant, and then preference tested with a novel cat and a novel dog, also randomly selected and different for each infant. The experimental design is depicted in Figure 7.3. By taking these precautions, the investigator increases the validity of the experiment as a study of category formation, one in which the infants must represent category-level information (e.g., features characteristic of the category as a whole), to perform at above-chance levels.

It should also be mentioned that claims of category formation by infants requires that two further conditions be met. First, it must be shown that the preference for the novel category instance did not occur because of an a priori, or pre-existing preference. The category formation study should thus be repeated with a control group of infants with one important difference: the infants would be presented with only the preference test exemplars and not the familiarization exemplars. In this way, one gains a measure of spontaneous preference for the exemplars that appeared on the preference test trials of the category formation study. An inference of category formation is permitted if the novel category preference observed in the experimental group is significantly greater than the spontaneous preference (for the same category) observed in the control group.

Given that categorization is defined as equivalent responding to a set of discriminably different instances, a second condition that must be met for category formation to be inferred is that the infants be shown capable of *within-category* discrimination. If the infants are not able to discriminate between the individual instances from the familiar category, then the category

Figure 7.2 Black-and-white examples of the cat and dog stimuli used in Quinn *et al.* (1993).

formation study would amount only to a demonstration of *between-category* discrimination, a process that may be considerably simpler than a categorization process that requires grouping of discriminably different instances together.

In order to demonstrate within-category discrimination, each infant in a separate control group is first familiarized with one exemplar from the familiar category and subsequently presented with a preference test pairing the familiar exemplar and a novel exemplar from the same category. The exemplar pairings would be randomly chosen and different for each infant in the control group. Positive evidence for discrimination in the form of a novelty preference that is reliably above chance would tell us that infants can discriminate between the different exemplars. This outcome then allows for the

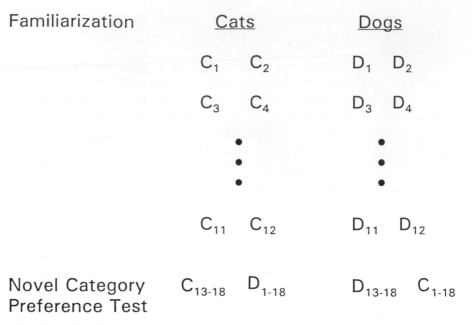

Familiarization   <u>Cats</u>   <u>Dogs</u>

$$C_1 \quad C_2 \qquad\qquad D_1 \quad D_2$$

$$C_3 \quad C_4 \qquad\qquad D_3 \quad D_4$$

$$C_{11} \quad C_{12} \qquad\qquad D_{11} \quad D_{12}$$

Novel Category $C_{13\text{-}18}$ $D_{1\text{-}18}$ $D_{13\text{-}18}$ $C_{1\text{-}18}$
Preference Test

Figure 7.3 Schematic depiction of the experimental design used to assess whether infants can form category representations for cats versus dogs.

conclusion that the infants in the category formation study had grouped together a class of discriminably different entities.

In addition to the familiarization/novelty-preference procedure, at least two other procedures are available for assessing categorization in infants. One is called the *sequential touching procedure*, and has been used with older infants and toddlers in the age range from 12 to 30 months of age (e.g., Mandler *et al.*, 1991). The sequential touching procedure involves presenting infants with a number of exemplars from two categories simultaneously. The exemplars are small, three-dimensional, toy models and are placed before the infant in a random arrangement. Categorization is inferred if the infant touches in sequence exemplars from one category before touching members of the other category.

A more recently developed procedure for assessing infant categorization is called *generalized imitation* (Mandler & McDonough, 1996; McDonough & Mandler, 1998). In this procedure, an infant is presented with a small model of a real-world object (similar to the stimuli used in the sequential touching studies) and an experimenter then models an action appropriate for that object (e.g., a dog drinking from a cup). Categorization is inferred if the infant generalizes the action to other members of the same category, but not to members of contrast categories. Like the sequential touching procedure, the generalized imitation procedure has been used with older infants and toddlers in the age range from 9 to 20 months.

What kinds of categories do infants represent?

Through the use of the three procedures described in the preceding section of this chapter—familiarization/novelty, sequential touching, and generalized imitation—infants have been shown capable of representing a variety of categories *at different levels of inclusiveness*. This observation means that, in the domain of *objects*, infants have been shown to represent instances of furniture and animals at both general, e.g., mammal, furniture, and more specific levels of inclusiveness, e.g., cat, chair (Quinn, 2001a). In the domain of *space*, infants have been shown to represent concepts for spatial relations such as *above versus below*, *between*, and possibly *left versus right*, as well as categories used in particular locations (at specific times), e.g., bathroom or kitchen items (Mandler *et al*., 1987; Quinn, 2001b).

Infants have also been shown to form category representations for attributes of objects, including *colour, orientation, form*, and *facial expression* (Bornstein, 1984; Quinn & Eimas, 1986; Nelson, 1987). In addition, it is possible to interpret the results of other studies in the infant cognition literature as evidence that infants possess physical concepts such as *support, containment*, and *causality* (Cohen & Oakes, 1993; Baillargeon, 1999). In view of the importance and utility of category representations as discussed in the introductory section of this chapter, it should not be surprising that infants can represent much of their experience at the category level.

Current issues

Researchers have begun to investigate a number of interrelated questions regarding *how* infants form category representations. Some of these questions are likely to have complex answers.

Information used to form category representations

One question concerns the basis for category formation by infants. It is possible that infants use *perceptual* attributes that can be found in the appearances of static exemplars of the category. For example, infants might form a category representation for mammals that includes instances of novel mammal categories, but excludes instances of furniture, on the basis of the presence versus absence of such features as faces, fur, tails, and *curvilinear* versus *rectilinear* (curved or straight) contours (Quinn & Eimas, 1996b). Alternatively, it is possible that infants may use more complex, *dynamic* attributes such as the fact that animals form a class of self-starters (i.e., being biological organisms they can move by themselves), whereas furniture items form a class of non-self-starters. Some have argued that such dynamic attributes are more conceptual in nature in that they permit the infant to begin to know 'animals' and 'furniture' as distinct 'kinds of things' as opposed to just knowing what the two classes look like (Mandler, 1992; but see Haith & Benson, 1998).

One strategy that has been used to identify the cue (or cues) that infants may use to form a particular category representation is to demonstrate that infants form the category representation when the cue is present, but do not form the category representation when the cue is absent. Such a strategy has been used to determine how, for example, infants form a category representation for cats that includes novel cats, but excludes dogs, and a category representation for dogs that includes novel dogs, but excludes cats (Quinn & Eimas, 1996a; Quinn et al., 2001a). Given that the two species of animals have considerable perceptual overlap—both possess facial features, a body torso, four legs, fur, and tails—this information is not an obvious indicator of the animal's category.

It is possible that subtle differences, not noticeable upon cursory visual inspection, in one attribute, the pattern of correlation across a number of attributes, or the overall **gestalt** or whole might be used to form the category representations. Interestingly, infants were found to form the category representations of cats versus dogs when the exemplars presented during familiarization and test trials displayed only information from the head region (minus the body region), and did not form the category representations when the exemplars displayed only information from the body region (minus the head region). Infants were also found to form the category representations based on the head region (and not the body region) when presented with whole cats or dogs during familiarization, and preference tested with a pair of hybrid stimuli: a novel cat head on a novel dog body and a novel dog head on a novel cat body (Spencer et al., 1997). Examples of the hybrid stimuli are shown in Figure 7.4. In this case, the novel category preference was found for the stimuli containing the novel category head. These studies thus suggest that information from the head region provides the infants with a necessary and sufficient basis to form a category representation for cats that excludes dogs, and a category representation for dogs that excludes cats. The importance of the face in infant perception of humans is discussed in detail in Chapter 10, and the present results suggest that it is important for animals as well.

Although the above research strategy was successful in demonstrating that head information is used by infants to form category representations for cats versus dogs, some limitations of the approach should be acknowledged. Given that the stimuli were static photographic exemplars of the categories, we do not know the extent to which infants might rely on head information when categorizing real-world instances of cats and dogs encountered in the natural environment. Real cats and dogs display different movement patterns, and it

Figure 7.4 Black-and-white examples of the cat-dog hybrid stimuli used in Spencer *et al.* (1997).

is possible that such movement patterns might also help indicate category membership. Some evidence already suggests that infants can use motion information to categorize more general categories such as animals and vehicles (Arterberry & Bornstein, 2001).

Another limitation of the studies demonstrating the importance of the head region in categorizing cats versus dogs is that we do not know the extent to which the head information would be relied upon by infants who are presented with different category contrasts. When cats or dogs are contrasted with birds, horses, or humans, for example, other cues such as the number of legs, the shape of the body, or the typical posture, may become important in the formation of exclusive category representations for cats and dogs.

These examples suggest that category representations may be anchored by multiple static and dynamic attributes, any one or subset of which may be relied upon or used by infants in a particular context. The task of determining those attributes and identifying the conditions in which they are diagnostic of category membership has begun, and will likely continue for some time, given the cognitive complexity created by the large number of categories, each of which must be differentiated from a large number of contrast categories.

Category formation versus category possession

Another current issue regarding the category representations of infants is whether they are formed on-line, i.e. during the course of an experiment (a case of category *formation*), or whether the experiment is simply tapping into category representations that were constructed (presumably on the basis of real-life experience) *before* the experiment began (an instance of *category possession*). One variable to consider in deciding whether a given experiment is demonstrating category formation versus category possession is the type of experimental task used.

The design of the familiarization/novelty-preference procedure lends itself to an interpretation couched in terms of category formation. Infants are presumed to construct the category representation as more and more exemplars from the familiar category are presented (Mareschal *et al.*, 2000, give a computational model of the on-line category formation process). In contrast, in the sequential touching procedure, exemplars from two categories are presented simultaneously, and spontaneous touching behaviour is recorded. This procedure would seem to tap category representations formed prior to the experiment. Another variable to consider is age. With increasing age, infants have more real-world experience, and are thus more likely to tap their own knowledge base, when performing in laboratory experiments.

Even with task and age as guidelines, it can often be difficult to determine the precise mixture of perceptual process and knowledge access that is occurring in a particular experiment. Consider, for example, the performance of young infants (2–4 months of age) presented with a mammal versus furniture contrast in a familiarization/novelty-preference experiment. Given that such young infants are not likely to have observed (at least directly) mammals such as elephants or hippopotamuses, or the particular furniture exemplars to be presented in the task, one might be tempted to say that the participating infants rely largely, if not exclusively, on perceptual processing, and that they are forming the category representation during the course of the familiarization trials. However, parents are known to read to their infants from picture books that may contain pictorial exemplars of animals, and infants are likely to have at least some visual experience with generic furniture items such as chairs and tables. Moreover, even young infants may be able to recognize that mammals such as elephants and hippopotamuses are more like other animals (including humans) than furniture items (Quinn & Eimas, 1998). Thus, even in an experiment that is designed as a study of concept formation, young infants may recruit from a pre-existing knowledge base that at least in part determines their preference behaviour.

Consider also the performance of older infants (14–22 month olds) presented with an animal versus vehicle contrast in the sequential touching procedure (Rakison & Butterworth, 1998). One would suspect that infants well into their second year of life have encountered a number of animals and vehicles, either through direct or indirect experience (e.g., picture books, television), and that such experience would support the construction of separate category representations for animals and vehicles—representations that could then be used as a basis for successful performance in the experiment. And indeed, this hunch appears to receive confirmation from experimental findings: older infants will spontaneously divide animals and vehicles into separate groupings in the sequential touching procedure. However, if one

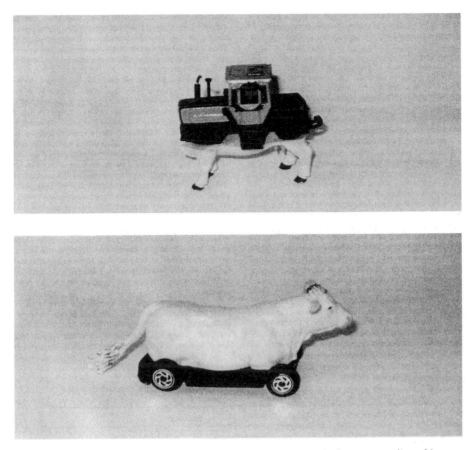

Figure 7.5 Black-and-white examples of the animal-vehicle 'switched parts' stimuli used by Rakison and Butterworth (1998).

removes the legs from the (toy!) animals, and the wheels from the vehicles, the differentiation does not occur. Likewise, if one switches the legs of the animals with the wheels of the vehicles for half of the exemplars (black-and-white examples are depicted in Figure 7.5), differentiation does occur, but it follows the *legs versus wheels* contrast, rather than the *animals versus vehicles* contrast.

Although one can argue that the infants in the Rakison and Butterworth (1998) studies are simply falling back on the use of whatever salient attributes provide a consistent break between two groups when stimuli become strange or unfamiliar, it is clear that the concepts for animal and vehicle are not so clearly established prior to participation in the experiment. If that had been the case, one would have expected the conceptual contrast between animals and vehicles to have been maintained despite the perceptual alterations to the exemplars. Overall, then, these examples are instructive because they cry out for caution when attempting to determine whether infant performance in a categorization experiment is governed primarily by perception or knowledge-based processing.

One- versus two-process frameworks for understanding category representation by infants

A further source of current debate concerns the processes that infants rely on to represent category information. One view has it that the category representations of infants develop gradually through a process of quantitative enrichment (Quinn & Eimas, 1997). By this *single-process* view, infants develop a category representation for animal or animal-like entities; for example, by encountering various animals over time, and joining together into a common representation their perceived attributes such as an elongated body shape, skeletal appendages, facial attributes bounded by a head shape, biological movement patterns, and communicative sounds.

The observable static and dynamic attributes that can be detected from the surfaces and trajectories of the exemplars by perceptual input systems can be supplemented by less apparent information regarding biological structures and functions such as 'has a heart' and 'can reproduce' that are acquired usually by means of language. Language in this view serves as an additional input system that can deliver information that further defines representations already established through vision (and other sensory modalities). As Quinn and Eimas (2000) summarize, 'a representation like animal that may begin by picking out relatively simple features from seeing and other sensory modalities comes over time to have sufficient knowledge to permit specifying the kind of thing something is through a single continuous and integrative process of enrichment' (p. 57).

An alternative *dual-process* framework for thinking about the category representations of infants begins with the idea that 'seeing is not the same as thinking' (Mandler, 1999). This view embraces the idea that category representations formed on the basis of static perceptual attributes are merely *perceptual schemas* that define what a group of things looks like (i.e., categories based on appearance), but that do not contain the content required to define the meaning of something. True category representations or concepts are formed through the analysis or redescription of continuous perceptual input—a process that produces output representations called *image schemas* (i.e., categories based on meaning). Image schemas are the forerunners of mature concepts and can be used to separate animals from non-animals by conceptual primitives or features such as whether the members of the concept are 'self-starters' or 'non-self-starters'. The dual process framework thus suggests that infants possess both perceptual schemas that can be used for *identifying* entities and image schemes that can be used for *conceptualizing* entities—different systems of representation for perception versus conception that operate in parallel.

Is there an order of emergence for category representations at different levels of inclusiveness?

In the opening section of this chapter, it was noted that category representations may exist at different levels of inclusiveness and form hierarchically organized systems of knowledge representation. Human adults can, for example, represent 'mammal' or 'animal' at a *global* or *superordinate* level of inclusiveness, cat at an *intermediate* or *basic* level of inclusiveness, and Siamese cat at a *specific* or *subordinate* level of inclusiveness. Likewise, in the domain of furniture items, furniture is superordinate, chair is basic, and lawn chair is subordinate.

Developmentalists have been interested in the order of emergence for category representations at different levels and whether development consists primarily of progressive differentiation of the basic and subordinate levels from the global level (i.e., from the highest to the lowest levels), or whether development reflects the grouping of specific subordinate representations into basic, and eventually, global levels (i.e., from the lowest to the highest level).

The conventional wisdom for a number of years was that the basic level was the first to be acquired by children, and that development consisted of grouping together basic-level representations to form the superordinate level, and differentiation of the basic level into separate groupings to form the subordinate level. The evidence supporting the *basic-to-superordinate* part of this claim came from a sorting task in which 3-year-olds were asked to identify which two of three simultaneously presented objects were alike (Rosch *et al.*, 1976). The main result was that children succeeded in the basic-level task involving, for example, two airplanes and a dog, but performed poorly in the superordinate level task involving, for example, an airplane, a car, and a dog. This finding provided the initial basis for the basic-to-superordinate view of early category development.

The data supporting the basic-to-superordinate view have been criticized because of the presence of a confound in the basic-level task (Mandler & Bauer, 1988). In particular, it has been pointed out that the basic-level task could be solved with basic-level knowledge (i.e., how much the two airplanes are alike), or with superordinate-level knowledge (i.e., how much the two airplanes are different from the dog), or both. The more appropriate test of the basic-to-superordinate view is to determine whether basic-level categories from the same superordinate category (i.e., airplanes versus cars, dogs versus cats) can be represented before two contrasting superordinate categories can be represented (i.e., vehicles versus animals). In a number of subsequent studies conducted in accord with this experimental design, infants from a variety of age groups, performing in looking, touching, and generalized imitation procedures, have provided evidence of global category representations earlier and more readily than basic-level representations (Mandler *et al.*, 1991; Mandler & McDonough, 1993, 1996; Younger & Fearing, 1999; Quinn & Johnson, 2000; Quinn *et al.*, 2001b). The results of these latest studies thus support a differentiation-driven, *global-to-basic* view of early category development (Quinn & Johnson, 1997).

Concluding remarks

Although concept formation has a history of being considered a late acquisition, dependent on the availability of language, logic, and instruction, studies conducted over the last 20 years suggest that preverbal infants possess abilities for developing category representations that later come to have conceptual significance. The discovery of these abilities has been made possible by advances and refinements in methodologies such as the familiarization/novelty-preference, sequential touching, and generalized imitation procedures. Current debates include the nature of the attributes that infants use to represent category information, the mix of on-line learning versus access of previously acquired knowledge, one- versus two-process models of category representation, and the order of emergence for category representations at different levels of inclusiveness. Given the importance of category representations for the efficiency and stability of cognition, future research investigations will continue on each of these fronts.

Acknowledgements

Preparation of this chapter was supported by National Science Foundation Research Grant BCS-0096300. The author thanks Alan Slater for his comments on an earlier version of the chapter, and Jason Parkhill from the Instructional Technology Center for Faculty Development at Washington and Jefferson College for his assistance in creating the figures.

Space and objects

TOM G.R. BOWER

Introduction

We human adults live in a world of objects arranged in space. At any point in time there are surfaces beneath our feet extending outwards. On these surfaces are objects, near and far, to right and left, some objects on top of other objects, some objects behind other objects, all instantly perceptible without any conscious thought. There is reason to believe that young children, particularly infants, do not possess our adult facility. The best known and most easily demonstrable example of this was discovered by Piaget (1937) nearly 70 years ago (also see Chapter 6). Suppose one places a desirable toy on a table in front of an infant of 6 or 7 months. Most infants will quite rapidly reach forward and take the toy. Suppose one retrieves the toy or gets another toy and puts it on the table. Before the infant can reach for it, place a screen in front of the desirable toy. Most infants will act as if the object no longer existed, paying no further attention to the place where the object is. It has long been thought that the infant's problem stemmed from the screen rendering the desirable object out of sight. However, while 'out of sight' may add to the infant's problem, it is not the true source of the problem, because one can render an object out of sight by switching the room lights off. The infant will then grab the toy even though it is out of sight (Bower & Wishart, 1972). Suppose instead of placing a screen in front of a toy one simply places the toy on another object. As Piaget pointed out we know that the young infant will respond to an object placed on another object in plain sight as if it no longer existed (see also Bresson *et al.*, 1977; Wishart & Bower, 1984, for a large-scale replication). It is clear that the core problem has to do with the spatial relations between objects.

The instance given above is simple and dramatic proof that the world of infants is not quite like the world of adults. There has been great interest in trying to discover just how much commonality there is between these two worlds. Consider the very simple picture shown in Figure 8.1. It can be seen as a trapezoid; however, most adults see it as a rectangle, partly rotated into the third dimension. Would infants see it as a rectangle or as a trapezoid? Consider Figure 8.2. Does it show the same face in three different spatial posi-

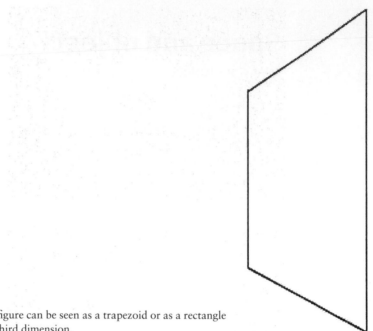

Figure 8.1 This figure can be seen as a trapezoid or as a rectangle
rotated into the third dimension.

tions? Two of the faces in that figure could be seen as very asymmetrical faces.
Most adults, however, would see all three as perfectly normal faces rotated in
the third dimension. When does the infant obtain this ability? An infant without this ability would live in a rather surprising world. The infant en face (facing his or her mother) must occasionally have to deal with mother turning her
face away. Would that be perceived as face distortion or as mother turning
away? There are theories and data about this and related abilities. Consider
the cylinder shown in Figure 8.3. The figure shown in 8.3b is actually much
smaller that the cylinder shown in 8.3a, but we adults see it as of the same size
but further away. The cylinder shown in Figure 8.3c is the same size as the figure shown in 8.3a, but we adults perceive it as further away and much bigger.
We adults are subject to illusions in this last case. Does the infant suffer from
the same illusions, or is his or her perception accurate? Again there is evidence
that we will discuss below.

Nature and nurture again: the problem of the missing dimensions

In recent years, a great many data relevant to these questions have been gathered. However, theorizing *preceded* data on young subjects, and theorizing to
some extent shaped the data gathering process! Of course, there is clearly a

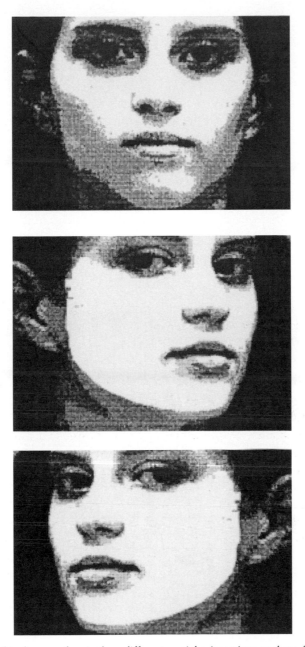

Figure 8.2 Is this the same face in three different spatial orientations or three different faces?

need for theory. We live in an ordered world of three dimensions with objects in it that remain more or less constant. None of our senses is inherently three dimensional. At first sight, at least, the ear seems perfectly adequate to detect order and time, but the ear seems to have no right and left and no third dimension (depth). The sensitive surface of the eye, the retina, is certainly capa-

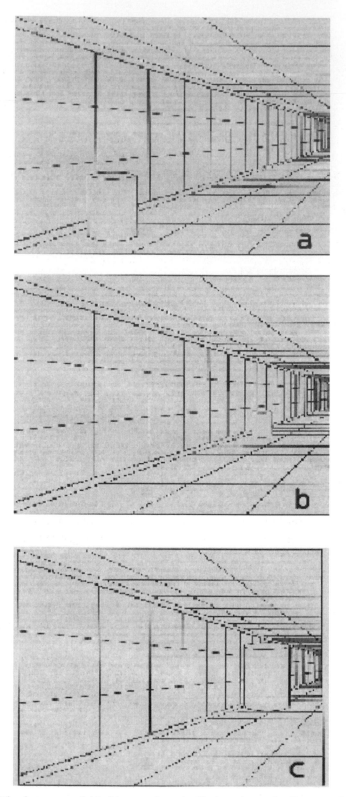

Figure 8.3 The three parts of this figure produce size illusions due to the distance information provided by the background.

ble of picking out right and left and above and below, but where does the third dimension of visual space come from? This is the *problem of the missing dimensions*. Our perceptual world seems to have more dimensions than our sense organs would allow us to have. Where do the missing dimensions come from? One important line of theorizing has maintained that the missing dimensions are created by our mind as a result of learning and hypothesis testing, all designed to give us a simple and coherent world to live in. As this line of theorizing assumes that learning and hypothesis testing take time, the theory necessarily predicts that young infants will live in a random, chaotic world until they have acquired enough experience to make sense of it. A contrary view maintains that there is more information available to our sense organs than first inspection would lead us to believe, and that—the long process of evolution has ensured that we are all born with mechanisms that make sense of the world around us. These two theories have given rise to a long and, at times, bitter controversy. For centuries the controversy went on in the absence of data. The last four decades have given us a plethora of data. We shall examine the impact of the data on the theories.

Smell

We shall begin with the simpler senses, which are also discussed in Chapter 5. First, consider the sense of smell. Odour molecules are drawn in through our nostrils. The characteristics of the molecules tell us a great deal about the source of the odour. However, they do not and cannot tell us where it is! The location of odour sources is an example of dimensions seemingly missing in the stimulus but present in our perceptual experience. The solution to the problem stems from the fact that we have two nostrils. An odour source on the right stimulates the right nostril more strongly than the left nostril. An odour source on the left stimulates the left nostril more strongly than the right nostril. An odour source that is straight ahead stimulates both nostrils equally and symmetrically. Front and back is easily specified by the changes in stimulation consequent on head movement. We adults are not particularly good at odour localization, certainly not in the class of dogs or cats; however, newborns are probably as good as we are. Thus it has been shown that newborns will turn their noses towards a breast pad taken from their own mother's bra, turning away from the pad of another new mother. This behaviour clearly indicates localization and even more strikingly, a degree of personal identification (MacFarlane, 1978).

Hearing

Our sense of hearing presents us with similar missing dimensions. The solution here is very similar. We have two ears. An object on the right stimulates the right ear earlier and more strongly than the left ear. A stimulus on the left stimulates the left ear earlier and more strongly than the right ear. A stimulus that is straight ahead stimulates both ears symmetrically. It has been shown that newborns will turn their heads towards the source of a sound, indicating that they are sensitive to the symmetry/asymmetry of auditory stimulation (Wertheimer, 1961).

The evidence from the studies mentioned above is extremely convincing, partly because the studies use simple, natural responses. It is very easy for us to infer what the newborn is perceiving from our observation of the newborns' behaviour, but subsequent studies of auditory localization in infants have raised a cautionary note about our interpretation of natural behaviour. It has been shown that some time after birth, infants stop turning towards sound sources that require a very large head movement, a head movement that may be too difficult for the baby to make (Bower 1982). Thus if we encounter an infant who does not turn toward the source of sound, the lack of behaviour may indicate prior learning rather than a hearing impairment of some kind (one should always check for a hearing impairment). The lack of behaviour may also indicate neural reorganization (Clifton *et al.*, 1981).

Seeing

The missing dimension of vision has attracted more interest than any other missing dimension. Our adult world is three-dimensional. Where does the third dimension come from? Clearly, a pair of eyes will give the infant a view of the world that contains depth, the missing third dimension; but how, and when, does the infant manage to extract the depth information?

Optical expansion patterns

One line of research presented newborns with stimuli that were approaching their faces or shadows that represented the same visual stimulation on its own, without any air movement. Here, the clue to distance is an increase in an object's perceived size. Under those circumstances newborns show a characteristic defensive pattern that includes head retraction (Bower *et al.*, 1970b; Yonas *et al.*, 1979). This again is a natural response, seemingly designed to pull the head away from the approaching object. The behaviour does not occur if the approaching object is actually on a miss path so that it would whiz harmlessly by the baby's head (Ball & Tronick, 1971). This indicates that babies are sensitive to the very specific information that differentiates an approaching object, one that is moving in the third dimension, from an object that is merely expanding. The infant's sensitivity goes beyond this. We get the same defensive reaction to the stimulus presentation shown in Figure 8.6, which is the shadow of an object rotating in the third dimension towards the baby's face. That behaviour is elicited by the very specific pattern of perspective changes produced by object rotation (Dunkeld & Bower, 1980).

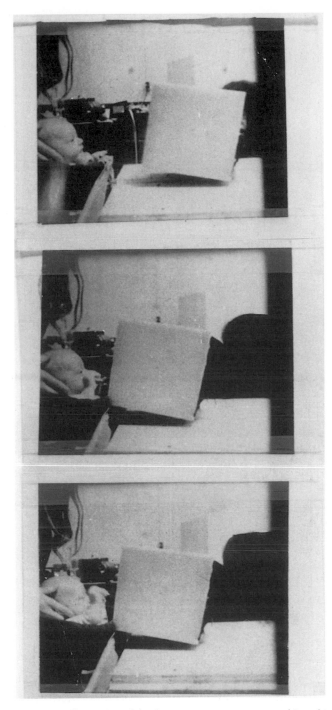

Figure 8.4 An illustration of newborn response to an approaching object.

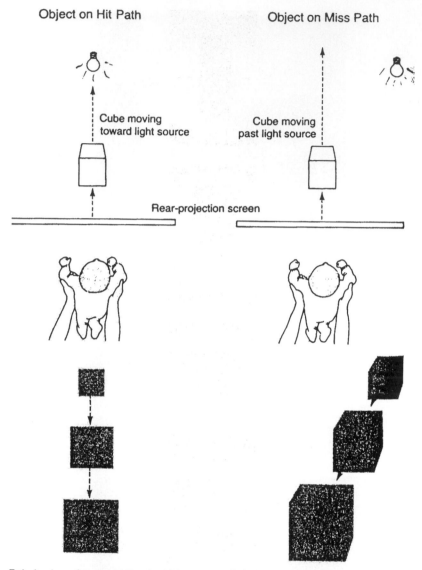

Figure 8.5 (a) The optical expansion pattern produced by an object on a hit pattern. (b) The optical expansion pattern produced by an object on a miss pattern. Newborns can tell the difference.

Binocular and monocular parallax

The examples given in the preceding paragraph are examples of the effects of the optical expansion pattern, a ver well studied stimulus for distance (Gibson, 1950; Schiff, 1965). There are, of course, many other stimuli that can specify distance. We have two eyes, and each receives a slightly different image

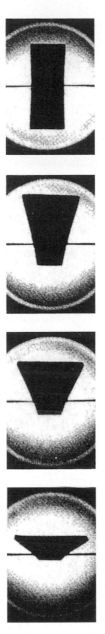

Figure 8.6 This figure shows the pattern of changes at the eye produced by an object rotating in the third dimension in such a way that its top edge will contact the viewer.

of the world, the combination specifying distance because the brain can take into account the difference between the two images. This *binocular* information is commonly referred to as *binocular parallax*, meaning that the two eyes, by being separated in space, get slightly different versions of the world. There is also a *monocular* form of parallax commonly referred to as *motion paral-*

lax. It is generated whenever the eye moves from one position to another. The difference between the views at the start and end of motion specifies depth and distance very convincingly to the adult eye. For example, even if you close one eye you will get a strong sensation of depth when looking from the window of a moving train: nearer objects move relatively faster than the distant ones.

It is clear that both binocular and motion parallax operate to some extent in the visual system of the newborn as well. The studies that have demonstrated this do not rely upon completely natural responses. They may rely on looking, which is a natural response, but in a constrained situation. Their interpretation is not as clear as in the studies described above. Suppose we present a newborn or older infant with an object that they have never seen before. They typically look at it and look away. Looking time typically increases as they become more familiar with the object and then declines as they become bored with it (Hunter & Ames, 1988; Barille *et al.*, 1999). After boredom has set in, looking declines, that is, the infant habituates. Presentation of a new object will stimulate more looking. Now one can choose to exploit the increase in looking with familiarity or its consequent, the decrease in looking with excessive looking, and the recovery due to novelty. Suppose one presents a newborn with a novel object until the newborn has become bored with it. Let us now rotate that object in the third dimension. If the infant showed a dramatic increase in looking we could assume that the newborn did not perceive the depth change but instead perceived the object as a whole new object. If instead there was no change or only a fleeting change we could assume that the newborn perceived the rotated object as the same boring, old object. There have been a number of studies of this kind all arguing that very young infants are sensitive to the stimuli that specify depth (Slater & Morison, 1985). Attempts to separate out binocular and motion parallax sensitivity have yielded conflicting information. However, the fact that newborns are capable of shape constancy does indicate that they are sensitive to one or other or both of these variables.

Painters' cues

What of the so-called '*painters' cues?*' If we adults close one eye and hold our head still, the world does not become flat. It retains its three-dimensional characteristics. That is because we are sensitive to a whole array of stimulus information of the kind that can be captured in paintings or photographs. These variables are often called the painters' cues. There is a definite consensus that newborns are not sensitive to painters' cues, sensitivities to these variables not emerging for some months (Slater, 1989). The reason for this delay has not been specified. This writer, for many years, believed that it was simply a matter of growth in the eyeball increasing the sensitivity of the visual system to the subtle variations that comprise the painters' cues. A recent study has perhaps reopened the question. In that study newborns were presented with three-quarter profile views of a female face. They were presented on a computer monitor so that no parallax information was available. However, all of the painters' cues were present. After brief exposure they were given the choice of looking at a full frontal view of that face or a full frontal view of a different face. As the exposure time had been brief, we would expect the familiar face to receive more attention than the novel face, and indeed it did. This result surprisingly seemed to indicate that newborns could recognize a face through rotation in the third dimension with nothing more to go on than the painters' cues. While alternative explanations for the babies' ability are possible, the investigators up to this point have been unable to substantiate any alternative hypothesis (Walton *et al.*, 1997).

Rapid learning in young infants, and sensory surrogates

While the above account has emphasized what seemed to be inborn abilities, it cannot be denied that newborn humans are capable of very rapid learning and that learning of a very special kind may play some part in the appearance of these early abilities. Recently, it has been claimed that newborns can learn to identify a face in eight-tenths of a second (Walton *et al.*, 1998). Faces are somewhat beyond the remit of this paper and covered in detail in Chapter 10, but rapid learning in one domain surely indicates that rapid learning in another domain is equally possible. Thus, it is clear that young infants whether blind or sighted can learn to use spatial information presented through a com-

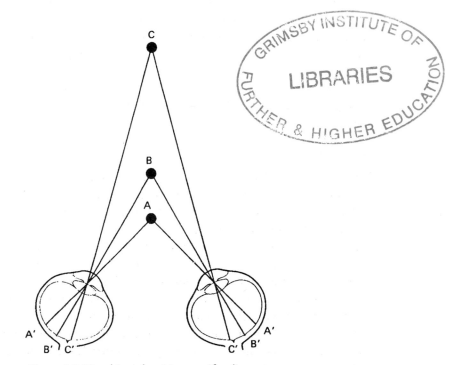

Figure 8.7 How binocular vision specifies distance.

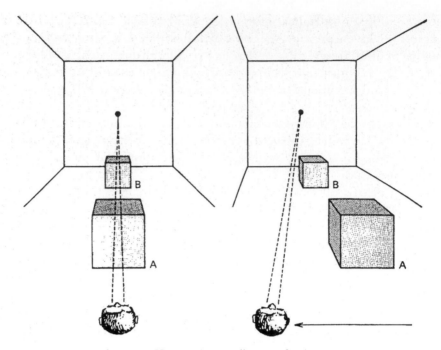

Figure 8.8 How motion parallax specifies distance.

pletely artificial sensory aid, like that shown in Figure 8.9 (Aitken & Bower, 1982; Sampaio, 1989). The information presented has no evolutionary history. It is a human artefact and yet babies, whether blind or sighted, can very rapidly learn to use the information provided by this machine. It has been argued that the rapidity of their learning depends on the fact that the artificial stimulation provided by the machine shares formal, abstract properties with the stimulation that is used by evolved sensory systems. None the less, learning is involved, learning that is rapid and easy for young infants, becoming somewhat more difficult or maybe impossible with increasing age. The certainty that there is rapid learning involved in the use of a sensory aid has not thus far led to any experimentation with natural or evolved stimuli. If we wish to truly pin down the role of learning and the role of evolved mechanisms in space perceptions such research will be necessary.

Similar considerations apply to cochlear implants (surgically implanted, electronic hearing aids) as a form of artificial sense (sensory surrogation). The input provided to the central nervous system by a cochlear implant is not precisely that supplied through the natural evolved mechanism. None the less there is evidence that the information provided can be put to good use. Most of the research thus far has focused on speech perception, but there are ongoing investigations of the utility of cochlear implants for precise auditory localization. The extant evidence indicates that there is a developmental factor in

Figure 8.9 A blind baby using one sensory surrogate, the sonic guide. This machine codes distance as pitch, with further away objects producing a higher pitch at the ear. Size is represented by the loudness of the signal, larger objects producing a louder sound. Hard surfaces produce clear sound, soft objects a fuzzy sound.

the use of cochlear implants, with younger children obtaining greater benefit than older children. The use of artificial information cannot, however, rely solely on evolved developmental mechanisms. Some kind of learning is necessarily involved.

For 50 years, the paradigm, or best example, of an evolved perceptual mechanism has been space perception in the frog. Sperry (1951) showed that the information provided through the frog's eye, what the frog's eye told the frog's brain, was totally impervious to experience or consequences. Sperry's work was behavioural; subsequent electrophysiological work has shown that the mapping of the world from the frog's eye to the frog's brain seems to be genetically fixed with no possibility of alteration by experience. While these results have proven to be extraordinarily robust, they do pose a theoretical problem. Changeux (1984) pointed out that there is not enough information in the genome (DNA) of the frog to specify the frog visual system as precisely as it is specified! That line of thinking is given even more point by the recent compilation of the DNA sequence of the human genome. The current best guess for the number of genes in the human genome is 80 000, well below the number that would be required for precise specification within the human visual system, much less all of the other sensory systems. Like it or not, there must be some experiential tuning of sensory systems. Thus, Gaze (1971) has shown that, even in the frog, the pattern of binocular connections is wholly under the control of experience, with experience playing a creative part rather than a simply destructive one. At present we have not even begun to conceptualize these problems for theories of perceptual development. As sensory surrogates extend and focus the role of experience, they may offer us an avenue of investigation for these deeply puzzling phenomena.

Object perception

Thus far this chapter has focused on space or objects in space rather than on objects themselves. Object perception is a fascinating but relatively little studied aspect of perception. Some aspects of object perception are very well-studied, such as size perception, shape perception, colour perception, perceptual identity, and so on. It would be fair to say that, from early on in life, infants perceive these attributes of objects more or less like adults. One striking characteristic of object perception by very young infants is that it is, from the beginning, *intermodal* (information from the different senses is used and combined). Thus, infants, as we saw above, defend themselves against an approaching object, or the shadow of an approaching object, indicating that they expect a visual event to have tangible consequences. Similarly, they turn their eyes towards the source of a sound, indicating that they expect there to be visible correlates of auditory experience. Meltzoff and Borton (1979) showed that 1-month-old infants could match a seen object with an object in their mouth. Kaye and Bower (1994) showed that newborns could match the shape of a pacifier in their mouth to a seen pacifier that was actually much larger but had the same shape. Bremner (1994) has suggested that the ability to detect a match or mismatch between a seen, speaking face. and the sounds it produces should be a very early intersensory or intermodal co-ordination. It certainly is, since newborns can demonstrate it (Aldridge *et al.*, 1999).

Objects and pictures

Despite the above, it is true to say that the stimulus characteristics that define an object as such are relatively understudied. In a fascinating paper, Michotte (1962) argued that we can get at the definition of an object by looking at why and how it is that adults do not confuse pictures of objects with objects. Michotte's criterion for this was simple. He recommended that we ask an adult to pick up a pictured object. The adult, he said, will look at us as if we were insane and will make no attempt to pick up the pictured object. Pictured objects thus lack some essential characteristic of real objects. It is relatively easy to fool the perceptual system into thinking that a pictured object is real if one is using binocular stereoscopic presentation. However, lacking such presentations it is very difficult to present a static picture that has the sufficient appearance of reality that anyone would attempt to grasp it. It can be done, but it is very difficult and almost necessarily involves the subject closing one eye as otherwise binocular information instantly informs the perceptual system that the object is flat and shares all its boundaries with the surface on which it is located. It has been shown that the young infant will treat a stereoscopically defined object as a real object, trying to grasp it and acting surprised that there is nothing there to be grasped (Bower *et al.*, 1970a). The writer spent many years trying to get young infants to grasp at pictured objects that were not stereoscopically defined in depth with no success whatsoever! As these studies led to the conclusion that young infants less than 6 months did not do something, the results were not thought worthy of publication, although they were alluded to in various other papers. These observations led the writer to propose that an object, a graspable thing, must be perceived as a bounded volume in space, with a top, a bottom, a left, a right, a front, and a back.

Reaching for pictures of objects

This definition was used to explain the strange phenomenon described by Piaget and discussed in the first paragraph of this paper. When one object is placed on another object, or in front of another object, or behind another object, it will typically lose one of its boundaries and so will no longer exist separately from the other object. On this view it would not be surprising that the young infant would act as if the original object no longer existed. Recently, that whole line of theorizing was thrown into disarray by DeLoache *et al.* (1998) who presented evidence that infants about 1 year of age would try to pick up a pictured object. It is clear from the paper that the infants did show appropriate hand movements for grasping. The behaviour appeared in two cultures, and certainly was fading out by 18 months of age, but its appearance at all is extremely puzzling. We have known for many years that recognition of pictures does not require learning (Hochberg & Brooks, 1962). Newborns can identify their mother's face even if it is presented on a computer monitor (Walton *et al.*, 1992). However, treating a picture of an object as a real object is really very different. At present the author has only one question about this study. Did the subjects show any surprise when they failed to pick up the pictured object? Were they at all disappointed in the pictured objects' lack of reality? If they were not surprised, then it is possible that what DeLoache *et al.* were describing was a precocious version of pretend play. The writer has certainly seen an older infant take a spoon and pretend to eat a picture of a dish of ice cream. If, however, the subjects of DeLoache *et al.* truly believed that the pictured objects were real, then we have a new theoretical paradox to deal with, a paradox that may alter many current theories of perception and its development.

In the light of the results of Deloache *et al.*, the object retrieval tasks described by Piaget become even more puzzling than before. Until we can understand the infant's definition of an object, we cannot truly advance our understanding of object perception. Indeed our understanding of the space the infant lives in far exceeds our understanding of the objects that fill that space.

Language development: from speech perception to first words

PETER W. JUSCZYK[1]

Introduction

When do infants begin to learn language? If you asked someone this question in the middle of the twentieth century, chances are that they might have answered 'at the end of the first year, when infants begin to say their first words' (note that the word 'infant' comes from the Greek *infans*, which means 'without speech'). Indeed, in his landmark book, *Child language aphasia and phonological universals* (1941/1968), the eminent linguist, Roman Jakobson, made a strong case for considering babies' babbling to be a pre-linguistic, rather than a linguistic, behaviour. At the time, the study of language acquisition was largely confined to collecting data about the developing child's production of language. Little consideration was given to the possibility that infants might be learning things about their native language before they could produce words and sentences of their own. To a large extent, researchers' preoccupation with the production of language had to do with the lack of suitable methodology for studying infants' perceptual capacities. This picture changed toward the end of the 1960s, when investigators began to devise a range of procedures that allowed them to test the perceptual capacities of infants in the first few months of life. The development of these new testing methods and the discoveries that they yielded led to a radically different view of the perceptual, cognitive, and linguistic abilities of young infants. Today, the most widely held view is that infants acquire considerable information about the nature and organization of their native language well before they actually begin to produce recognizable words. In the remainder of this chapter, we focus on the kinds of things that infants learn about their native language during their first year of life.

[1] Peter Jusczyk passed away on 23rd August 2001, shortly after he finished this chapter. His contribution to our understanding of speech and language development is unequalled. Information about his death was accompanied with the following words: 'With his passing we have lost a pioneer and prolific researcher in infant speech perception and language development whose impact on the field has been enormous'.

Perceiving distinctions among speech sounds

Prior to the first infant speech perception studies, a widely held view suggested that infants might not be able to discriminate differences between speech sounds until they actually had some experience in producing sounds. To understand why someone might hold this view, it is necessary to consider an important phenomenon that investigators discovered about the way adults perceive speech sound differences. When presented with two speech sounds that differ minimally, such as [ba] and [pa], adults' perception of this distinction is said to be 'categorical'—that is, we perceive different speakers' production of [ba] as falling in one category, and their production of [pa] as falling in a distinctly different one.[2] However, the sounds [ba] and [pa] differ only in what linguists refer to as voicing; [ba] is said to be voiced because when it is produced, the vocal cords tend to be vibrating when the lips are released. By comparison, [pa] is described as voiceless because the lips are released before the vocal cords begin vibrating.

As with any human motor activity, the timing of the vocal cord vibration relative to the lip release often varies from one production to the next, meaning that there are lots of slight variations from speakers uttering the same sound. However, listeners' abilities to detect these timing differences are only about as good as their abilities to label the sounds as 'ba' or 'pa'. In other words, they are poor at discriminating timing differences between two different sounds that they would label as 'pa', yet they are very good at distinguishing a [ba] and a [pa] that differ by an equivalent timing difference. This finding is surprising because, for most acoustic stimuli, listeners typically discriminate many more distinctions between stimuli than they can provide distinct labels for. Pollack (1952) found that average listeners could discriminate about 1200 pitch differences between 100 Hz and 8000 Hz, but only consistently used about seven labels within this pitch range.

It was believed that categorical perception of speech sounds developed as speakers learned to ignore the slight timing differences that they heard in their own productions of sounds. Thus, when Eimas *et al.*, (1971) used the high-amplitude sucking procedure to investigate 1- and 4-month-olds' abilities to discriminate [ba] and [pa], they also tested whether their perception of this phonetic contrast is categorical. Their findings showed that, although the infants could discriminate a timing difference as small as 20 ms for sounds that adults labelled as 'ba' and 'pa', they did not discriminate an equivalent timing difference either between two different 'ba' syllables or two different 'pa' syllables. In other words, like adults, their perception of this voicing contrast is

[2] [Ba] and [pa] are both syllables and each is made up of a consonant sound and a vowel sound. A consonant is any sound that involves a stoppage of the stream of air in speech—[b], [c], [d], [f], etc.—whereas a vowel involves narrowing of the airways but no stoppage—[a], [e], [i], [o], [u].

categorical, suggesting that categorical perception is not learned, but rather a natural consequence of the capacities that infants have for discriminating speech sound differences.

Many subsequent studies were undertaken to determine the extent of infants' capacities for discriminating phonetic contrasts.[3] Research focusing on infants' abilities to discriminate distinctions involving consonants indicated that even in the first few months of life, infants can discriminate a wide range of phonetic contrasts, including ones between [b] and [d] (Morse, 1972; Eimas, 1974), [r] and [l] (Eimas, 1975), [m] and [n] (Eimas & Miller, 1980b), [w] and [y] (Jusczyk *et al.*, 1978), and [b] and [w] (Eimas & Miller, 1980a). Although the critical phonetic differences that infants had to detect in these studies occurred in the initial positions of syllables, other studies showed that infants could discriminate many of the same contrasts when they occurred as the final segments of syllables (Jusczyk, 1977; Williams, 1977), or as the middle segments of bisyllables (words with two syllables, such as 'doctor', 'garden', etc.) (Williams, 1977; Jusczyk *et al.*, 1978; Jusczyk & Thompson, 1978). Other investigations demonstrated that during the same period infants are also able to discriminate different contrasts between vowels such as [a] versus [i] (the vowel in 'see') and [i] versus [I] (the sound in 'sit') (Trehub, 1973; Swoboda *et al.*, 1976, 1978; Kuhl & Miller, 1982). Thus, the results of these studies indicated that infants have the ability to discriminate a wide range of phonetic differences that are used to distinguish words in their native language.

Coping with variability

Discriminating differences among speech sounds is important in order to distinguish one word from another. An infant who is not able to distinguish [b] from [d] could never correctly respond to words such as 'buck' and 'duck' or 'bad' and 'dad'. However, because the production of speech depends on the nature of one's articulators and the shape of one's vocal tract, the same word produced by different talkers will vary somewhat in its acoustic characteristics. Moreover, there is much evidence that even within the first few months of life, infants are able to distinguish speech sounds produced by different talkers (Mehler *et al.*, 1978; DeCasper & Fifer, 1980; Miller *et al.*, 1982). Thus, different talkers' renditions of the same word are likely to be perceptible for infants. Yet, while attention to such differences is undoubtedly helpful in identifying who produced the word, in order to respond appropriately to the word's meaning, it is important that infants be able to recognize the word

[3] Phonetic contrasts are distinctions between any two different speech sounds (phonemes).

regardless of whether it is produced by talker A, B, C, etc. In other words, perceptual constancy is not only important when recognizing visual objects in the world, it is also important for correctly perceiving what was said.

Even though they are able to distinguish different talkers, infants also display some ability to recognize the same speech sound when produced by a range of different talkers. This ability was first identified in a study Kuhl (1979) conducted with 6 month olds. Kuhl used the **operant conditioned headturn procedure** (see Chapter 2) to train infants to respond to a contrast between the vowels [a] and [i] produced by a single talker. One of these vowels was played repeatedly as a background stimulus. Every once in a while, the background stimulus was changed to the other vowel for three repetitions, and then returned to the original background stimulus. If infants turned their head during the interval when the new vowel was playing, they got to see an interesting visual display. Once the infants learned to respond correctly to the vowel change, Kuhl tested them again on the same contrast using tokens (utterances of the sounds) produced by a number of different male and female talkers. Note that in the latter situation, it is not sufficient for infants to turn their head to *any* change in the background stimulus (such as a change from one talker to another). Rather, they had to respond to the right kind of change based on the phonetic identity of the vowels. The infants were able to respond correctly to the vowel contrast despite the fact that the talkers' voices were constantly changing. Thus, 6 month olds demonstrate some perceptual constancy for speech sounds. Subsequently, Jusczyk *et al.* (1992) found that even 2 month olds display some ability to cope with talker variability. Specifically, the infants detected the phonetic distinction between 'dug' and 'bug', even when listening to six male and six female talkers' productions of these syllables.

Talker differences are not the only source of acoustic variability in the production of speech sounds. The acoustic characteristics of particular speech sounds are also affected by changes in speaking rates. Certain types of speech contrasts are especially affected by speaking rate changes, such as the distinction between [b] and [w]. Miller and Liberman (1979) found that the same acoustic information that led adults to identify a sound as [b] at a slow speaking rate was identified as [w] at a fast speaking rate. Thus, adults normally compensate for speaking rate in their identification of speech sounds. Eimas and Miller (1980a; Miller & Eimas, 1983) found that 2–3 month olds, too, show evidence of compensating for speaking rate differences in their perception of the sounds [b] and [w]. Thus, not only do young infants have the capacity to discriminate a wide range of speech contrasts, but, like adults, they also are able to adjust to the variability that occurs in the production of speech sounds.

The role of experience in the development of phonetic categories

The infant's biological endowment for language

It is clear that infants only a few months old possess some sophisticated abilities to perceive the sounds of their native language. However, since the beginning of research in this area, researchers have wondered about the role that infants' experience of listening to spoken language plays in the development of their abilities. On the basis of their findings with infants as young as 1 month, Eimas *et al.* (1971) suggested that these perceptual capacities for discriminating speech contrasts are part of one's biological endowment for language. Indeed, a number of studies since that time suggest that the ability to perceive phonetic contrasts is part of the perceptual capacities that infants are born with. For example, Bertoncini *et al.* (1987) found that even within the first 4 days of life, infants exhibit an ability to discriminate phonetic contrasts, such as the one between [b] and [d].

Other researchers have investigated the role of linguistic experience in a different manner, by testing infants on phonetic contrasts that do not occur in their native language environment. For instance, Streeter (1976) tested the ability of 1–4-month-old Kikuyu-learning infants to perceive the [ba]–[pa] distinction. Despite the fact that this contrast does not occur in Kikuyu (a Kenyan language), the infants were able to perceive it. Similar kinds of findings were reported for English-learning infants' abilities to perceive contrasts that occur in Czech and in French, but not in English (Trehub, 1976). As a result of these kinds of findings, it is generally believed that in the first few months of life, infants are capable of discriminating any phonetic distinction that occurs in any of the world's languages.

The role of experience

However, in the long run, experience listening to a particular language does affect infants' abilities to discriminate phonetic contrasts, in the sense that they can get worse! Werker and Tees (1984) first demonstrated this in an investigation with English-learning infants. They tested these infants on three different phonetic contrasts: the English [ba]–[da] contrast, a contrast between [ta] and [Ta] from Hindi, and a contrast between [k'i] and [q'i] from Nthlakapmx (a North American Indian language). Infants, aged 6–8 months, discriminated all three types of contrasts. However, at 8–10 months, the (English) infants still discriminated the English contrast, but only some of them discriminated the Hindi and Nthlakapmx contrasts. By 10–12 months, the infants all discriminated the English contrast, but none of them now discriminated either of the non-native language contrasts.

Additional experiments that Werker and Tees conducted with Hindi-learning and Nthlakapmx-learning 10–12 month olds showed that these infants were able to discriminate the particular contrast that came from their native language. Thus, the English learners' decline in discriminating the Hindi and Nthlakapmx contrasts seems to stem from their lack of experience with these contrasts in the linguistic input. A similar finding has been reported for Japanese infants' sensitivity to the English [ra]–[la] contrast. At 6–8 months, Japanese learners give evidence of discriminating this contrast, but by 10–12 months, they no longer discriminate it (Tsushima *et al.*, 1994). In Janet Werker's expression, the infants had become 'native listeners'! (Werker, 1989).

Although lack of experience with a particular phonetic contrast sometimes leads to a decline in sensitivity to that contrast, this is not always true. Best *et al.* (1988) found no decline in English learners' ability to perceive a contrast between two Zulu click sounds. Similarly, English-learning 10–12 month olds can discriminate a place of articulation distinction for different ejective sounds in Ethiopian.[4] Although Best *et al.* (1995) found that English-learning 10–12 month olds discriminate such ejective contrasts, they also found that infants at this age showed a significant decline in discriminating a voicing contrast in Zulu between lateral fricatives (turbulent consonant sounds produced at the roof of the mouth by drawing the edges of the tongue down).

The perceptual assimilation model

Why sensitivity declines for some, but not for other, non-native contrasts may have to do with how these contrasts relate to ones in the native language (Best, 1995; Eimas, 1991; Werker, 1991; Flege, 1995). The **Perceptual Assimilation Model** was proposed by Best (1995) to explain why sensitivity declines to some non-native contrasts, but not for others. According to this model, there are three important distinctions.

1. When two sounds correspond to, or are very similar to, two *different* native language phonemic categories, they will remain easy to distinguish—thus, as [ba] and [pa] fall in different categories in English they are easily distinguished by English learners.

2. When two sounds *do not* correspond to any native language categories, they will be less likely to undergo a decline—so that English speakers remain able to distinguish Zulu click sounds as these do not correspond to phonemes in the native language.

---

[4] Place of articulation refers to the location at which the vocal tract is most constricted in producing a sound (e.g., the place of articulation for [b] is the lips, whereas for [d], it is at the alveolar ridge (just behind the teeth). Ejective sounds, which appear in about 18% of the world's languages, are consonants produced by upwards movements of the glottis (the opening between the vocal cords and the windpipe).

3. However, when two sounds map to, or are part of, the *same* phonemic category in the native language (so that both are perceived as variants of the
   same sound), then infants (and adults) lose the ability to discriminate between them. Thus, in Japanese [ra] and [la] map to the same category and
   the ability to discriminate between them is lost.

Thus, as infants begin to attend more closely to the way that sound categories are organized in their own native language, they may begin to focus
more on the acoustic properties that distinguish those sound categories. This
tendency would lead them to ignore selectively other acoustic properties that
are less relevant for making the distinctions among these categories, leading
to a decreased tendency to detect differences in these less relevant acoustic
properties (Jusczyk, 1993, 1997).

The 'perceptual magnet effect'

It has been suggested that linguistic experience affects speech perception
capacities in another way. Kuhl (1993) has argued that, by 6 months, infants
develop prototypes for certain native language vowel categories. Her claim is
based on 'a perceptual magnet effect' (Kuhl, 1991). This phenomenon refers
to the fact that listeners often show an asymmetry in their ability to discriminate different tokens (spoken versions) of a particular vowel (e.g., [i]). In particular, their ability to discriminate the vowels depends on whether they must
distinguish (1) a more prototypical (or 'ideal') instance of the vowel from less
good instances, or (2) to distinguish a less good instance from other instances
of the same vowel. Listeners are less likely to discriminate the vowel tokens in
the first case (1) than in the latter (2) (Kuhl, 1991). Kuhl argues that this asymmetry occurs because the prototype acts as a perceptual magnet. In effect, the
prototype pulls poorer instances closer to it.

In a cross-linguistic study comparing English- and Swedish-learning 6
month olds, Kuhl *et al.* (1992) compared the discrimination performance on
two types of contrasts—one involved the English [i]; the other involved the
Swedish [y]. The infants gave evidence of a perceptual magnet effect only
when they were tested on the vowel from their own native language (i.e., the
Americans showed the effect for [i], and the Swedes showed the effect for [y]).
Thus, Kuhl *et al.* concluded that linguistic experience leads to the formation
of native language vowel prototypes by 6 months of age.

More recent research with adults (Iverson & Kuhl, 1995; Sussman &
Lauckner-Morano, 1995; Lively & Pisoni, 1997; Thyer *et al.*, 2000) has
raised some important questions about the robustness of perceptual magnet
effects (i.e., whether such effects occur for all or only some vowels) and their
nature (i.e., whether it is the prototype or more distinctive instances of a vowel
that provide the most attraction for other instances). Moreover, other research
with 6 month olds has provided evidence of similar asymmetries in vowel dis-

crimination by American and German infants for both native and non-native language contrasts (Polka & Bohn, 1996). Because infants in the latter study were as likely to display perceptual magnet effects for vowel contrasts that they had no prior experience with, as for ones in their native language, such effects may reflect some general characteristics of human auditory processing; for instance, a tendency to disperse perceptual categories to make them as distinctive as possible may result in new instances being drawn to more extreme regions of the perceptual space that vowels are located in. Clearly, further research is necessary to determine exactly how linguistic experience affects the formation of native language vowel categories.

How linguistic experience affects other aspects of speech processing

To this point, our focus has been on how infants process one aspect of the sound structure of language, phonetic segments, which are the elementary sound units used in building words. However, within a language, there are particular restrictions on the way that sounds can be combined in forming words. Thus, English does not allow two stop consonants to begin a word, but such sequences are acceptable in Polish, which includes words such as 'dba' and 'kto'. Linguists refer to the sequences of phonetic segments that are permitted in words and syllables in a language as its **phonotactic organization**. Thus, in addition to discovering which phonetic segments appear in words in the language, infants must also learn about the phonotactic organization of the language. Furthermore, the sounds of a language are organized with respect to units that are much larger than phonetic segments, what linguists refer to as its **prosody**. Prosodic characteristics of a language refer to the rhythms, intonation contours, stress, variations in pitch and tone features of utterances.

Sensitivity to prosodic differences in utterances

Languages vary considerably in their prosodic organization. For instance, some languages, such as English, tend to alternate between accented (stressed) and unaccented (unstressed) syllables in forming words. Other languages, such as French, give more or less equal emphasis to each syllable in a word. In terms of their rhythmic organization, the former types of languages are said to be **stress-timed**, whereas the latter are said to be **syllable-timed**. Once again, infants must learn about the prosodic organization of their native language.

Some of the earliest investigations in the field demonstrated that infants are sensitive to prosodic differences in utterances. Morse (1972) demonstrated that 2 month olds are able to distinguish syllables with a rising pitch from ones with a falling pitch (see also Kuhl & Miller, 1982). Other studies demonstrated that infants at the same age are able to discriminate two bisyllables such as [daba] and [daba], which differed only in whether their first or second syllable was stressed (Spring & Dale, 1977; Jusczyk & Thompson, 1978).

Distinguishing one language from another

Such studies indicated that infants are able to detect the prosodic characteristics of utterances, which is a necessary prerequisite for learning about the particular prosodic organization of native language utterances. However, insights as to when infants might begin to learn about native language prosodic organization only came about when investigators began to explore infants' abilities to distinguish utterances in one language from those in another. This issue was first explored in an investigation with French newborns and American 2 month olds using recordings from two fluent bilingual speakers; one of whom spoke French and Russian, the other of whom spoke Italian and English (Mehler *et al.*, 1988). The infants were exposed to excerpts of narratives produced by one of the speakers in each of her languages. Because the excerpts changed from trial to trial and the speaker always remained the same, infants could detect a change in the languages only if they extracted out the common properties shared by utterances from a particular language. The French and American infants succeeded in discriminating utterances in their native language from those in the other language.

Many different properties could be used to discriminate the utterances of one language from the other (e.g., differences in the phonetic elements or vocabulary, the sequences of segments that are permissible, and prosodic properties such as rhythm, pitch contours, and intonation patterns). To eliminate some of these possibilities, Mehler *et al.* tested infants on low-pass filtered versions of the same materials. Low-pass filtering eliminates most information about phonetic segments, while preserving prosodic properties. The infants still discriminated the utterances from the two languages, suggesting that prosodic properties of the utterances were sufficient to distinguish them.

Three different rhythmic categories of language: stress-timed, syllable-timed, and mora-timed

Other studies gave further evidence of infants' abilities to discriminate utterances from different languages (Bahrick & Pickens, 1988; Moon *et al.*, 1993; Dehaene-Lambertz & Houston, 1998). However, infants' use of rhythmic properties to discriminate utterances from different languages was first explored by Nazzi *et al.* (1998). The starting point for their investigation was linguists' classification of languages into three types of categories: stress-timed, syllable-timed, and mora-timed.

As noted above, languages that alternate stressed syllables, such as English and Dutch are said to be *stress-timed*, whereas ones that give each syllable equal emphasis, such as French and Spanish, are *syllable-timed*. *Mora-timed* languages are ones such as Japanese and Tamil. The mora is a rhythmic unit that can either be a syllable or part of a syllable. In English, a mora roughly corresponds to a CV (consonant–vowel) syllable with a short vowel (e.g., 'the' as opposed to 'thee', which has a long vowel, or to 'them', which ends with a consonant. 'Thee' and 'them' each consist of two moras).

Distinguishing between languages from different rhythmic classes

Nazzi *et al.* (1998) hypothesized that infants might be born with the ability to distinguish two languages belonging to different rhythmic classes, even when neither language is their native language. Consistent with their hypothesis, French newborns discriminated two languages from *different* rhythmic classes (e.g., English from Japanese), but not two languages from the *same* rhythmic class (e.g., English from Dutch). To determine whether rhythmic differences were the key to infants' success in discriminating utterances from different languages, they conducted an additional experiment. They mixed utterances from two languages and tested whether infants discriminated these from a mixture of utterances from two other languages. For some infants, the utterances were chosen from languages within the same rhythmic class (i.e., English and Dutch versus Italian and Spanish); for other infants, the mixed utterances came from languages that did not belong to the same rhythmic class (i.e., English and Italian versus Dutch and Spanish). When there was a rhythmic basis for discriminating the utterances (i.e., as in the first grouping), the newborns were successful; otherwise they were not.

Discriminating languages from the same rhythmic classes

It appears, from the studies cited above, that newborns' ability for discriminating utterances from different languages is limited to situations in which the languages belong to different rhythmic classes. For example, 2 month olds do not seem to discriminate two languages from the same rhythmic class, even when one of these is the native language. Hence, British infants did not distinguish English from Dutch utterances (Christophe & Morton, 1998). Thus, newborns appear to begin with a broad categorization that allows them to distinguish the major rhythmic classes, but not to make distinctions among languages belonging to the same class.

How might infants' sensitivities to the rhythmic properties of languages develop? One possibility is that they learn about the specific rhythmic properties and organization of their native language, which then allows them to distinguish utterances in it from utterances in other languages within this rhythmic class. What is learned in this case is similar to what one learns about the phonemic categories in one's native language. In particular, one learns about the specific organization of the language. In other words, not only does the infant become a 'native listener' in phonemic discrimination, as discussed earlier, he/she also becomes a 'native language expert' with respect to many other properties of the native language. Recent findings indicate that the developmental pattern most resembles this possibility.

Infants first display some ability to distinguish between languages belonging to the same rhythmic class between 4 and 5 months of age. Bosch and Sebastián-Gallés (1997) tested the abilities of infants from Barcelona to discriminate a number of different language pairs. As in earlier investigations, the infants discriminated two languages from different rhythmic classes. However, infants at this age also discriminated their native language from another language in the same rhythmic class. Specifically, the infants discriminated Spanish and Catalan, both of which are syllable-timed languages.

More information about older infants' abilities to discriminate languages from within the same rhythmic class comes from an investigation by Nazzi *et al.* (2000). They showed that American 5 month olds' discrimination of languages from within the same rhythmic class is limited to the class to which their native language belongs. Thus, these infants discriminated English from Dutch (both stress-timed), but not Spanish from Italian (both syllable-timed). Perhaps even more surprising, American 5 month olds distinguished their own native dialect of English (i.e., American English) from another dialect (British English).

To determine whether the infants had developed specific knowledge about the rhythmic properties of their native language or a more general knowledge of the rhythmic properties of languages in the stress-timed rhythmic class, Nazzi *et al.* (2000) tested infants on two unfamiliar languages from this rhythmic class, German and Dutch. The infants did not discriminate these languages, suggesting that the knowledge they have developed about rhythmic organization is specific to the rhythmic structure and organization of the native language that they are acquiring. Indeed, their knowledge of these rhythmic features is sufficiently specific to permit them to distinguish their own native dialect from another dialect of the same language.

In sum, infants discriminate between the three different rhythmic classes of languages apparently from birth, but only discriminate between their native language and another language from the same rhythmic class at about 4–5 months.

Learning about the phonetic and prosodic organization of the native language

There do appear to be some important similarities, as well as some apparent differences in how infants learn about the phonetic and prosodic organization of their native language. In both cases, infants appear to start life with some ability to categorize the input in ways that enable them to discover the sound organization of their language at each of these levels. At first glance, it may appear that infants possess more fine-grained abilities to distinguish phonetic features than prosodic features. For example, they appear to be able to discriminate all possible phonetic contrasts, but only three broad rhythmic classes of organization.

However, the types of investigations that have been carried out on infants' sensitivity to rhythmic organization of the language are ones that demand infants correctly extract the regularities from utterances that differ on many *different* dimensions. By comparison, evidence of infants' ability to detect phonetic contrasts typically involves the presentation of sounds that differ on a *single* dimension. In this respect, a more relevant comparison is to contrast the acquisition of native language prosodic organization with the acquisition of native language phonemic categories. When we do so, it becomes apparent that infants give evidence of learning about the nature of the prosodic organization of the native language (at about 4–5 months of age), well before they display any similar knowledge of how sounds are organized into native language phonemic categories (perhaps at 8–10 months at the earliest). This pattern of sensitivity developing to prosodic characteristics of the native language prior to its phonetic characteristics is evident when infants begin to learn about the sound properties of words in their native language. For example, Jusczyk *et al.* (1993b) found that 6 month olds did not distinguish native language words from non-native language words on the basis of their phonetic or phonotactic properties. However, infants at the same age were able to distinguish native from non-native language words on the basis of their prosodic properties.

Extracting and learning the sounds of words

In order to speak and understand any language, one has to be able to learn its words. Given young infants' abilities for discriminating phonetic differences and coping with variability in the way that speech is produced, it may seem that word learning should be a relatively easy task for infants, just a matter of pairing a sound pattern with a particular meaning and then retaining this relation in memory. Indeed, infants are known to respond to the sound patterns of their own names, as opposed to other infants' names, by 4.5 months of age (Mandel *et al.*, 1995). Moreover, by 6 months, they respond appropriately to 'mommy' and 'daddy' by looking at the correct picture of a parent that they hear named (Tincoff & Jusczyk, 1999). Why then, does vocabulary growth appear to proceed at such a relatively slow pace until the child reaches 18 months or so? One possible factor may have to do with the fact that most of the words that infants hear are likely to occur in multiple word utterances (van de Weijer, 1998). Identifying individual words in multiword utterances does not pose any particular difficulty for fluent speakers of a language.

However, consider your own experiences when listening to someone speaking an unfamiliar foreign language. It is often difficult to tell where one word ends and another begins. This phenomenon occurs because in fluent speech, speakers tend to run words together. We have success in segmenting words from our native language because we have learned to pick up certain cues to word boundaries. The cues that are most effective for locating word boundaries depend on the sound organization of a particular language, which helps to explain why we have an easier time segmenting words in our own language than an unfamiliar one. Because word segmentation cues vary across languages, infants must identify the right cues for the language that they are learning.

Segmenting words from fluent speech

The issue of how and when infants are able to segment words from fluent speech only began to be studied recently when researchers developed suitable testing methods to examine this issue. Jusczyk and Aslin (1995) used the head-turn preference procedure to familiarize 7.5–month olds with a pair of words, such as 'feet' and 'bike' (or 'cup' and 'dog'). Then they played infants four different six-sentence passages, two of which contained the words that infants had heard during the familiarization period. The infants listened significantly longer to the passages that contained the words from familiarization, suggesting that they were able to pick out these words when they occurred in the fluent speech contexts. Moreover, Jusczyk and Aslin obtained a similar result when they tried familiarizing 7.5-month olds with two passages, and then testing them on repetitions of isolated words, two of which had occurred in the familiarization passages. By comparison, 6 month olds showed no ability to segment the familiarization words from fluent speech. Hence, Jusczyk and Aslin concluded that infants first begin to segment words from fluent speech at about 7.5-months of age.

Using the sound organization of the native language

The results of many subsequent studies suggest that infants use the knowledge that they have acquired about the sound organization of their native language in segmenting words. For example, Jusczyk *et al.* (1993a) reported that between 6 and 9 months, English-learning infants develop a preference for listening to words with the predominant word-stress pattern of the language (i.e., an initial stressed syllable followed by one or more unstressed syllables). In fact, in fluent conversational speech, more than 80% of content words (words containing meaning such as nouns) used by English-speakers are likely to have stress on the word-initial syllable (Cutler & Carter, 1987). Thus, it has been suggested that, as a first pass strategy, listeners might assume that each stressed syllable marks the onset of a new word in fluent speech (Cutler & Norris, 1988). To determine whether English-learning infants might also rely on the location of stressed syllables in segmenting words, Jusczyk *et al.*

(1999b) tested infants' abilities to segment words that began with either a stressed (e.g., 'doctor', 'candle', etc.) or unstressed (e.g., 'guitar', 'surprise', etc.) syllable. At 7.5-months, the infants were able to segment correctly the words that began with a stressed syllable. However, infants at this age failed to segment the words that began with an unstressed syllable. In fact, they tended to mis-segment the latter items at the stressed syllables in these words. Thus, an infant listening to a passage about a guitar, was more likely to respond to 'tar' than to 'guitar'. Thus, at least during the early stages of learning to segment words from fluent speech, English-learning infants appear to treat stressed syllables as marking the beginnings of new words (see also Morgan, 1994; Morgan & Saffran, 1995; Echols *et al.*, 1997).

Sensitivity to word boundaries

English learners who use the location of stressed syllables to indicate the onsets of words in fluent speech would be able to segment many words correctly, but they would also mis-segment a number of words such as 'of', 'beret', 'unhappy', etc. Segmentation of these kinds of words requires the use of other kinds of cues to word boundaries. It has been suggested that sensitivity to the phonotactic organization of the language may provide listeners with useful word boundary cues (Brent, 1997; Cairns *et al.*, 1997). In particular, certain phonetic sequences (e.g., [fh], [vt] in English) are much more likely to occur *between* words in utterances than they are to occur *within* words. Consequently, a listener encountering such a sequence would have good reason to infer a word boundary in the middle of these phonetic sequences. English-learning infants display an increase in sensitivity, between 6 and 9 months of age, to the frequency with which certain phonotactic patterns appear within native language words (Jusczyk *et al.*, 1994). Perhaps, it is not surprising then that, by 9 months, English learners are able to use phonotactic cues in segmenting words from fluent speech (Mattys *et al.*, 1999; Mattys & Jusczyk, 2001).

Allophones

Another potential source of information about word boundaries in fluent speech has to do with the occurrence of particular spoken variants (what linguists refer to as allophones) of phonemes in the language. For example, there are a number of different allophones of the English phoneme /t/, some of which are restricted with respect to the position that they can occur inside a word. Thus, the allophone of /t/ occurs in the initial position of a word in English differs from the one that typically occurs at the end of a word. Sensitivity to this difference in allophones could provide listeners with a useful word segmentation cue (Church, 1987). Similarly, other kinds of allophonic differences may be useful in signalling the existence of word boundaries. For instance, the allophones of the initial /t/ and following /r/ in 'nitrates' differ from the ones in 'night rates'. Jusczyk *et al.* (1999a) found that, although 9 month olds were not able to use these kinds of allophonic differences to segment the correct words from fluent speech, 10.5-month olds were able to do so. Thus, by 10.5-months, English learners show some ability to use allophonic cues in word segmentation. Interestingly enough, it is at this same age, when English-learners are able to use both allophonic and phonotactic cues in word segmentation, which they also show some ability to segment words that begin with unstressed syllables (Jusczyk *et al.*, 1999b). Hence, by this age, infants are able to draw on multiple sources of information in segmenting words from fluent speech.

From sounds to meaning

The fact that infants begin segmenting words from fluent speech does not necessarily imply that they have 'learned' these words in the sense that they have identified these sound patterns with their appropriate meanings and stored this information away in their memory. Nevertheless, there is evidence that suggests that infants do retain information about the sound patterns of words that they segment, even when they may not know what meanings are associated with these sound patterns. Jusczyk and Hohne (1997) found that 8 month olds who heard the same three stories on audio tape for 10 days, showed recognition of the sound patterns of words that had frequently appeared in the stories, when they were tested in the laboratory 2 weeks later. These findings suggest that when infants are beginning to develop a lexicon (vocabulary) for their native language, they may sometimes store information about the sound patterns of potential words first, and then add information about their meanings at some later point. (For further information on word learning, see Chapter 14 by Vikram Jaswal and Anne Fernald.)

Statistics and rules

The study of language acquisition has long been marked by debates concerning the roles of innate capacities and linguistic input in developing the ability to speak and understand a native language. As the preceding discussion indicates, infants are born with some important perceptual capacities that help them to categorize and process speech sounds and to begin to make sense of their linguistic input. A long period of prior exposure listening to linguistic input is not necessary in order for infants to perceive phonetic distinctions.

At the same time, languages differ considerably with respect to the elementary sound categories they use and in how these sounds are organized to form words. Infants clearly have to detect the regularities in their linguistic input that provide them with clues as to the sound organization that is particular to their native language. As the studies reviewed here demonstrate, infants learn a great deal about the sound organization of their native language within the first year of life. How do they manage to do so?

Infants are good statistical learners

Infants appear to be good *statistical learners*. That is, they show an ability to pick up patterns in their speech input, and separate out individual words. To see how this might work, consider a baby whose name, let's say, is Jodie. The baby will hear her name on many occasions, but embedded in a different speech context—'Hello Jodie how are you?'; 'Don't worry Jodie mommy's here'; 'Where's Jodie's sock?'. In all these, and countless other sentences, the one constant is the bisyllable 'Jodie'—the syllable 'Jo' is always followed by the syllable 'die'. The baby will learn that this is a separate speech sound—and she will learn later that this is called a 'word', and that it is her name!

Infants as young as 8 months can do this in a very short space of time. In a series of investigations by Saffran *et al.* (1996), 8 month olds heard several trisyllabic 'nonsense words' (sets of syllables that aren't proper words in the English language, such as 'pabiku' and 'tibudo'), and these 'words' were presented with no stress on any of the syllables, and no cues to word boundaries (such as stress or pauses between 'words') other than statistical cues. A short time later they recognized these 'words' in that they liked to listen to them more than the same syllables ('pa' 'bi' 'ku' 'ti' 'bu' 'do') in a mixed up sequence. So, when no other speech cues to word boundaries are present, infants can use statistical regularities in the input to segment possible words from a stream of speech.

The ability to use these statistical cues to segment the speech stream is not a mechanism unique to humans. In a recent replication of this study Hauser *et al.* (2001) found that monkeys (cotton top tamarins) were also able to segment the speech streams in the same way as human infants! They conclude that 'Future work must now show where humans' (adults and infants) and non-human primates' abilities in these tasks diverge' (p. 53).

Sensitivity to non-speech statistical regularities

Unlike the other word segmentation cues considered in the previous section, the ability to use statistical cues to appears not to be specific to speech or language. Eight month olds are also sensitive to statistical regularities that occur in sequences of non-speech tones (Saffran *et al.*, 1999). Thus, statistical learning appears to be a general cognitive ability to detect regularly occurring features in the environment. This observation is important to keep in mind when considering the role that statistical learning abilities play in language acquisition. Newport and Aslin (2000) have pointed out that it is necessary to identify the situations and circumstances in which infants are able to extract regularities from the input. Many types of regularities occur in the linguistic input that infants hear, but not all are equally informative about the underlying organization of the language. Yet infants seem to choose the right kinds of regularities to focus on, rather than ones that might mislead them and make language acquisition more difficult. One possible reason why infants are successful is that their innate perceptual capacities may interact with their statistical learning abilities in the selection of the type of information to count in the input. This type of interaction between inherent capacities and information in the environment is referred to as *innately guided learning* (Gould & Marler, 1987; Marler, 1990; Jusczyk, 1997). In this respect, it is interesting that when statistical cues conflict with other types of speech cues to word boundaries (such as word-stress), infants appear to favour the segmentation that is suggested by the speech cues (Johnson & Jusczyk, 2001).

Patterns and rules

Finally, some types of patterns that occur in language cannot be acquired by the kinds of mechanisms thought to be responsible for statistical learning. Marcus *et al.* (1999) have examined infants' abilities to learn such patterns. They found that 7 month olds were able to extract a general pattern from a series of trisyllables that varied from instance to instance, such as the A–B–A pattern that holds for items of the form 'wo–fe–wo', 'de–li–de', 'ha–so–ha', etc. Infants generalized from this type of sequence to new instances containing syllable sequences, such as 'ga–ti–ga', that they had not heard during familiarization. Thus, infants can form generalizations about patterns in the input that go beyond the ordering of specific items that they have been exposed to.

Similarly, in a study using considerably more complex patterns, Gomez and Gerken (1999) exposed 12 month olds to a subset of strings produced by one of two artificial grammars, and found that even when generalization to new strings involved new vocabulary items entirely, the infants correctly discriminated grammatical from ungrammatical strings. The ability to extract patterns of this sort and to make appropriate generalizations has long been associated with symbol manipulation and rule learning (Marcus, 2001). Such findings raise the possibility that infants may have different types of mechanisms available to them for acquiring the structure and organization of their native language. Clarifying the roles that statistical learning and rule learning play in language acquisition is certainly an important goal for future research in this area.

Overview

The infant's first meaningful world is usually uttered at about 1 year of age and, although prior to this time infants can be described as being *preverbal*, they are definitely not *prelingual*, as it is clear that they are attentive to and learning about their native language well before they produce words and sentences of their own.

Response to speech sounds begins in the womb, and in the first few months from birth infants display an innate ability to discriminate between any phonetic discrimination that occurs in any of the world's languages. This discrimination is categorical, in the sense that they can recognize the same sound even when produced by different talkers—like adults, young infants are able to adjust to the variability that occurs in different speakers' (and sometimes the same speaker's) production of the same speech sounds.

Experience with the native language soon has an effect on speech perception. We have seen that experience *in utero* results in a preference for the mother's voice at birth, and experience affects the infant's perception of language in that they become particularly attuned to the sounds of their native language—in the period 8–12 months infants become 'native listeners'.

The world's languages can be divided into three categories—stress-timed (e.g., English), syllable-timed (e.g., Spanish), and mora-timed (e.g., Japanese). Soon after birth infants can discriminate languages from *between* these categories, but it is only at about 4 or 5 months that they can discriminate their own native language from another within the same class (e.g., between English and Dutch).

In order to speak and understand any language one has to be able to learn its words. Infants respond to their own names by $4\frac{1}{2}$ months, and by 6 months they respond appropriately to 'mommy' and 'daddy', but it is not until about $7\frac{1}{2}$ months that they really begin to segment or distinguish words from fluent speech. In this respect they are 'language detectives' and they pick up on several cues. These include: word stress (words in English tend to begin with a stressed syllable); sensitivity to cues indicating word beginnings and ends; statistical regularities (the syllables in individual words always go together); and other rules of language such as rhyme, alliteration, and other rules. From about 8 months infants begin to attach meanings to words, and begin the business of developing a lexicon.

As we can see, an awful lot of learning about the native language has taken place before infants speak their first word, so that this 'milestone' represents a continuation in language development, not its beginning. Of course, one of the main purposes of language is to help us to communicate with each other, and the story of how the infant learns to communicate is described in Chapter 14.

Acknowledgements

Preparation of this manuscript was facilitated by a Senior Scientist Award from NIMH (01490) and a Research Grant from NICHD (15795) to PWJ. In addition, the author would like to thank Ann Marie Jusczyk for helpful comments on a previous version of this chapter.

Social and emotional development

10 How infants perceive faces

JENNIFER L. RAMSEY and JUDITH H. LANGLOIS

Introduction

Imagine going to a big party. You enter and find the room filled with people in lively conversation. Like most guests, unless you are really hungry, you will spend more time looking at people's faces than at the food on the *hors d'oeuvres* table. As you scan the faces in the room, you almost instantaneously determine the gender, race, age, and physical attractiveness of the other guests. You ascertain whether or not you recognize anyone's face as familiar. You guess what type of mood people are in based on their emotional expression. Also, you make a judgement about who is and isn't friendly, interesting, intelligent, and approachable based on social cues you 'read' from faces.

Now imagine a newborn infant in the same room filled with people. Would the infant perceive the faces the same way as you just did? What abilities are infants born with and what are acquired as a result of experience with faces? Understanding face perception in infants has interested researchers over the past four decades. This chapter summarizes much of the research in this area. We start with research investigating whether or not faces constitute a 'special' class of objects and are preferred by infants over other objects. Next, we discuss memory for faces and the development of face recognition. We then turn to the topics of whether or not young infants have preferences for certain types of faces, how infants perceive emotional expressions, and the role of faces for social development.

Before proceeding, however, let's briefly review the visual capabilities of infants in relation to face perception (for a more in-depth review, see Chapter 5). At birth, faces appear somewhat blurry to newborns even when the face is relatively close to the infant. Despite the fuzziness, however, there is still enough information available for newborns to see and perceive faces (Figure 10.1). During the next 6 months of development infants' visual acuity rapidly improves, and over the next 30 months their visual acuity gradually continues to improve until it becomes similar to that of an adult (Courage & Adams, 1990). Thus, even at birth, infants can perceive faces (albeit in a blurred fashion) and they rapidly become adult-like in their perception of faces.

Figure 10.1 What do newborns see? The picture on the left portrays an adult's view of Liz Taylor's face, whereas the picture on the right portrays a newborn's view of her face.

Are faces special to infants?

Much research has shown that infants pay a lot of attention to faces. Is this because faces are 'special' to infants, in ways that other complex stimuli such as checkerboard patterns are not? Scientists can define faces as 'special' if the following two conditions are met: (1) infants respond to faces in a qualitatively different manner than non-face-like objects, and (2) there is a specific mechanism in the brain that directs infants' attention toward faces and processes facial information (e.g., Kleiner, 1993). If these two conditions are not met, then faces are *not* defined as special objects to infants; thus, some explanation other than a face-specific processing mechanism is necessary for understanding why infants are so interested in faces. Because infant face perception researchers are divided on the issue of whether or not faces are special, we'll review the evidence that supports each side of the argument.

Faces are special

Several researchers have proposed that faces are special because even newborns prefer faces over other objects (e.g., Goren *et al.*, 1975; Johnson *et al.*, 1991; Mondloch *et al.*, 1999). For example, Goren *et al.* (1975) found that newborns tracked with their eyes and turned their head further to follow a moving schematic face than a moving scrambled or blank face (Figure 10.2). Johnson *et al.* (1991) later replicated this result and suggested that the newborn brain is predisposed to attend to face-like patterns. Because the preference for faces appears at birth, Morton and Johnson (1991) proposed infants are born with an innate mechanism that specifically directs their attention

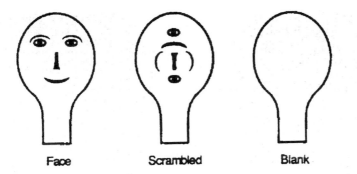

Face   Scrambled   Blank

Figure 10.2 What do newborns prefer to look at? Several researchers have found that they prefer to look at the schematic face more than the scrambled or blank face. Figure from 'Newborns' preferential tracking of face-like stimuli and its subsequent decline' by M. H. Johnson, S. Dziurawiec, H. Ellis, and J. Morton in *Cognition*, copyright © 1991 by Elsevier Science Publishers, reproduced by permission of the publisher.

toward facial configurations. They named this mechanism CONSPEC, which is derived from the word *conspecific*, and refers to infants' ability to recognize and attend to human face-like configurations. Morton and Johnson (1991) suggest that CONSPEC receives input from a less mature part of the brain, the subcortex, because the newborn's brain is not yet fully developed.

Interestingly, Johnson *et al.* (1991) also found that infant preferences for faces briefly disappears sometime between 1 and 2 months of age, but then re-emerges sometime between 2 and 3 months of age. Thus, there is a very short period of time during infants' development that they show no preferences for faces. As the infant's brain rapidly develops during the first few months, CONSPEC declines or is inhibited as a working mechanism and is replaced shortly thereafter by a mechanism that is dependent on more mature brain development. Morton and Johnson (1991) termed this mechanism, CONLERN, because it develops as infants *learn* about faces through their exposure to them. Whereas CONSPEC is present at birth and requires no experience with faces, CONLERN develops because of experience with faces. Therefore, according to Morton and Johnson (1991), faces are special because infants show preferences for faces over other non-face-like objects and these preferences are directed by the face-specific processing mechanisms, CONSPEC and CONLERN.

Further support for the idea that faces are special comes from studies assessing infants' reactions to upside-down faces. An upside-down face contains all the same features as an upright face, but no longer comprises a normal facial configuration (e.g., the eyes are at the bottom rather than the top area of the face). Thus, an upside-down face may not be perceived as a face. Indeed, researchers have found that adults and infants approximately 3 months of age and older process and respond differently to upside-down and upright faces (e.g., Fagan, 1972; Farah *et al.*, 1998). For example, although infants are interested in and look at upside-down faces, they smile less at upside-down faces and at faces rotated more than 45° from upright (Rach-Longman, 1991; cited in Muir *et al.*, 1994). Also, infants have more trouble discriminating among facial movements produced by upside-down versus upright faces (Stucki *et al.*, 1987). Last, infants have difficulty recognizing faces when they are presented upside-down after initially seeing them presented upright (Fagan, 1972). Infants may respond differently to upside-down and inverted faces because they are either born with a predisposition to recognize faces in their most frequent orientation (Stucki *et al.*, 1987), or because they acquire this predisposition through experience with faces.

Faces are not special

Despite the evidence suggesting faces are special, there is also evidence suggesting they are *not* special. Other researchers have tried to replicate Goren *et al.*'s (1975) and Johnson *et al.*'s (1991) results and the findings have not been consistent (see Maurer, 1985 for a review). Whereas most researchers have been able to demonstrate that infants prefer schematic faces over blank objects, the findings have been equivocal when it comes to demonstrating that infants prefer schematic over scrambled faces. For example, Easterbrook and her colleagues (1999a,b) recently found that newborns showed no differences in their eye movements and head turns to follow objects containing face-like features, regardless of the featural arrangement (e.g., scrambled, normal, or inverted). Importantly, Easterbrook *et al.* (1999b) also demonstrated that newborns could discriminate between the schematic and scrambled face to ensure that newborns could tell the difference between the two patterns. Because newborns in this study, as well as others (see Maurer, 1985 for a review), expressed no preference for faceness, Easterbrook *et al.* (1999a,b) do not support the idea that newborns are born with a mechanism orienting their attention toward faces.

According to researchers who argue that faces are not special, infant interest in faces is first driven by a combination of the physical properties of faces (e.g., the patterns and areas of high contrast), and the development of the infant's visual system (e.g., Easterbrook *et al.*, 1999a,b). After some experience with faces, infant interest is then driven by the high exposure to and meaningfulness of faces (e.g., Kleiner, 1993). Thus, there is no need for a separate mechanism specifically geared toward face processing. For example, Maurer and Salapatek (1976) found that 1-month-old infants rarely fixate a face and when they do, they usually look at the external features of the face, such as the chin or hairline, rather than the internal features. However, 2-month-old infants spend a significant amount of time fixating internal features of faces, particularly the eyes and mouth (Figure 10.3). This is because features such as the eyes and mouth are in high contrast (i.e., they stand out more) compared

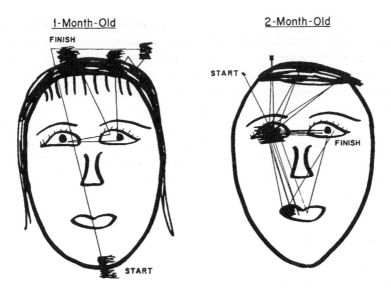

Figure 10.3 How do 1- and 2-month-old infants scan the features of faces? One month olds tend to scan the external features of the faces whereas 2 month olds tend to scan the internal features of the face. Figure from 'Basic visual processes' by P. Salapatek in *Infant perception: from sensation to cognition*, edited by L. B. Cohen and P. Salapatek, copyright © 1975 by Academic Press, reproduced by permission of the publisher.

with the rest of the face, and 2 months of age is the point in development when infants' contrast sensitivity increases (Banks & Salapatek, 1981). Contrast sensitivity refers to infants' ability to detect differences in brightness between the darkest and lightest parts of patterned objects. A zebra's black and white stripes are an example of something that is high contrast and easy for an infant to detect, whereas the wood gratings on a desk are an example of something that is low contrast and difficult for an infant to detect. Thus, faces become appealing to infants at about 2 months of age because they prefer high contrast patterns and are able to detect the contrast between the eyes and mouth in comparison with the rest of the face.

By the time the infant is 3 months of age, however, Dannemiller and Stephens (1988) suggest infants' interest in faces is no longer exclusively determined by the physical attributes of faces, such as contrast patterns, but is also influenced by the meaningfulness of faces or prior experience with faces. Over the first 3 months of life, therefore, infant preferences for faces become based less on the ability to detect high contrast areas of faces and more on the facial configuration or pattern (eyes above the nose and mouth; Kleiner, 1993). Thus, the differential responses infants 3 months of age and older exhibit toward upright and upside-down faces may occur because they've had more experience with upright faces, and thus have more expertise processing upright versus upside-down faces.

After 3 months of age, infants' experience with faces and the social meaningfulness of faces continues to influence infant responses toward faces. For example, Lewis (1969) investigated 3-, 6-, 9-, and 13-month-old infants' responses to a regular face (a photograph of a male face), a cyclops face (a face created by placing one eye over the area where the two eyes normally are on a male face), a schematic face (a line drawing of a face), and a scrambled face (a line drawing with the facial features misplaced). He found that the younger infants looked longer at the regular face compared with the other faces, but as they got older this preference went away and they looked at all the various 'faces' with equal interest. This finding suggests that by 13 months of age, infants have become relatively familiar with regular faces and find more novel objects equally as interesting (Lewis, 1969). Despite infants' decrease in looking time toward regular faces during development, their smiling and vocalization toward regular faces increases with development, suggesting that they have a greater understanding of the role of faces in social interactions.

Conclusions regarding the specialness of faces

Despite the extensive amount of research in this area, the field still lacks agreement about whether or not faces are special to infants. What we can conclude is that young infants do respond differently to faces than other objects even though researchers disagree on when this begins in development and why this occurs. Also, by 3 months of age, both sides of the debate agree that experience with faces directs infant attention toward faces. Those who think faces are special suggest this occurs because CONLERN develops as the infant's brain becomes responsive and sensitive to faces. Those who don't think faces are special suggest this occurs because infant experience with faces during social interactions causes infants to become 'face experts' and faces become more meaningful.

Infant face recognition

Now that we have some background regarding infants' interest in faces, the next question to ask is, 'When can infants recognize their parents and when can babies tell the difference among the faces of strangers?' This section differs from the previous section in that it focuses on infants' recognition of particular faces rather than infant recognition of 'faceness' (i.e., recognizing that a particular object is a face). Not only do these two abilities differ conceptually, but neurobehavioural evidence strongly suggests that there are separate brain systems for processing representations of individual faces and 'faceness,' although some overlap may exist between the two systems (de Schonen & Mathivet, 1989; de Schonen & Deruelle, 1994).

Recognition of the mother's face

Because the mother tends to be the infant's primary caregiver and her face is one of the first faces that the infant sees, it is the most important and most likely face for an infant to recognize early in development. Indeed, there is evidence that newborns can visually recognize their mothers shortly after birth (e.g., Walton *et al.*, 1992; Pascalis *et al.*, 1995). For example, Field *et al.* (1984) found that 2-day-old newborns preferred to look longer at their mother than at a female stranger during a live presentation. However, olfactory cues may have helped the newborns recognize their mothers, so two similar studies were conducted that masked olfactory cues with a strong air freshener. Both studies found that 2–4-day-old infants still recognized their mother's face (Bushnell *et al.*, 1989; Pascalis *et al.*, 1995). Another study enabled newborns to control whether a videotaped image of their mother or a female stranger was presented by varying the rate at which they sucked on a pacifier. Newborns sucked significantly more to see an image of their mother's face than an image of the stranger's face (Walton *et al.*, 1992).

The above studies suggest that visual recognition of the mother is acquired shortly after birth. This preference for the mother's face is more dependent on infant recognition of the mother's external features, such as her hairline, rather than internal features, such as her eyes and nose, because when mothers and strangers cover the outer contour of their heads with a scarf, newborns no longer prefer to look at their mother (Pascalis *et al.*, 1995). This finding is consistent with information from the previous section that suggested infants generally don't scan the internal features of the face until 2 months of age.

Given newborn infants' remarkable ability to recognize their mother's face shortly after birth, some researchers have suggested that this ability is an evolutionarily adaptive process that ensures proximity between newborns and their mother (e.g., Field, 1985). Others have suggested infants may have a special system for recognizing their mother's face that differs from the system for recognizing other faces (de Schonen & Mancini, 1995, cited in de Haan & Nelson, 1999). Although it's difficult to determine the exact mechanism newborns use to recognize their mother, it's clear that only a brief amount of experience with her face is necessary for the recognition to occur, because Field *et al.* (1984) found newborns could recognize their mothers after spending only four discontinuous hours with them.

At about 1 month of age, infants begin looking longer at strangers' faces than at their mother's face, at least when these faces are accompanied by their mother's or a stranger's speech (Burnham, 1993). This developmental change in looking preferences does not mean that infants now prefer strangers more than their mothers, but rather that babies are now very familiar with their mother's face and are interested in learning about other faces. Despite the decrease in looking time toward their mother's face, infants still show more affect in their facial expressions and movements when looking at their mother versus a stranger (Burnham, 1993).

By 3 months of age, infants can recognize and discriminate their mother's face from a female stranger's face when presented via photographs, even when the two faces are very similar looking (Barrera & Maurer, 1981c). Furthermore, when bathing caps and scarves are used to mask external features of the mother's and a stranger's face, infants are able to recognize the difference between them, suggesting that they now recognize their mother's internal features and they rely less on outer contours (de Schonen & Mathivet, 1990). Interestingly, at 6 months of age, infants show no differences in looking time to their mother or a female stranger when pictures of these two are paired together. However, differences in event-related potentials (ERPs), suggest that the brain reacts to the familiar face of the mother as different than the female stranger's face, regardless of whether this face is similar or dissimilar looking to the mother's face (de Haan & Nelson, 1997). ERPs are electrical responses of the nervous system that can be used to investigate how infants cognitively respond to particular stimuli (Misulis, 1994). Thus, de Haan and Nelson's (1997) findings suggest that ERPs may be used to detect certain infant face perception abilities that can't be found by comparing looking times with different faces.

Recognition of the father's face

Given that infants are able to recognize their mother's face shortly after birth under certain circumstances, it seems likely that they would also learn their father's face early in development. However, little research has been conducted to address this question. Walton *et al.* (1992) tested a very small number of newborns for recognition of their father's face, and found no significant differences between how long newborns sucked a pacifier to view a videotape of their father's face versus a male stranger's face. Another study tested 4-month-old infants' preference for their father's face over an unfamiliar male's face and found no visual preferences or differences in affective responsiveness to the two videotaped faces (Ward *et al.*, 1998). Clearly, more studies are needed to address this issue, but currently it appears that recognition of the father's face develops much later than recognition of the mother's face, and it is unclear at what point in development this occurs.

Recognition of other faces

We've discussed infant recognition of their parents' faces, but what about their ability to recognize the faces of relatives, such as their grandparents, whom they may see only occasionally? Older studies found that infants do not begin to recognize faces previously unfamiliar to them until about 5 months of age, and that recognition of faces occurs most easily when the face to be recognized is paired with a physically, dissimilar looking face, such as a male face paired with a female face (e.g., Cornell, 1974; Fagan, 1976; Dirks & Gibson, 1977; Fagan & Singer, 1979). However, one reason infants in these studies may have had trouble recognizing a face when it was paired with a similar looking face is because they were not given a sufficient amount of time to look at and learn about the face (Barrera & Maurer, 1981a). When first becoming familiar with a face, infants may focus more on external features than internal features, thus making it more difficult to note specific differences between similar looking faces during a short period of time (Dirks & Gibson, 1977). However, when infants are able to look at a face for as long as they like when first becoming familiar with it, even 3 month olds can later tell the difference between that face and a very similar looking face (Barrera and Maurer, 1981a).

Similar to the way that an infant's brain responds differently to seeing their mother's face versus a female stranger's face, the ERPs in infants as young as 3 months of age differ when they are shown a novel face versus a face they've seen previously (Pascalis *et al.*, 1998). To find this difference in ERPs, young infants need to be given sufficient exposure to a face they are seeing for the first time. By 8 months of age, however, infants' ERPs for novel faces and faces they've seen previously will differ even if the exposure to the face they saw previously was brief, suggesting they now need less time to process faces (Nelson & Collins, 1992).

The above studies tested infants' ability to recognize a face when the face was shown in the same orientation and view as the one initially presented, but can infants recognize faces when they see them in different orientations and views? For example, when can infants recognize someone's profile after seeing only a frontal view of the face (Figure 10.4)? Pascalis *et al.* (1998) investigated 3- and 6-month-old infants' ability to recognize a novel view of a female face (e.g., a frontal smiling view) after seeing other views of the face (e.g., a frontal neutral view, a smiling profile view) either 2 minutes or 24 hours earlier. All the 6-month-old infants, but only the 3-month-old males, were able to recognize the face in its novel view. These results suggest that by at least 6 months of age, infants can recognize faces from different orientations (Pascalis *et al.*, 1998).

How do infants recognize faces? What mechanisms allow the infant to accomplish this difficult task? Maturation of both the visual system and the brain contribute to the acquisition of this ability. As infants' visual acuity improves, allowing them to see more easily individuals who are farther away, infants begin to display the ability to recognize faces other than their mothers. Also, as the infant's brain develops, lateralization begins, meaning that the left and right hemispheres begin to specialize. Starting at about 4–5 months of age, infants use their right hemisphere more than their left hemisphere during face recognition, suggesting that, like adults, their right hemisphere has become specialized in recognizing faces (de Schonen & Mathivet, 1989; 1990).

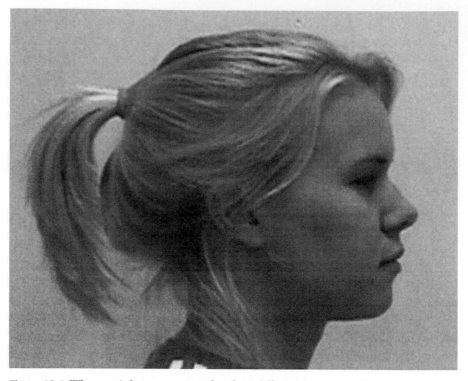

Figure 10.4 When can infants recognize a face from different orientations? By 6 months of age, infants can recognize the frontal view of a face after seeing only the profile view.

Because infants more easily recognize faces using their right hemisphere, but show no advantage for recognizing *non-face* objects using either their left or right hemisphere (Deruelle & de Schonen, 1991), this suggests there may be a special system for recognizing faces. One other possibility, however, is that infants have greater expertise for processing faces than other objects, and thus show a more specialized recognition response (de Haan & Nelson, 1999).

Categorization of faces

As infants begin to recognize faces, they start to notice commonalities among faces belonging to the same category. For example, by 9 months of age, infants can categorize faces according to gender (Leinbach & Fagot, 1993). This means that after being exposed to a series of different male or female faces, infants can recognize that a new face of the same gender belongs to that category and that a new face of the other gender does not belong to that category. Thus, as infants recognize and learn about faces, they begin to group certain faces together. The ability to categorize faces into common groups facilitates information processing of faces. See Chapter 7 for more on infants' categorization abilities.

Figure 10.5 Do infants recognize their own face (top left) when paired with an unfamiliar peer's face (top right) or an object with facial features (bottom left and right)? Between 5 and 8 months of age, infants show evidence that they can recognize themselves. Figure from 'Five- and eight-month-old infants recognize their faces and voices as familiar and social stimuli' by M. Legerstee, D. Anderson, and A. Schaffer in *Child development*, copyright © 1998 by the Society for Research in Child Development, reproduced by permission of the publisher.

Recognition of their own face

While learning about other faces, it's not surprising that infants also begin to recognize their own face. Recent evidence suggests this ability emerges some-time between 5 and 8 months of age (Legerstee *et al.*, 1998). Legerstee *et al.* (1998) showed 5- and 8-month-old infants videotaped or static images of themselves paired with a videotaped or static image of an unfamiliar peer or an object with facial features (Figure 10.5). Eight month olds looked longer at images other than themselves regardless of who they were paired with, sug-gesting they were familiar with their own face and more interested in other faces. Five month olds also looked longer at images other than themselves when shown on videotape, but looked longer at themselves when shown as static images, suggesting they found their own face familiar only when it was moving. It's likely that infants use movement to learn about their faces, and the younger infants were either surprised to see their faces not moving or did not recognize their faces during the static condition. By 8 months, however, infants can recognize a non-moving image of themselves.

Conclusions about the development of face recognition

From this section, we can conclude that infants are able to recognize their mother's face shortly after birth, given some experience with her face. However, it's not clear what the specific mechanism is that permits newborn recognition of their mother's face. Through development, this ability progresses from being able to recognize their mother via a live presentation or videotape to being able to recognize their mother via a static photograph. A similar progression of development is seen in infants' recognition of themselves. It may be that movement cues and external features help infants initially recognize faces and through development they begin to rely more on internal features. Development of the visual system, hemispheric lateralization, and experience with faces allow the infant to more easily process faces, distinguish between similar looking faces, and learn about them during briefer presentations.

Infant preferences for different types of faces

We just discussed how infants prefer their mother's face early in development and then prefer novel faces later in development. However, infants do not respond to all novel faces in a similar manner. Infants look longer at some faces more than others. We will now describe what types of faces infants prefer, offer explanations for their preferences, and speculate about how these preferences may serve as rudiments of stereotyping based on facial appearance.

Infants prefer attractive faces

An infant may respond differently to particular faces based on their experience with those faces, but what happens when an infant is presented with two novel faces? Research shows that infants respond differently if the faces vary in attractiveness (e.g., Langlois et al., 1987; Samuels & Ewy, 1985). Like adults and older children (e.g., Dion, 1973; Berscheid & Walster, 1974; Langlois & Stephan, 1977), infants as young as 2 months of age, and even newborns only a few days old, prefer attractive faces and look longer at faces rated as attractive by adults than at faces rated as unattractive (Langlois et al., 1987, 1991; Samuels & Ewy, 1985; Slater et al., 1998; Figure 10.6). This preference for attractive faces applies to many different types of faces, including

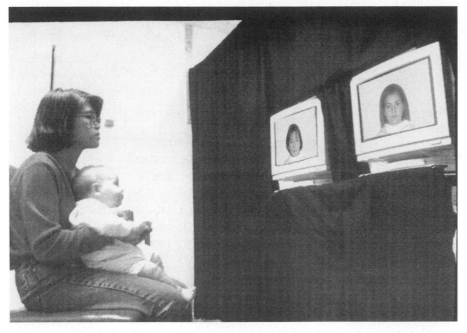

Figure 10.6 What types of faces do infants prefer? Like adults, infants prefer looking longer at the more attractive face on the right than the one on the left.

male and female, Caucasian and African-American, and adult and infant faces (Langlois *et al.*, 1991). Preferences for attractive faces are based more on internal, rather than external, features of the face (Slater *et al.*, 2000).

By 12 months of age, infants not only look longer at attractive faces, but they play with and show more positive affect toward an attractive stranger than toward an unattractive stranger. Infants also avoid unattractive strangers more than attractive strangers (Langlois *et al.*, 1990). These results demonstrate that facial attractiveness guides infants' looking during early infancy, and elicits differential social responses to strangers as the infant gets older. Given that most infants are not watching television or reading fashion magazines, these findings dispute previous suggestions that attractiveness preferences are caused by socialization and the media. If infants aren't learning who is attractive from these sources, from where do their attractiveness preferences originate?

Origins of attractiveness preferences

To understand what makes a face attractive and why preferences for attractive faces emerge so early in development, Langlois and Roggman (1990) proposed two complementary theories. First, because of stabilizing selection, in which evolutionary pressures operate against the extremes of the population

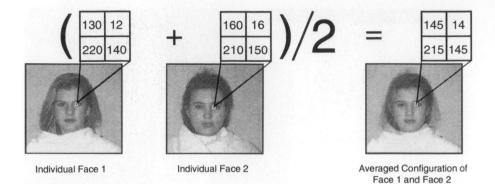

Individual Face 1   Individual Face 2   Averaged Configuration of
                                                            Face 1 and Face 2

Figure 10.7 How are faces averaged together? Digitized images of faces are made up of small dots called pixels. Each of these pixels has a numerical value reflecting the darkness or lightness of that pixel. Thus, all the pixel values of two individual faces can be added together and then divided by two to create the pixel values comprising the 'averaged' face. Figure from 'What is average and what is not average about attractive faces?' by J. H. Langlois, L. A. Roggman, and L. Musselman in *Psychological science*, copyright © 1994 by Blackwell Publishers, reproduced by permission of the publisher.

causing physical characteristics close to the average of the population to be selected, the average values of many population features should be preferred to extreme values. Thus, individuals with facial configurations close to the mean of the population should be preferred and thus considered attractive. Note that by average facial configurations, Langlois and Roggman (1990) do not mean average in attractiveness, but rather average in the size of facial features and their placement from one another. Second, research in cognitive psychology suggests individuals prefer prototypes, which are defined as the central tendency or mean of a population. Facial configurations close to the average of the population should thus be considered attractive because they are more prototypical than configurations that deviate from the average of the population.

To test their theory that faces with configurations close to the population mean are preferred and considered attractive to adults, Langlois and Roggman (1990) first averaged together digitized images of faces (Figure 10.7) and had the resulting composite faces rated by adults for attractiveness. Langlois and Roggman found that averaged faces composed of 16 or more faces were rated as more attractive than most of the individual faces used to create the averaged face (Figure 10.8). Thus, these researchers supported the theory that averaged faces (faces with configurations close to the mean of the population) are preferred and considered attractive by adults.

Langlois and her colleagues then tested whether averaged faces were preferred by infants (Rubenstein *et al.*, 1999). Rubenstein *et al.* (1999) showed infants pairs of Caucasian, female faces that included an averaged face and a

2-FACE COMPOSITE

4-FACE COMPOSITE

8-FACE COMPOSITE

16-FACE COMPOSITE

32-FACE COMPOSITE

Figure 10.8 What makes a face attractive? As more and more faces are averaged together, the resulting composite face more closely resembles a facial configuration close to the population mean. Adults rate an 'averaged' face comprised of 16 or more faces as more attractive than the original faces used to create the composite, and infants look longer at the 'averaged face' than less attractive faces.

face with a low attractiveness rating. Infants looked longer at the averaged face than the less attractive face suggesting that, like adults, they prefer averaged faces.

Other explanations

Some researchers have suggested that individuals prefer certain faces because of their symmetry (e.g., Grammar & Thornhill, 1994), eye size (e.g., Geldart *et al.*, 1999a), or feature height (Geldart *et al.*, 1999b) rather than their 'averageness.' Samuels *et al.* (1994) tested the symmetry theory by showing infants photographs of attractive and unattractive faces that were either altered to be more symmetrical or shown in their original form. They found that altering the symmetry of the faces had no effect on infants' preferences for the faces. Infants preferred attractive over unattractive faces, regardless of symmetry, suggesting that symmetry alone cannot account for infants' attractiveness preferences. Langlois *et al.* (1994) found similar results when testing the effects of symmetry on adults' preferences for faces. Geldart *et al.* (1999a) tested the theory that large eyes influence infants' interest in faces, but found only a subtle effect. Geldart *et al.* (1999b) also tested how the height of internal features on an individual's face affected attractiveness ratings (Figure 10.9), and found inconsistent results in how infants and adults responded to the faces. Thus, none of these alternate explanations can appropriately account for infants' and adults' preferences for certain faces.

How do preferences for attractive faces develop?

Evolutionary theory suggests that infants may be born with a mechanism that detects faces close to the mean of the population and this 'averageness' detector may be present at birth, meaning that no experience with faces is necessary for attractiveness preferences to emerge. Cognitive theory suggests individuals may be born with a mechanism that allows them to average examples within a category, such as faces. Category members resembling the averaged product or prototype should be more preferred than category members less like the prototype. Because facial prototypes are formed through our experience with

high height   **medium height**   **low height**

Figure 10.9 How does the height of internal facial features affect attractiveness ratings? Adults rate faces with their features at the low height (left picture) or medium height (middle picture) as more attractive than faces with their features at the high height (right picture), whereas infants prefer to look longer at faces with their features at the high height. Figure from 'Effects of the height of the internal features of faces on adults' aesthetic ratings and 5-month-olds' looking times' by S. Geldart, D. Maurer, and H. Henderson in *Perception*, copyright © 1999 by Pion Press, reproduced by permission of the publisher.

faces, the cognitive theory suggests experience with faces is necessary for developing attractiveness preferences.

Are infants born with preferences for attractive faces?

Several researchers have attempted to determine whether preferences for attractive faces are present at birth or are acquired after having some experience with faces (Slater *et al.*, 1998; Kalakanis & Langlois, 2000). Slater *et al.* (1998) found that newborns looked at attractive faces longer than less attractive faces. However, the newborns in his study were between 14 and 151 hours old, so it's difficult to determine whether these preferences were present at birth or learned shortly after as a result of the neonates' experience with faces. Kalakanis and Langlois (2000) tested 15-minute-old newborns in two different studies and found that very young newborns tracked attractive and unattractive faces equally. Given the inconsistent results, it is premature to conclude whether or not attractiveness preferences are present at birth and further research is necessary to resolve this issue.

Do infants average across faces to form prototypes?

To investigate whether 6 month olds can form prototypes of faces, Rubenstein *et al.* (1999) showed infants eight different, attractive, female faces in order to familiarize them with the faces. They then tested whether a prototype, created by averaging the eight female faces together, seemed familiar to the infants. According to prototype theory, if babies have the ability to form prototypes by averaging together faces they have seen, the prototype face should seem familiar even though the baby has technically never seen it before. The prototype face should seem even more familiar than any of the faces the baby saw because it is similar to each of the faces and is thus easily recognized by virtue of this similarity (e.g., Hayes & Taplin, 1993). Indeed, this is exactly what Rubenstein *et al.*'s (1999) study found. Prototype faces were more familiar to the infants than either a novel female face or the individual faces the infants originally saw. These results show that by 6 months of age infants have the ability to create prototypes of female faces. Walton and Bower (1993) have demonstrated that even newborns have the ability to form prototypes of faces, suggesting this ability is present at birth. Because we know that babies can average across faces and we know that they prefer averaged faces, the cognitive prototyping mechanism is a plausible cause of infants' preferences for attractive faces.

Rudiments of a stereotype: 'beauty is good'

In addition to preferring attractive faces, adults and children also assign positive traits to attractive individuals and negative traits to unattractive individuals (e.g., Dion, 1973; Berscheid & Walster, 1974; Langlois & Stephan, 1977). This is known as the 'beauty is good' stereotype and may begin developing during infancy. However, before infants begin associating positive or negative traits with attractive and unattractive faces, most theories suggest that infants must first categorize faces according to attractiveness, meaning they should group attractive faces together and unattractive faces together (e.g., Zebrowitz-McArthur, 1982).

Indeed, by 6 months of age, infants are able to categorize faces according to their attractiveness (Ramsey *et al.*, 2000). Ramsey *et al.* (2000) found that after seeing a series of attractive female faces, 6 month olds treated novel attractive faces as familiar, but treated novel unattractive faces as different. Conversely, after seeing a series of unattractive faces, 6 month olds treated novel unattractive faces as familiar, but treated novel attractive faces as different. These results suggest infants categorized attractive faces as one group and unattractive faces as another group.

Given that 6 month olds categorize faces according to attractiveness, when do infants begin associating positive traits with attractive faces and negative traits with unattractive faces? Rubenstein and Langlois (2000) found that 12 month olds, but not 9 month olds, looked longer at attractive faces while a positive-sounding voice played and they also looked longer at unattractive faces while a negative-sounding voice played. This matching of pleasant voices with attractive faces and non-pleasant voices with unattractive faces suggests that by the end of their first year of life, infants display some evidence of stereotyping individuals according to facial attractiveness.

Overview of the development of attractiveness preferences

From this section, we can conclude that infants demonstrate reliable and clear preferences for attractive faces very early in development. Their preference for attractive faces may be innate or may require some experience with faces. As infants continue to develop, they show their preferences for attractive faces through differential social responses to attractive and unattractive individuals, and they also begin to associate positive traits with attractive faces and negative traits with unattractive faces. Thus, by the end of their first year of life, infants' preferential looking at attractive faces has transitioned to the rudiments of 'beauty is good' stereotyping.

Perceiving emotional expressions

Infants' differential social responses are not only elicited by facial attractiveness, but also by emotional expressions. As infants develop, they begin to look to their caregivers for cues about how to react during novel situations, such as whether to approach or avoid a stranger. For example, a mother's smiling face tells a young infant that she/he can safely approach a person or object, whereas a mother's fearful face tells the baby to stay away. This phenomenon is called *social referencing* and is one more reason why infants attend to faces more than other objects in the environment.

Discriminating emotional expressions

Before infants understand facial expressions and what emotions they signify, babies must be able to recognize the featural or configural differences among facial expressions. Using live models, newborns as young as 1–2 days old can discriminate and imitate certain facial expressions, such as happy, sad, and surprised (e.g., Field *et al.*, 1983). By 3 months of age, infants can use pictures of faces to discriminate between their mother or a female stranger posing different facial expressions, such as smiling and frowning (Barrera & Maurer, 1981b). Moreover, studies assessing 7 month olds' ERP responses show that their brains react differently to happy and fearful expressions (Nelson, 1993; Nelson & de Haan, 1996). Although young infants can recognize that one facial expression is different from another, this does not mean that they actually understand the meaning of the emotions associated with different facial expressions. Rather, it's more likely that infants are responding to some change in features (e.g., teeth showing versus not showing) and the ability to detect these featural changes allows them to later associate emotion with these different expressions in a meaningful way (Nelson, 1987).

Categorization of emotional expressions

Although it is important for infants to detect changes in the facial expressions of the particular individuals with whom they interact, it is also important for babies to recognize that similar facial expressions displayed by different individuals signify the same emotion. For example, infants need to recognize that smiling faces belong to the same category (happiness), regardless of the particular face displaying smiling happiness, regardless of whether or not teeth are showing, and regardless of whether or not the smile is intense or mild. Most researchers suggest that infants are able to categorize *some* emotions between 4 and 7 months of age (e.g., Nelson, 1987; Serrano *et al.*, 1992, 1995).

Infants do not learn all categories of emotion at the same point in development. For instance, Nelson and Dolgin (1985) found that 7-month-old infants can categorize happy faces, but not fearful faces. Infants may categorize happy facial expressions before fearful facial expressions because, on average, they are more familiar with happy than with fearful facial expressions (Ludemann & Nelson, 1988). Thus, infants categorize familiar emotions first and then categorize less familiar emotions later in development. This suggests that, although some ability to recognize emotions may be innate, some experience with particular emotions, or perhaps faces in general, is necessary for infant categorization of facial expressions to develop (Ludemann & Nelson, 1988).

Infants 7 months of age and older can categorize across facial expressions even when they vary in intensity (Figure 10.10), meaning that they recognize that faces varying in mild versus extreme happiness belong to the same category (Ludemann & Nelson, 1988). However, facial expressions do need to be prototypical (i.e., a good example) for infants younger than 10 months to recognize that particular facial expressions belong to the same category. A facial expression is considered prototypical when the majority of adults who view the face are able to classify accurately the emotion that is being portrayed (Ludemann, 1991). Infants younger than 10 months cannot categorize faces according to *general* affective tone; they do not group together different types of positive facial expressions nor do they group together different types of negative facial expressions. For example, infants younger than 10 months do not categorize happy and surprised faces as belonging together (positive emotions), or angry and fearful faces as belonging together (negative emotions). Rather, infants less than 10 months tend to categorize according to specific facial expressions (e.g., happy faces), which suggests they require a high degree of featural consistency in order to recognize the similarities among different people displaying the same emotion (Ludemann, 1991).

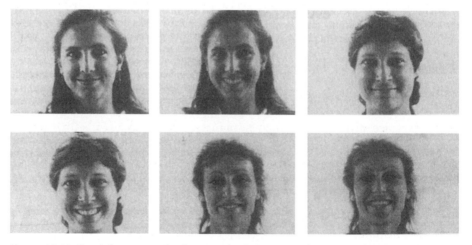

Figure 10.10 Can infants recognize faces varying in intensity of expression? By 7 months of age, infants can recognize these faces belong to the same category (i.e., happy expressions) even though they differ in intensity of smiling. Figure from 'Categorical representation of facial expressions by 7-month-old infants' by P. M. Ludemann and C. A. Nelson in *Developmental psychology*, copyright © 1988 by the American Psychological Association, reproduced by permission of the publisher.

This brings us to the question of how infants are able to categorize emotional expressions. Most infants under 8 months of age rely upon featural information (such as whether teeth are showing are not) to categorize facial expressions. By 8 months of age, however, infants use both featural and expressive aspects of the faces (Caron *et al.*, 1985). To illustrate, Caron *et al.* (1985) found that 8- and 9½-month-old infants attended to both the presence or absence of teeth as well as the type of expression (smiling versus angry) when categorizing facial expressions. Kestenbaum and Nelson (1990) further investigated this phenomenon and found that 7-month-old infants will use configural information (i.e., the type of expression) to categorize emotions when this is the only information available. However, when changes in salient features, such as toothiness, are available, this will override infants' use of expression when categorizing emotions. Although toothiness has been mentioned as the feature infants focus on while categorizing emotional expressions, they also use other features, such as the eye and brow areas. When the mouth is covered, 7-month-old infants can accurately categorize facial expressions by attending to changes in the eye and brow areas (Walker-Andrews, 1986). The actual facial features used to categorize particular expressions will differ according to the faces being seen and which features vary with the change in expression (Nelson, 1987).

Understanding emotional expressions

Although we've discussed infants' abilities to discriminate and categorize particular emotional expressions, this does not in and of itself mean that they understand the affective tone these expressions convey. Thus, behavioural studies that assess infants' knowledge of the emotion or how the emotion affects the infant are necessary to investigate their understanding of emotion.

One way researchers have investigated infants' understanding of emotion is by testing their ability to match a facial expression with a sound (Walker-Andrews, 1986; Phillips *et al.*, 1990) or a voice (Soken & Pick, 1999) depicting that particular emotion. For example, a recording of a person speaking in an angry voice was played through a speaker while infants were presented with two faces on either side of the speaker, one depicting a happy face and one depicting an angry face (Walker-Andrews, 1986). Seven-month-old infants in these studies looked longer at a face displaying the same emotional expression as the sound or voice being played than at a face displaying a different emotional expression. This matching of the face and voice, which is called *intermodal matching*, suggests that infants at this age may construe meaning from emotional expressions (Phillips *et al.*, 1990).

Another way researchers have assessed infants' understanding of emotion is by coding their behavioural responses to different facial expressions (Serrano *et al.*, 1995). Serrano *et al.* (1995) found that infants aged 4–6 months showed more positive behaviours in response to happy facial expressions, more negative behaviours in response to angry facial expressions, and no difference between positive and negative behaviours in response to neutral expressions. These results suggest that even 4-month-old infants have some understanding of the affective meaning of different facial expressions.

Overview of the development of the perception of facial expressions

During the first 3 months of life, infants can detect changes in an individual's facial expression. Sometime between 4 and 7 months of age, they can categorize some facial expressions, meaning that they can recognize the same facial expression among different individuals. Infants first learn more familiar categories of emotional expressions and they rely upon simple featural information to categorize faces based on emotional expression. As they develop, infants begin using configural information to categorize facial expressions, allowing them to recognize smiling expressions regardless of whether or not the teeth are showing. Finally, as infants develop categorical knowledge of facial expressions, they also develop an understanding of what emotions some of these expressions signify starting sometime around 4–6 months of age. Research suggests infants may be born with an ability to detect differences in emotional expressions, but that they also require experience with faces to obtain categorical knowledge and meaning from these expressions.

Role of faces for social development

Recognizing and understanding emotional expressions are not the only way infants learn to guide their social behaviour. Social interactions also teach infants the natural flow of 'give and take' during social exchange. As a result, infants begin to expect caregivers to respond reciprocally and consistently with eye gaze and facial expressions during these interactions.

Eye contact and eye gaze

Toward the end of the second month, infants begin to look at faces much more frequently, particularly within the eye region of the faces (Haith *et al.*, 1977). This increase in looking and shift in gaze to the eye region suggests that infants now perceive the face (or at least the eyes) as something particularly meaningful and the exchange of eye gaze between infants and their caregivers plays an important part in the development of their social bond. Support for this idea comes from evidence that infants look more at the eye region when an adult is talking, which encourages the adult to continue talking and participate in a social exchange because the infant is paying attention (Haith *et al.*, 1977).

Because infants look at the eyes of the person with whom they are interacting, it is important for the interacting person to maintain their gaze with the infant. When the interacting person shifts their direction of gaze away from the infant's eyes during an interaction, infants smile less (Hains & Muir, 1996a; Symons *et al.*, 1998) and sometimes decrease their looking at the adult (Symons *et al.*, 1998). These shifts in gaze do not need to be extremely large, but they do need to indicate a disruption of the social interaction. For example, small shifts in gaze by the adult from the infant's eyes to one of the infant's ears can cause the infant's behaviour to change. However, small shifts in gaze to the infant's head or chin do not cause the infant's behaviour to change because shifts to these areas of the face can help determine a person's emotional expression and may be perceived as a normal part of social interactions (Figure 10.11). Thus, infants are particularly sensitive to small deviations in the interacting person's eye gaze and they seem to depend on this information for directing social interactions (Symons *et al.*, 1998).

Social expectations

Although breaking eye contact with infants alters how they behave within a social interaction, it does not appear to produce as much negative impact as when adults' facial behaviour changes unexpectedly during their interaction with the infant (Hains & Muir, 1996a). Early in development, infants depend upon their caretakers to structure their interactions. During these interactions, the caretaker and infant take turns gazing and smiling at each other's face (Mayes & Carter, 1990). Based on their experience with these interactions, it appears infants begin to form expectancies about social exchanges (Carter *et al.*, 1990). Thus, a violation of these expectancies should affect the infant.

The most common way researchers investigate disruptions in social

Figure 10.11 What happens if you stop looking directly at an infant's eyes while interacting with them? If a person interacting with an infant shifts their eye gaze to the right or left as shown by the first two faces, infants smile less and react to this change in eye gaze as a disruption of the social interaction. However, if a person interacting with an infant shifts their eye gaze up or down as shown by the last two faces, infants do not react to this change in eye gaze.

exchange is through a method known as the *still-face situation*, which was originally developed by Tronick *et al.* (1978). Generally, researchers investigate 1–6-month-old infants in such situations and the sequence of events is as follows: the mother and infant play together for several minutes; the mother then poses with an expressionless face for several minutes; and this is followed by a 'reunion' session during which the mother and infant play again for several minutes to restore normal interactions (e.g., Tronick *et al.*, 1978; Carter *et al.*, 1990; Mayes & Carter, 1990; Hains & Muir, 1996b; Weinberg & Tronick, 1996). Infants' reactions to the still-face situation are of interest to face perception researchers because their reactions appear to be driven more by changes in the mother's facial expression than by changes in tactile or vocal expression (Muir & Hains, 1993).

How exactly do infants respond to such situations? Most infants display positive affect and look at both their mothers and objects in the room during the first play session (Weinberg & Tronick, 1996). During the still-face portion, however, most infants display neutral affect, although some infants respond with protest and negative affect (Mayes & Carter, 1990). They also look at their mothers very little and look around the room or focus on objects when their mothers are expressionless. Infants make pick-me-up gestures, twist and turn in their infant seat, and hiccup and spit up more during the still-face portion. Their heart rate also tends to increase during this episode. It appears that infants first start off with the goal of resuming normal interaction during this situation, but when they are unsuccessful, they withdraw from the interaction and look around the room (Weinberg & Tronick, 1996). Finally, during the reunion play episode, infants display both positive and negative affect, greatly increase their looking to their mother's face, and show little interest in looking at objects in the room. At this point, most infants are happy to have their mothers resume normal interactions, but this happiness tends to be mixed with the emotions carried over from the still-face episode (Weinberg & Tronick, 1996).

Although most studies have investigated the effects of the still-face situation using the mother in a live setting, similar effects occur with the use of videos (Muir & Hains, 1993), with fathers (Braungart-Riker *et al.*, 1998), and even with strangers (Hains & Muir, 1996b). As mentioned earlier, the still-face effects appear to be driven primarily by changes in facial expression, but these effects do not seem to occur simply due to the adult's face changing from dynamic to static (Muir & Hains, 1993). Rather, they seem to occur because the initial play session with the adult sets up expectancies in the infant concerning the quality of the interaction. Thus, the changes in infant affect and attention that occur during the still-face episode appear based on how infants perceived the person's facial expressions during that interaction compared with the previous one (Hains & Muir, 1996b). This important skill of perceiving social interactions depends on the infant's basic abilities to perceive and understand faces.

Conclusions

Now that you have finished reading this chapter, think back to the party discussed at the beginning and the question, 'How would a newborn perceive faces at the party?' As long as the faces are close enough to see, newborns will show much interest in the guests' faces. Aside from their mother, it's unlikely newborns will recognize anyone else in the room. Newborns may spend more time looking at the attractive guests if they can see several guests who differ in attractiveness. They most likely can detect changes in the guests' facial expressions, even though they probably do not know what these expressions signify. Last, newborns may be starting to form expectancies of facial behaviour during social interactions. To review more, think about how you would answer the above question if the infant was 3, 6, 9, or 12 months of age. Consider what face perception abilities change and how these develop. It's amazing what types of information babies get from looking at faces by the end of their first year of life.

Acknowledgements

The authors would like to thank the following companies and individuals for permission to reproduce published material: Elsevier Science Publishers and Mark H. Johnson (Figure 10.2); Academic Press (Figure 10.3); The Society for Research into Child Development and Maria Legerstee (Figure 10.5); Blackwell Publishers (Figure 10.7); Pion Limited, London, and Sybil Geldart (Figure 10.9); and Charles Nelson (Figure 10.10).

11

Early emotional development

MICHAEL LEWIS

Introduction

For many people, emotions are what define human beings. When and how do our emotional lives develop? If we observe newborn infants, we see a rather narrow range of emotional behaviour. They cry and show distress when pained or lonely, or in need of food and attention. They look attentive and focused on objects and people in their world. They appear to listen to sounds, to look at objects, and to respond to being tickled. Moreover, they seem to show positive emotions, such as happiness and contentment. When fed, picked up, or changed, they show a relaxed body posture, they smile, and they appear content. Although they show a wide range of postural and even facial expressions, the set of discrete emotions that they exhibit is rather limited. Yet, in a matter of months and, indeed, by the end of the third year of life, these same children display a wide range of emotions. For example, they show shame when they fail a task and pride when they succeed. Indeed, some have suggested that by this age almost the full range of adult emotions can be said to exist (Lewis, 1992b). In 3 years, the display and range of human emotions goes from a few to the highly differentiated many.

In order to understand emotional development, we need to look at infant and toddler behaviour in both the emotional and cognitive domains, for emotions and their developments are completely tied to cognitive developments. In fact, we often use emotions to infer **cognitions** and cognitions to infer emotions. For example, when young infants see a midget walking toward them they show a face that can be scored as a surprise face. What are they surprised at? They are not surprised when they see a young child or an adult walking toward them, but are when it is a midget (Lewis & Brooks-Gunn, 1982). Surprise reveals to us who observe infants that the infant knows (has cognitions about) the relationship between facial configuration and body height. A midget, after all, has the height of a young child but the face of an adult. This discrepancy is what elicits surprise and informs us that the infant knows about the face and body relationship.

One particular cognition that is most important to the development of human emotions is that of self-knowledge (sometimes called a *meta-*

representation, meaning a representation or understanding of oneself) or idea that 'this is me' (Lewis, 1999). This idea of me is the same as consciousness. We measure it by observing whether infants/toddlers recognize themselves in mirrors. The emergence of self-knowledge or consciousness alters old emotions and gives rise to new ones. To understand emotional development, then, means that we have to understand cognitive changes and, in particular, the development of self.

In the discussion of emotional development, we can think of two broad types of emotions, those that we call basic or **primary emotions** and those that we call **self-conscious emotions**. The former are emotions that most likely are present in humans and other animals. The latter, self-conscious emotions, require elaborate cognitions, including the central one having to do with consciousness; that is, the idea of 'me'. Charles Darwin, in his famous work *The expression of emotions in man and animals* (1872/1965), was the first to make the distinction between these two types. He believed that a **self** was necessary in order for these later emotions to emerge. Moreover, he thought that they emerge at about 3 years in the human child. He described blushing—a reddening of the facial skin—and suggested that blushing was a measure of these self-conscious emotions, which, for him, involved elaborate cognitions involving 'the self thinking about others, thinking of us. . . . which excites a blush' (p. 325).

A model of emotional development

Most of emotional life emerges over the first 3 years. Although not all emotions appear, the majority are present in the 3 year old. This is not to say that other emotions do not emerge past 3 years of age, or that the emotions that have emerged are not elaborated more fully. They do; however, the major framework exists by 3. In our discussion of development, we will divide the chapter into three sections, one following the other: (1) early or primary emotions; (2) self-consciousness; and (3) self-conscious emotions. Figure 11.1 presents our model of emotional development. We can see that in the first 6 months, the primary emotions appear and are the first to emerge. About the middle of the second year of life, consciousness emerges, which gives rise to the first set of self-conscious emotions. In the middle of the third year, or at about 2½ years, the child acquires and is able to use societal standards and rules in order to evaluate their behaviour. This second cognitive milestone, along with consciousness, gives rise to the second set of self-conscious emotions, ones that are called self-conscious evaluative emotions.

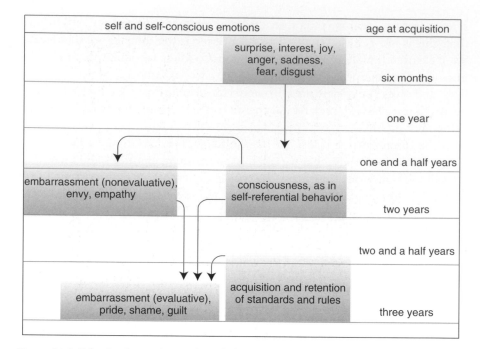

self and self-conscious emotions	age at acquisition
surprise, interest, joy, anger, sadness, fear, disgust	six months
	one year
	one and a half years
embarrassment (nonevaluative), envy, empathy	consciousness, as in self-referential behavior
	two years
	two and a half years
embarrassment (evaluative), pride, shame, guilt	acquisition and retention of standards and rules
	three years

Figure 11.1 Behavioral experiments have led to a model of the emergence of self-conscious emotions. Some noncognitive, primary emotions are evident at birth; others emerge by the age of six months. Sometime in the middle of the second year, the child develops a sense of self, as evidenced by the type of self-referential behavior seen in the right-hand panel of Figure 5. At this time emotions such as envy and empathy emerge. The child will also express self-conscious embarrassment when he or she is looked at, pointed at or singled out in some way. Between the ages of two and a half and three years, the child starts to incorporate a set of standards, rules and goals. The child also develops a sense of success and failure and the ability to determine whether he or she has lived up to expectations. At that point, between the ages of two and a half and three years, the child shows signs of complex self-conscious emotions. The child can express shame in its extreme forms and in its milder manifestation of embarrassment, as well as pride and guilt.

Early or primary emotions

Joy, sadness, disgust, anger, fearfulness, and surprise

These early emotions are present within the first 6 months or so of life. Following Bridges (1932), we assume that at birth the child shows a bipolar emotional life. On the one hand, there is general distress marked by crying and irritability. On the other hand, there is pleasure marked by satiation, attention, and responsivity to the environment. Attention to the environment and interest in it appears from the beginning of life and we can place this either in the positive pole or, if we choose, we can separate this, thus suggesting a tripartite division with pleasure at one end, distress at the other, and interest as a separate dimension (see Figure 11.1).

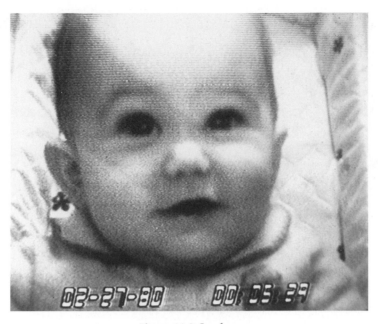

Figure 11.2 Joy face.

By 3 months, **joy** emerges. Infants start to smile and appear to show excitement/happiness when confronted with familiar events, such as faces of people they know or even unfamiliar faces. Very early smiling to people and sounds appear to be reflective in nature. For example, both sighted and blind infants do not differ in their smiling behaviour in the first 3 months of life (Fraiberg, 1974). Afterwards, however, smiling becomes more associated with pleasant events that the infant sees, such as the face of its mother, father, or older sibling. Smiling also now takes place when the infant is played with. Therefore, smiling after 2 months is not reflective and is related to the emotion of joy or happiness.

Also by 3 months, **sadness** emerges, especially around the withdrawal of positive stimulus events. Three-month-old infants show sadness when their mothers stop interacting with them. For example, when mothers sit opposite their 3 month olds and play with them, smiling faces, even laughter, can be observed. However, this laughter and smiling turns to sadness when the infant's mother turns away from them. At this point the child often becomes sad and in some cases even starts to cry. This sad expression disappears once the mother starts again to interact with the child.

Disgust also appears in its primitive form, a spitting out and getting rid of unpleasant tasting or smelling objects placed in the mouth. This disgust face appears to be a defensive reflex designed to help get rid of some food that does not smell or taste good to the infant. Given that there is little hand–mouth and grasping co-ordination, the infant's ability to spit out something unpleasant is a highly adaptive response. As we will see, this early form of disgust becomes

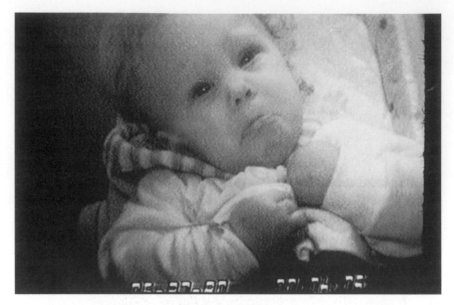

Figure 11.3 Sad face.

utilized later and now reflects learned taste and smell aversion, such as specific and personal food preferences. Thus, by 3 months, children are already showing interest, joy, sadness, and disgust, and exhibit these expressions in appropriate contexts.

Anger has been reported to emerge between 4 and 6 months (Stenberg *et al.*, 1983). Anger is manifested when children are frustrated, in particular when their hands and arms are pinned down and they are prevented from moving. However, Lewis *et al.* (1990) have shown anger in 2-month-old infants when a learned **instrumental act** was blocked. For example, a 2-month-old child can be taught that when they pull their arm, to which a string has been attached, a slide appears on the screen. Thus, every time the child pulls, a picture goes on. After only 3–5 minutes, most 2 month olds learn the association between moving their arm and a picture appearing. Once they learn this, they show anger if we arrange it so that the picture does not come on. This study demonstrates the earliest known emergence of anger. Anger is a particularly interesting emotion as, from Darwin (1872) on, it has been associated with unique cognitive capacities. Anger is thought to be both a facial and motor/body response set designed to overcome an obstacle. Notice that in this definition of anger, the organism has to have some knowledge about the relation between the arm pull and picture going on. For anger to be said to be adaptive it has to be a response whose function is to overcome a barrier blocking a goal. In some sense then, means–ends knowledge has to be available and the demonstration of anger at this early point in life reflects the child's early knowledge acquisition relative to this ability (Lewis, 1991).

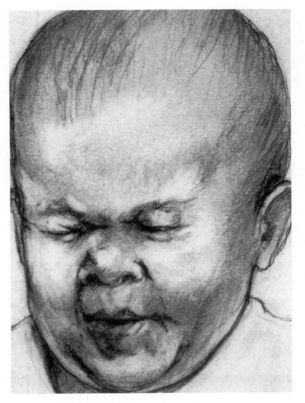

Figure 11.4 Disgust face.

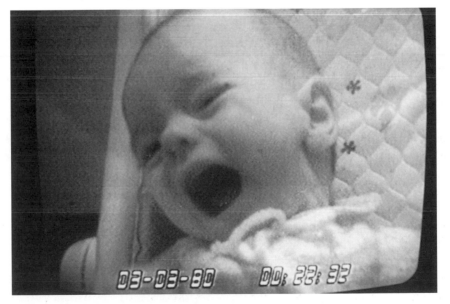

Figure 11.5 Anger face.

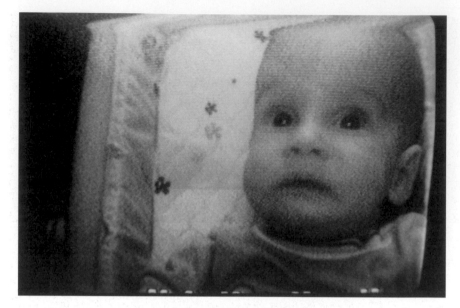

Figure 11.6 Fear face.

Fearfulness seems to emerge still later. Our best guess is that it is about 6–8 months, although it appears to reach its peak at 18 months, when measured as fearfulness at the approach of a stranger. Again, fearfulness reflects further cognitive development. For example, Schaffer (1974) has shown that in order for children to show fearfulness they have to be capable of comparing the event that causes them fearfulness with some other event. For example, in stranger fear, the infant has to compare the face of the stranger coming toward it with that of its internal representation or memory of faces. Fear occurs when the approaching face is found to be discrepant or unfamiliar relative to all other faces that the child remembers. Children's ability to show fearfulness in these situations cannot emerge until a comparison ability appears. Children, at about 6–8 months, begin to show this behaviour, although it has been reported by some to occur even earlier, especially in children who seem to be precocious.

Surprise also appears in the first 6 months of life. Children show surprise when there are violations of expected events; for example, when infants see a midget (a small adult) walking toward them, they are reported to show interest and surprise rather than fear or joy (Lewis & Brooks-Gunn, 1978). Surprise can be seen when there is violation of what is expected or as a response to discovery as in an 'aha' experience. Lewis *et al.* (1984) have shown that when children were taught to pull a string in order to turn on a picture, they showed surprise at the point when they discovered that the arm pull is what caused the picture to appear. Surprise here reflects insight.

Figure 11.7 Surprise face.

In the first 6–8 months of life, children's emotional behaviour reflects the emergence of the six early emotions—joy, sadness, disgust, anger, fearfulness, and surprise—called by some primary emotions or basic emotions (see, e.g., Tomkins, 1962; Izard, 1978). The cognitive processes that underlie these early emotions consist of perceptual abilities, including discrimination and short-term memory, and are representative abilities of some sort. Although these cognitive processes are necessary, it is likely that many species in the animal kingdom possess them. They do not require the elaborate cognitions that are involved in the next set of emotions. For example, anger is elicited in animals as well as infants when a learned response to obtain a goal is blocked. Infants show anger when the string pull does not produce the picture and rats show anger when the learned path to food is blocked.

Self-consciousness

States and experiences

As we have tried to indicate, the development of the early or primary emotions requires some cognition. One cognition that they do not have in the first 6 months, but do acquire in the middle of the second year, is the cognition related to self or what we have called consciousness. Infants younger than

8–9 months of age show all the basic emotions. The question is, do they experience them? If we think of facial expressions representing an internal emotional *state*, then we can say that infants have a happy *state*. However, before consciousness emerges, they may have the *state*, but do not *experience* the *state*. For example, emotional experiences require that the child knows it is having the emotional *state*. Consider that when we say 'I am frightened,' or 'I am happy,' the subject and object is the same, one's self. Thus, the statement, 'I am happy,' implies two things. First, it implies that I have an internal *state* called happiness, and second, that I perceive that internal *state* of myself. Until the child is capable of consciousness, the ability to *experience* the primary emotions does not exist. Consider this example:

Susan, a 7-month-old, sits in a chair watching a stranger move toward her. When the stranger reaches over to touch her hand, Susan pulls it away and begins to cry.

Susan's behaviour, her crying, pushing away, and fearful face, suggests she is in a *state* of fear. However, if we ask whether she is conscious of being fearful, we would have to conclude that she is not. From a variety of studies we know that consciousness does not emerge until the second half of the second year. As such, we may say that, although Susan is in a *state* of fear, she is *not aware* of herself as being fearful. Thus, from a developmental perspective, it is reasonable to believe that Susan has a disassociation between the *emotional state* and her *experience* of that state. That *state* and *experience* of emotions can be disconnected is easily seen in adults who possess both state and consciousness.

Michelle is driving a car on a highway and as she is travelling at 65 mph, her left front tire blows. For the next 20 seconds, Michelle's attention is focused on getting the car to a safe spot off the road. Only when she has finally stopped the car does she *experience* her fearfulness.

We would hold that while Michelle was in a *state* of fear prior to stopping her car, she could not *experience* her fear (was not conscious of it) until she could focus her attention on herself. Thus, as in the case of the 7-month-old child, there is a dissociation between *state* and *experience* (Lewis & Michalson, 1983).

The idea of consciousness, our ability to experience ourselves, is best captured by looking at R. D. Laing's book, *Knots* (1970). Laing argued for the importance and uniqueness of the human capacity for self-reflexive behaviour. Such behaviour can be observed in verb usage, for example, the difference when one makes reference to washing oneself as opposed to washing anything other than self. In French the sentence structure would be *se laver* for washing oneself as opposed to *faire la vaisalle* for washing the dishes. Such reflexive behaviour is seen as well in the social knots as described by Laing. Consider the example: 'I know my wife knows that I know that she knows that I bought a new tie.' Such an example of reflexive behaviour implies that not only do I have knowledge of myself, but also I have knowledge of someone else's self having knowledge of myself. Such complex recursive behaviour is what must be considered when we discuss consciousness or experience, especially from a developmental perspective. Consciousness, that is, thinking about the self, does not emerge until the second half of the second year of life. Moreover, we have been able to demonstrate that the emergence is dependent on a certain level of general mental maturity.

Rouge on the nose test

We study this by looking at infants' responses to mirrors. We place children in front of the mirror and look at what they do. For the most part, they look briefly and then turn away. After this initial exposure, we place a red dot on the child's nose and place the child back in front of the mirror. At this point, the child has two possible responses; they can touch the mirror and the image or they can use the mirror to direct their fingers to touch their own noses. No child before 15 months old touches their nose, while at 15 months approximately 20% do so. If the children are normally developing, 100% will touch their own noses by 24 months (Lewis & Brooks-Gunn, 1979). At the same time and in conjunction with this self-recognition, two additional features of their knowledge about themselves emerge. First, the development of personal pronouns such as 'me' and 'mine' and second, pretend play where the child pretends that the crayon is an airplane, even though they know it is not!

When consciousness emerges, and there is reason to believe that this is a maturational process common to all humans, the next set of emotions—the self-conscious emotions—start to appear.

Self-conscious emotions

Empathy, jealousy, and exposure embarrassment

Figure 11.1 shows the next step in emotional development. Once consciousness emerges so do at least three new emotions. These include empathy, jealousy, and exposure embarrassment. These emotions require, at least, a sense of self. For example, empathy, by definition, involves the ability to put *yourself* in the role of another. So, for example, if I know that I am likely to feel unease in a strange social situation, I am able to utilize my own feeling to assume that you (another person) are also likely to feel unease. In one of the only studies to look at this association, Bischof-Kohler (1991) found that only after infants gain the ability to recognize themselves in mirrors were they able to show empathy, both on their faces (as in a sad expression), as well as in their actions (such as tapping the back of someone they imagine is sad). Likewise, for jealousy. We need to have consciousness for jealousy, as jealousy is the emotion associated with wanting for the self what someone else has. Without a self or consciousness, it would not be possible to have jealousy.

Finally, the emotion of embarrassment is dependent on consciousness. We will discuss two kinds of embarrassment, the first one we call exposure embarrassment, while the second one we call evaluative embarrassment. We will leave the evaluative embarrassment until later as it requires cognitions, which only appear after 2 years of age.

In certain situations of exposure, people become embarrassed. It is not related to negative evaluation, as is shame. Perhaps the best example is the case of being complimented. The phenomenological experience of those who appear before audiences is that of embarrassment caused by the positive comments of the introduction. Consider the moment when the speaker is introduced: The person introducing the speaker extols his or her virtues. Surprisingly, praise, rather than displeasure or negative evaluation, elicits this type of embarrassment!

Another example of this type of embarrassment can be seen in our reactions to public display. When people observe someone looking at them, they are apt to become self-conscious, look away, or touch or adjust their bodies. When the observed person is a woman, she will often adjust or touch her hair; men are less likely to touch their hair, but may adjust their clothes or change their body posture. In few cases do the observed people look sad. If anything, they appear pleased by the attention. This combination—gaze turned away briefly, no frown, and nervous touching—looks like this first type of embarrassment.

A third example of embarrassment as exposure can be seen in the following experiment: When I wish to demonstrate that embarrassment can be elicited just by exposure, I announce that I am going to point randomly at a student. I repeatedly mention that my pointing is random and that it does not reflect a judgement about the person. I close my eyes and point. My pointing invariably elicits embarrassment in the student pointed to.

In each of these examples, there is no negative evaluation of the self in regard to standards or rules. In these situations, it is difficult to imagine embarrassment as a less intense form of shame. As praise cannot readily lead to an evaluation of failure, it is likely that embarrassment resulting from compliments, from being looked at, and from being pointed to has more to do with the exposure of the self than with evaluation. Situations other than praise come to mind in which a negative evaluation can be inferred, although it may not be the case. Take, for example, walking into a room before the speaker has started to talk. It is possible to arrive *on time* only to find people already seated. When you are walking into the room, eyes turn toward you, and you may experience embarrassment. One could say that there is a negative self-evaluation: 'I should have been earlier; I should not have made noise (I did not

Figure 11.8 Embarrassment figure.

make noise).' I believe, however, that the embarrassment in this case may not be elicited by negative self-evaluation, but simply by public exposure. Above we see the face and body posture associated with embarrassment.

These three emotions, at least, require the emergence of consciousness but do not require that the child be able to evaluate their behaviour against some standard or rule that they have learned from the people around them. This occurs only later.

Self-conscious evaluative emotions

The self-conscious evaluative emotions depend on the development of a number of cognitive skills. First, children have to have absorbed a set of standards, rules, and goals. Second, they have to have a sense of self. And finally, they have to be able to evaluate the self with regard to those standards, rules, and goals and then make a determination of success and failure.

As a first step in self-evaluation, a child has to decide whether a particular event is the result of their own action. If, for example, an object breaks while the child is using it, he might blame himself for breaking it, or he might decide the object was faulty to begin with. If he places the blame on himself, he is making an internal attribution. If he doesn't blame himself, he is likely to go on to the next step of evaluation.

Whether a child is inclined to make an internal or an external attribution depends on the situation and on the child's own characteristics. Some people are likely to blame themselves no matter what happens. Dweck and Leggett (1988) studied children's attitudes toward their academic records. They found that some children attributed their success or failure to external forces. Others were likely to evaluate success and failure in terms of their own actions. Interestingly, strong sex differences emerged: Boys are more apt to hold themselves responsible for their success and others for their failure, whereas girls are apt to do the opposite.

Psychologists still do not entirely understand how people decide what constitutes success or failure after they have assumed responsibility for an event. This aspect of self-evaluation is particularly important, because the same standards, rules, and goals can result in radically different emotions, depending on whether success or failure is attributed to oneself. Sometimes children assess their actions in ways that do not conform to the evaluation that others might give them. Many factors are involved in producing inaccurate or unique evaluations. These include early failures in the self system, leading to narcissistic disorders, harsh socialization experience, and high levels of reward for success or punishment for failure (Kohut, 1977; Morrison, 1986; Hoffman, 1988). The evaluation of one's own behaviour in terms of success and failure plays a very important part in shaping an individual's goals and new plans.

In a final evaluation step, a child determines whether success or failure is global or specific. Global attributions come about when a child is inclined to focus on the total self (Abramson *et al.*, 1978). Some children, some of the time, attribute the success or failure of a particular action to the total self: They use such self-evaluative phrases as 'I am bad (or good).' On such occasions, the focus is not on the behaviour but on the self, both as object and as subject. The self becomes embroiled in the self, because the self-evaluation is total. There is no way out. Using such global attribution results in thinking of nothing else but the self. During these times, especially when the global evaluation is negative, a child becomes confused and speechless. The child is unable to act and is driven away from action, wanting to hide or disappear (H.B. Lewis, 1971).

In some situations children make specific attributions, focusing on specific actions. Thus it is not the total self that has done something wrong or good; instead, a particular behaviour is judged. At such times children will use such evaluative phrases as, 'What I did was wrong, and I must not do it again.' Notice that the child's focus here is not on the totality of the self but on the specific behaviour of the self in a specific situation, in interactions with objects or people, on the actions of the self, or the effect on other selves.

The tendency to make global or specific attributions may be a personality style (Beck, 1979). Global attributions for negative events are generally uncorrelated with global attributions for positive events (Abramson *et al.*, 1978). It is only when positive or negative events are taken into account that relatively stable and consistent attributional patterns are observed (Kaslow *et al.*, 1988). Some children are likely to be stable in their global and specific evaluations under most conditions of success or failure. Such factors are thought to have important consequences for a variety of fixed personality patterns. For example, Beck (1979) and others have found that depressed people are likely to make stable, negative, global attributions, whereas non-depressed individuals are less likely to be stable in their global attributions.

Shame and guilt

Of all the self-conscious emotions, shame, until recently, has been the most undervalued in its power to motivate human behaviour. Earlier theorists tended to attribute certain actions to guilt, but many psychologists now believe that shame is the more appropriate underlying emotion (Janoff-Bulman, 1979; Buss, 1980; H.B. Lewis, 1987; Lewis, 1992a,b).

Shame results when a child judges her actions as a failure in regard to her standards, rules, and goals and then makes a global attribution. The child experiencing shame wishes to hide, disappear, or die (H.B. Lewis, 1971; Lewis, 1992a,b). It is a highly negative and painful state that also disrupts ongoing behaviour and causes confusion in thought and an inability to speak. The body of the shamed child seems to shrink, as if to disappear from the eye of the self or others (see Figure 11.9). Because of the intensity of this emotional

Figure 11.9 Shame face.

state, and the global attack on the self-system, all that children can do when presented with such a state is to attempt to rid themselves of it, often by hiding.

Some children try to dissociate the shameful feelings from themselves. The most severe manifestation of this is in people with multiple personality disorder, where a child tries to create other selves to bear the shame (Ross, 1989). Often it is the child who has seriously traumatic incidents such as childhood abuse. It is not the abuse that creates the disorder; it is the shame brought about by the abuse (Hilgard, 1977; Lewis, 1992a,b).

Shame is not produced by any specific situation, but rather by an individual's interpretation of an event. Even more important is the observation that shame is not necessarily related to whether the event is public or private. Failure attributed to the whole self can be public or private, and can centre around moral as well as social action.

If shame arises from a global attribution of failure, guilt arises from a specific attribution (Ferguson *et al.*, 1991; Tangney, 1995). Guilt and regret are produced when a child evaluates her behaviour as a failure, but focuses on the specific features of the self that led to the failure. A guilty child is likely to consider actions and behaviours that are likely to repair the failure. Guilty individuals are pained by their evaluation of failure, but the pain is directed to the cause of the failure or the object of harm. Because the cognitive attributional process focuses on the action of the self rather than on the totality of self, the feeling produced is not as intensely negative as shame and does not lead to confusion and the loss of action. In fact, guilt almost always has associated with it a corrective action that the child can take (but does not necessarily take) to repair the failure and prevent it from happening again (Tangney, 1990; Barrett, 1995). In guilt, the self is differentiated from the object. The emotion is thus less intense and more capable of dissipation.

Guilt and shame have different physical manifestations as well. Whereas a shamed child hunches over in an attempt to hide or disappear, a guilty person moves in space as if trying to repair the action. The marked postural differences between guilt and shame are helpful both in distinguishing these emotions and in measuring individual differences.

Hubris

Self-consciousness is not entirely a negative thing. Self-evaluation can also lead to positive and even overly positive emotions. Hubris, defined as exaggerated pride or self-confidence, is an example of the latter. Hubris is the emotion elicited when success with regard to one's standards, rules, and goals is applied to a child's entire self. It is the global condition. Children inclined to be hubristic evaluate their actions positively and then say to themselves: 'I have succeeded. I am a success.' Often, hubris is considered an unlikable trait that should be avoided.

Hubris is difficult to sustain because of its globality. The feeling is generated by a non-specific action. Because such a feeling is alluring, yet transient, children prone to hubris ultimately derive little satisfaction from the emotion. Consequently, they seek out and invent situations likely to repeat this emotional state. According to Morrison (1989), this can be done either by altering their standards, rules, and goals or by re-evaluating what constitutes success.

A child who considers himself globally successful may be viewed with disdain by others. Often the hubristic person is described as 'puffed up' or, in extreme cases, grandiose or narcissistic (Kohut, 1977; Morrison, 1986). The hubristic child may be perceived as insolent or contemptuous. Hubristic children have difficulty in interpersonal relations, as their hubris likely makes them insensitive to the wishes, needs, and desires of others, leading to interpersonal conflict. Moreover, given the contemptuousness associated with hubris, other children are likely to be shamed by the nature of the actions of the hubristic person. Narcissists often derive pleasure in shaming others by claiming their superiority.

Pride

If hubris is the global emotion that follows a positive assessment of an action, then pride is the specific emotion. A child experiencing pride feels joyful at the successful outcome of a particular action, thought, or feeling. Here the focus of pleasure is specific and related to a particular behaviour. In pride, the self and object are separated, as in guilt, and unlike shame and hubris, where subject and object are fused. Heckhausen (1984, 1987) and Stipek *et al.* (1992) have made a particularly apt comparison between pride and achievement motivation, where succeeding at a particular goal motivates activity. Because the positive state engendered by pride is associated with a particular action, individuals have available to them the means for reproducing the emotion. Notice that pride's specific focus allows for action.

Embarrassment

Embarrassment as a consequence of evaluation of one's actions, called evaluative embarrassment, is closely related to shame. Embarrassment is distinguished in contrast to shame by the intensity of the latter. Whereas shame appears to be strong and disruptive, embarrassment is clearly less intense and does not involve disruption of thought and language. Furthermore, children who are embarrassed do not assume the posture of someone wishing to hide, disappear, or die. In fact, their bodies reflect an ambivalent approach and avoidance posture. An embarrassed person alternatively looks at people and then looks away, smiling all the while (Edelman & Hampson, 1981). In contrast, the shamed child rarely smiles while averting their gaze. Thus, from a behavioural point of view, shame and embarrassment appear to be different.

Figure 11.10 Pride figure.

The difference in intensity can probably be attributed to the nature of the failed standard, rule, or goal. Some standards are more or less associated with the core of self; for me, failure at driving a car is less important than is failure at helping a child. Failures associated with less important and less central standards, rules, and goals result in embarrassment rather than shame.

Overview: the major developments of emotional life

There are other types of evaluative self-conscious emotions, but these, pride, hubris, shame, guilt, and evaluative embarrassment, have been the ones most studied. The emergence of this class of emotions completes the major development of emotional life, creating in children both a wide array of different emotions, some more complex than others. It also includes the developmental shift from emotional *states* to emotional *experiences*, thus giving the human child the extra capacities to both have particular emotions and to be aware that they have them. Thus, by 3 years of age, the emotional life of a child has become highly differentiated. From the original tripartite set of emotions, the child comes within 3 years to possess an elaborate and complex emotional system. While the emotional life of the 3 year old will continue to be elaborated and will expand, the basic structures necessary for this expansion have already been formed. New experiences, additional meaning, and more elaborate cognitive capacities will all serve to enhance and elaborate the child's emotional life. However, by 3 years of age, the child already shows those emotions that Darwin (1872/1965) characterized as unique to our species—the emotions of self-consciousness. With these, the major developmental activity has been achieved.

12 Social development

MICHAEL LEWIS

Introduction

How does the infant develop into a social animal? In order to understand social development, we need to remember that social development is connected both to emotional as well as to cognitive development. For example, the nature of the infant's social life is highly dependent on those cognitions that allow for empathic behaviour, as without empathic behaviour the child's relationships with others cannot involve the same level of intimacy that is found when empathic behaviour is present. Consider that a newborn infant will cry when she hears the cry of another child. This crying cannot be supported by empathic behaviour as the newborn does not have the cognitive capacity for such a process. Rather, we say that the newborn's cry is produced by contagion; that is, an automatic response that has very little cognition associated with it. It is a well known fact that contagion is a process to be found in all social creatures, not only in humans. Birds on a wire fly away when they see another bird flying away. Women who live together synchronize their menstrual periods. In the same way, newborns cry when they hear the cry of another infant. However, once empathy is established, at about 2 years (see Chapter 11 on Early emotional development), the emotional response of another can produce an empathic response in the toddler. Thus, her sadness over the sadness of another child, and her attempt at comfort, is based not on contagion but on the toddler's being able to 'place herself in the role of the other.' This cognitive ability, associated with the emergence of consciousness and the idea of 'me,' leads to social behaviours not present until such cognitive capacities emerge.

Understanding social development also requires that we consider a child as imbedded into a large network of people and activities and that to understand social development we need to include not only the relationship of the child to its mother but the other important relationships that the infant engages in from the beginning of its life. This embeddedness services many needs, including protection, play, learning, and the like. It is to this network of people and needs that the newborn child must adapt and in which social development occurs.

In this chapter, then, we will first address the nature of the entire social nexus or network in which the child is born. Then we shall map out how social relationships undergo developmental transformations as a consequence of the development of cognitive capacities; in particular, the development of consciousness. Finally, we will discuss the social network and how we might understand infants' social development.

Social nexus

By nature, humans are social animals. From the moment of birth the child is surrounded by other conspecifics, a small portion of which share the child's gene pool, a larger portion of which will influence and in turn be influenced by the child, and finally the largest portion, which forms the background in which these other interactions will take place. The smallest segment we call the family; the larger comprises lovers, friends, acquaintances, and even strangers; and the largest segment is the culture.

Human newborns are surrounded by a large and diverse social network, and it is within this array that the developmental processes of the organism occur. Given that the major task of the newborn is the adaptation to this environment of people, it seems reasonable to assign to humans the feature of sociability. Not only must the newborn adapt to this world, but there is considerable evidence that many of the sensory and cognitive abilities of infants centre around making sense of their social environment.

Social development is important as suggested by all the skills and biological structures that appear to be in its service. For example, much sensory processing seems keyed to social needs. Infants' discriminatory ability is greater for social than for non-social stimuli. By 12 weeks of age and perhaps earlier, English-speaking children can distinguish between social stimuli such as the speech sounds *pa* and *ba* (see Chapter 9). This discriminatory ability appears to be a function of social experience as infants who are not raised in an English-speaking environment become unable to distinguish these subtle differences. Moreover, although young infants are little interested in non-social stimuli, they are considerably more attentive—as measured by heart rate changes—to social stimuli. Even brain structures appear more attuned to social than to non-social events. For instance, hemispheric differentiation for sound appears to be divided by social or speech sounds and non-social or all other sounds. Of equal importance to the social competence of children is the control of biological functions through social interactions. Important organizational processes, including the regulation of sleep–wake cycles, appear to result from the social interactions between caregivers and infants.

The amount of knowledge that children acquire about their social environment is incredibly vast, and the acquisition occurs rapidly. Lewis and Brooks-

Gunn (1979) have shown that by 9 months infants already have some rudimentary knowledge about themselves. Moreover, children's knowledge about others also is highly developed. By 1 month some infants and by 3 months most infants have some understanding of the relationship between people's faces and voices and infants interact differentially with familiar persons and strangers as early as 5 weeks of age (McGurk & Lewis, 1974). Sometime between 3 and 6 months, children acquire knowledge about human faces, and by 7 months they demonstrate discrimination of emotional expressions (Caron *et al.*, 1982). By 3–4 months infants begin to respond differently to children and adults, and by 6–8 months they show differential fear responses to people on the basis of gender and age. By 6–8 months infants are surprised at the appearance of a small adult (i.e., a midget) and seem to understand that the height–facial feature integration is unusual in these people (Lewis & Brooks, 1974). Recently, we have found that by 10 months, infants are using the facial expression and tonal quality of their mothers in their interactions with strangers. Infants are more friendly to strangers who are treated in a positive manner by their mothers (Feinman & Lewis, 1983).

People in the infant's life

Mothers are the primary focus in attachment theory, but children form important relationships and attachments with individuals besides their mothers. In this section we first discuss the relationship to mothers but also consider others such as fathers, siblings, grandparents, and peers.

Mothers

Mothers play a primary role in the infant's life. The role of the mother was first clearly articulated by Sigmund Freud in his theory of socio-emotional development. Psychoanalytic thought established the mother–infant bond as the primary social relationship of the child, although the conflict between the child and his mother and father, known as the **Oedipus complex,** also was seen as important. It was not until the object relation theorists, such as Melanie Klein (1930), W. R. D. Fairbairn (1952), D. W. Winnicott (1959), and Karen Horney (1939), that the idea of the mother–child dyad as the primary social relationship upon which all other social relationships were built became the central focus of study.

The attachment of the infant to its mother has been likened to a love affair and has been called attachment. John Bowlby (1969) described this relationship as an affectional tie and it constitutes after the first year of life a model or representation of the child's social–affective relation with people. The initial representation of this attachment occurs in the first 3 months of life and has been called a dance-like interaction. During this time, the infant and its primary caregiver engage in a dance, learning how to interact with one another. The movement of this dance consists of the physical movements of each, gaze behaviour, and affective attunement where the behaviour of one leads to the response of the other. Soon after birth the infant clearly discriminates between his mother and others (see Chapter 5), and by the end of 9 months is often upset at the appearance of those he is not familiar with. This phrase has been called *stranger anxiety* and is marked by attention toward the stranger, a kind of wariness, and in the extreme, fearfulness and upset when the stranger approaches. Thus, the infant is now highly selective toward those he knows and those he does not.

The final phase of this attachment can be seen at 1 year of age where the infant shows a desire to be near their mother, is upset by her absence, and can use her as a secure base from which to explore their world. Bowlby, like Freud (1948), saw the infant's relationship to his mother as unique without parallel, established unalterably for a whole lifetime as the first and strongest love digest and as the prototype of all later love relations.

Bowlby's work on attachment was further developed by Mary Ainsworth (1969) who created a paradigm for measuring attachment when the child is 1 year old, known as the *strange situation* (described in Chapter 2). In this situation, the mother, child, and stranger are seen together in nine 3-minute episodes. The two episodes where the child is left alone and then the mother returns, are the two episodes used to measure the infant's attachment. The child's response to the mother's return, after she has left the infant alone in a strange room, is used to assess the type of attachment the child shows. Originally three types were described: (A) ambivalent, (B) secure, and (C) avoidant attachments. More recently, a fourth type, (D) disorganized attachment has been added. Most work on attachment distinguishes between secure (B) and all others called insecure.

The work on attachment in humans has its parallel in the work of Harry Harlow with monkeys (Harlow, 1969) and Jane Goodall with chimpanzees (Goodall, 1988). Harlow, in particular, showed that monkeys raised without their mothers turned out to have poor peer relationships when they were older and also made poor mothers (Harlow, 1969). This work has recently been criticized as Harlow raised his monkeys in social isolation (Harlow & Harlow, 1965). Thus, not only were the babies without their mothers, they were also without any other contact. When baby monkeys are raised without mothers but in the companion of other babies, many of the problems that Harlow reported in terms of the child's subsequent social problems are not present. In fact, most recent work reveals that while the early mother–infant relationship in the first year of life is important, it does not mark the child for life. In fact, Lewis (1997) has shown the child's ongoing and often changing relationship with its mother and others, such as its father, siblings, peers, and teachers, contribute to the child's social development. While the emphasis on the mother and infant relationship in the early years of life is important, without understanding the child's *total* social nexus, it is not possible to understand the social development of the child.

Fathers

Twenty years ago, a visitor from Mars reading the developmental literature would hardly know that American and European babies usually had fathers living in the same household! The more recent research literature, although still dominated by studies of mother–child interactions, has brought into focus some of the roles fathers play in children's lives. Four questions have been directed toward the father–child relationship.

Can fathers do what mothers do?

One important question raised about fathers is whether there is any biological difference between mother's and father's care for the very young. Perhaps mothers take care of infants better than fathers? Lamb's (1976) work with fathers and infants demonstrate that fathers' care, that is, the interaction patterns between fathers and children, is similar to mothers' care. Thus, one would say that fathers can care for their very young infants. While fathers can care, it is apparent that, in general, they do not, especially in the case of the young infant under 9 months or so. Their daily contact remains low. In spite of the social milieu that makes contact acceptable, the sex-role-appropriate male behaviour does not include the care of the very young. It has been demonstrated that even the increased multiple roles assumed by the mother (mother, worker-out-of-the-house, wife) have not led to much of an increase in father involvement.

What do fathers do that is different from mothers?

While fathers have been shown to be equally capable of caring for young children, there are differences that distinguish them from mothers. Mothers' behaviour is likely to centre around child-care activities, such as feeding, changing diapers/nappies and clothes, and bathing; fathers' interactions are more likely to include physical playful activities. Lamb has shown fathers to engage in more rough and tumble, bouncing, and tickling activities than mothers. Moreover, as the children become older, the father's role is likely to increase, mostly as a function of the declining need for caregiving activities and the increasing needs for exploration, play, and self-initiated action or efficacy, namely, the physical environment. Mackey (1985) has shown that across many cultures, fathers interact more and are more likely to hold their infants and young children in public places (zoos, museums, public streets) than they do when they are at home.

What are the indirect effects of the father?

Fathers also affect their children's lives indirectly by affecting the lives of their wives. These indirect effects include emotional support of the mother. The interdependent nature of the child–parent and parent–parent subsystems has been amply demonstrated. A woman's successful adaptation to pregnancy is associated with the husband's support. Support can include other factors than emotional support. Studies have shown that mothers without husbands on a regular or temporary basis feel busier, more harassed, and more depressed as well as more oriented to immediate goals (Lynn, 1974).

Are the children attached to their fathers?

Surprisingly, the question of whether children are attached to their fathers is rarely asked. Perhaps because theory is oriented toward attachment to the mother, it took many years even to ask the question. The answer is: Of course, children are attached to their fathers. Children direct equal social behaviour to each, the only difference being that fathers received somewhat more distal behaviour (i.e., more 'indirect' contact such as playing and less 'direct' contact such as hugging).

Siblings

Thinking about Western myths pertaining to siblings, we come first to the story of Cain and Abel. This story is a prototype of the negative relationship, with competition, rivalry, and even hate between siblings as the prevailing moods. Indeed, there are many of these negative attributes associated with siblings. However, there are also many positive features, which tend to be downplayed. Siblings can affect the child's behaviour and the child's relationship with and view of the family (Dunn & Kendrick, 1979). Even the child's view of itself is affected by siblings. Siblings play a variety of roles, namely, one another. Siblings protect and help one another. Many mothers note that when they are punishing one of their children the other will protect that child even if the punishment concerns a sibling conflict. Siblings help each other if their mother cannot help. For example, younger siblings depend on older siblings for help with homework or when they need an ally. Siblings provide important social models for each other. Children learn how to share, cooperate, help, and empathize by watching their siblings. Siblings spend their early lives sharing a variety of objects, experiences, and people. Thus, siblings share not only the same parents and grandparents and roughly the same genetic heritage but also possessions (toys, books, clothes, pets), space (sleep in the same room, use the same bathroom, live in the same space), people (mutual playmates, baby-sitters, teachers, doctors, etc.), and even the same life histories (go to the same camps, vacation together, experience disasters together, etc.). They often serve as playmates to one another and when they have friends often involve their siblings with their friends.

Moreover, and most important, siblings seem to form important and long-lasting attachments with each other, although it appears that younger siblings are more often attached to older siblings than the reverse. In a recent survey, we asked over 60 adults with siblings which sibling was more likely to call the other. More than 80% reported that the younger is more likely to initiate the call to the older, 10% said the older, and 10% said there was no difference. Infants appear upset by the loss of siblings, or even when the siblings stay away from home overnight or for weekends. Siblings show strong affective bonds, and these relationships show continuity over time.

Given these positive features, it is curious to note the negative view often assigned to sibling relationships. In part, this may be due to an adult-parent perspective in which sibling rivalry is seen as a predominant factor, neglecting the positive features. Moreover, negative sibling behaviour is likely to display itself under (or even be provoked by) the attention and focus of the parents; that is, siblings may be more likely to fight and quarrel in the company of their parents than when alone. In any event, it is clear that sibling aggression, competition, and rivalry do exist. Certainly they must compete for a limited resource, the most important of which is the parent. While it is in the parents' interest that all children survive, it has been suggested by Trivers (1974) that sibling rivalry is unavoidable given that siblings must share the same parents and given that the attention of a parent increases one sibling's likelihood of survival while decreasing the likelihood for the others. According to this account, this is an evolutionary reason why physical aggression, including hitting, biting, and pushing, occurs between young siblings.

Grandparents

The failure to consider the possible role of the grandparents in children's development, like that for other social objects, is based on a particular view of social development. The neglect is surprising given the obvious facts that parents of parents exert a strong influence on children's development, if for no other reason than that they influence the parents. Even the name 'grandparent' should make it obvious that such a role carries with it importance for both child and grandparent. Why have grandparents been neglected? Mostly because grandparents, in general, at least in the United States, do not even live in the same home as the child, so how can we focus on only direct effects? It is clear that the lack of study of influence of grandparents on development reflects a culture that does not value age, that is highly age segregated, and in which intergenerational learning is not encouraged. In cultures such as that of Japan today, cultures where many grandparents, parents, and children live together, the role played by grandparents is more obvious.

Grandparents generally have contact with their adult children (the parents of the child) at least once a week. Hospital visits by grandparents at the time of the infant's birth are quite high: more than 90% see the child on the first or second day, in spite of the geographic mobility of the child's family (Wilson & Tolson, 1983)! Parents of mothers are seen more frequently than the parents of fathers. This reflects the well-documented point that in general mothers are the 'kin keepers'; that is, that they arrange and maintain family contact. This role of kin keeper also gives rise to the findings that the mothers' parents (maternal grandparents) are seen more often by infants than are the paternal grandparents (Hill *et al.*, 1970). Grandmothers are more directly involved in the child's activities than grandfathers, reflecting sex-role differences as an intergenerational phenomena.

Children can observe how their parents interact with their parents and thereby learn about how adult children behave. This effect does not involve the child directly. The other indirect effects of grandparents should mirror those of the father except that the grandmother–daughter relationship may supply special support for children through affecting their mothers. Given the mother–daughter relationship and its unique role throughout the life cycle, it should be the case that grandmothers' approval and support have particular importance for mothers, certainly more so than for sons.

Aunts, uncles, and cousins

Simply stated, there is no research literature on the role of aunts, uncles, or cousins in the development of the child. Within anthropology and animal behaviour, the role of these others is well recognized. In many groups, lion prides for example, the social structure of the group includes the female relatives: mothers, aunts, daughters, and female cousins (if such terms can be used in this context). Moreover, the role of uncles, the father's brother and mother's brother has been recognized. In fact, Frazer (1915) points out that at the death of the father, the father's brother (uncle) becomes responsible for the family. Jocasta's brother Creon becomes king when Oedipus blinds himself. Hamlet's uncle Claudius becomes king and marries Gertrude when Hamlet's father dies. Thus, there is ample evidence for the role of uncles in the lives of families; the role of aunts is more unnoticed.

Because aunts and uncles are in close contact, their children (cousins) should also be in close contact. In fact, for many children, their first peer contacts and long-lasting ones are with cousins. Thus, cousins are likely to play an influential part, and the social network data indicate considerable rate of cousin contact. Cousins are viewed as so close, at least genetically, that in many states there exist laws against marriage between them. For aunts, uncles, and cousins, differences similar to those already reported for grandparents and siblings are likely to appear. Female cousins and aunts are more likely than uncles and male cousins to maintain contact, a sex-role difference that should appear throughout the social network structure. Moreover, the role of grandparents in the maintenance of sibling contact is probably important. That is, aunt and uncle (and therefore cousin) contact is more likely in some families than in others. The exact nature of the relationship that facilitates this is not well understood.

Peers

Beyond family members there are any number of social objects that play an important part in children's development. Peers are surely the most important, for it is in peer relationships that most of adult social life exists. For this reason, of all social objects beside mothers, early peer relationships have been most studied. For a more complete review of peers, see Chapter 13 on Infant play.

The belief that infants had no social or emotional interest in peers, due in part to the prevailing view that the social–emotional life of the child primarily involved only the mother, also prevented the study of early peer relationships. The role of peers has been shown to be equally important as it is encouraged or inhibited by the social structure. Cultural differences in peer contact is the primary factor affecting the degree and amount of social–emotional involvement (Lewis & Rosenblum, 1975). In some cultures, peers are given more direct roles in child care (Whiting & Whiting, 1975). On the Kibbutz in Israel and in Russia, China, and Cuba, for example, we would expect more and earlier peer emotional–social interactions than where group child care is not a part of the culture (e.g., Japan or the United States, although this is changing even now). Peers show interest, enjoyment, and emotional involvement from the earliest opportunities provided in the first year of life. Peer attachment has been shown to exist especially in the absence of adults (Freud & Dann, 1951; Gyomrai-Ludowyk, 1963).

Like siblings, peers perform both positive and negative functions. Peers are good for play and for modelling one's behaviour as they share equal or nearly equal abilities and are most like the self. They are also good at teaching, especially somewhat older peers, as their abilities do not differ too markedly. Peers protect each other and, most importantly, peers are capable of forming attachments to each other.

The negative features of the peer relationship revolve around the lack of the adult perspective. Thus, for example, while an adult may be able to give up a need for the sake of a child, such behaviour may be beyond the ability of young peers. Disputes, therefore, are often settled by power status variables such as strength, age, and gender rather than by true prosocial behaviour. Aggressive behaviour between peers represents another negative feature, with high physical interaction and direct aggression being two noticeable examples. Given that peer relationships themselves are embedded in cultural rules, the study of peer behaviour needs to be considered in the context of the entire social network. The absence of peer contact in a culture that does not promote contact cannot be taken as evidence for the unimportance of peers in early life.

Teachers, day-care personnel, and baby-sitters

Even during the first few months, infants are often exposed to non-related adults who care for the child while the mother is at work, in school or college, or at play. Given the large number of mothers who work out of the home and the changing family structure, the majority of infants and children are cared for daily by people other than relatives. There was some concern about infant day-care being harmful to the infant; they were without their mothers for a large portion of the day and attachment theorists thought this harmful. Evidence from the American National Institute of Child and Human Development (NICHD) Daycare Studies indicates that young children are capable of forming important relationships with day-care personnel and that the relation with them does not negatively affect the child's social or emotional development (NICHD, 1994, 1996). In fact, day-care experiences with teachers, etc. may mitigate some of the difficulties created by the abusing or neglecting mother (Lewis & Schaeffer, 1981).

The failure to study the children's attachment to other adult caregivers may rest on our general bias, which holds to the importance of a single adult attachment figure. Bowlby (1969) did not recognize the multiple-attachment capability of the human infant, and because of the emphasis on the mother, relatively little research with others has been done. Cross-cultural research, such as that of Konner (1975) and Greenbaum and Landau (1977), shows that even in the first few weeks infants interact with many adults, including non-relatives to whom they may become attached. Given this possibility and the changing nature of child care, it is necessary that we focus on the effects of multiple attachments and the child's relationship to adult caregivers other than parents and relatives.

From this review, it is clear that the infant enters into a large social nexus in which his mother, as well as others, play important parts. The neglect of the other people reflects the bias we have that places the mother as the only and most important person in the child's social as well as emotional development. It is the emphasis on attachment to the mother that has until recently limited the scope of our understanding of children's social development.

Types of relationships

Interestingly, only 1-year-old infants' attachment relationships to their mothers have been studied in detail, although friendship patterns have received some attention in regard to play and peers (see Chapter 13). Given that there are many people in the infant's social world, it would be good to look at the type of possible relationships we adults have. It is these types of adult re-

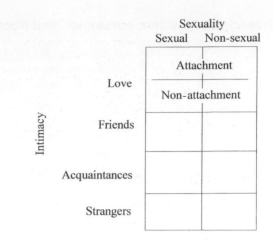

Figure 12.1 Types of relationships.

lationships that the child will ultimately have and, except for the sexual aspects of relationships, has even in infancy.

The social space of the child is made up of a potentially large number of social objects, including inanimate objects, such as security objects, plants, trees, and so on, and animate objects, including animals and a wide range of people. So a first division is between objects and people. When considering people, we see the possibility of different types of social relationships. Figure 12.1 presents two-dimensional space, including sexuality and intimacy. While the space describes eight cells, there is no clear separation between them and, in fact, movement between cells in either direction is possible.

Love relationships

First consider love relationships that take place within the family as well as outside of it. Love relationships may be of two kinds: those that are attachment relationships, that is, those that provide a secure base, and those that need not, for it is not clear that a secure base is a necessary part of all love relationships. For example, parents love their children, but children do not necessarily offer a secure base for parents. Love relationships also are divided by sexuality. In some love relationships sexuality will play an important part, such as with a spouse, while in others, such as with mothers, fathers, and children, sexuality is absent. Thus, within love relationships the dimensions of secure base (attachment) and sexuality form a complex structure for a variety of different love relationships, all of which exist in our experience. The four cells within love relationships created by an attachment and sexuality matrix might contain: mates as an example of attached and sexual; parents as an example of attached, non-sexual; boy- or girlfriend as non-attached and sexual; and parent to child as non-attached and non-sexual. Whether such a complex set of love relationships exists for all children is unknown. However, children can and probably do have strong love relationships that both have and do not have an attachment dimension. For example, children love both their parents and their siblings, but they are probably attached to the former and not the latter, especially if the sibling is younger.

Friendship relationships

Friendship relationships are different from love relationships and, although this may be difficult to describe, it is indicated by the language itself. Friendship relationships also vary along different dimensions and at times may merge with love relationships. Like love, friendship may or may not involve sexual behaviour. Friendship relationships tend to vary with the age of the participants; thus, they may involve same-age peers or they may exist between older and younger persons, such as between a teacher and student. Like love, friendship relations can be enduring and can exist even without extended interactions.

Acquaintance relationships

Acquaintance relationships are those relationships that tend to be the least enduring and the most specific to the particular interactions that bring them into existence. They usually occur as a consequence of particular and highly structured social exchanges such as with a storekeeper or bank clerk. These relationships vary along a dimension of familiarity, from those in which the members recognize one another, know each others' names, and exchange information (such as between employers and employees or between a shop owner and a customer) to those less familiar interactions with the ticket collector on a train or with people whom we greet casually in passing on the street.

Although people do not have relationships with strangers, our analysis requires that this category of non-relationships be included, especially as so much attention has been paid to children's social interactions with strangers. Strangers are, by our definition, those people with whom we have no relationship and who are unfamiliar to us. Yet even in this category of non-relationships there are variations that may be of some importance to our analysis. For example, strangers who possess particular characteristics may elicit different interactions than strangers without those characteristics. Thus, strangers of the same sex or racial background as the child are likely to evoke different interactions than strangers of the opposite sex or of another racial background (Lewis, 1980).

For any complete study of social development, it is necessary to recognize that children do have relationships with people other than their parents and to trace the development of these relationships from the child's early social interactions. A complex array of relationships exists early in infancy.

The development of relationships

Infants certainly appear to form relationships early. They smile when their mother or father appears, they follow their older siblings around as soon as they are able to move around in the house, and they move away from and become weary of strangers when they are 8–9 months old. But are these relationships as we mean them when referring to adults or are they some primitive form of these, perhaps not too dissimilar from other mammals that interact with their young?

Robert Hinde, a biologist now retired from Cambridge University, wrote that relationships should be characterized as having goals, a diversity of

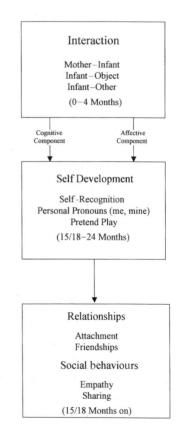

Figure 12.2 Transformational Model of the Development of Relationships.

different interactions and reciprocity (1976). The feature most important for our discussion is his belief that relationships require mental processes that allow members of an interaction to think of the other member as well as of themselves.

Notice that for Hinde, as for Lewis (1991), relationships require elaborate cognitions, cognitions that require a self and knowledge of other selves. These cognitions are not likely present until the end of the second year of life. We see social development dependent on the growth of particular cognitions, which is present in Figure 12.2. In this model, what is commonly referred to as the mother–child relationship(s) is really a set of social interactions. These interactions grow out of the basic capacities of the human genome; so for example, the baby is not taught how to smile, although his smiling behaviour is very much influenced by his social environment. How and when people smile will influence how and when he will smile, but his smiling itself is not learned.

These early social interactions, smiling (mother–infant smiling), vocalizing (infant–mother talking) are in place by the 3–6-month period. As attachment theorists indicate, these interactions constitute a kind of dance. However, unlike others who think this means a relationship, the model of Figure 12.2 suggests that they are not relationships. Because of the absence of sufficient cognitions, these are complex interactions and are the material for relationships once the concept of self or what we have called consciousness occurs.

As the development of consciousness has been already described in Chapter 11, we will only say that at between 15 and 24 months, infants indicate through the use of personal pronouns, 'me' or 'mine,' and self-recognition in the mirror, that the self has emerged. With its emergence comes such capacities as empathy and sharing behaviours, behaviours absolutely necessary for the emergence of relationships.

Once the infant has formed a rudimentary concept of self and established particular habits, the next stage in the transformation is the utilization of these skills to form relationships. As stated, the mediating cognitive structures necessary for relationships are: (1) a self-schema, and (2) from the self-schema the development of two social affective skills, empathy and sharing. Having discussed the emergence of the self-schema (see Chapter 11), let us attend next to the emergence of empathy and sharing. One would agree that empathy (and sharing) is possible only through the recognition of the existence of two selves—oneself and another's self—each having a separate identity and a separate set of needs. Such an analysis requires that we understand both the development of a self-schema and the development of the understanding of the separate nature of selves. The process of growth by which children *decentre*, that is, begin to consider that all selves are not like oneself, has been discussed (Piaget, 1952; Flavell & Miller, 1998). The timing of this decentring is still unclear. Piaget (1952), for one, did not see these processes as occurring much before 4–6 years, while others see this process as occurring at earlier ages, indeed, as young as 3–5 years (Wellman *et al.*, 2001). Whatever age we ultimately find as appropriate, it does seem that egocentric thought, that is the use of self to infer actions, thoughts, and feelings of others, and then decentred thought are both necessary for the formation and maintenance of empathy and sharing, the basis of relationships.

In this regard, our age timing for the movement from self to relationships is used to imply the initial formation of relationships that occurred in the later part of the second year of life. Certainly by 2 years, the child's use of no and the onset of the 'terrible twos' should alert us to the existence of two selves (child and parent) and the beginning of relationships based on negotiation between them.

To reiterate, from an *ontogenetic* (the development of the individual) point of view, the mediating structure between interaction and relationships is the development of self. Even beyond its developmental role, the sense of self may play an important part in interactions and relationships. Relationships are based on interactions but require a sense of self and an integration of a self with others as in empathy to give them meaning. This is particularly true when we think of the recursive nature of thought. Not only can I think about how I behave to you and how you behave to me, but I can think about how I think you think I behave toward you, and you to me.

The social network

The attachment model argues that the earliest relationship with the mother is the single most important aspect for subsequent behaviour. Social development is seen as a transformation of this earliest relationship into all other relationships. Peer interpersonal behaviour is a consequence of present peer experiences and the secure attachment.

The notion of a social network systems model argues instead that the causes of social behaviour and development are to be found in the structure of the social system itself and the past experience. An example of the interplay between an individual's behaviour and a social network will underscore this difference between the two views. Rosenblum and Kaufman (1968) studied both bonnet macaque and pigtail macaque monkeys. Bonnet macaques cluster together in matriarchal groups so that a mother, her sisters, her adult daughters, and their babies might all be found huddled in close proximity. Pigtail macaques, on the other hand, are much more isolated. There are no groups, just the adult female and her baby. Thus, in the former case the baby is in close proximity to a large number and varied set of others besides its mother, while in the latter case the baby and mother are alone. The bonnet baby interacts daily and forms relationships with mother, aunts, grandmother, and cousins while the pigtail baby only interacts and forms relationships with its mother, only later forming relationships with others.

When separated from its mother, the pigtail baby first shows marked distress, calling and moving about. This is followed by a state of deep depression. The bonnet baby shows a markedly different pattern. It too is distressed by the withdrawal of the mother; however, it soon recovers as it is 'adopted' and cared for by familiar others. This illuminates the effects of the social network. In a system where there is only the mother, her loss constitutes an enormously significant event, one from which the infant is not likely to recover. In Bowlby's (1951) attachment model, the loss of the mother is a life-threatening event. In a system where there are other people, the loss of the mother, while perhaps significant, no longer becomes a life-threatening event, and in fact, given the proper care from others, appears to cause relatively little subsequent disruption. Similar findings have been reported by Robertson and Robertson (1971), Rutter (1979), and Tizard and Tizard (1971), among others, when human infants are studied.

Likewise, in a system where there is only the mother as caregiver, the child's first (and only) relationship will be with her. Other relationships must be sequential (after this first one) and, in part, dependent on this first one. This sequential, deterministic feature (the hallmark of the attachment view) does not have to be a biological necessity for the species as Bowlby has argued. There is little support for the notion that such a structure of mother as sole caregiver is necessary or indeed historically, culturally, or evolutionarily correct. For example, some cultures promote the use of multiple caregiving in the form of both mother and older female sibling or friend (Whiting & Whiting, 1975). In the United States the majority of infants and children are in day-care settings with multiple adults and children. A social network systems approach appears as an important alternative to the attachment view.

Description and measurement of the social network

As an area of research, the study of social networks is about 40 years old. Bott's (1957) seminal work *The Family and Social Network* is widely known to both sociologists and psychologists. Bott reported that—contrary to popular belief—middle-class couples did not live in isolation but formed coalitions with other middle-class couples in a network of social kinship. In interviews with couples, Bott discussed with both husbands and wives the type and frequency of contact with people in the categories of relatives, friends, neighbours, and organizations (e.g., school, clubs, unions, religious groups, etc.). Couples also kept diaries that helped the researchers determine the nature of the social networks. One interesting result from Bott's work involved the relationship between social network and family roles. Although networks have been examined in regard to adults, relatively little work has been done on networks, roles, and infants' and children's development. An extensive literature exists that employs quantitative techniques for describing and specifying the characteristics of social networks. In addition, information about the needs satisfied by which members of the social network has been obtained and informs us about the relations between people in the child's network and the roles they serve.

Social matrix as a measure of the social network: the relation between people and needs

We have seen that even in infancy and early childhood, children are likely to have multiple relationships. We also know that infants have many different needs; for example, needs such as protection, love and attention, play, learning, etc. We need to develop a model that describes how these multiple people and needs interact.

In the model depicted in Figure 12.3, people form the Y (vertical) axis while needs form the X (horizontal) axis. Together they form a matrix of objects and functions. In this figure, the set of people includes self, mother, father, peers, siblings, grandparents, aunts, plus any other people such as teachers, etc. to be considered. The array of people is determined by a variety of factors. The needs consist of protection, caregiving, nurturance, and so forth. These are

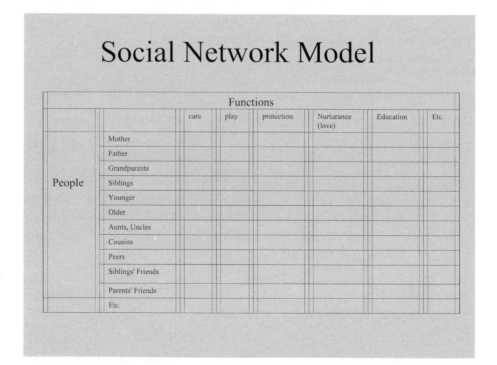

Figure 12.3 Social Network Model.

broad needs that can be broken down further. For example, under caregiving, feeding and changing could be included, while under nurturance, emotional behaviours such as kissing or responsivity might be considered. The general form of this model provides a framework for considering the complete array of people and needs that describe the child's social network. By examining the matrix one can determine which people are present, which needs are being satisfied and, most important, which needs are achieved by what person. By examining the horizontal axis of the matrix, one can obtain an idea of what needs are characteristic of a particular person within this particular network. This axis will inform us whether mothers are predominantly concerned with caregiving and fathers with play. On the other hand, by examining the vertical axis of the matrix, one can study the different needs that characterize the network of a particular child. While all of the listed needs are presumed to be important, it might be that for some children caregiving, play, and learning are equally important. Likewise, a child whose network is predominantly concerned with protection will be quite different from one raised in a network concerned with nurturance. However, in order to determine the relationship of people to need, we must turn our attention to the individual cells of the matrix.

The matrix raises the general question of whether the satisfaction of a need by a particular person are more important for the child's development than others. For example, what is the consequence of having an older sibling as caregiver as well as the mother instead of just the mother? Or, what is the consequence of having a caregiver as giver of care (as in day care) in addition to the mother instead of just the mother?

In an attempt to determine whether the matrix is applicable to young children, Edwards and Lewis (1979) explored how young children perceive the distribution of needs and people (see also Dunn & Kendrick, 1979). Persons were represented by dolls of infants, peers, older children, and parent-aged adults. Social needs were created for the child in the form of a story. In the two studies to be discussed, children in the age range of 3–5 years were asked to choose which person they wanted to interact with in a specific social activity. In all the studies, the functions were: (1) being helped, (2) teaching about a toy, (3) sharing, and (4) play. For help, the adults were selected, while for someone to play with, children chose adults and infants last and peers and older children first. For teaching, specifically, how to use a toy, older children were selected, while for sharing, there was no preference among social objects. In a second study, children were asked to point to photographs of infants, peers, older children, adults (parent-aged), and grandparents in response to the questions. For example, we asked the child to point to the photograph of whom you would go to for help, play with, or share a toy. The results indicated that older persons were chosen for help. The teaching need result was like the first study in that older children were preferred for teaching. There was no difference in the person chosen for sharing, a replication of the earlier findings. Interestingly, the data on grandparent-aged adults are most similar to that for parent-aged parents.

These specific people–needs relationships exist by 1 year of age. At 1 year of age, infants play with peers more than with strange adult females or mothers, and mothers are sought after for protection and nurturance more than strange females and peers. Such findings suggest that the discrimination of persons and needs begins very early in life.

The construction of the people–needs matrix provides us with a model for understanding the child's social network. The variety of people and needs that comprise this network alters at least as a function of the child's age and culture. Until recently, the focus of most research has been restricted to examining particular cells of the matrix—such as the mother and caregiving needs. At the same time, certain needs and persons have been assumed to be synonymous. Moreover, by using the attachment model, researchers have assumed that the lack of a particular people–need relationship leads to harmful consequences. If we consider the entire matrix, however, it may be possible to determine whether there are specific people–need relationships, for example, whether mother and mothering are synonymous. In addition, it can be determined whether certain functions can be safely substituted for by others without harmful consequences, as, for example, whether a teacher or a peer can be substituted for a mother for the satisfaction in the needs of nurturance or teaching. Recent research indicates that this is the case (NICHD, 1997, 1998, 1999).

The social network model may best characterize the child's social world as well as reflecting ontogenetic, cultural and idiographic differences. In the child's life there exists a variety of significant people. Which people constitute the important relationships for the child depends on the structure and values of the particular culture. We view the social network as a system. The network is established by the culture for the transmission of cultural values. The composition of the network, the nature of the people, the needs they fulfil, and the relationship between people and needs are the parts of the vehicle through which the cultural values are determined. In fact, this structure may be as important as the specific information conveyed; indeed, it may constitute the information itself. Finally, these comments should alert us to the dangers of assuming that the care of children represents some unchanging and absolute process. The care of children is the primary social activity of any society as it represents the single activity wherein the values of the society are preserved. Child care must reflect the values of the culture at large; therefore, one should expect it to change as these values change. The issue of social values must be addressed in order for us to deal with the ideal relationship (if any) between people and needs and their interaction. The research tasks are to characterize various networks and to determine the outcome of various people–need relationships in regard to a set of goals and values rather than to argue for some ideal biological state.

13 Infant play: functions and partners

CATHERINE S. TAMIS-LEMONDA, JILL C. KATZ, and
MARC H. BORNSTEIN

Introduction

All humans, and even non-human primates, play. This observation led
developmental and evolutionary scientists to speculate that play is a distinct
motivational/behavioural system that might serve diverse adaptive functions
(Power, 2000). Many early theorists of play focused on the functions of children's solitary play and play with peers (e.g., Piaget, 1952; Freud, 1959) or
underscored the importance of adults and other social partners in play to supporting the development of children's thought (e.g., Vygotsky, 1962). What
are the roles of different social partners in interactive play, and how do those
roles change over infancy? Most research has been focused on a specific play
partner, notably mother, at an isolated age, rather than comparing young
children's play with adults, siblings, and/or peers (but see Martlew et al.,
1976; Dunn & Dale, 1984; Vandell & Wilson, 1987; Dale, 1989; Youngblade
& Dunn, 1995; Perez-Granados & Callanan, 1997). Few researchers have
examined the roles of different play partners at different ages (but see Haight
& Miller, 1992; Howes, 1992; Farver & Wimbarti, 1995), despite the fact
that children are embedded in and affected by a rich social network from early
infancy (Lewis, 1987). In this chapter we provide an integrative review of
the various play functions of different play partners during the child's first
2–3 years of life.

Broadly speaking, play serves functions in five major domains of development: **psychological, mastery, cognitive, social**, and **cultural**. In the psychological domain, play is a medium through which children regulate arousal,
express a range of emotions, and resolve conflicts and traumas. In the mastery
domain, play has been associated with attention span and task-directed behaviour in structured and unstructured tasks. In the cognitive domain, play
enables children to acquire information and skills, engage in creative and
divergent thinking, and advance in representational abilities. In the social domain, play supports the development of *reciprocity* (giving and receiving) and
intersubjectivity (taking account of other people's thoughts and intentions in
deciding what to do), both of which provide a foundation for mature forms of
social understanding. Lastly, in the cultural domain, play is a vehicle for the

transmission of social roles and cultural values. As we see, numerous persons inhabit the lives of infants and contribute to the complexity of early socialization (Lewis, 1987); play provides a prominent context for socialization across this array of partners.

Psychological functions of play

Play affords a stage for children to regulate arousal (Ruff & Lawson, 1991), express a range of emotions (Stern, 1993; Singer, 1995), and resolve conflicts and traumas (Fein, 1981; Gordon, 1993). We consider the contributions of different partners to each of these functions.

Regulation of arousal

From the first months of life, social play in the form of face-to-face playful exchanges between caregivers and their young helps infants regulate their arousal. Infants offer and avert their gaze to initiate and terminate play interactions, thereby taking an active part in maintaining optimal levels of arousal (Stern, 1985). Partners who respond appropriately to their infants' need for more or less stimulation help contribute to infants' self-regulation capacities. In turn, infants who are better able to regulate arousal are more apt to experience pleasure during play interactions and to be able to reduce negative states. Younger infants in particular rely on their partners to interpret their signals. Suggesting that it is adult caregivers who might best support infants' regulatory functions. Indeed, mothers are more likely to respond contingently to 6- and 9-month-old infants than older siblings or peers (Vandell & Wilson, 1987). This suggests that play with parents takes place at levels of stimulation that are tolerable and pleasurable for the infant.

In the second year, play with adult caregivers continues to support children's self-regulation. For example, mothers who spend more time engaged in joint attention with their 2 year olds during play have children who more effectively engage in self-soothing strategies when frustrated (Raver, 1996). Moreover, time in joint attention accounts for infants' self-soothing strategies separate from their temperament. Although this relation does not necessarily demonstrate a causal connection, it does suggest that infants' movement toward autonomous emotional regulation may be rooted in early play experiences with their mothers.

Expression of emotions

In addition to the function of arousal regulation, play serves to expand the range of emotions that infants express by enabling them to experience positive feelings, such as fun, excitement, and pleasure, as well as negative emotions, such as anger, sadness, and fear (Singer, 1995). Bruner (1972) contended that play also allows the young of the species to experiment with a full range of emotions by displaying behaviours that might not be safe in real or mature life, for example, mock anger or aggression.

From the first days of life, mothers support their babies' experience of joy by playing with facial expressions, vocalizations, and touch, and evoking gazing, smiling, and laughing from their infants. According to Stern (1993), the progressive escalation of excitement inherent in mother–infant game rituals boosts infants to higher levels of joy than they might achieve on their own. It is the infant's growing awareness of the contingency in these interactions that adds to feelings of pleasure, in addition to enabling greater tolerance for higher arousal states (Roggman, 1991). The finding that mothers are more contingent with infants than are siblings or peers (Vandell & Wilson, 1987) suggests that attuned adults are best able to amplify and prolong the infant's experience of pleasure in the first months of life.

By the end of the first year, infants' positive emotional exchanges extend to peers. Eckerman *et al.* (1975) found that the play episodes of peers between 10 and 24 months contained behaviours indicating positive emotions. At younger ages, positive feelings towards peers were expressed through smiling, vocalizing, and touching; offering and accepting toys were positive behaviours that increased with age. At all ages, positive emotions outweighed negative emotions, as expressed through fussing and crying.

Play interactions between older infants and siblings or peers may allow for the expression of an ever-wider range and greater intensity of emotions than play interactions with mothers. Specifically, 17–20 month olds have been found to smile more frequently at peers than at mothers when both are present (Rubenstein & Howes, 1976; also see Morgan *et al.*, 1991). Similarly, Farver and Wimbarti (1995) found that there was significantly more laughing and smiling in play between siblings than in play between mothers and children at 18, 24, and 36 months in Javanese families. Play with siblings was also more likely to incorporate exciting and frightening themes than was play with mothers, suggesting that siblings engender a greater intensity of both positive and negative emotions.

These studies suggest that mothers are more effective than siblings and peers at all ages in *regulating* their infants' emotions by adjusting levels of stimulation and containing emotions in play. However, after the first year, play interactions with peers and siblings increase in prevalence and may be more intense and affectively charged than those with mother.

Resolution of conflicts and traumas

Freud (1959) was one of the first to suggest that play helped children resolve conflicts and traumas and to vent forbidden impulses. More recent theorists speculate that play helps children generate multiple solutions to hypothetical situations and to test alternative outcomes to conflicts and trauma (Gordon, 1993; Singer, 1995).

Case material from child psychoanalysis suggests that children as young as 2 years of age use play to represent conflicts or traumas symbolically (Winnicott, 1977). However, because representational abilities are still rudimentary at this stage, interpretation of play activities by an attuned adult is necessary to facilitate conflict resolution. Others suggest that play only begins to help children resolve conflicts after the age of 3, because they are not able to substitute thought for action until then (Lewis, 1993). Because 3 year olds are unable co-ordinate social pretence without expert help, adult partners continue to best support the use of play for conflict resolution (Stockinger Forys & McCune-Nicolich, 1984).

Although older siblings are capable of providing expertise to facilitate pretence, they are less likely than mothers to follow younger siblings' lead (Dale, 1989). Thus, unless conflictual material or traumas are of mutual interest, older siblings may not allow younger ones enough independence to play out disturbing material. In addition, the rigid quality of post-traumatic play (Terr, 1981) implies dependence on an exceptionally motivated and flexible play partner—qualities that are more likely to be found in adults. In the first years of life, therefore, adults best support children's ability to represent and resolve conflicts and traumas through play because of their combined support for children's representational play skills and their tendency to support children's choices of play themes.

Mastery functions of play

The mastery functions of play are those that help children achieve a sense of self-efficacy and motivation to persist toward goals. Pretend play enables children to master a novel, complex environment in a miniaturized form (Singer, 1995). Empirically, play sophistication is associated with greater attention span (Tamis-LeMonda & Bornstein, 1990) and persistence on problem solving tasks (Power et al., 1985).

Mastery motivation in structured tasks

In infancy, the concept of mastery motivation is captured by infants' curiosity about and exploration of objects (Morgan et al., 1991). During this stage, adults are more effective in focusing infant's attention to social and non-social stimuli than are peers or siblings (Vandell & Wilson, 1987). In addition, mothers are able to shift infants' attention from interpersonal to object play (Jacobson, 1981; Vandell & Wilson, 1987), thereby facilitating their exploration of the environment. For example, mothers who encourage their 2 month olds to orient to and explore objects in the environment have infants who explore objects more at 5 months (Bornstein & Tamis-LeMonda, 1990), and parents' stimulation and responsiveness to infants at 6 months predicts infants' persistence on problem-solving tasks at 13 months (Yarrow *et al.*, 1984).

Between 1 and 2 years of age, children's goal-directed behaviours increase as they practise emerging skills and attempt multipart tasks. During this period, adult play partners continue to foster children's sense of efficacy and persistence on structured tasks. Twelve- and 20 month olds persist more on challenging tasks when mothers support their autonomy (Grolnick *et al.*, 1984; Frodi *et al.*, 1985), and mothers who physically aid their 18 month olds when playing have children who persist on structured tasks (Morgan *et al.*, 1991). Positive mother–toddler attachment has also been linked to persistence (Maslin *et al.*, 1987; Morgan *et al.*, 1988).

Mothers' early advantage in supporting mastery motivation on structured tasks may be due to their responsiveness to children's initiatives, accuracy in assessing their need for help, and/or the effectiveness of their assistance. Mothers are highly attuned and responsive to the level of their toddlers' play sophistication at both 13 and 21 months, which may serve to optimize infants' attention and interest during play (Tamis-LeMonda & Bornstein, 1991; Damast *et al.*, 1996). Specifically, mothers prompt play at levels that match or are slightly above their toddlers' own play, and rarely encourage their toddlers to engage in play below the level spontaneously exhibited. Thus, adults' expert support allows children to perform within their 'zone of proximal development' (Vygotsky, 1978).

Mastery motivation in unstructured play

Although mothers support sustained attention best for all forms of play during infancy, peers seem better able to support sustained attention in unstructured, physically active play during toddlerhood (Morgan *et al.*, 1991). Rubenstein and Howes (1976) suggested that peers are particularly adept at maintaining mutual interest and excitement in joint episodes of push-pull, chasing, climbing, sliding, and swinging and joint episodes of open-ended object exploration During pre-school, unstructured pretend play with peers yields longer episodes than with mothers (Haight & Miller, 1992). It may be that after infancy the joint enthusiasm that characterizes peer play best supports continued engagement, as long as children can manage the cognitive and social demands of the task independently.

Cognitive functions of play

When babies are at play, more than meets the eye is going on. The cognitive functions of play are those that serve the acquisition of information, divergent thinking and creativity, and representation. Here we examine the contribution of social partners to these functions.

Acquisition of information and skills

Throughout childhood, mother–child play partnerships serve a didactic function. For example, Kugiumutzakis's 1992 study (as cited in Trevarthen, 1993) showed that mothers use sound play with 2 month olds to reinforce babbling sounds related to speech, thus preparing the infant for future communication. Mothers also use play to stimulate and sustain their infants' interest in objects and the environment. In the latter part of the first year, mothers support their children's efforts to practise new skills and succeed on multipart tasks (Morgan *et al.*, 1991).

During the second year, mothers continue to use joint play as an opportunity to teach, by increasingly encouraging their children to use toys in conventional ways. For example, Fiese (1990) found that 15–24 month olds increased the use of toys in functionally appropriate ways when playing with mother as compared with playing alone. Mothers also use pretend play to model a 'right' way of doing things, and to correct children's violations of reality, for example, protesting (seriously or playfully) when youngsters drink tea from the teapot instead of the cup (Howes, 1992). Dale (1989) also found that mothers of 2 year olds initiate and sustain pretend play by focusing on objects and their functional uses. A mother might prompt her toddler to pretend to talk on a toy telephone by handing the phone to her child and saying 'Daddy wants to talk. Say hello'.

The didactic role that parents take during collaborative play is less predominant when siblings play together. Mothers are more likely than siblings to instruct their 2 and 3 year olds about object use, to set up models for them to copy, and to correct their behaviours while playing (Farver & Wimbarti, 1995). Peers are even less likely than siblings to take a didactic role in play with age-mates, perhaps due to their limited competence.

Adult caregivers' more prominent role as teacher during play does not negate the role of peers and siblings, however. Towards the end of the first year children watch and imitate peers' actions with toys (Hanna & Meltzoff, 1991; Verba, 1994), and are sometimes more prone to imitating other children than adults (Eckerman *et al.*, 1975; Rubenstein & Howes, 1976). Toddlers use imitation to initiate pretend play with siblings 38% of the time, but never use this strategy to initiate pretend with mothers (Dunn & Dale, 1984).

As imitation is an early learning strategy, peer and sibling play clearly helps children acquire new skills after the first year. However, the skills emphasized by mothers are different from those generated in sibling and peer play. Mothers are more likely to convey information about the real world and encourage conventional object use and convergent thinking. Mothers use play as a vehicle for learning, whereas siblings and peers are motivated by play itself.

Divergent thinking and creativity

Bruner (1972) suggested that the ability and opportunity to 'play' with learned behaviours outside of their real context allows the young of a species the freedom to combine actions and objects in novel ways, thereby engendering a flexible mindset. Play has been correlated with success on divergent problem-solving tasks and measures of creativity; the opportunity to play freely with materials has been linked to innovative uses for objects, a flexible approach to problem-solving, and better performance on divergent-thinking tasks (Rubin *et al.*, 1983). Imaginative play, in particular, has been causally linked to measures of creativity such as unique responses on the Rorschach Ink Blot test (Rubin *et al.*, 1983; Singer, 1995). Researchers speculate that the act of pretence fosters flexible thinking because it involves a shifting in and out of the play frame from real to imagined identities of people, situations, and objects (Rubin & Howe, 1986; Singer, 1995; Lillard, 1998).

During the second year, peers and siblings support flexibility, creativity, and divergent thinking in both exploratory and pretend play. Siblings and peers often demonstrate novel actions in their play, perhaps because their play is less prescribed or rigid than that of adults. One study revealed that 17–20-month-old children engage in more creative or unusual uses of objects during play with peers than during play with mothers (Rubenstein & Howes, 1976). Similarly, toddlers express more diverse themes when engaged in pretence with older siblings than with mothers (Dunn & Dale, 1984; Youngblade & Dunn, 1995). Dunn and Dale (1984) found that 2- and 3-year-olds' pretence with older siblings often involved the creation of imaginary situations, whereas pretence with mothers more often involved realistic situations. Siblings might be more likely to pretend about Superheroes; mothers might be more likely to encourage their toddlers to put teddy bears to sleep.

Representational thinking

Both Piaget (1962) and Vygotsky (1967) emphasized the importance of play in the development of representational thinking. The capacity to simulate events out of their real context frees children from the here-and-now, and allows them to reflect on the past and anticipate the future, through symbolic gestures and the use of language. This notion is supported by associations between children's pretend play and measures of language development, including vocabulary, verbal fluency, semantic diversity, and complexity of language structures (Tamis-LeMonda & Bornstein, 1990, 1994; Singer, 1995).

Symbolic play

During the second year of life, children begin to re-enact activities in non-literal ways (e.g., by pretending to drink from a cup, or use a block as a telephone). These advances reflect children's progress toward greater decontextualization of thought in three ways: (1) play becomes distanced from self (e.g., as children move from pretending toward self to pretending toward others); (2) play becomes distanced from the tangible properties of objects (e.g., as children move from pretending with literal replicas of objects to using substitutive objects); and (3) play becomes distanced from overt actions (e.g., as children move from enacting active themes to more emotive ones) (Tamis-LeMonda & Bornstein, 1996). Between 1 and 2 years, adults best support these emerging abilities in children's pretence. Howes (1992) noted that, when children are between 12 and 15 months, mothers interpret concrete actions as pretence, thereby assigning symbolic meaning to children's actions. For example, a mother might respond, 'You're patting the baby!' as her child touches a doll. It is thus unsurprising that toddlers' symbolic play with mothers is more complex, diverse, and sustained than is their solitary play (Dunn & Wooding, 1977; O'Connell & Bretherton, 1984; Slade, 1987; Haight & Miller, 1992; Bornstein *et al.*, 1996).

Moreover, variation in mothers' play sophistication is linked to variation in children's pretence abilities. Mothers who demonstrate and solicit more symbolic play with 13 and 20 month olds have toddlers who engage in more symbolic play. Over this 7-month period, mothers who increase in the frequency of their symbolic play have toddlers who demonstrate rapid gains in their symbolic play; mothers who show no change or decrease in their symbolic play have toddlers who show little symbolic gain (Tamis-LeMonda & Bornstein, 1991).

During the second year, play with siblings is less supportive of children's emerging pretence. Older siblings attempt to direct their younger siblings' play and elicit their compliance, and peers imitate each others' actions, but they are not yet capable of communicating pretence to each other (Howes, 1992). By 2–3 years of age, however, older siblings become important, supportive partners in children's symbolic play, and pretend play with siblings increases in prevalence. In one study, US children engaged in pretend play more often with older siblings than with mothers by 33 months of age (Youngblade & Dunn, 1995). In Javanese families pretend play has been found to be more frequent with siblings than with mothers at 18, 24, and 36 months (Farver & Wimbarti, 1995).

Studies with toddlers suggest that mothers scaffold play in concrete ways, whereas siblings engage in more abstract transformations (Dunn & Dale, 1984; Dale, 1989). On the one hand, mothers' tendency to focus on toy objects and their functions may provide better support for the emerging symbolic abilities of 2 year olds. By 3 years of age, siblings' use of a combination of objects, pretend actions, and imaginary discourse may provide better support to children as they advance in representational abilities. Indeed, as the age of the older sibling increased, the frequency of role play of 33-month-old younger siblings increased (Youngblade & Dunn, 1995). This suggests that most children still depend on a partner's expertise to foster role play towards the end of the third year. For this reason, 3-year-old peers are not yet capable of the joint role play that characterizes siblings' play (Howes, 1992).

Language development

The representational abilities reflected in the emergence of symbolic play during the second year are reflected in concomitant language gains. As with symbolic play, adult caregivers hold a privileged position in fostering language development during this stage.

Research indicates that mother–child play contains more continuous verbal interactions than play between toddlers (Rubenstein & Howes, 1976), and facilitates the use of more complex language than play with either siblings or peers (Perez-Granados & Callanan, 1997). Additionally, mothers' language during play is closely linked to toddlers' language gains. Mothers who are more verbally responsive during play with their 13 and 21 month olds have toddlers with larger receptive and productive vocabularies at both ages (Tamis-LeMonda *et al.*, 1996) and who express a greater range of meanings as reflected in their semantic language abilities at 21 months (Tamis-LeMonda & Bornstein, 1994). Mothers who respond to their 9- and 13-month-olds' language initiatives during free play, particularly by imitating/expanding on infant vocalizations and prompting symbolic play, have toddlers who imitate, express first words, achieve a vocabulary spurt, use sentences, and verbally express memories up to 6 months sooner in development than children of less responsive mothers (Tamis-LeMonda *et al.*, 1998, 2001). Mothers who are attuned to their 9-month-olds' emotional expressions during play have children who achieve language milestones earlier (Nicely *et al.*, 1999), perhaps due to the fact that mothers' attuned responses foster intersubjectivity (Stern, 1993).

Towards the end of the pre-school years, siblings and peers begin to support the development of symbolic play. During this same period, adults continue to support the growth of children's language abilities through their responsive engagements with toddlers during collaborative play. After the age of 3, children quickly develop communicative competence with a variety of partners. Garvey (1990) noted that pre-schoolers practise complex language skills while playing with peers. Thus, the cognitive benefits of mother–child play are salient early on, extending to peer and sibling play by age 3.

Social functions of play

The social functions of play are those that foster children's understanding of others' feelings, intentions, and perspectives, thereby fostering successful social interactions and relationships. Early forms of mother–infant play are thought to build reciprocal patterns of communication (Bruner & Ratner, 1978) and intersubjective understanding (Trevarthen, 1993), both of which underpin and motivate later collaborative activity. Role play, in particular, has been linked to the ability to understand feelings, mental states, and others' perspectives (Rubin & Howe, 1986; Dunn, 1987; Youngblade & Dunn, 1995). Rubin and Howe (1986) suggested that role play enhances perspective-taking ability, because the constant shifting from reality to pretence may strengthen children's ability to consider multiple points of view. Perspective-taking ability has been positively associated with social competence, although this relation is not causal (Light, 1987). Here we examine how different partners support these social functions in infancy.

Reciprocity

Communicative reciprocity involves conversational turn-taking and respond-ing in a way that is topically related to a partner's prior communication. In infancy, play with adult caregivers is fundamental to the development of communicative reciprocity. For example, at 6 and 9 months, a greater number and longer durations of turn-taking exchanges characterize infants' play interactions with their mothers when compared with that with siblings or peers (Vandell & Wilson, 1987). Towards the end of the first year, games such as 'peek-a-boo' reinforce reciprocal communication (Bruner & Ratner, 1978). Although co-ordinated exchanges between peers, such as giving and accepting toys, appear at this time, they are brief and relatively rare (Eckerman *et al.*, 1975; Didow & Eckerman, 1991; Eckerman & Didow, 1996).

During the second year, adult caregivers continue to extend turn-taking ex-changes during play by directing children's attention to their actions or link-ing their responses to children's actions (Howes & Unger, 1992). Towards the end of the second year, peer communication during play becomes increasingly reciprocal, reflecting a growing awareness of peers' needs and intentions. There is an escalation in the frequency of temporally related talk (i.e., turn taking) when 20 and 24 month olds play together, although responses related to the prior topic are infrequent (Eckerman & Didow, 1996). By 29–38 months, peers are more likely to respond contingently to each other, although responses are not necessarily verbal (Howes & Unger, 1992). As language increases, communications between peers becomes increasingly verbal, leading to greater understanding of feelings and intentions not bound to the immediate context.

Intersubjectivity

Intersubjectivity motivates play partners to convey their own and seek under-standing of others' thoughts and feelings. According to Trevarthen (1993), the origins of intersubjectivity are affective or emotion-related and are evidenced during the first months of life in early forms of communication between mothers and infants, called 'protoconversations.' If either mother or infant fails to respond with appropriate emotional expression, play is disrupted. During later infancy, mother–infant play also involves 'teasing games and rituals' that help the infant practise negotiation skills that build more intricate intersubjective understanding (Trevarthen, 1993). Gönçü (1993, p. 187) asserted that 'the intersubjectivity attained in mother–infant interactions prepares children to share meanings with peers' later on. Others have shown that both secure mother–infant attachments and secure teacher–toddler relationships shape current and future social competence and positive peer interactions in children (Elicker *et al.*, 1992; Howes, 1997) and predict social adjustment in children up to 9 years of age (Howes *et al.*, 1998).

In older infants, pretend play with both mother and siblings supports the development of children's understanding of feeling states, such as pain, distress, sleepiness, hunger, or sadness. Infants as young as 18–24 months are able to take on the perspective of a feeling state other than their own in pretend play with siblings (Dunn, 1987). Research indicates that toddlers derive feelings of social support, trust, and intimacy from peers (Howes & Tonyan, 1999) and respond to the crying of another child if that child is a friend (Howes & Farver, 1987).

The emerging ability to engage in role play with mothers and siblings also appears to support understanding of others' mental states. Youngblade and Dunn (1995) found that more social pretending at 33 months predicted better performance on a task measuring affective understanding at 40 months, whereas greater participation in role enactment predicted better performance on a task measuring children's understanding of false beliefs. Others have also suggested that pretend play, even in toddlers, supports the later development of a theory of mind by offering children opportunities to practice, use, and manipulate their own and their partners' representations of situations (Lillard, 1993, 1998).

During later infancy, peers are not yet capable of joint pretence, but they do enjoy simple collaborative play that enables them to practise communicating about common goals. Children as young as 13–17 months show evidence of collaborative, goal-directed play (Verba, 1994). Eckerman and Didow (1996) suggested that at between 16 and 32 months age-mates use non-verbal imitation to create mutual understanding of the joint nature of activities. In a year-long case study of two female playmates, Budwig *et al.* (1986) found that between the ages of 2 and 3 years the girls needed a great deal of help from their caregivers to understand one another's perspectives during play interactions. At the same time, Gönçü (1993) reported that children between 18 and 36 months communicate the idea of pretence with 'exaggerated movements, facial gestures, and voice inflection, as well as brief verbal exchanges' (p. 194). These findings indicate that toddlers make attempts to convey complex states of mind with age mates.

In sum, adult caregivers build reciprocity and intersubjectivity through early social play with infants. These abilities constitute the interpersonal and intrapsychic building blocks of successful social negotiations. In the second and third years, pretend play with peers, siblings, and mothers lays a foundation for understanding others' feelings and mental states, as reflected in the development of a theory of mind.

Cultural functions of play

Play has long been thought to serve a variety of cultural functions. In 1898, Groos suggested that role play helps children practise behaviours they will need as adults in their society. In the 1930s, Mead proposed that role play helped children to first understand and then acquire societal standards and beliefs (see Damon, 1983). Later theorists stressed the active socialization process that takes place when children experiment with roles and behaviours during play. Chick and Barnett (1995) emphasized the transformations in values that occur when groups of children play together over time, suggesting that social play helps children learn traditional ways of thinking and behaving, while also inspiring cultural innovations. In this section, we examine how different partners support the cultural functions of play.

Expectations about the roles of different individuals within a society are communicated to infants and children merely by virtue of *who* is deemed to be an appropriate play partner—parents, relatives, siblings, or peers. In some cultures, parents avoid play with children. Mexican mothers reputedly attach no particular value to play and likewise do not believe that it is important to play with their children (Farver & Howes, 1993). Guatemalan mothers reportedly laugh with embarrassment at the idea of playing with their children, as play is considered the territory of other children and occasionally grandparents (Rogoff *et al.*, 1993). Similar attributions have been made about Indonesian (Farver & Wimbarti, 1995) parents. In Italy, mothers regard child play as inevitable, and not requiring adult intervention (New, 1994).

In other cultures, parents consider play with children to be central to parenting and take an active part in children's play. Middle-class American and Turkish parents think of themselves as play partners for their children (Göncü *et al.*, 1991), and consistent with such beliefs, promote and participate in pretend play with their children (also see Tamis-LeMonda *et al.*, 1992; Bornstein *et al.*, 1996). In some societies (e.g., the USA), direct teaching is often criticized as being developmentally inappropriate for very young children, and play is regarded as a preferable path to promoting competence and academic success. Cultural constraints on children's play is equally regarded as a means to other related goals such as self-regulation, and social competence with peers (e.g., Howes, 1992).

Although many studies emphasize the cultural functions of play that are evidenced *after* the infancy period, the past decade has been characterized by a surge of research underscoring the importance of interactions in infancy for cultural socialization. Parents' playful engagements with infants in societies as far flung as Argentina and Japan communicate expectations about societal roles and cultural ideologies (Bornstein & Tamis-LeMonda 1990; Bornstein *et al.*, 1990, 1992, 1999; Tamis-LeMonda & Bornstein, 1996). For example, cross-cultural research demonstrates that Argentine and Japanese mothers foster collectivist values, whereas American mothers foster individualist values in play with their young infants (Tamis-LeMonda *et al.*, 1992; Bornstein *et al.*, 1999).

In one investigation, mothers in Tokyo, Japan, and New York (USA) were videotaped interacting with their 4–5-month-old infants (Bornstein *et al.*, 1985–86). When engaged in play with their infants, mothers in Japan more often encouraged infants to attend to themselves, whereas mothers in the USA more often encouraged their infants to attend to objects in the environment. This difference accords with a collectivistic versus individualistic characterization of Japanese versus US American cultures. In a second study, various forms of play and other interactions were coded in Japanese and US mothers playing with their 13-month-old toddlers (Tamis-LeMonda *et al.*, 1992). Japanese mothers more often engaged in 'other-directed' pretence play with their children, for example by prompting them to bow to or feed dolls. In contrast, US mothers more often encouraged their toddlers to engage in independent, concrete play (e.g., placing shapes in shape sorters), and they used the play setting as a forum for labelling and describing objects and events. In line with these differences in parental play, Japanese toddlers engaged more frequently in pretence play (particularly 'other-directed' pretence) and US toddlers were more advanced in their receptive and productive vocabularies. These findings suggest that, during the period when toddlers' representational abilities are emerging, parents emphasize different modes of representation in their play, that preferred modes accord with traditional cultural values, and that they exert an early and telling influence on children's developmental achievements.

After the second year, pretend play increasingly becomes a vehicle for transmitting information about cultural roles, routines, and conventions. Adult caregivers are critical conveyers of information about roles and routines as they help children elaborate their play ideas. For example, Miller and Garvey (1984) studied the development of the mother/baby role in children's play from 18 months to 3 years. In the earliest stages, mothers provided dolls and other props to their children (i.e., clothing, dishes, bottles) and gave a great deal of instruction about mothering behaviours. Similarly, Dunn and Dale (1984) found that mothers are far more likely to engage in play around nurturing themes and household activities with daughters than with sons, and much more likely to engage in action play with sons than with daughters when their children were toddlers. Interestingly, Fagot and Hagan (1991) found that parents were more likely to respond in sex-differentiated ways to their children at 18 months than they were at 12 or at 60 months of age. As such, play with toddlers may be a particularly salient context for transmitting gender-typed information.

Like mothers, older siblings and peers are also a source of information and modelling of social roles and conventions, particularly in the toddler and pre-school years. In hunter–gatherer and agricultural societies, children rather than adults are primary playmates even of toddlers (Edwards & Whiting, 1993; Power, 2000). Lloyd (1987) found that gender-typed toy and activity preference exists when same sex peers (19 and 42 months) played together, despite the fact that 2 year olds did not yet demonstrate stable representations of gender on a series of cognitive tasks. In this same study, she found that cross-gender toy use and activity were more frequent when boys and girls played together.

In overview, the play partners of infants and toddlers vary across cultures, and these differences themselves communicate information about cultural norms concerning the role of peers and adults as well as the role of the child in the larger society. In societies in which adults frequently engage in play with infants, social roles and cultural values are transmitted to infants from the first days of life. During infancy, peers are less likely to transmit directly specific social roles or values through role play, both because of a lack of competence in co-ordinating social pretend and because of a lack of knowledge of social and cultural values. Using gender-typed behaviour as one example of how cultural values are transmitted through play, it seems that adult caregivers reinforce gender-typed behaviour most strongly during the toddler years, whereas peers become more influential during the pre-school years.

Conclusions

The psychological, mastery, cognitive, social, and cultural functions of infant play are all significant and all supported by adult caregivers, siblings, and peers. Not surprisingly, the role of adult caregivers in each of these play functions is paramount during early infancy. By 2–3 years of age, however, peers' and siblings' contributions to certain play functions (e.g., divergent thinking, perspective taking) begin to outweigh those of adults. Thus, different play partners have unique characteristics and play styles that support different functions at different developmental periods.

Parent–child play holds a special place in infancy, in that it is a stage when the intrinsic pleasure and excitement of play predominates (Bornstein, 2001). During playful interactions, adult attunement and responsiveness to the infant's signals and needs are critical. For the infant, tactile, vocal, and visual theme-and-variation play with mothers supports the interrelated functions of regulation of arousal, expansion of emotion, mastery motivation, and primary intersubjectivity. Over time, adults increasingly use play as a vehicle for teaching children how to master the use of objects and how to communicate with others. Mothers *qua* teachers stimulate their children intellectually as they prompt and support their children's cognitive achievements. As mothers transmit information to their children, they foster achievements in language, convergent thinking, and self-efficacy, while also communicating cultural expectations. Thus, by the time infants become toddlers, the pleasure care-givers derive from playing with their children has shifted from 'sheer delight' (Roggman, 1991) towards supporting cognitive and social competencies within a cultural context.

Sibling–child partnerships have certain characteristics that are similar to adult–child partnerships and others that are similar to peer–child partner-ships. Like adults, older siblings normally possess more expertise than their younger siblings and therefore are capable of modelling higher levels of play. Research suggests that older siblings play a strong role in supporting symbolic play when their younger siblings are between 2 and 3 years of age (Dunn & Dale, 1984; Dale, 1989; Farver & Wimbarti, 1995; Youngblade & Dunn, 1995). At this time, children are still too young to engage successfully in mu-tual pretence with peers, and therefore benefit from their older siblings' ex-pertise and ability to share experiences. Moreover, when they pretend, older siblings engage in more role play and abstract transformations than mothers, perhaps fostering representational abilities in their younger siblings. The shared experiences of older siblings, as well as their enhanced tendency to engage in role play, sets the occasion for younger siblings to participate more effectively in pretend play about familiar routines. Because older siblings are more motivated by the sheer pleasure of play than by the desire to teach, play between siblings appears to be more affectively charged than play with mother. By 2–3 years, play between younger and older siblings is character-ized by greater shared experiences and pleasure than is adult–child play.

Unlike caregivers or older siblings, peers are playmates who share similar developmental levels and relate to each other horizontally without an estab-lished hierarchy. Play partnerships between peers foster more sustained atten-tion, pleasure, and excitement during joint episodes of physically active play than do mother–child partnerships. With each new form of play that is mastered (i.e., goal-oriented tasks for 3 year olds and advanced and sustained levels of symbolic play for 4 and 5 year olds), play with peers continues to be more engrossing and emotionally intense than mother–child play.

This integrative review underscores the changing nature of play functions and partners across infancy. It is simplistic to contend that certain play part-ners (e.g., mothers) support children's developmental achievements better than do others (e.g., peers). Rather, different social partners contribute in unique, and often complementary, ways to children's psychological, mastery, cognitive, social, and cultural advances in play. The functions that are served in play, and the roles of different partners in supporting those functions, change in parallel with developments in children's cognitive, verbal, and social–emotional abilities.

14 Learning to communicate

VIKRAM K. JASWAL and ANNE FERNALD

Introduction

The ability to communicate is essential for all animals living in social groups. Some social species such as ants and bees communicate through intricate but relatively inflexible behaviours that change little over the lifespan. At the other end of the spectrum, primates depend on the adaptable use of continuously varying communicative behaviours that change fundamentally between infancy and adulthood. As different as they are, ants, bees, chimps, and humans have all inherited the need and the potential to interact successfully with *conspecifics* (members of the same species), although the behaviours and mental faculties required for communicative competence in these species are obviously very different. In contrast to the fixed behavioural patterns of social insects, the development of communication in primates requires an advanced capacity for learning. Young chimps and humans learn to convey information relevant to their needs through vocal, facial, and motor behaviours, and learn to monitor the behaviours of others in order to read their intentions and make sense of their actions, skills crucial for success in the complex social worlds in which they live. By the end of their first year, human infants move beyond the non-verbal behaviours shared with other primates, toward a medium of communication that is incalculably more powerful and flexible. This chapter focuses on how human infants learn to communicate, at first through voice, face, and gesture, and gradually through the use of language.

Infants are social creatures from the beginning, by virtue of being born into communities concerned for their survival. Caretakers in every culture tend to interpret babies' cries as a sign of discomfort and to respond accordingly, although the cry of the newborn is certainly not an intentional communication. In his theory of attachment (see Chapter 12), John Bowlby drew on insights from animal behaviour to interpret the social capabilities of human newborns from an evolutionary perspective. Bowlby pointed out that the cries and other reflexive behaviours of the young in many species serve an evolutionary function by alerting caregivers to the infant's needs. Such signals are particularly important in species where the young require a prolonged period of parental support. In '*precocial*' species such as horses, sheep, and geese, the young are born motorically well developed, able to move around on their own, and seek food and protection by following the parent shortly after birth. However, in *altricial* species such as cats and robins, the young remain helpless for a period and need the parent to stay close by to provide food and protection. Although infants in altricial species are too motorically immature to maintain proximity by following the parent, species-specific social signals enable them to achieve that goal by other means. The gaping mouth of the herring gull chick elicits feeding behaviour from the parent, and the ultrasonic distress cry of the rat pup inspires the mother to return to the nest and lick the pup, both examples of the complementary evolution of infant behaviours matched by appropriate parental behaviours. Bowlby extended these ethological observations to humans, the most altricial species of all, reasoning that the earliest social signals are cries, smiles, and other reflexive behaviours indicative of the infant's internal state. These communicative signals have evolved as the involuntary tactics of the helpless newborn for keeping the parent close at hand.

What is communication?

Although biologists, linguists, psychologists, and engineers still debate about how best to define communication (Mellor, 1990), they generally agree that communication occurs when a signal given by one organism is perceived by and influences the behaviour of another organism. But what exactly is a signal? When the uneven gait of an injured zebra reveals vulnerability to a hungry lion, is this a social signal? Signals convey information, and the zebra's behaviour is certainly informative. However, most ethologists (scientists interested in natural behaviour) would agree that the wounded animal's gait is a direct consequence of a physical condition, not a signal specialized for communication. What about the pheromone released by a sexually receptive female cat that attracts all the male cats in the neighbourhood? Some would consider this a social signal because it reflects an evolved mechanism for broadcasting important information to conspecifics, although others might object that it too is a by-product of the female's physiological condition. The alarm call of a frantic monkey on seeing a predatory snake also conveys information about the monkey's state of arousal; however, this behaviour more clearly qualifies as a social signal because it has evolved to convey information to conspecifics and because it is turned on and off in particular circumstances (Hauser, 1996). How do the cries and smiles of the human infant compare with these examples? In the first months of life, cries and smiles are behaviours that are closely linked to the infant's physiological states and can be perceived and interpreted reliably by other humans. Thus they are informative and can strongly influence the behaviour of conspecifics, as in the example of the female cat. However, unlike the monkey's alarm calls, these early cries and smiles do not yet relate to anything in the outside world beyond the infant's immediate sensations.

Although in terms of their communicative competence human newborns may start out roughly at the level of a cat in heat, they begin to overtake the monkeys within the first months of life. The monkey's alarm call seems different from the behaviours of the zebra and the cat, somehow closer to human communication, but why? Several questions come to mind: Did the monkey realize the snake might attack? Was the alarm call a deliberate warning to others in the troop informing them of potential danger? Did the monkey understand that the alarm call would cause the other animals to seek safety? Did the other monkeys understand that the caller had seen a snake? These questions get at whether the monkey's communicative signal was intentional, was perceived by others as intentional, and was motivated by assumptions about the intentions and future actions of others. In the case of a human shouting 'Watch out for the snake!' the answer to all these questions would be positive, although with monkeys it is much less clear (Cheney & Seyfarth, 1990). This example makes the point that intentionality and an understanding of the mental states of others are critical in distinguishing human from animal communication.

In the first year of life, human infants move beyond their early reflexive cries and smiles toward an understanding of other minds that enables them not only to interpret the cries and smiles of others, but also to begin to communicate through language. Although the awareness of other points of view and the ability to make sense of meanings through spoken language emerge only gradually over this period, the speechless infant is still fully engaged in human communication on other levels. Infants express their sociability in the early months not only through their own emotional expressions, but also by their intense interest in the voices and faces of others. Bowlby referred to this as a universal stage of 'indiscriminating' social awareness, because months before infants develop strong emotional attachments to particular individuals, they appear to be fascinated by people in general. This observation has now been substantiated by 30 years of experimental studies exploring infants' early sensitivities to faces, voices, gestures, and the dynamics of social interaction, to be reviewed briefly in the following sections. Six month olds may not yet understand that other people have emotions that lead them to act in certain ways and not others; however, by this age they are already very attentive to the emotional signals that will ultimately enable them to make such inferences.

Listening to voices

While still *in utero* (in the womb), infants are able to hear the intonation of the mother's voice: in Chapter 3 it was noted that the mother talking will be readily heard by the fetus, and her voice is an auditory signal potentially rich in information. After hearing a voice for only a few seconds, experienced listeners make rapid judgements about whether the speaker is a friend or a stranger, male or female, young or old, perhaps also concluding that the speaker is angry or tired or ill. Research with newborns shows that even listeners with minimal experience encode socially relevant characteristics of vocal signals. DeCasper and Fifer (1980) asked whether infants can recognize their mother's voice at birth, testing newborns in a conditioning procedure where they learned to adjust their sucking response in different ways to produce either their own mother's voice or the voice of another woman. Infants only a few hours old chose more often to listen to the recording of their own mother. As the newborns had almost no postnatal experience hearing the mother speak, and no opportunity to associate her voice with pleasurable experiences such as nursing, the listening preference for the familiar voice was apparently based on prenatal experience.

Do these results show that newborns can recognize the mother through her voice? Certainly not in the sense that an adult can identify an individual speaking on the phone, nor even in the sense that an 8 month old shows recognition by smiling in response to the mother's voice and looking toward the door in anticipation of her appearance. In these examples, 'recognition' implies that the familiar voice is part of a complex schema based on extensive experience with the individual. For the inexperienced newborn, however, the mother's voice is merely an auditory stimulus that has been experienced before but not yet in association with any other aspects of her identity in postnatal experience. Although this study demonstrated recognition in only a limited sense, the DeCasper and Fifer (1980) findings were exciting because they were the first to show that even before birth, infants are attentive to human voices. These researchers also showed that newborns can distinguish two verses spoken in the same voice, one read aloud by the mother several times during pregnancy and the other a verse never heard before (DeCasper & Spence, 1986). Given this choice, newborns chose to listen to the verse they had heard while *in utero*. As the mother was the speaker in both cases, the two verses could not be discriminated on the basis of acoustic characteristics unique to her voice, but only on the basis of rhythmic and other prosodic differences peculiar to each. Newborns can also distinguish one language from another, preferring to listen to the language they have been hearing prenatally (Mehler *et al.*, 1988; Moon *et al.*, 1993). These findings reveal that newborns are already capable of extracting information from voices along multiple dimensions that will be socially and linguistically relevant in postnatal life.

After birth, the infant begins to experience voices in the context of increasingly rich forms of social stimulation. In many cultures, adults interacting with infants use a special form of speech that is more lively and musical than the speech typical of adult conversation. Figure 14.1 shows the vocal melodies of an American mother speaking to her 4-month-old child in the infant-directed (ID) speech style (sometimes called *Motherese*), and also speaking to an acquaintance in the adult-directed (AD) speech style. Note how the intonation contours of ID speech are greatly expanded in pitch range. Analyses of ID speech in British and American English, French, German, Italian, Japanese, and Chinese show that ID speech in these languages is typically higher in pitch with more exaggerated intonation contours, shorter utterances, and longer pauses than in AD speech (Griesser & Kuhl, 1988; Fernald *et al*., 1989). When given the choice of hearing ID or AD speech in an auditory preference experiment, infants listen longer to ID speech (Fernald, 1985) and show more positive emotion (Werker & McLeod, 1990). Through social interaction over the early months, the melodies of the mother's voice become associated with playful interaction, comforting, feeding, and many other pleasurable aspects of parent–infant interaction, which may account in part for the listening preference for ID speech shown by 5 month olds. However, even newborns show this preference (Cooper & Aslin, 1990), suggesting that the vocal melodies of ID speech are appealing in themselves without extensive experience.

Through experience, however, these intonation patterns take on meaning for the infant because parents in different languages tend to use characteristic intonation patterns in particular interactional and emotional contexts

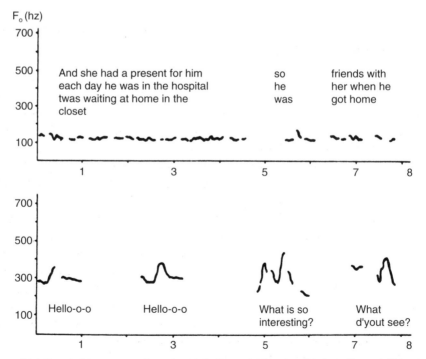

Figure 14.1 Intonation contours from the adult-directed (above) and infant-directed (below) speech of an American mother. Graph shows the movements in fundamental frequency (F_o), which corresponds to the pitch of the mother's voice.

(Fernald, 1992). For example, the intonation contours used to praise an infant are typically wide in pitch range with a rise–fall pattern, quite different from the typical contours used for warning or prohibition, which are shorter, more abrupt, and lower in pitch. Contrast how you might say 'What a good baby!' with how you would say 'No! That's not for you to play with!' By the age of 5 months, infants respond distinctively to these different contour types, even in a language they have never heard before. When English-learning infants heard 'praise' and 'prohibition' contours in German and Italian ID speech, they smiled more in response to the vocalizations that were positive in tone and looked wary in response to the negative vocalizations (Fernald, 1993). As the words were unintelligible in any case and were spoken in an unfamiliar language, these findings show that certain culturally widespread features of ID intonation are effective in eliciting emotion in preverbal infants. However, even though 5 month olds respond appropriately to intonation contours associated with communicative intentions such as praise and prohibition, we cannot conclude that they *understand* anything about the speaker's intentions at this age. In terms of communicative competence, these early selective responses based on intonation show an increasing sensitivity to emotion in the voice, but they are still not fundamentally different from the selective responses of monkeys to alarm calls.

Making sense of faces

Infants find faces as fascinating as voices from the beginning, and facial expressions provide another rich source of social information in human communication. Chapter 10 reviews the questions scientists have asked about how infants first process faces as visual stimuli and then gradually learn to interpret the emotional information available in facial expressions. Are infants biologically predisposed to find human faces interesting, or does the 'specialness' of faces emerge through experience? Given the poor visual acuity of infants in the early months, what kinds of visual information can they extract and remember when looking at faces? When are infants able to categorize and interpret emotional expressions in the face? These questions are all relevant to the development of communication, for an obvious reason: the ability to recognize individual faces and to interpret facial expressions is only useful when another person is present, i.e., in the context of social interaction. Building on the research described in Chapter 10, we consider another important question: How do infants begin to *use* their growing knowledge about faces in the process of communicating with other people?

By the age of 8 months infants can tell that happy faces are different from angry faces in terms of their visual features (Ludemann & Nelson, 1988). While this ability may be necessary for interpreting the emotional meaning of these expressions, it is far from sufficient. To interpret an expression in the flow of social interaction requires integrating information from multiple sources and making rapid inferences about what just happened and what will happen next. For example, when you see a big, sudden smile on your friend's face as she looks behind you, your response is not to conclude dispassionately 'Oh, the position of Sarah's mouth just changed' and leave it at that. Most likely you will make several automatic and instantaneous attributions, inferring that Sarah's expression indicates an internal state of pleasure, that she has seen something that caused the change in state, that whatever she has seen is something she regards positively, that she is more likely to approach than to flee from whatever it is she is looking at, and so on. As you make these rapid inferences you will probably also turn to follow her gaze so you can share her focus of attention. Without a word spoken and in a fraction of a second, you have processed several kinds of information from your friend's face that enabled you to make assumptions about aspects of the situation that you did not (and could never) experience directly, i.e., how Sarah is feeling, what made her feel that way and why, and what she might do in response. This kind of 'mind-reading' pervades human communication on every level, and by the end of the first year infants are well on their way to developing the complex mental abilities necessary for understanding other minds.

In the example above, at least three kinds of information could be extracted from what was happening on Sarah's face: first, the change in expression, marking the onset of the causal event; second, the expression itself, indicating the nature and intensity of her internal emotional state; and third, the direction of her gaze, indicating attention to something presumably involved in the change of state. Co-ordinating these different sources of information in a moment and initiating an appropriate response is a challenging task that demands much more than the ability to categorize static facial expressions. In their pioneering study of 'social referencing', Campos and Stenberg (1981) were the first to explore how 12-month-old infants use these emerging mind-reading skills in action. Infants were placed on a 'visual cliff', an apparatus originally developed for testing depth perception, which gives the compelling illusion of a sudden drop. In fact the chasm is spanned by a sturdy plexiglass surface to support the infant, but most 12 month olds stop at the brink and refuse to venture further. Positioned on the other side of the gap, the infant's mother was instructed to pose one of two facial expressions—a big smile or an exaggerated fear face—when the infant stopped at the brink and looked across at her. If the mother smiled, most infants overcame their hesitation and proceeded across the chasm; however, if the mother displayed fear, all of the infants retreated from the edge and refused to cross. Campos and Stenberg concluded that in situations of uncertainty, infants check the mother's face to see her appraisal of the situation and then decide how to respond depending on the emotion she is displaying. This compelling phenomenon was dubbed *social referencing* because infants appeared to be referring to a social partner for non-verbal guidance, modifying their behaviour based on the mother's positive or negative appraisal of a potentially dangerous situation.

Research on social referencing suggested that by the end of their first year, infants can engage in complex reasoning processes, which integrate many sources of non-verbal information to make inferences about the mother's emotional state. On the surface, these conclusions might seem plausible, but there are reasons to prefer a more cautious interpretation. For example, imagine a wary infant who hesitates to approach a fascinating but unfamiliar mechanical bear; the infant then turns to the mother who displays fear as she looks at the same toy. If the child avoids the bear after looking at her face, can we really conclude that this response is guided by inferences about the mother's internal state? We can assume that the mother's fear expression, a kind of visual alarm call, is motivated by more complex processes than the monkey's alarm call because she is not actually afraid of the toy herself. However, the infant's avoidance response may result directly from discomfort at seeing the strange expression, or from past experience with fear faces followed by unpleasant events. These explanations do not presuppose any implicit reasoning about the mother's emotional state, i.e., that if the mother has this particular facial expression as she looks at the bear, she must be afraid of the toy and thus it should be avoided. If simpler explanations can account for the infant's avoidance of the toy, they imply no more (or less) mind-reading ability than monkeys use to flee in response to the alarm call of a conspecific.

We cannot resolve these complex questions here (see Baldwin & Moses, 1996), but the example serves to make some important points. First, while the 3-month-old infant looks to the mother's face purely for the pleasure of interacting with her, the 12 month old may look to the mother's face to seek information about something in the world beyond their interaction. Second, while the response of the 12 month old may seem simple and straightforward, it represents an enormous advance in communicative competence, although the mental processes involved are complex and difficult to tease apart. And finally, our insights into the cognitive and emotional mechanisms underlying the development of communication over the first 2 years do not result from any one study or paradigm; rather, they emerge slowly from many convergent studies of different behaviours, which all reveal the infant's gradual progress in understanding other minds.

Appreciating intentions

Already in the first year of life infants begin to understand that the actions of others are usually purposeful, or goal-directed, and that much of human behaviour is motivated by desires and beliefs (Wellman, 1990). For example, if you were frantically opening and closing the drawers of your desk, rifling through their contents, your room-mate would likely infer that you wanted to find something, and that you believed it might be in your desk. Even if no words are exchanged, your room-mate will attempt to interpret your behaviour, just as you would attempt to interpret the cause of the big smile on your friend's face described earlier.

Infants could not possibly interpret accurately the reason why you were searching through your desk, as they have no experience with desks, losing things, or searching for them. This is not to say, however, that they lack the drive to interpret the behaviour of other humans. In a series of clever studies by Woodward (1998), infants watched as a hand repeatedly reached toward and grasped a ball in a display containing a ball on one side and a stuffed bear on the other. Recall from Chapters 2 and 5 that infants will lose interest (habituate) when watching the same display repeatedly. Once they had habituated to this action, the locations of the ball and the stuffed bear were switched. If infants paid attention simply to the *path* of the hand as it reached toward an object, they should dishabituate if the hand now reaches toward the new location (which is where the ball now is). However, if infants paid attention to the object or *goal* of the reach, they should dishabituate if the hand reaches toward the stuffed bear, now located at the old location. In fact, this is exactly what infants did: infants as young as 6 months looked longer when the hand reached toward a new goal, but not when it simply reached toward the same goal in a different location. (The same results were obtained when the bear was the first item reached for, and the ball the second.) In other words, 6-month-old infants apparently considered a change in goal to be more noteworthy than a change in path. Even more interesting, when the same study was conducted with a mechanical claw doing the reaching and grasping rather than a human hand, there was rarely a looking preference, but when there was, it tended to favour the new path rather than the new goal. This suggests that by 6 months, infants can distinguish between human-produced behaviour and machine-produced behaviour, and that for behaviours produced by humans, it is the goal that is important.

This early ability to interpret the intentions of other humans in terms of goals is quite striking. However, it is important to caution again against attributing too much to the infant. Even pre-schoolers err on mind-reading tasks that would seem trivial to an adult, often because they can understand behaviour in terms of desires, but have yet to grasp the notion of belief (Wellman, 1990). For example, 3 year olds understand that someone who wants a piece of candy will look for it, but they expect that the person will look for it in the location where it actually is rather than where he or she believes it to be. Thus, if Sally left a chocolate in one location and, unbeknown to her, Anne moved it to a second location, 3 year olds expect that Sally will look for it in the new location—even though she could not have known that Anne moved it (Wimmer & Perner, 1983)! Despite such limitations, an early sensitivity to cues relating to intentionality can help infants as they learn to communicate.

Following gaze and pointing gestures

Prior to about 9 months, infants respond directly to salient sources of stimulation, crying in response to a loud noise or producing a charming smile in response to a game of peekaboo, without attempting to share their experiences with anyone else. At about 9 months, however, things begin to change, as infants try to communicate *about* things to other people For example, while a 6 month old might smile in response to a wind-up toy, a 14 month old would also be likely to look to his mother while smiling, as if to say 'Isn't this cool?' This is an important transition in a child's development, marking the beginning of intentional communication and an understanding of intentional communication by others (Bates, 1979). When older infants vocalize, these signals are often deliberate and may serve no other purpose than to gain the attention of their partner in interaction, quite unlike the cries and babbling of the younger infant. This section focuses on the development of two hallmarks of intentional communication: gaze-following and pointing.

Gaze-following

Following the gaze of another person is a deceptively simple activity. When you stare at an object, it is trivial for another adult to figure out what you have focused your attention on. Once both of you are looking at the same object and thus have established 'joint reference', you can communicate about that object, talking about its features, whether each of you likes it, and so on. Before an infant reaches 8 months, the adult is the one responsible for following the gaze of the infant in order to establish joint reference. That is, when the infant chooses to focus on something, the adult then follows in, frequently labelling and/or commenting on the object of the infant's attention (Collis & Schaffer, 1975). If the adult looks at something different and tries to call attention to it, young infants will frequently look only at the adult's face, apparently unaware of the object of reference.

By about 12 months, however, infants have learned to follow an adult's gaze under most circumstances; if an adult across from the infant looks to the right or left, the infant will generally look in the appropriate direction (Butterworth & Grover, 1988). Interestingly, by 12 months, infants will also turn to follow the look of a decidedly non-human object, provided that the object provides cues to indicate that its actions might be intentional. To demonstrate this, Johnson *et al.* (1998) showed infants a round, fuzzy object that turned either to the left or to the right. The question was whether infants would follow the 'gaze' of this strange object. When the object had what could best be described as eyes, like the object on the right in Figure 14.2, infants did follow its gaze, turning to look in the same direction. Even when the object did not have eyes, like the object on the left in Figure 14.2, infants mirrored its turns, so long as

Figure 14.2 Schematic drawing of the novel object with (right) and without (left) eyes. Infants always followed the gaze of the object with eyes, but only followed the gaze of the object without eyes if it had responded contingently to their behaviour. From Johnson *et al.*, 1998; artwork by Kirsten O'Hearn.

it had earlier beeped in response to their vocalizations and flashed attached lights in response to their movements. (Imagine the robot R2D2 from 'Star Wars.') However, in another condition where the object lacked eyes *and* failed to respond contingently, the babies did not follow its 'gaze.' Thus, what drives infants to follow another's gaze seems to be cues related to that individual's intentionality—in this case, eyes and/or contingent responsiveness. By 12 months infants have learned that things with certain cues (i.e., ones human adults construe as intentional) are more likely to provide meaningful information about things in the environment than things without such cues.

Chimpanzees, our closest non-human relatives, can also follow the gaze of others (Povinelli & Giambrone, 2001), suggesting that they may be sensitive to the same cues signalling intentionality as human infants. However, we must bear in mind the caveat from the social referencing work described earlier: infants and chimps alike may use intentional cues to attend to potentially meaningful things in the environment without imputing anything like intentionality to the person (or object) emitting those cues. Eventually, humans do use intentionality to make inferences (e.g., Why is she smiling? Why is he looking in the wrong place?), but the picture is much less clear with chimpanzees (see Premack & Woodruff, 1978; Heyes, 1998). In fact, in experimental tests, chimps do not seem to understand the link between visual perception and knowledge at all: for example, they are as likely to request food from a human trainer wearing a blindfold over her eyes as a trainer wearing a blindfold over her mouth, as if they fail to infer that food would only come from the individual who could see the request (Reaux *et al.*, 1999). Some scientists have argued that the ability to understand another's behaviour as intentional—whether it be through eye gaze or some other action—is, in fact, what enabled human communication as we know it to emerge (Tomasello, 1999).

Figure 14.3 Infants begin to point as early as 9 months. Photo by Karen Thorpe.

Pointing

Pointing gestures are another cue that adults frequently provide when direct-ing a child's attention. As with gaze-following, the ability to interpret a point develops early in the second year of life. Prior to about 12 months, infants tend to look at the pointer's hand rather than at the object being pointed to (Butterworth & Grover, 1988). As with gaze, interpreting a point is simpler in some situations than in others: For example, 9 month olds may be able to fol-low a point as long as the target object is close to the end of the finger, there are no intervening objects, and so on. However, infants are much more flexi-ble by 14 months and can generally follow most pointing gestures successfully (Murphy & Messer, 1977). It is interesting to note that even for adults, point-ing in a cluttered environment may not completely disambiguate an object of reference; however, pointing can be helpful in combination with words, which 14 month olds are beginning to understand (Schaffer, 1984).

Some infants begin to use pointing gestures themselves as early as 9 months (Figure 14.3), and most are regularly pointing by 14 months (Schaffer, 1984). Younger infants may point at things even when they are on their own and no social partner is present, suggesting that the earliest form of this behaviour is actually non-communicative (Bates, 1979). However, pointing clearly serves a communicative function a few months later, when the infant not only points but also looks to check that the adult is attending to the point. Bates (1979) has shown that early communicative pointing, where the infant checks with the adult for confirmation, correlates with a number of language measures of both comprehension and production. Based on these correlations, Bates argues that pointing is really a gestural form of naming and thus is closely related to the development of language skills.

Learning to communicate through language

First sounds

Long before infants produce recognizable words, they spend a good deal of time vocalizing, or babbling—an activity that provides them with valuable practise using the vocal modality. Indeed, the consonants that make up the first 50 words spoken by a child are typically created from sounds that occur frequently in babbling, suggesting that babbled sounds may provide the foundation for the production of a child's first words (Vihman *et al.*, 1985; Vihman, 1992). The development of babbling unfolds in five stages (Oller, 1980; Locke, 1993; Stoel-Gammon, 1998), with transitions from one stage to another depending on the development of neural mechanisms and the vocal tract as well as the practise the child receives in each stage.

In **stage 1** (0–2 months), infants produce reflexive vocalizations, including crying, sneezing, and burping—sounds directly related to their physical state. These vocalizations account for about 90% of all vocalizations at 2 weeks, dropping to 50% by 8 weeks (Stark *et al.*, 1993). In **stage 2** (2–3 months), infants begin 'cooing', so-called because 'coo' is one of the few sounds infants first attempt to produce. In **stage 3** (4–6 months), they start to experiment with the wide array of possible noises they can make with their vocal tract, resulting in a variety of vowel-like sounds as well as hoots and squeals. In **stage 4** (6–7 months), babbling begins in earnest with the appearance of what are called *canonical syllables*. The term 'canonical' can mean 'true to life' and canonical syllables are the first babbling sounds that sound like real words. These consist of a restricted set of alternating consonants and vowels, such as the stereotypical 'gaga,' or 'mama' and 'dada.' Although 'mama' and 'dada' sound like the conventional names for parents in English (and many proud parents treat them as such), we would not call them true words until infants demonstrate an understanding of the correspondence between the sound and its meaning. This is an important caveat to keep in mind, and is related to our earlier discussion emphasizing intentionality as criteria for human communication. At 11–12 months reduplicated babbling ('gaga') gives way to variegated babbling, which involves stringing together different syllables ('bagoo'). Finally in **stage 5** (12 months), infants begin a period of 'jargon' babbling, producing longer strings of consonant–vowel combinations with differing intonation and stress patterns. By this age the rate of babbling is already comparable with the rate of adult conversational speech (Kent & Bauer, 1985). Infants typically produce their first words at about 12 months, just when they are also beginning to use jargon babbling. For several months, babbling and conventional words occur together, but beginning at about 19 months, as children's facility with conventional language increases, the amount of babbling drops off (Stoel-Gammon, 1998).

The restricted set of syllables in early babbling is fairly consistent across linguistic environments and is made up of sounds that occur frequently in the majority of languages (Locke, 1993). This suggests that the range of babbled sounds may be limited more by anatomical or physiological constraints than by environmental factors. However, the ambient language does influence the relative rate at which various sounds appear in babbling (de Boysson-Bardies *et al.*, 1992). For example, babies raised in languages that make frequent use of final consonants (e.g., English) tend to use final consonants in their babbling more than those raised in other languages (e.g., Japanese).

Deaf children also go through a period of vocal babbling, although they seem to be slightly delayed in the onset of reduplicated babbling, and to have a reduced repertoire of sounds. Deaf babies also go through a period of manual babbling, which shares many of the characteristics at the same ages as the vocal babbling of hearing infants (Petitto & Marentette, 1991). In particular, the manual babbling of deaf (but not hearing) infants includes a restricted set of manual babbling gestures, reduplication, and even continuity between the forms used in manual babbling and the first symbolic signs.

First gestures

In addition to early vocal communication, hearing infants also communicate through a host of gestures such as showing, giving, pointing, and ritual requests before they begin to speak their first words (Bates, 1979). These gestures are non-symbolic because they are not used to 'stand for' something else. Despite this, they can still be intentional and communicative if the infant demonstrates an awareness of the effect a particular gesture could have on a conversational partner and persists until the effect is obtained (Bates, 1979). For example, if a 12 month old reaches up repeatedly for a favourite toy high on a bookshelf as her father watches, she might demonstrate intentional communication by looking back and forth between the father and the toy on the shelf, or by vocalizing until the desired goal is achieved. Many of infants' gestures meet these criteria by the age of 10 months. Even after infants begin producing words, they continue to support their linguistic communication with gestures, so gestural schemes are not simply replaced by verbal ones.

Just as babbling may be related to language development in that it provides practise with the communicative modality, regular production of some gestures may be related to language development in that it provides practise communicating via conventional signals. For example, as mentioned earlier, communicative pointing seems to be correlated with word comprehension at the beginning of the second year, perhaps because both pointing and word comprehension involve establishing joint reference to an external object (Bates, 1979).

Infants may also be able to communicate via symbolic gestures, or gestures that actually do stand for things. In fact, some researchers have suggested that infants can learn to produce symbolic gestures before producing words (Meier & Newport, 1990). One study showed that hearing infants exposed to American Sign Language (ASL) began producing signs at about 8.6 months, 3 months before most children begin producing words (Bonvillian *et al.*, 1983). The gestural modality may show this advantage for a number of reasons, including that motor control of the hands may develop more quickly than control of the articulatory system; signs might be more recognizable by parents than underarticulated words; and many early signs have a high degree of iconicity (Acredolo & Goodwyn, 1990). By iconicity is meant that the sign might look like what it refers to, so that an early sign for 'I'm hungry' might be bringing the hand to the mouth. Before accepting a sign as a symbol, however, we must apply the same standards we require of an early word: it must be intentional and relatively context-independent. When these same standards are applied to the same group of children, the first symbolic signs and the first words both emerge around the age of 12 or 13 months.

For infants who are experiencing difficulty with vocal communication, Acredolo and her colleagues have argued that training them in sign may provide them with a useful communicative outlet (Acredolo & Goodwyn, 1990; Goodwyn & Acredolo, 1993). In one study, they trained mothers to make daily use picture books and other materials in order to demonstrate target gestures (e.g., lip-smacking for 'fish', arm-flapping for 'bird', etc.) to their pre-verbal 11 month olds. Biweekly interviews were conducted to collect information about the children's production and comprehension of these signs as well as the conventional words. On average, infants produced both gestures and words at about the same time, although there was substantial variability among children. In short, some children will progress faster with sign, some with speech, and some will produce words and signs at the same time.

Early comprehension

As you know from Chapter 9, infants have learned an enormous amount about the sounds of their language during the first year. By 8 months infants are attuned to the phonological (sound) system of the ambient or surrounding language (Kuhl, *et al.* 1992; Polka & Werker, 1994), and can recognize recurrent patterns in sequences of speech sounds (Jusczyk & Aslin, 1995). These skills are all essential for recognizing words in fluent speech, which must be processed at a very rapid rate. However, identifying a sequence of syllables as familiar is just the first step in word recognition, which also requires learning an association between the sound sequence and a particular meaning. Moreover, this sound–meaning association must be more than just a conditioned response to a verbal routine to count as true comprehension.

The question of when comprehension begins has been debated since the earliest scholarly studies of language development 200 years ago. In a diary study published in 1877, Hippolyte Taine noted that when his 11-month-old daughter heard 'Where is Mama?', she always turned toward her mother. This example echoed an observation by Dietrich Tiedemann (1927/1787) published 100 years earlier, whose baby diary was referred to in Chapter 1; when asked to 'Swat the fly', his 8-month-old son also made appropriate gestures, although a different interpretation was offered. While Tiedemann claimed that such responses showed how his son had 'learned to comprehend' simple sentences, Taine was more conservative, suggesting that 'there is nothing more in this than an association'. When his daughter was 12 months old, however, Taine was convinced she demonstrated true comprehension of the word *bébé*. Although her understanding did not appear to coincide with the conventional meaning, Taine claimed that *bébé* nevertheless had 'a general signification' for her which went well beyond a limited association between a sound pattern and a gestural response. These informal observations suggesting that infants begin to demonstrate understanding of words by the end of the first year have been verified by numerous studies in many different languages (e.g., Bloom, 1973; Casselli *et al.*, 1995). One way of gathering data on early comprehension is to ask parents to fill out standardized checklists to keep track of which words their child appears to understand in daily interactions in the home. Figure 14.4 shows that, on one such checklist, infants understand an average of about 50 words by their first birthday, and over 150 by the age of 16 months (Fenson, *et al.*, 1994). As the figure shows, however, there is considerable variability among children on these measures.

While checklists give an estimate of changes in the size and extent of the child's receptive vocabulary over time, they don't reveal anything about important developments in the child's ability to recognize and understand familiar words in continuous speech. If a mother indicates on the checklist that her infant understands the word 'ball' at 12 months, she is likely to check the same box again at 15 months, although in the intervening months there have been dramatic changes in speech processing efficiency that are not obvious in the child's spontaneous behaviour. You are probably not aware of this, but as a fluent language user you typically process 15–30 different speech sounds every *second* in following a casual conversation! How do infants develop the skill to understand spoken language with such remarkable speed and efficiency?

The early development of competence in word recognition has been studied by tracking infants' eye movements as they listen to spoken sentences

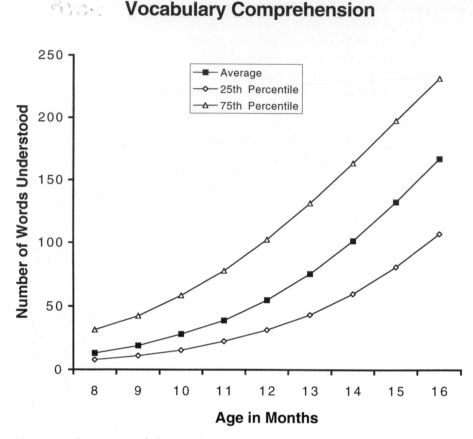

Figure 14.4 Receptive vocabulary size from 8 to 16 months. This figure shows the average number of words infants at various ages understand, and also includes the 25th and 75th percentile range in order to show the large amount of variability in early vocabulary size. Adapted from Fenson *et al.*, 1994.

containing familiar words. Sitting on the parent's lap, infants are observed in a booth where they look at pictures while hearing speech naming one of the pictures, as shown in Figure 14.5. The infant's eye movements are video-recorded during the test session, and then analysed later in slow motion, frame-by-frame, to measure very precisely how quickly the infant's eyes moved to the named picture. By tracking infants' gaze patterns in the process of understanding, it is possible to document impressive progress in the efficiency of spoken word recognition occurring over the second year of life (Fernald *et al.*, 1998). Figure 14.6 shows the average speed of response, or reaction time, for infants at 15, 18, and 24 months of age, as they orient to the appropriate picture in response to hearing the name of the picture. The bar graph in this figure is aligned with the waveform from one of the stimulus sentences, showing the time course of infants' responses in relation to the famil-

Front View of Infant Testing Booth

Images   **Curtain**

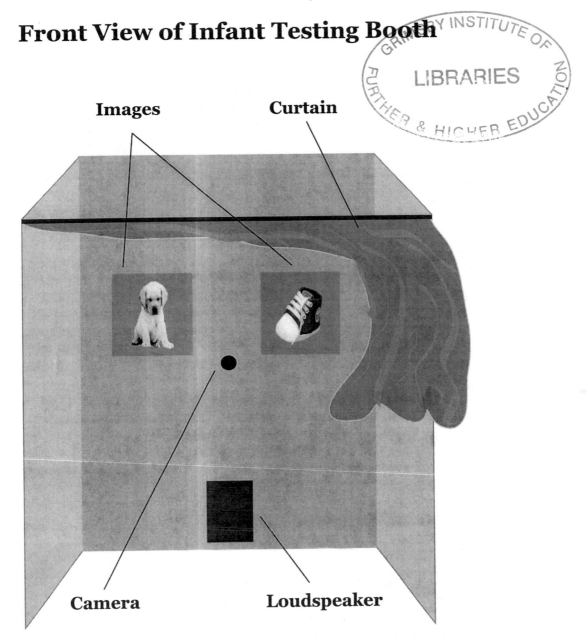

Camera   **Loudspeaker**

Figure 14.5 Experimental set-up used by Fernald *et al.* (1998). Infants listen to speech naming one of the pictures. Does the infant look at the named picture?

iar target word 'baby'. Note that 15 month olds shifted their eyes to the picture of the baby *after* the target word was spoken. By 24 months, however, infants were several hundred milliseconds faster to respond, identifying the word 'baby' after hearing only the first syllable, *before* it was completely spoken. Other studies show that by 18 months infants are already becoming

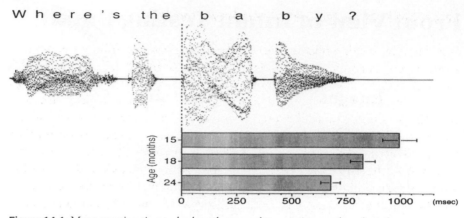

Figure 14.6 Mean reaction time to look at the named target picture when the infants were initially looking at the 'wrong' picture. Fifteen month olds take about a second (1000 milliseconds) and reaction time gets quicker with age. (From Fernald *et al.*, 1998.)

highly efficient in spoken language processing; like adults they can recognize familiar words based on incomplete acoustic information, a skill that is essential for the rapid and reliable processing of fluent speech (Fernald *et al.*, 2001).

Word learning and social understanding

Around the first birthday many infants begin to speak their first words, although some start a bit earlier and others don't talk for another 6 months (Fenson *et al.*, 1994). The first words spoken by most infants have a lot in common across different languages and cultures (Bloom, 1973; Casselli *et al.*, 1995). These include words used in social routines such as *bye-bye* and *peek-aboo*, names for family and pets such as *Mama* and *Fido*, lots of names for animals and common objects of interest to the child, such as *doggy, shoe*, and *train* (or *choo-choo*), along with a few action words such as *eat* and *push*. The infant's first utterances consist of single words, although some of these may be amalgams such as *gimmee*, which the child treats as a single word.

Many studies have investigated how children figure out the meaning of new words (P. Bloom, 2000). This might seem like a simple enough task: when the mother hands a new toy to the child and says 'This is a yo-yo', shouldn't it be obvious what *yo-yo* refers to? Actually it's not so obvious, because the new word could refer to many different features of the unfamiliar object. *Yo-yo* might mean *red*, or *round*, or *plastic*, or *string*, or *this-red-round-plastic-thing-with-a-string*. Questions about infants' cognitive strategies in guessing what new words refer to have been a research topic of considerable interest (e.g., Markman, 1989). But just as interesting are questions about how infants use their emerging knowledge of other minds to help them learn new words.

Emerging knowledge that others have minds

For example, we described earlier how children learn to follow the gaze of another person, and to understand that gaze can be indicative of that person's focus of attention. What role might gaze-following play in word learning? Considering the cluttered world most infants live in, adult gaze direction could be a valuable source of information to figure out what is being talked about. If an infant is playing with a fascinating toy car and hears his mother say 'Look at this yo-yo,' it would clearly be an error for the infant to assume that *yo-yo* referred to the car. Only by looking up to check and follow his mother's gaze could he make the correct association between the new word and the object it referred to. In fact, this is exactly what infants did in an experiment by Baldwin (1991). As the infant played with one toy, the adult said, 'It's a modi,' while looking at a second toy. At that point, most infants looked up to check the speaker's focus of attention. Later the children were shown both toys, the one they had been playing with and the one the speaker was looking at. When asked to choose the 'modi', 18 month olds chose the toy the speaker had been looking at, as if they understood that this was the one the speaker had *intended* to refer to.

As we have been stressing throughout, the ability to read the intentions of others has important implications for human communication. Someone who is unable to interpret social signals indicative of intent might therefore be expected to have difficulty learning to communicate. In fact, autistic children do seem to have trouble making use of social signals such as eye gaze, and, in an experimental study such as the Baldwin (1991) one described above, they also tend to make just the kind of mapping errors that non-autistic 18 month olds avoid (Baron-Cohen *et al.*, 1997).

Communication is very much a social skill, requiring the ability to interpret and understand the feelings, intentions, and mental states of others. Although infants can demonstrate an early understanding of some aspects of intentionality, it is worth emphasizing again that understanding intentionality is not an all-or-none ability. Carpenter *et al.* (1998) argue that prior to about 12 months, infants begin to recognize only *that* other people have intentions, although they are still unable to determine what those intentions are or how they come about. As a result, infants younger than 1 year can engage in activities where they share attention with another individual, but only as long as they do not have to follow another's attention or provide purposeful cues to direct another's attention. Only later, at about 12–13 months, do infants begin demonstrating an understanding of *what* other people's intentions are, which allows them both to follow another's attention and to consciously manipulate it. This new understanding enables word learning to begin in earnest, as infants can now treat a word uttered by another person as specifically intended to refer to a particular referent. Thus, in the Baldwin (1991) study described earlier, an 18 month old can recognize that a speaker intended to refer to one

Table 14.1 Average age at which infants first begin to demonstrate fundamental skills related to the emergence of communicative competence

Sharing of attentional focus with another person	9.0 months
Use of gestures to communicate	10.3 months
Following the attention of another person	11.5 months
Learning through imitation	11.9 months
Referential use of language	>15 months
(from Carpenter, Nagell, and Tomasello, 1998)	

object even though the infant's own attention was focused on a different object.

Another impressive example of young children's ability to use a speaker's intentions to learn new words is provided by Akhtar and Tomasello (1996). In their study, 2 year olds participated in a finding game where they opened four containers and discovered an interesting object in each one. Importantly, these were objects that the children would not already have names for (e.g., a bike horn, a beanbag frisbee). After repeating this activity a few times, the children observed a speaker say 'Let's find the toma!' while unsuccessfully trying to remove one of the objects from a container that now appeared to be locked. Later, when the 2 year olds were shown the four objects and asked to select the 'toma,' they tended to select the object that had been in the locked container. Even though they had never seen that object labelled directly with the word 'toma,' they inferred from the speaker's unsuccessful attempts to open the locked container that he or she intended to refer to that object.

Conclusions

Human infants start out life capable only of involuntary signals closely tied to their physiological condition at the moment, not unlike other animals with a limited repertoire of inflexible social behaviours. From an evolutionary point of view, these primitive signalling behaviours serve a vital communicative function, because more mature and experienced humans are able to interpret them reliably as indices of the infant's needs and internal condition. But unlike other animals, the human infant's communicative skills expand and change continually from day to day, with experience and the development of new cognitive capacities that enable the child to extract socially relevant information from the voices, faces, and gestures of other people. By the end of the first year, the infant has moved well beyond the more limited capabilities of other primates, able to communicate intentions through symbolic gestures and words and to read the intentions of others through their social signals. During this period the young infant demonstrates increasing knowledge of other minds through continual transitions in many dimensions—the transition from looking into the mother's eyes with delight to following the direction of her gaze for information, the transition from smiling in response to the mother's voice to calling her attention with a smile to something unexpected, the transition from babbling single syllables to using words symbolically to influence the behaviour of other people. Although a sophisticated understanding of others' thoughts, feelings, and intentions will still take several years to mature, the mind-reading ability that distinguishes humans from all other animals develops gradually over the first year, manifested first in non-verbal communication and then more clearly in the child's emerging ability to speak and understand language.

Part 5

Early interventions and social policy implications

Early interventions: programmes, results, and differential response

CRAIG T. RAMEY, SHARON LANDESMAN RAMEY, and
JANICE N. COTTON

Introduction

Early intervention programmes are receiving a great deal of public attention because of the increased interest in young children's brain development—the concern that many children are inadequately prepared to meet successfully the rigors of school, and research findings from model programmes and publicly funded programmes such as *Head Start* demonstrating the efficacy of early intervention programmes. Many would suggest that excellent early intervention programmes have the potential to change the life course of children with identified developmental disabilities or at risk for developmental delay. The purpose of this chapter is to provide an overview of the need for early intervention programmes, a brief review of the origins of these programmes, and the scientific evidence of which programmes are successful and why.

Rationale for early intervention

The rationale for providing early intervention services is clear. It is estimated by the Centers for Disease Control that in the United States at least 300 000 individuals under 21 years of age have poor cognitive development and can be considered mentally retarded (IQ below 70) (C. T. Ramey & Ramey, 1998). An *epidemiological catchment area survey* completed by Boyle *et al.* (1994) showed that risk for mental retardation in these individuals might have been prevented through the provision of early and continuous intervention services, especially for children from families with the lowest socio-economic status and in particular children whose mothers' educational level is below the 10th grade (about 15 years). Therefore, early intervention services are needed not only for children and families with developmental disabilities, but also for those considered to be at high-risk for mental retardation and poor school readiness. Thousands of children enter school each year unprepared to meet the intellectual challenges of the academic environment. Poor school readiness can lead to **grade retention** (a failure to move up from 1 year to the next because of poor performance), special education placement, low levels of academic achievement, and ultimately school dropout. Unfortunately, school dropouts often repeat this intergenerational cycle (Carnegie Task Force, 1994).

It is reasonable to assume that it may be possible to prevent learning disabilities, mental retardation, and school failure if the right early interventions are provided. Shore's (1997) summary on the significance of early experience on brain development, found in *Rethinking the brain: new insights into early development*, provides a strong argument for systematic efforts to strengthen children's development and learning opportunities in the first 3 years of life. As the quality of the relationship a child has in the first years of life has a lasting impact on how the brain develops, it is imperative that children experience enriched, appropriate environmental stimulation on a daily basis in order to nurture healthy brain development. The new synthesis of research shows that the right kind of experiences enable the central nervous system to become properly wired and to function optimally (Zuckerman & Kahn, 2000). In other words, experience matters. Efforts made to enhance the development of children in Romanian orphanages illustrates the importance of early experience.

A group of young Romanian children living in an orphanage participated in an intense systematic early childhood programme that previously had been proven in 10 separate randomized trials in the United States to be effective in preventing developmental delay and mild mental retardation (S. L. Ramey & Ramey, 2000). This treatment was provided 6 hours a day for 5 days a week by trained and supervised caregivers. After a year of this intensive enrichment, it was found the children made steady developmental gains, compared with a control group, yet there was no evidence that the children's gains were adequate to correct for earlier delays associated with lack of stimulation. In other words, these children could not catch up for what was missing in the first year or two of their life, but they did show the capacity for developing *at a normal rate* when they received massive additions on a daily basis in the quality, amount, and appropriateness of interactions with people and objects in their environment (S. L. Ramey *et al.*, 1995).

The work of Furstenberg *et al.* (1987) further illustrates the importance of early experience, particularly as related to children being adequately prepared for school. They reported that economically impoverished children have lower performance than other children, even if the economic situation of their parents improves in later years. Unfortunately, it is difficult, at present, to reverse the effects of major deprivation associated with lack of appropriate amounts of positive early learning experiences for these children. For example, public sector efforts to train low skilled workers have yielded very small returns. Analyses conducted by Heckman (1999) show that even with a 10% return on investment, it would take at least $50 000 to increase the wages of a welfare mother $5000 per year from $10 000 to $15 000 (Currie, 2000).

Further, low income *per se* is not the causal factor for the children's delay, but rather a marker for increased exposure to multiple life conditions, including low levels of parental education and language, poor housing, neglect, lack of early literacy experiences, chaotic living and child care conditions, maternal stress and depression, geographical and social isolation, increased family violence and substance abuse, and inadequate health care.

Is early intervention effective?

Does early intervention have a positive influence on children's development? In the last 40 years, a large and consistent body of research has accrued regarding the efficacy of early intervention. Reviews of this literature include the work of Bryant and Maxwell (1997), the Carnegie Task Force on Meeting the Needs of Young Children report (1994), Farran (1990), the edited volume by Guralnick (1997), and the work of Haskins (1989), Karweit (1989), C. T. Ramey and Ramey (1998), S. L. Ramey and Ramey (1999), and White and Boyce (1993). The literature is clearest for those children living in poverty who are at risk for cognitive and language development delays and for children who are biologically at risk due to low birth weight and premature birth. The evidence shows that early intervention programmes can yield modest to large effects (known as 'effect size') on children's cognitive and social development during the pre-school years. Larger effect sizes are noted for improved academic performance and even into the early adult years, especially when schools are of good quality (Lazar *et al.*, 1982; Schweinhart *et al.*, 1993; Reynolds, 2000; Campbell *et al*, 2001). On the other hand, there is little empirical research using randomized controlled trials that early intervention for children with developmental disabilities results in demonstrable benefits (C. T. Ramey & Ramey, 1996; S. L. Ramey & Ramey, 1999).

Origins of early intervention programmes

Examination of how early experiences and intervention might impact children's healthy development has been underway for about 70 years. A group of psychologists firmly grounded in learning theory, including Donald Hebb (1949), J. McVicker Hunt (1961), and Harry Harlow (1958), began to explore the role and consequences of early experiences on children's cognitive, social, and emotional development and other psychologists followed with scientific experiments. In the 1930s and 1940s a series of notable studies focusing on infants and young children living in orphanages showed that the care provided to children in institutions was woefully inadequate when compared with the loving, attentive care typically provided by a family. The work of Bowlby, Dennis, Goldfarb, Skeels, Skodak, and Spitz, among others, raised concern about the lasting harm caused by the lack of care and stimulation found in institutions. The seminal work of Skeels and Dye (1939) proved that early experience had the power to alter the development of intelligence and the life course of institutionalized retarded children. Their work launched vigorous scientific examination of what children need in order to ensure healthy growth and development (S. L. Ramey & Sackett, 2000). A series of carefully controlled experiments using animal models were implemented that uniformly varied the type and timing of early experiences. The first set of findings from these studies revealed that deficits in social and sensory experiences produced aberrant social, emotional, and learning behaviour in animals who otherwise were born healthy and with a good genetic foundation (c.f., Sackett *et al.*, 1999).

A second set of experiments sought to understand how children responded to non-optimal environments and the extent to which stimulation could reverse or minimize the negative effects of early deprivation, including institutionalization (Landesman-Dwyer & Butterfield, 1983; Landesman & Butterfield, 1987). The work from these studies showed that not all individuals respond in a similar way to the same environmental conditions. In social ecology, this principle is referred to as the Person X Environment interaction, which means the impact of what occurs depends upon the person as well as the event (e.g., Bronfenbrenner, 1979; Landesman & Ramey, 1989). In other words, individual experiences, not just the mere exposure to environmental conditions, serve to mediate and moderate the effects of early deprivation. Factors such as biological and genetic differences, the age when a child first experiences deprivation, and the child's own behavioural propensities theoretically can contribute to varying *individual* responses to similar environments.

In the early 1960s, a third line of investigation was a proactive effort to prevent suboptimal development and developmental delay in children living in poverty. The work of these studies was propelled by a national awareness of the devastating conditions of poverty in the United States, the inequality of educational opportunities for children living in poverty, and scientific findings from the fields of child development and mental retardation. Key findings included:

1. Evidence that rates of mental retardation, most especially mild mental retardation with no identified biomedical cause, were elevated among very poor families (c.f. Garber, 1988 for a review of epidemiological findings). It was also found that this form of mental retardation had a strong familial pattern (Zigler, 1967) and had a time-distributed onset with progressive mental retardation (Deutsch, 1967; Klaus & Gray, 1968).

2. Strong associations between the quality of a child's home environment—as measured by the responsiveness and sensitivity of the mother to her child, the amount and level of language stimulation, and direct teaching—and the child's intellectual and problem-solving capabilities (e.g., McVicker Hunt, 1961; Vygotsky, 1962; Hess & Shipman, 1965; Bee *et al.*, 1969). This finding has been confirmed in hundreds of studies conducted in the last four decades (e.g., see reviews by Maccoby & Martin, 1983; Cowan *et al.*, 1994; Huston *et al.*, 1994).

3. Confirmation that very young infants are capable of learning, which disputed the once prevailing view that infants were passive and incapable of learning at such an early age (see Osofsky, 1979, first edition of *The handbook on infant development* for an early summary of these findings). These studies identified a multitude of ways infants could learn and how these experiences impacted their responses to subsequent learning experiences (C. T. Ramey & Ramey, 1999).

The findings from these studies prompted the creation of early enrichment programmes, most notably the American national programme, Head Start, based on a broad platform of empirical findings and theoretical support (C. T. Ramey & Ramey, 1998; C. T. Ramey & Ramey, 2001). (The British equivalent of Head Start is Surestart, and similar programmes are to be found in most Western societies.) The original and continuing goal of these programmes has been to discover the value of early educational intervention as an antidote for environmental deprivation (McVicker Hunt, 1964).

Early scientific studies

The first set of experiments testing the efficacy of providing enriched experiences for children at risk from impoverished homes was conducted in the late 1960s and early 1970s. Most took place in university child development centres, although they differed considerably in the amount and types of services provided, the age when children were enrolled, and the extent of risk among participants. Today, these programmes are often labelled as compensatory in nature, in that they sought to offer elements found in many middle class families, including responsive, educated caregiving; educational materials such as toys and games; nutritious meals; and a safe, stimulating environment where young children's thinking and problem solving are actively encouraged. While compensatory programmes have sometimes been criticized because they implied a deficit model, in fact these programmes appeared to be enacted with great care and concern for participants and were well received by the families. The Consortium for Longitudinal Studies was one such effort.

The Consortium for Longitudinal Studies

The Consortium represented a collaborative effort involving 11 systematic studies that used experimental or quasi-experimental designs to determine the efficacy of early intervention programmes for children at risk, based on socio-demographic characteristics (Darlington *et al.*, 1980; Lazar *et al.*, 1982). Several key findings evolved from this study. The first finding reaffirmed earlier reports that children participating in these high-quality early intervention programmes made significant gains in intellectual and cognitive performance. In addition, there were long-lasting effects in terms of their academic school competence, attitudes and values, and impact on the family. The second and more controversial finding was that IQ scores for children were highest at the end of the intervention and were maintained for 3 or 4 years, but began to decline over time. This phenomenon is widely referred to as the 'fade-out' effect. Somewhat disappointing is that this second finding is often the only one cited, rather than acknowledging the lasting benefits on children's real world indicators, such as lower rates of grade retention (i.e., dropping back a grade or class) and decreased rates of placement in special education.

Longitudinal early intervention studies

In the 1970s, a number of model early intervention programmes that were typically funded at higher levels and supervised more closely than large publicly funded programmes were started. Five of these programmes incorporated randomized trial research designs, which is considered the 'gold-standard' of research (Currie, 2000). Randomized trials provide a more rigorous test of the impact of a new treatment by randomly assigning comparable types of children with treatment and control groups, thus eliminating potential selection bias factors. The utilization of randomized trials helps researchers be reasonably certain that there are no pre-existing and uncontrolled differences between the two groups. In addition, these five programmes were relatively free of attrition (i.e., children withdrawing from the study) and gathered information on the children at least into the middle school years. These programmes are the *Abecedarian Project* (C. T. Ramey & Campbell, 1984; Campbell & Ramey, 1994; C. T. Ramey *et al.*, 2000), the *Infant Health and Development Program* (Infant Health and Development Program, 1990; C. T. Ramey *et al.*, 1992), the *Milwaukee Project* (Garber, 1988), the *Perry Preschool Project* (Weikert *et al.*, 1978; Schweinhart *et al.*, 1985, 1993), and *Project Care* (Wasik *et al.*, 1990; C. T. Ramey *et al.*, 1995; Burchinal *et al.*, 1997). All of these programmes were multi-pronged and provided at least one full year of intervention prior to the time children were 5 years of age. These programmes differed in their enrolment selection criteria, the age children entered the programme, and the amount and nature of the services.

The Abercedarian Project

In 1972, the *Abecedarian Project* was launched at the Frank Porter Graham Child Development Center on the campus of the University of North Carolina at Chapel Hill. This single-site randomized controlled trial focused on determining if co-ordinated high-quality services of early childhood education, paediatric care, and family social support could improve the intellectual and educational competence of participating children. Children were enrolled from birth and were selected for the programme based on a 13-item high-risk index (C. T. Ramey & Smith, 1977). Overwhelmingly, these children came from poor and undereducated families, but all were biologically healthy and had no known genetic or infectious links to mental retardation (C. T. Ramey & Campbell, 1992; C. T. Ramey & Ramey, 1998). The conceptual framework for the intervention programme was based on developmental systems theory (e.g., Bertalanffy, 1975), which articulates how instrumental and conceptual learning is facilitated through a stimulating, positive, and responsive environment (C. T. Ramey & Finklestein, 1981).

The Abecedarian Project enrolled 111 families, with half randomly assigned to the comparison group who received free nutritional supplements for the infants, social services, and free or low cost paediatric follow-up services. The other half were assigned to the treatment group and received the same services as the comparison group plus they participated in an educational intervention for a full day, each weekday for 50 weeks per year in the child development centre on the university campus. The children began participation in the pre-school educational programme by at least 4 months of age, prior to any developmental delays, and continued until they entered public school kindergarten (S. L. Ramey & Ramey, 1999).

The educational programme was staffed by teachers who had formal training, teaching experience, and demonstrated skill and competence in working with young children. A strong emphasis was placed on developing language competence and providing positive response–contingency learning experiences, as it was hypothesized that in the majority of the children's homes, these were limited due to high maternal risk factors (C. T. Ramey et al., 1981). The curriculum for infants and toddlers was based on the *Partners for Learning* educational programme with activities promoting development for cognitive-fine motor, social-self, motor, and language development (Sparling & Lewis, 1979, 1984). A preliteracy curriculum was also provided for the older pre-school children (Wallach & Wallach, 1976).

The results from the Abecedarian Project showed that beginning at 18 months of age and at every assessment age thereafter through age 21, the children in the treatment group showed significant IQ benefits. In the pre-school years, the IQ difference between the treatment and comparison group was 10–15 points higher than the comparison group. Follow-up assessments at 12, 15, and 21 years showed the difference between the treatment and comparison groups narrowed, yet the treatment group continued to have higher average cognitive scores that are educationally meaningful.[1] Perhaps even more importantly, at all ages from 5 to 21, the treatment group had significantly higher academic achievement scores in both reading and mathematics, were less likely to be placed in special education, and were less likely to retained in grade than children in the comparison group (C. T. Ramey *et al.*, 2000).

The Infant Health and Development Program

The *Infant Health and Development Program* (IHDP) enrolled 985 infants that had both low birth weight (below 2500 grams) and were premature or less than 37 weeks gestational age. The sample varied widely in their social risks, yet the demographics reflected premature, low birth weight babies in general with a disproportionate number of low income, socially at risk and minority families (IHDP, 1990; C. T. Ramey *et al.*, 1992). Infants were randomly assigned with approximately one-third of the sample to the intervention group (number of infants, $n = 377$) and two-thirds to the follow-up group ($n = 608$). IHDP operated from hospital discharge to 3 years of age and used home visits only in the first year and home visits plus early childhood education in a child development centre from 1 to 3 years of age. Each of the eight sites established and operated a full-day child development centre with home visitors co-ordinating centre and home activities.

The goals of the home visit programme were: (1) to provide emotional, social, and practical support to parents, as adults; (2) to provide parents with developmentally timed information about their low birth weight child's development; (3) to help parents learn specific ways to foster their child's intellectual, physical, and social development; and (4) to help parents discover ways to cope with the responsibilities of caring for a developing and, initially, vulnerable child (C. T. Ramey *et al.*, in press). A major component of the home visiting programme were the *Early Partners* curriculum for 24–40-week gestational age low birth weight infants (Sparling *et al.*, 1992) and the *Partners for Learning* (Sparling & Lewis, 1984) curriculum for infants to 36 months.

A number of findings were derived from this study. First it was found that at age 3, when the intervention ended, the probability of a child functioning in

---

[1] The 21-year follow up has not yet appeared in a peer-reviewed journal; therefore, this discussion is taken from the Executive Summary of the Carolina Abecedarian Project, which is available on the Frank Porter Graham web site, www. fpg.unc.edu/verity.

the borderline intellectual range or lower decreased significantly with increasing degrees of family participation (C. T. Ramey *et al.*, 1992). Second, infants in the *heavier* birth weight group had average higher IQ scores by 13 points as compared with no-intervention controls, while the group differed 6.5 IQ points from those in the intervention group who had lighter birth weights. This might be explained by greater effects of biological conditions among the lighter premature children, perhaps indicative of early central nervous system damage *in utero* (in the womb). A third major finding showed that among heavier low birth weight children, 23% of the children in the comparison (no intervention) group had IQ scores of 70 or below at 3 years of age, compared with only 8% of the children in the treatment group (S. L. Ramey & Ramey, 1999). Fourth, mothers with lower maternal education and/or maternal IQ benefited to a much greater degree than those with higher educational levels and IQ levels (Landesman & Ramey, 1989; Brooks-Gunn *et al.*, 1992). This has been reported elsewhere as well (Martin *et al.*, 1990). Interestingly, there were negligible or no effects for children born to college educated mothers. It is hypothesized that higher educated parents provide their low birth weight infants with additional care and special services in their own homes and appropriate community-based supports.

Longitudinal analyses of these children's development showed that by 5 and 8 years of age, the overall IQ differences between the treatment and comparison (no-intervention) groups decreased to such an extent that it was no longer educationally significant (Brooks-Gunn *et al.*, 1992; McCarton *et al.*, 1997). However, it is noteworthy that the *heavier* low birth weight children continued to have significantly higher IQ scores at age 5 and by age 8 the early intervention group scored 4 4 points higher than the comparison. The scientists involved in this study concluded that early cessation of services at age 3 was likely to have contributed to the loss of early benefits and that additional interventions are indicated for low birth weight infants to sustain earlier gains.

The Milwaukee Project

The *Milwaukee Project* began in the 1960s and was located in an inner city. This programme enrolled only children whose mothers had an IQ below 75. An educational programme with a strong emphasis on language development was provided throughout the pre-school years and continued as the children entered kindergarten. Training was provided for the mothers on employment skills and parenting. At the conclusion of the programme, significant main effects of the early intervention on children's intelligence were detected. In fact, the Milwaukee Project produced the largest IQ group differences of any of the longitudinal studies discussed in this chapter. At 18 months of age, differences were first noted in the development of the treatment and control groups. At the conclusion of the treatment period, there was an astounding 30 IQ points difference between the treated and control groups, plus the treated group had superior verbal and expressive behavioural repertoires. The scientists noted in observations of the mother–child dyads that the experimental children supplied more verbal information to the mother, initiated more verbal communication than the control group, and actually took control of the verbal exchange with the mother. It appeared the children actually directed the communication through questioning or teaching the mother, which benefited not only the child but the mother as well (Garber, 1988). In addition, the Milwaukee Project provided more direct support for the children's learning experiences and the families than any other randomized controlled study.

At age 10, the treated children in the Milwaukee Project continued to have higher IQ scores (104 for the treated group and 86 for the control group), although the differences were not as great as at the conclusion of the pre-school and kindergarten programme. Surprisingly, there were no differences in the academic performance of the two groups, yet the treated group was significantly less likely to be placed in special education or referred for special services. Garber attributed the lack of difference in school performance to the poor quality of the inner city public schools the children attended, and other educational policies that may have impacted their school performance (in marked contrast to the generally high quality of the public school system in Chapel Hill, North Carolina for the Abecedarian Project). This finding illustrates that factors other than IQ contribute to a child's success in school, thus suggesting a narrow focus in early intervention programmes on just increasing IQ scores is misguided; in contrast, a broader set of indicators of children's adjustment is recommended.

The Perry Preschool Project

The *Perry Preschool Project* is one of the best known early intervention programmes, having followed its participants to 27 years of age. It was based in Ypsilanti, Michigan, USA in the early 1960s and was designed to serve 3- and 4-year-old children who already showed developmental delay (i.e., IQs between 70 and 85). Perry Preschool provided 1 or 2 years of a 2_ hours/day educational pre-school programme 5 days/week for 8 months plus a weekly 90-minute home visitation programme to promote positive parenting skills. Like the other programmes, low child/teacher ratios were maintained; further, all teachers had masters degrees and training in child development (Schweinhart *et al.*, 1985, 1993).

Significant differences in cognitive development were found between the groups at age 5 with a mean IQ of 95 for the treated group and 84 for the control group. Although this IQ advantage disappeared by age 15, with both control and treated groups having IQs in the low 80s, the children in the treatment group showed significantly greater academic achievement in the eighth grade (about age 13–14) and significantly higher literacy scores at age

19 than the control group. In addition, 71% of the treated group versus 54% of the control group graduated from high school or received a General Education Development Certificate. Grade retention rates (reflecting failures to advance grades or move up year classes) and special education placement rates were also significantly lower for treated children than the control children. The most substantial benefits from participation in the Perry Preschool Project were those referred to as 'real-world,' notably their decreased school dropout and unemployment, increased college attendance, reduced teen pregnancy, higher income status, and decreased criminal activity at age 27 years. A cost–benefit analysis of this study estimates that for every dollar invested in this early intervention programme, it resulted in a long-term savings of approximately 7 dollars (Barnett, 1985, 1995).

Project CARE

Project CARE systematically compared two forms of intervention: a centre-based programme identical to the Abecedarian Project and a home-based programme of weekly home visits for the first 3 years of life, followed by biweekly visits for the next 2 years. Additionally, children received a family-based intervention from infancy to school age. This project enrolled 63 children from poverty families with additional social risk factors such as teen mother, mother with an IQ below 90, and low maternal education (High Risk Index: C. T. Ramey & Smith, 1977). Children were randomly assigned to one of three treatment conditions: (1) centre-based educational intervention plus home visits; (2) home visits only; or (3) control (see Wasik *et al.*, 1990, for more details). All Project CARE children assigned to either the centre-based programme plus home visit or home visit only groups also participated in a treatment involving a home–school resource teacher during the first 3 years of elementary school.

This project was very favourably received by the community, the mothers, and the home visitors (who were community individuals who received extensive training and ongoing supervision and support for their work). The results for the early educational programme plus home visit group replicated those from the Abecedarian Project, with significant benefits in cognitive performance from the second year of life on as well as long-term group differences in reading and mathematics achievement through adolescence (Wasik *et al.*, 1990).

It was disappointing, however, that child development outcomes on a wide array of measures did *not* detect any benefits for children in the home visiting only group. In addition, the home visiting family education component did not significantly improve the home environment, the parents' attitudes, or the children's or parents' behaviour. These findings cause serious pause, to the importance of considering the magnitude of differences in children's environments—whether in the home or in a centre. Although the same curriculum materials were available in the home and the centre settings, the use of and delivery of the materials may have varied greatly. The children in the educational child centre setting spent time with well-trained and experienced child-care staff whose main purpose was to provide a stimulating environment and a systematic curriculum. The changes that might have occurred in parenting behaviour and in parent–child interactions may not have been early enough and intensive enough (quantity) to equal what was received in centre-based optimal educational care. Unfortunately, follow-up of these families in terms of the development of later born children did not occur to determine whether there might have been carryover effects in terms of subsequent parental competence (C. T. Ramey *et al.*, 2001).

Overview of the five studies

The results of these five studies all demonstrate benefits of early intervention for children at risk for developmental disabilities in terms of significant improvements in cognitive development and reduced rates of mental retardation during the pre-school years. These benefits persisted in varying degrees well into middle childhood and, when evaluated, into the early adult years. The advantage in cognitive development demonstrated in the pre-school years persisted for the treated groups in the Abecedarian Project, Project Care, and the Milwaukee Project in terms of IQ gains. Treated groups, with the exception of some of the low birth weight premature children in the Infant Health and Development Program, also benefited in terms of improved school achievement (with the exception of the Milwaukee study) and reduced rates of special education placement and grade retention (S. L. Ramey & Ramey, 1999). In addition, the 21-year follow-up of the young adults who participated in the Abecedarian Project, showed they had significantly higher mental test scores and reading and mathematics achievement test scores; were more likely to be enrolled in college and employed in higher skill jobs; and were older when they had their first child than those in the comparison group (Campbell *et al*, 2001). The Perry Preschool Project follow-up at age 27 also found multiple real-world benefits at age 27 (Schweinhart *et al.*, 1993).

Factors for success

What are the factors that appear to determine an early intervention programme's success in preventing developmental delay, mental retardation, and poor school achievement? Four factors appear to make a critical difference: (1) timing and duration of the intervention; (2) intensity of services provided and received; (3) use of direct versus indirect learning experiences; and (4) the provision of comprehensive services in addition to educational programming.

Timing and duration

The majority of early intervention or 'school readiness' pre-school pro-grammes for at-risk, low-income children begin at 4 years of age. The evidence, however, shows that the earlier an intervention is started and the longer it is maintained, the more likely it is to produce greater benefits for participants. Successful experimental model programmes such as the *Abecedarian Project* (C. T. Ramey & Ramey, 2000), *Brookline Early Education Project* (Hauser-Cram *et al.*, 1991), *Project Care* (Wasik, *et al.*, 1990), and the *Milwaukee Project* (Garber, 1988), enrolled children in infancy and continued at least until they entered elementary school. All produced significant benefits on children's cognitive, academic, and/or language performance. The National Head Start programme now recognizes the need for providing strong early intervention programmes at an earlier age and has funded over 500 Early Head Start programmes for families with infants and toddlers (with a subsample being evaluated for efficacy). In 1999, the American Congress appropriated over 4 billion dollars for Head Start programmes with almost 350 million dollars used for Early Head Start programmes (Head Start, 2000). In conclusion, high-quality programmes that begin earlier and continue longer afford greater benefits to the participants than those that start later and do not last as long.

Intensity of services

Unfortunately, there are many early intervention programmes that do not demonstrate change in children's intellectual and academic performance. An examination of these programmes show they are not intensive, as indicated by the hours per day, days per week, and weeks per year of educational services provided. The Utah State Early Intervention Research Institute conducted 16 randomized trials of early intervention programmes for special needs children and found that none of the programmes produced significant effects on children's development. It must be noted that *none* of the 16 programmes provided a full-day, 5-day per week programme. Scarr and McCartney (1988) also failed to produce positive cognitive effects when they provided a parent-oriented, one time per week intervention with economically impoverished families in Bermuda. Two home visiting programmes, however, showed that intense programmes can make a difference. First, an early intervention home-visit programme that provided services 3 days/week produced significant benefits, while the same programme offered at a less intense level was not successful (Powell & Grantham-McGregor, 1989). Second, the Brookline Early Education Program (Hauser-Cram *et al.*, 1991) found that *only* the most intensive two-generation model they provided was adequate to benefit children at risk for school difficulties, while the lowest intensity programme had no measurable consequences.

The *Infant Health and Development Program* (1990) examined intensity at the individual level. Based on a daily, weekly, and monthly monitoring of the variations in the amount of intervention each child and family received over a 3-year period, it was found that the amount of services received had a strong positive relationship to the child's social and intellectual development at 36 months of age (C. T. Ramey *et al.*, 1992). In fact, the group that had the highest participation rate had a ninefold reduction in the proportion of low birth weight children who were mentally retarded compared with the control group who received only paediatric follow-up services. For the intermediate participation group, retardation was reduced by a 4.9-fold factor, while the low participation group was only 1.3-fold. It must be noted that this variation did not appear related in any simple fashion to family variables such as ethnicity, parental education, family income, or the child's birth weight status.

Direct versus indirect services

Successful early interventions can be provided to children and/or families in a variety of forms. Some offer *direct services* to children in the form of classes in a child development centre. Others may offer early intervention services to children in a more indirect method, most often a home visiting programme where trained personnel work with parents to inform them about how to promote children's development or where parenting classes (groups) are offered. Some programmes provide a combination of these types of services. The scientific literature examining the effects of these strategies are clear: indirect methods are far less powerful than direct approaches in terms of enhancing children's intellectual and social development (Madden *et al.*, 1976; Casto & Lewis, 1984; Scarr & McCartney, 1988; Wasik *et al.*, 1990). This holds true for disadvantaged children and high-risk children, including biologically disadvantaged children, economically disadvantaged children, and high-risk children with both environmental and individual risk conditions.

The first experimental study comparing the value of direct versus indirect forms of early intervention underscores this conclusion. As described above, *Project CARE* (Wasik *et al.*, 1990) found that combining daily centre-based intervention with weekly home visits produced significant gains in cognitive development, while the group that had regular home visits (indirect method) over a 5-year period had *no* documented benefits on children's cognitive and social development, parent attitudes or behaviour, or the quality of the home environment. In fact, the home visit group was no different than the children in the control group who received nutritional supplements, medical surveillance, and social services, *even though the parents were highly satisfied with the home visitation component*. Home visitation programmes are very popular in the United States and are used extensively to support and promote children's development. While it is important to recognize and celebrate the role of parents in their children's development, careful consideration should be given to whether such programmes actually produce adequate positive child benefits. The findings of Powell and Grantham-McGregor (1989), pointed out earlier in this chapter, do provide some promise that three home visits per week can produce significant child outcomes.

Comprehensiveness of services

Early interventions that adopt a broad, multi-pronged approach to working with children and families in order to enhance children's development are more effective than those that have a more narrow focus. The Abecedarian Project, the Brookline Early Education Project, Project CARE, the Milwaukee Project, the Infant Health and Development Program, and the Mobil Unit for Child Health (Gutelius *et al.*, 1977) all provided comprehensive services for families and used multiple routes to enhance children's development. These services included ongoing health and social services, transportation, assisting families with meeting urgent needs, other types of parental support, individualized neurological therapies as needed, parent education components, in addition to strong educational programming. For example, significant cognitive effects were found in the 3-year Mobil Unit for Child Health Project where prenatal counselling, well-baby care, infant stimulation activities with an emphasis on language, educational toys, and family education were combined. Schorr and Schorr (1988) summarized the importance of providing comprehensive services to families and children at risk for developmental delay:

Programs that are successful in reaching and helping the most disadvantaged children and families typically offer a broad spectrum of services. They recognize that social and emotional support and concrete help (with food, housing, income, employment, or anything else that seems to the family to be an insurmountable obstacle) may have to be provided before a family can make use of other interventions, from antibiotics to advice on parenting (p. 257)

Hundreds of early intervention programmes have been developed by local, state, and federal groups to prepare children for successful school entry, to prevent developmental disabilities, and to address identified special needs. Unfortunately, not all early intervention programmes are effective and even children within the same programme respond differently to the intervention. Generally speaking, those children and families that have the greatest needs benefit the most if the intervention is comprehensive, co-ordinated, intensive, and of sufficient duration. Furthermore, if the benefits children and families derive in high-quality early intervention programmes are going to endure over the long-term, children and families must continue to experience highly supportive environments.

16 Social policy and the enhancement of infant development

ANNE E. BRADY, FRANCINE H. JACOBS, and
RICHARD M. LERNER

Introduction: Social policy affects real children and families

Social policy affects real children and families. Consider these two American families:

The Alvarez family

Mary and Pedro Alvarez live in a suburb of Grand Rapids, Michigan. Both graduated from college and Pedro has a master's degree in education. They married three years after their college graduation. They are both employed full-time; their annual income is $65,000 per year. Both of their employers offer full benefits packages, but Pedro's comes at a lower monthly cost for a family and is more comprehensive, so they use his. They have been married for one year and are both 26 years old. Their first child, Juanita, is two weeks old. Just before Juanita's birth they moved to a new town to be closer to Pedro's job; most of their family and friends live about 30 miles away in another suburb of Grand Rapids.

The McManus/Brown family

Jeanne McManus and Robert Brown live in a semi-rural community in New York State. Neither Jeanne nor Robert attended college. Jeanne became pregnant with their first child at the end of eleventh grade and dropped out when the baby was born. Krissy is now six years old. Jeanne has never completed her diploma but hopes to get her high school Graduate Equivalency Diploma (GED) someday. Jeanne and Robert started living together two years after Robert's high school graduation and have been cohabitating for three years; they are now both 23 years old. Robert works full time in a cement plant. Jeanne works part-time as the assistant manager of a local supermarket. Their yearly income is $30,000 and their rent is $500 per month. Their second child, Bobby, is expected in one week. Their family and many friends live nearby.

If you have read this book from the beginning then you have just read 15 chapters on infant development, including the previous chapter on the role of intervention in children's development (a major social policy issue), and you have now met the Alvarez and the McManus/Brown families. How have the previous chapters helped you understand what kinds of public support and interventions these two families may need to do a good job raising their children? Where are the connections between infant developmental theory and action the most obvious, the most imperative?

As explained by Lewis (1997), who notes the rich and systemic interrelation of theory and practice, the social value of developmental theory lies in its connection to action—in its promise to enhance child-rearing practices, or to help shape programmes and policies for children and families. To parents, practitioners and advocates, it is important to pose 'so what?' questions to researchers: 'So what if we know that infant cognition is affected by nutrition if our government is not able or willing to provide infants with these necessary nutrients?' they might ask. 'How will defining the initial stages of language development help us better prepare our children for school?' Such questions are at the heart of this chapter.

Programmes and policies for infants and toddlers reflect the life circumstances of young families, the values and beliefs of the larger society, and current scientific and theoretical understandings of how children develop and families function. Using the United States as a sample case, we begin this chapter with a discussion of *the context for child and family policy* and, in the second section—*snapshot of young families in the United States*, a snapshot of American families.

In the third section—*The current United States policy environment*—we describe, in broad strokes, major programmes and policies currently available for this population, focusing on social policies. There are many other policies that affect young children and families equally powerfully; for example, policies pertaining to medical care or child nutrition, but the focus here is on the core *social* policies.

In the fourth and final section—*A vision for the future: How to get there from here*—we draw conclusions about the nature of the current relationship between what we know and what we do, and follow with our recommendations for an integrated approach to programmes and policies for infants and toddlers.

As we have noted, the emphasis in this chapter is primarily on federal child and family policy in the United States. However, even here we are necessarily only providing a sample of what exists. Policy activity occurs at several levels of political organization—municipal, county, state, and federal—and within both the governmental and private, non-profit worlds. Indeed, many of the most exciting policy initiatives are found in states and localities, not in Washington, DC. We offer this chapter, then, as a case example of how social policies for young families develop, and where developmental theorists and researchers can make significant contributions.

The context for child and family policy

Social policy is a subset of public policy; it represents governments' intentions to improve life for their citizens, particularly the vulnerable among them. One might expect that social policy begins with the question, 'given our economic capabilities and constraints, how can we do best by our people?' Although it appears that some nations do initiate certain social policy debates from this vantage point, many—including the United States—apparently do not.

Each country's set of social policies is rooted in that nation's particular political culture—the values and beliefs about the proper role of government that 'animate the principal institutions of a society' (Feldman & Zaller, 1992). In the United States, these core values and beliefs include the virtues of autonomy, personal industry and achievement, self-sufficiency, individual freedom, and privacy. A relatively limited view of government's role, then, has emerged. In a country as wealthy and full of opportunity as ours, the argument goes, being poor or otherwise disadvantaged is essentially one's own fault (Katz, 1989; Piven & Cloward, 1993).

US child and family policy is a particularly impoverished subset of our social policy. This is for two primary reasons. To begin, the family is seen as a private domain—a holdover, perhaps, from the days when children and wives were considered by law to be *owned* by fathers and husbands. The image of government intrusion into this sanctuary is nightmarish to many. Secondly, the decision to have children is seen as private one, and one that, in the twenty-first century, is easily and efficiently controlled by the individual. As the benefits of having children are privately enjoyed, the responsibilities should be privately borne (Jacobs, 1994).

Infants and toddlers are considered the most 'privately owned and controlled' of all children. The compulsory education laws for children ages 7–16 in the United States suggest a compelling societal interest in an educated populace that overrides belief in the sanctity of the family. But if we read our social policies correctly, there appear to be no compelling reasons to regularly 'violate' familial boundaries before children reach middle childhood. Babies belong with their mothers, and mothers belong at home. The arguments made in other countries, and in many quarters in the United States—that demographics (e.g., maternal employment patterns), and research (e.g., in early brain development, in parent–child relations, in developmental disabilities) support public investment in families with infants and toddlers—fall largely on deaf ears. An irregular patchwork of public programmes for these children and their families is the result.

Dimensions of child and family policies

Child and family policies, including those for infants and toddlers, can be understood with reference to several core characteristics (Jacobs, 1994). Are the policies and programmes under review available to all infants and toddlers (a universal service definition), or are there eligibility criteria that include certain children and families and exclude others (a targeted service definition)? Do policies serve children exclusively (child centred), or are other family members, and the family as a unit (family centred) also considered appropriate beneficiaries? Do policies primarily support the fiscal obligations of families towards their young members (economically oriented), or do they support the nurturing roles that families play (caregiving oriented)? Do policies focus on correcting or rehabilitating existing problems with children or in families (treatment oriented), or do they attempt to head these problems off beforehand (prevention oriented)?

A fitting set of policies would array programmes across these continua. At best there would be a wide array of choices for families to consider. The current approach in the United States with all children and families, however, indicates an over-reliance on economically defined, targeted, treatment-oriented programmes within the relatively narrow band of programmes available. As you follow the Alvarez and McManus/Brown families, see if this diagnosis holds true for them, and for other families with very young children.

Race, class, and gender

Considerations of race, class, and gender also must be included in any investigation of the development, effectiveness, and worthiness of child and family policies (Davies & Jacobs, 1994). As we have noted, US social policies in general usually respond to existing, fairly dire, problems. But problems are 'socially constructed,' and what appears as a problem for one population subgroup may not be for another. Too often the majority community gets to define these terms. For example, spokespersons for poor communities, and communities of colour, have argued persuasively that youth violence was not viewed as a public problem until it affected life in white, middle-class neighbourhoods. The nature of particular programmes (how services are delivered, by whom, and where) may also encourage or discourage participation; sometimes these preferences reflect the idiosyncratic tastes of individual parents and children, but often they are based, at least in part, in class, gender, or racial distinctions. In addition, policies and programmes can have differential outcomes by race, income, and gender; these must be factored into the decision to promote or derogate any public initiative.

Developmental theories

As stressed by Lewis (1997), the ways in which policies relate to the current knowledge base about child and family development also must be considered. Theories of development integrate facts about human behaviour as it changes across age and, if they are useful, they also result in ideas for the collection of new information about development. Theories also may serve applied purposes (Lewis, 1997). Kurt Lewin (1943) is noted for pointing out that there is nothing as practical as a good theory; one practical application of theory is to serve as a frame for public policies.

For instance, attachment theory (e.g., Ainsworth *et al.*, 1978; Lamb & Easterbrooks, 1981; and see Chapter 12) stresses that sensitive caregiving is important for the development of the cognitive and emotion capacities involved in positive (or 'secure') relationships between the infant and his or her caregivers, and for healthy subsequent development. The emphasis on the significance of such early experiences for infant and later childhood development embodied here suggests that social policies aimed at improving the quality of child and family life should promote programmes and invest resources in the first year of life. Examples might be family leave policies to insure that a parent is sufficiently available to foster healthy attachment relationships from birth through 12 months and parent education programmes to enhance caregiver sensitivity, or, in cases where mothers work, training of child-care providers to provide sensitive caregiving.

In turn, contemporary theory and research pertinent to early brain development (c.f., Nelson, 1999) emphasizes that, while early experience is important for positive infant and later childhood cognitive and emotional development and social relationships, human development is characterized by 'plasticity' (i.e., the potential for systematic change) across the life span. Public policies, then, should invest in promoting healthy behaviour and development across life. That is, 'as dramatic as brain development is in the first few years, we should think of these years as analogous to building a foundation for a house' (Nelson, 1999, p. 237).

One reason that plasticity occurs is because the brain, and, in fact, the whole individual are linked interactively to variables from the multiple levels that comprise the ecology of human development (Bronfenbrenner, 1979; Bronfenbrenner & Morris, 1998). Processes within the person (e.g., cognition, personality) are integrated with processes involving other people, social institutions (e.g., families, schools), communities, cultural influences, and the physical settings of life. All of these are changing interdependently ('systemically') across time. These reciprocal relations are the province of developmental systems theories (e.g., Sameroff, 1983; Lerner, 1998; Magnusson & Stattin, 1998; Thelen & Smith, 1998). Developmental systems theories suggest that resources should be focused on strengthening key individual-context *relationships*, for example, between an infant and his or her parents, a child and his or her school, or a family and the community within which it lives (for example, see Lewis, 1997).

Snapshot of young families in the United States

The Alvarez and McManus/Brown families are typical, in many ways, of young families across the United States. Let's take a moment to learn more about the characteristics of such young families.

In recent years, there have been broad-based reductions in the poverty rate. These reductions were particularly evident for children. While 21% of children were poor in 1996, 16.9% were classified as poor in 1999 (Dalaker & Proctor, 2000).[1] In 1999, 18% of children *under age 6* were living in poverty (Dalaker & Proctor, 2000). While these rates represent an improvement, the United States has far to go in equalizing the rates of poverty of children and adults; the poverty rate for children is much higher than it is for adults (16.9% versus 9.7%; Zedlewski, 2000).

Children in single-parent families are disproportionately likely to be poor. In the United States in 1999, approximately 25% of children lived in a single-parent family, while 4% lived with other, non-parental adults. The proportion of two-parent families was lowest for black children (29%) and highest for white children (72%). Hispanic children lived in two-parent families in 60% of cases (Staveteig & Wigton, 2000). Almost three times as many low-income children (41%) were from single-parent families as were higher income children (14%; Vandivere *et al.*, 2000).

Racial and ethnic differences in the poverty rate persist despite overall economic improvement in the United States. The poverty rate is lowest (7.7%) in white non-Hispanic families and is highest in black non-Hispanic families (23.6%) and families of Hispanic origin (22.8%; Dalaker & Proctor, 2000). About 24% of white families are classified as low income[2] compared with 50% of black families and 56% of Hispanic families (Staveteig & Wigton, 2000).

Maternal employment

In 1997, approximately 57% of mothers with young children under the age of 3 were employed (US Department of Health and Human Services, 2000d). This rate corresponds to a steady increase in maternal employment rates since 1980. Between 1997 and 1999, the employment rate for low-income single parents increased from 63% to 67%, while it decreased slightly, and not significantly, for low-income married parents (from 66% to 65%; Zedlewski, 2000). In the low-income population, black adults were the only group to

---

[1] Federal poverty threshold in 1998 (NSAF) in terms of income earned per year: One adult with no children = $8480; One adult with one child = $11 235; One adult with two children = $13 133; Two adults with no children = $10 915; Two adults with one child = $13 120; Two adults with two children = $16 530.

[2] Low income is a family income less than 200% of the poverty rate.

experience an increase in employment (from 56% to 60%); employment rates for white and Hispanic adults decreased slightly (Staveteig & Wigton, 2000).

Participation in child care

In 1999, approximately 61% of children under age 4 in America were in regular child care. This figure includes 44% of infants under 1, 53% of 1 year olds, and 57% of 2 year olds (National Research Council and Institute of Medicine, 2000). In 1997, 41% of children under 5 whose mothers worked were cared for by people other than their parents for 35 hours a week or more (US Department of Health and Human Services, 2000a).

Entry into child care in the United States tends to occur at a very early age. The average age of entry into non-parental care is 3.31 months; about 72% of infants experience *some* non-parental care in their first year of life (NICHD Early Child Care Research Network, 1997). Nearly one-quarter of infants and toddlers of working mothers are cared for by other relatives. For those infants and toddlers not cared for by relatives, 7% have a nanny or babysitter who provides care in the home. Of the 39% of infants and toddlers who receive care outside of the home, 22% are in centre-based care, while 17% are in family child care arrangements (National Research Council and Institute of Medicine, 2000).

Thus, whether a baby is born into a single-parent or a two-parent family will have an effect on the trajectory of his or her life. The racial group into which a child is born affects his or her chances of growing up healthy. If the child is born to a family with a certain income, he or she is starting off advantaged or disadvantaged. Even the state and the region of the country into which a child is born affects that child's life trajectory. They are all babies, but every baby is not born equal.

The current US policy environment

The Alvarezes and McManus/Browns change with the birth of their infants. What is currently available to help them negotiate this next phase in their families' lives?

The Alvarezes

Mary returns to work when Juanita is three months old. Child care costs $1,000 per month. Juanita develops serious health problems after Mary has been back at work for two months. Since Pedro earns more than Mary, they decide that he should keep working while Mary cares for Juanita. After recovering from the acute phase of her illness, Juanita displays some developmental delay. Mary decides that it isn't feasible for her to work full-time from now on.

The McManus/Browns
Bobby is born healthy. Jeanne returns to work when he is six weeks old, and her mother provides child care for both Krissy and Bobby. Jeanne's mother announces that she has to return to work when Bobby is five months old. The family is forced to find another way to care for the children. The cement plant where Robert has worked since high school closes, and Robert has to accept a succession of lower paying jobs. The family's annual income drops to $20,000. Robert leaves Jeanne and moves out six months after he loses his job. The family income drops to $13,000 per year.

Early care and education

What programmes are available to address the need of these families and children? Policies currently in place in the United States offer a diverse array of early care and educational services.

Child care

There is no comprehensive federal policy on child care in the United States, but child care considerations touch the lives of the majority of children and families in the country. In 1996, the landscape of federal child care assistance for *low-income* families shifted with the passing of the Personal Responsibility and Work Opportunity Reconciliation Act of 1996 (PRWORA):

The legislation eliminated federal child care entitlements and consolidated the major sources of federal child care subsidies for low-income children into a single block grant to states—the Child Care and Development Fund (CCDF). That block grant gives states greater flexibility in designing their child care assistance programs, providing an opportunity to streamline the complex child care system that was in place before PRWORA and to design a system of assistance that better meets the states' child care needs and objectives. (Long *et al.*, 1998, p. 1)

CCDF provides subsidized child care to eligible families (those with low income, receiving temporary public assistance, or making a transition from public assistance to work or training/education) through certificates or contracts with providers. Parents can select any legally operating child care provider. Child care providers serving families with CCDF funding must meet *basic* health and safety requirements set by the states and, where applicable, tribal authorities (US Department of Health and Human Services, 2000b).

The vast majority of children with working mothers in low-income families receive no subsidies. In 1998, only 15% of children eligible for CCDF received help through the programme (National Research Council and Institute of Medicine, 2000). As a result, families of modest means spend a greater proportion of their income on child care and are 'priced out' of higher-cost forms of care (centres and licensed family day care homes) in many locales.

Much research has focused on the developmental effects of child care. Both the amount of time children spend in child care and the quality of that care have effects on child development. According to the National Institute of Child and Human Development (NICHD) Study (NICHD Early Child Care Research Network, 1999a, 1999b), more hours in child care are related to less harmonious mother–child interaction, a higher incidence of insecure attachment in children, and more behaviour problems when children are 2-year-olds.

More important that the absolute quantity of child care used (hours in care) is the *quality* of the child care settings in which children are placed. Child care quality encompasses three broad characteristics of programmes:

- the child–provider relationship;
- the structural features of care—training and education of providers, ratios, group size, and adult work environment; and
- the surrounding community and policy context (National Research Council and Institute of Medicine, 2000).

High-quality child care relates to a variety of positive outcomes (National Research Council, 1998; Cost, Quality and Outcomes Study Team, 1999; NICHD Early Child care Research Network, 1999a,b; Currie, 2000): better mother-child relationships; fewer insecurely attached infants; fewer reports of children with problem behaviours; higher cognitive performance; and higher level of school readiness. Lower quality relates to more negative outcomes in the same areas.

Most studies indicate that about 10–20% of child care arrangements in the United States fall below the definition of *merely adequate* care (Galinsky *et al.*, 1994; Cost Quality and Outcomes Study Team, 1995). The NICHD Study indicates that many (between 19% and 26% depending on the indicator in question) child care settings did not provide positive caregiving (NICHD Early Child Care Research Network, 1996). Oftentimes, children from poorer and, therefore, more highly stressed homes are in lower-quality care than are other children (National Research Council and Institute of Medicine, 2000). 'Among families using child care centers, the working poor and those whose incomes hover just above the poverty line receive poorer-quality care than either families living in poverty or families with solidly middle and upper incomes' (National Research Council and Institute of Medicine, 2000, p. 321).

Early Head Start

The Early Head Start (EHS) programme was initiated in 1995. EHS is a federally funded community based programme for pregnant women and low-income families with infants and toddlers. Its mission is to promote healthy prenatal outcomes for pregnant women, enhance the development of very young children, and promote healthy family functioning, 'supporting the family and primary educators of their children during the critical first three years of the child's life' (Kisker & Love, 1999, p. 2). As of December 1999, 547 EHS programmes were in operation (Kisker & Love, 1999).

Family income is one key factor in determining eligibility for EHS. Federal poverty guidelines are used to evaluate family income. EHS programmes may elect to target their services to a particular population to best meet the unique needs of families and children in their community. A tiny fraction of eligible children are enrolled (about 4% or 35 000 children; US Department of Health and Human Services, 1999b).

EHS is intended to enhance children's development, parents' ability to be caregivers of and teachers to their children, and parents' ability to meet their goals for themselves (US Department of Health and Human Services, 1999a). Each local EHS programme provides strengths-based services, including early education in and out of the home, home visits, parent education, comprehensive health services, nutrition services, and case management and peer support for parents (US Department of Health and Human Services, 1999a).

Early intervention

The Education for All Handicapped Children Act Amendments of 1986 (PL 99–457) was the predecessor to the current Individuals with Disabilities Education Act (IDEA) and 'was the most important legislation ever enacted for developmentally vulnerable children in the United States' (Meisels & Shonkoff, 2000, p. 20).

PL 99–457 was reauthorized in the 1997–98 legislative session as the IDEA (Meisels & Shonkoff, 2000). Part C of the IDEA establishes a requirement for states to facilitate the development of a comprehensive system of services for infants and toddlers with disabilities or developmental delays. All children through age 2 with developmental delays are entitled to services under the law. In the statute, early intervention is defined as 'developmental services which . . . are designed to meet a handicapped infant's or toddler's developmental needs in any one or more of the following areas: physical development; cognitive development; language and speech development; psychosocial development; or self-help skills' (Individuals with Disabilities Education Act, Amendments of 1997, Part C).

'As a federal initiative, the law provides for states to exercise considerable discretion regarding organizational and programmatic decision making' (Meisels & Shonkoff, 2000, p. 20). The law prescribes *minimum* components for each state-wide, comprehensive system of early intervention services for infants and toddlers.

In 1997, 197 376 infants and toddlers were served under IDEA, Part C. About one-half of these children were 2–3 years of age; one-third were 1–2 years of age (US Department of Education, 1999). The system of early intervention has shown some positive effects on the children and families it has served. Children have displayed developmental accomplishments in functional mobility; independence in feeding, dressing, and toileting; communication; and play. Their functioning with regard to vision, hearing, and motor co-ordination has improved. Child engagement—how children interact with their environment—has changed significantly. Child behaviour—social play, aggressiveness, tantrums, sleep difficulties, etc.—also has improved (Hebbeler & Wagner, 1998).

Family support services

According to the Family Support America website, 'family support is a set of beliefs and an approach to strengthening and empowering families and communities so that they can foster the optimal development of children, youth, and adult family members.' Family support programmes are meant to be ecologically based, preventive in orientation, and rooted in children's and families' strengths, not problems. These programmes are known by many other names—parent education, newborn home visiting, and parent–child activity groups, to cite a few (Weiss, 1988). Publicly administered family support programmes exist in schools, child protective agencies, public health centres, courts, and mental health facilities. However, the vast majority of individual family support and parent education programmes originated, and still reside, outside the formal public system, operated on relatively little money by private non-profit agencies, churches, and other organizations of personal affiliation (Kagan & Weissbourd, 1994; Abt Associates, 1996).

Although states and localities have been supporting these services for almost two decades, significant federal funding for family support is a relatively recent phenomenon. In 1993, Congress passed the Family Preservation and Support Services Program (FPSSP). The FPSSP was intended primarily to prevent child abuse and neglect, and to forestall or prevent the placement outside of their homes (e.g., in foster care) of those children who had suffered serious abuse and/or neglect. In 1997, a new piece of child welfare legislation—the Adoption and Safe Families Act—was passed; within it, the FPSSP was replaced by the Promoting Safe and Stable Families Program (PSSFP). Continued funding for family support and family preservation has been available through PSSFP, but the emphasis of this present legislation is on children from the most troubled families. It is doubtful that many of the programmes funded through PSSFP ascribe to the family support principles noted above.

Free-standing family support programmes, and family support as components of other services, such as early intervention or child care, are available and well-utilized in some locations, and not in others. There is no co-ordinated system for offering and monitoring these popular programmes.

Economic policies

In addition to the child care subsidies discussed above, there are public financial assistance programmes for families that meet certain criteria.

Earned Income Tax Credit

The Earned Income Tax Credit (EITC) is intended to offset certain living expenses and other taxes for low-income and lower middle-income families. The EITC is refundable, so eligible families receive the full amount of the credit even when that amount exceeds the amount of taxes owed (Friedman, 2000). In 1999, the maximum credit a family with one child could receive was $2313; a family with more than more qualifying child received a maximum credit of $3816 (Internal Revenue Service, 1999).

Each year a large number of the families eligible for the EITC do not participate. Many eligible families do not file tax returns or are not aware of their eligibility (Friedman, 2000). While the participation rate for the EITC is less than perfect, the programme has a significant effect on those who participate. In 1999, over 4 million people in low-income families were lifted out of poverty by virtue of the EITC; almost 19% of these individuals were children under age 6 (derived from data presented in Dalaker & Proctor, 2000).

Family and Medical Leave Act

In 1993, after a 7-year struggle, the Family and Medical Leave Act (FMLA) was passed (Karr-Kaitin, 1994). The law requires employers with 50 or more employees to offer job-protected leave of up to 12 weeks (to employees who have worked at least 1250 hours in the past year and have been employed for 12 consecutive months) to care for a newborn, newly adopted, or seriously ill child, parent, or spouse (Frank & Zigler, 1996).

About 89% of private-sector work places, and 53.5% of private-sector employees, are not covered by the FMLA (Commission on Family and Medical Leave, 1996). From 1994 to 1995, only 17% of eligible employees took leave (Cantor *et al.*, 1995). Nearly 66% of those workers who did not take a needed leave noted that they could not afford to lose their pay during that period.

Temporary Assistance for Needy Families (TANF)

In 1996, the PRWORA was signed into law and replaced the previous welfare system with Temporary Assistance to Needy Families (TANF); the programme provides financial assistance to needy families. PRWORA states that TANF recipients must work within 2 years of receiving benefits and may receive TANF benefits for no more than 5 years for their entire lifetime. Parents with infants may be exempted from this work requirement. At the same time, the law does not require that states make child care available to TANF recipients; 33 states guarantee child care, and 32 guarantee transitional child care for 12–36 months to recipients leaving TANF for jobs (US Department of Health and Human Services, 2000c).

The PRWORA was strongly criticized as unrealistic—even mean-spirited and dangerous—when it was first proposed and later passed given the lack of availability of suitable job training, subsidized child care slots, and jobs that could pay a living wage (c.f., Edelman, 1997). Increases in child poverty, homelessness, and occurrences of child abuse and neglect were predicted. Preliminary data, however, provide modest support for a work-based approach to reducing public dependency by young families.

A surging economy has added to the PRWORA's apparent success (Besharov & Germanis, 2000), but many remain concerned about what will happen when an economic downturn occurs. Others note the variability in results across TANF families. For example, poverty rates have *increased* among the poorest 20% of female-headed households with children (Primus *et al.*, 1999), and the least able mothers, who have not yet found employment, are now reaching their time limits for benefit receipt (Danziger, 2000). Attention to the PRWORA's effects on child development and family life, and on particular subgroups (for example, new immigrants) is critical (Zaslow *et al.*, 1998; Blum & Berrey, 1999).

Our families revisited

As the Alvarez and McManus/Brown families survey this landscape of available public supports for infants, toddlers, and families, what do they see? There are no universally available, preventive services in the policy domains that affect their lives—all services are targeted or 'reserved' in some way. Meeting eligibility requirements is no guarantee of programme participation.

Excellent infant/toddler early care and education options, built on real understandings of child development and family functioning, do exist. But as our two families will come to understand, much depends on where you live, where you work, whether or not your child has a particular constellation of special needs, and whether a particular programme for which you qualify is available in your community. At best, most families of modest or moderate means get by, cobbling together a collection of public and private supports. The arrangements that the Alvarezes and the McManus/Browns have managed to establish, typical of families in their circumstances, are summarized below:

The Alvarezes
Mary is able to take an additional three-month-long job-protected leave when Juanita is ill. Pedro's job allows for a paternal leave for the same purpose, but he and Mary decide he should continue to work since he earns a higher salary than she. Mary returns to work part-time after Juanita's recovery. The family is no longer able to afford the child care center they had arranged for Juanita and are forced to place her in lower quality care. When Juanita's developmental problems arise, her pediatrician refers the family to the local early intervention program. Through early intervention, they receive developmental services for Juanita, through home visits and infant/toddler groups, and emotional support for Mary and Pedro.

The McManus/Browns
Jeanne's employer allows six weeks paid and six weeks unpaid family leave. Jeanne takes a six week paid leave when Bobby is born, but cannot afford to take the addi-

tional six weeks. When Jeanne's mother returns to work, Jeanne and Robert are eligible for but unable to find subsidized child care slots through the CCDF; they are forced to leave the children in an uncertified family day care center while they work. When Robert leaves, Jeanne enters the TANF programme while she tries to find a better job. Because she lives in New York State, she must continue to work while she is on the TANF rolls, and Robert must pay child support. Jeanne finds that it is hard to get a better paying job without a high school diploma and enters a GED program. She is away from her children for more than 45 hours per week as a result. After Robert leaves the family, Jeanne finds that life is much more stressful but is unable to find some supports to help her negotiate this difficult time.

Are these public supports sufficient to promote the development and well-being of the Alvarez and McManus/Brown family members? Is this the best we can do?

A vision for the future: how to get there from here

The United States can certainly do better to promote the development and well-being of young children and families. Perhaps the first step is public acknowledgement of the circumstances for families with infants and toddlers: over half the mothers of children under 1 year of age are in the labour force, including those required to be by their participation in TANF. Unless we are willing to consider new economic supports to these families so that mothers can stay home with their children, we simply must abandon our old notion of the inviolability of 'mothercare.' And we must work to change the dominant political culture that considers family a private domain, and independence the ultimate virtue.

Instead, we must insist on the construction of a comprehensive, integrated system of publicly supported early care and education. This system would consider both the economic and caregiving roles of parents. It would weigh the requirements of both typically and atypically developing children; well-functioning families and those under stress. It would knit concerns for parents and extended family members together with those for children. It would anticipate what infants and toddlers might need in the future, and ease the transitions to school and programmes for older children. It would help families in their interactions with other service systems, health care, for example. It would constantly refresh itself with the newest research on child development and family functioning.

Much of the necessary scaffolding for this new system is already in place: model programmes for children and families, an experienced cadre of professionals to staff them and to train additional personnel, a growing theory and research base that credits the importance of early development and hints at necessary programme and policy elements, and evaluation results that, in some areas, identify successful interventions ripe for replication. What is needed is a commitment to significant 'new investments' in this field (National Research Council and Institute of Medicine, 2000), and to responsible, thoughtful, stewardship of these efforts by policymakers and citizens alike. Winning funding for this initiative is the necessary third step.

Funds should not, and likely will not, be forthcoming without careful attention to the delivery mechanisms for this comprehensive, co-ordinated system, and those are not obvious. Attending to the process of implementing such a system, including building collaborative relationships across involved parties, is as important as knowing what kinds of programming to undertake.

Continued theory development and applied developmental research is critical as well; these efforts should be supported through both public and private sources.

Improving the theory–practice connection

Earlier in the chapter we discussed the ways in which theories of development may suggest ideas pertinent to policies aimed at enhancing infant development and/or the role of infancy in positive development across life. While we believe that policies about infant development should be predicated on the best theory-based research available, this ideal is rarely met (e.g., Bronfenbrenner, 1974; Lerner *et al.*, 1999), as you have observed.

Often, policy makers find theory and research cast in terms too opaque to be useful and/or find that it is difficult to obtain a consensus for action among scholars. In addition, there is often a lack of fit between the way a researcher casts a 'problem' about infant development (e.g., 'What are the precise characteristics of a stimulus array that will enable a six-month-old to solve an object constancy problem?') and the way in which a policy maker may cast such a problem (e.g., 'What are the most fiscally responsible actions that can be taken to ensure that the infants of my constituents will have experiences that support their early cognitive development?').

When policy makers do not rely on theory and research to guide their actions, scholars often express frustration and cynicism about the motives of elected officials (Bronfenbrenner, 1974). However, it is rarely the case that scholars recognize that the validity of their work can be significantly enhanced if it is made more accessible to policy makers and the other people in communities (e.g., parents, teachers) invested in the positive development of infants and children. From a developmental systems perspective (Lerner, 1998; Lewis, 1997), the community is an 'expert system' in regard to the influences on infant development present in specific families, neighbourhoods, and cultural settings.

If scholars can learn to make better use of this wisdom of communities (e.g., see Rogoff, 1998), then the theory–policy connection may be substantially improved. Scholars would act to understand and refine knowledge about the influences identified by the community as important, and the community would better understand, place more value on, and be likely to be more invested in the theory and research of scholars. As such, policy makers, who would be part of this collaborative community, would have the support of their constituency for using such scholarship as a basis for the actions they support. There are several examples that such scholar–community partnerships are in fact feasible (Chibucos & Lerner, 1999; Ralston *et al.*, 1999), and that they result in information congenial to and of growing influence among policy makers (e.g., Engler & Binsfeld, 1998; Chiles, 1999; Kennedy, 1999; Thompson, 1999).

Conclusions

In this chapter, we have introduced you to two American families as they progress through the early years of their children's lives and encounter a patchwork of policies and programmes to help them handle the challenges they encounter. As is evident, the current system is not adequate to promote the development of their children, and of other young children across the nation. But many of the rudiments are in place. Our job, then, is to muster the 'political will' to initiate and sustain the necessary changes in policy, practice, and research. As the National Research Council and Institute of Medicine assert,

The charge to society is to blend the skepticism of a scientist, the passion of an advocate, the pragmatism of a policy maker, the creativity of a practitioner, and the devotion of a parent—and to use existing knowledge to ensure both a decent quality of life for all of our children and a productive future for the nation. (National Research Council and Institute of Medicine, 2000, p. 15).

Responsibility for this action rests with all of us.

References

Abel, E. L. (1989). *Fetal alcohol syndrome: fetal alcohol effects*. New York: Plenum Press.

Abramson, L., Seligman, M. E. P., & Teasdale, J. (1978). Learned helplessness in humans. Critique and reformulation. *Journal of Abnormal Psychology*, 87, 49–74.

Abt Associates. (1996). National Evaluation of Family Support Programs: Design Report. Cambridge, MA: Author.

Acredolo, L. P. & Goodwyn, S. W. (1990). Sign language in babies: The significance of symbolic gesturing for understanding language development. In R. Vasta (ed.), *Annals of child development*, Vol. 7, pp. 1–42. London: Jessica Kingsley.

Adolph, K. E. (1997). Learning in the development of infant locomotion. *Monographs of the Society for Research in Child Development*, 62, (3, Serial No. 251).

Ainsworth, M. D. S. (1969). Object relationships, dependency, and attachment: A theoretical review of the infant-mother relationship. *Child Development*, 40, 969–1026.

Ainsworth, M. D. S., Bell, S. M., & Stayton, D. J. (1974). Infant-mother attachment and social development: 'Socialisation' as a product of reciprocal responsiveness to signals. In M. P. M. Richards (ed.), *The integration of a child into a social world*, pp. 99–135. London: Cambridge University Press.

Ainsworth, M. D. S., Blehar, Waters, E., & Wall. S. (1978). *Patterns of attachment: A psychological study of the strange situation*. Hillsdale, NJ: Erlbaum.

Aitken, S. & Bower, T. G. R. (1982). Intersensory substitution in the blind. *Journal of Experimental Child Psychology*, 33, 309–323.

Akhtar, N. & Tomasello, M. (1996). Two-year-olds learn words for absent objects and actions. *British Journal of Developmental Psychology*, 14, 79–93.

Aldridge, M. A., Braga, E. S., Walton, G. E., & Bower, T. G. R. (1999). The intermodal representation of speech in newborns. *Developmental Science*, 2, 42–46.

Alessandri, S., Bendersky, M., & Lewis, M. (1998). Cognitive functioning in 8-to-18-month-old drug exposed infants. *Developmental Psychology*, 34, 565–573.

Alessandri, S. M., Sullivan, M. W., & Lewis, M. (1990). Violation of expectancy and frustration in early infancy. *Developmental Psychology*, 26, 738–744.

Anand, K. J. S. & Hickey, P. R. (1987). Pain and its effects in the human neonate and fetus. *New England Journal of Medicine*, 317, 1321–1329.

Arterberry, M. A. & Bornstein, M. H. (2001). Three-month-old infants' categorization of animals and vehicles based on static and dynamic attributes. *Journal of Experimental Child Psychology* (in press).

Bahrick, L. E. & Pickens, J. N. (1988). Classification of bimodal English and Spanish language passages by infants. *Infant Behavior and Development*, **11**, 277–296.

Baillargeon, R. (1987). Object permanence in 3.5- and 4.5-month-old infants. *Developmental Psychology*, **23**, 655–664.

Baillargeon, R. (1993). The object concept revisited: New directions in the investigation of infants' physical knowledge. In C. Granrud (ed.), *Visual perception and cognition in infancy*. Hillsdale, NJ: Lawrence Earlbaum.

Baillargeon, R. (1999). Young infants' expectations about hidden objects: A reply to three challenges. *Developmental Science*, **2**, 115–132.

Baillargeon, R., & DeVos, J. (1991). Object permanence in young infants: Further evidence. *Child Development*, **62**, 1227–1246.

Bakeman, R. & Gottman, J. (1989). *Observing interaction: An introduction to sequential analysis*. New York: Cambridge University Press

Baldwin, D. A. (1991). Infants' contribution to the achievement of joint reference. *Child Development*, **62**, 875–890.

Baldwin, D. A. & Moses, L. J. (1996). The ontogeny of social information gathering. *Child Development*, **67**, 1915–1939.

Ball, W. & Tronick, E. (1971). Infant responses to impending collision: Optical and real. *Science*, **171**, 818–820.

Banks, M. S. & Salapatek, P. (1981). Infant pattern vision: A new approach based on the contrast sensitivity function. *Journal of Experimental Child Psychology*, **31**, 1–45.

Barille, Armstrong, E. S., & Bower, T. G. R. (1999). Novelty and frequency as determinants of newborn preference. *Developmental Science*, **2**, 47–52.

Barker, D. J. P. (ed.). (1992). *Fetal and infant origins of adult disease*. London: BMJ.

Barnett, W. S. (1985). Benefit-cost analysis of the Perry Preschool program and its long-term effects. *Educational Evaluation and Policy Analysis*, **7**, 387–414.

Barnett, W. S. (1995). Long-term effects of early childhood programs on cognitive and school outcomes. *Future of Children*, **5**, 25–50.

Baron-Cohen, S., Baldwin, D. A., & Crowson, M. (1997). Do children with autism use the speaker's direction of gaze strategy to crack the code of language? *Child Development*, **68**, 48–57.

Barrera, M. & Maurer, D. (1981). The perception of facial expressions by the three-month-old. *Child Development*, **52**, 203–206.

Barrera, M. E. & Maurer, D. (1981a). Discrimination of strangers by the three-month-old. *Child Development*, **52**, 558–563.

Barrera, M. E. & Maurer, D. (1981b). The perception of facial expressions by the three-month-old. *Child Development*, **52**, 203–206.

Barrera, M. E. & Maurer, D. (1981c). Recognition of mother's photographed face by the three-month-old infant. *Child Development*, **52**, 714–716.

Barrett, K. (1995). A functionalist approach to shame and guilt. In J. Tangney & K. Fischer (eds), *Self-conscious emotions*, pp. 25–63. New York: Guilford.

Bates, E. (1979). *The emergence of symbols: Cognition and communication in infancy*. New York: Academic Press.

Bates, J. E. (1983). Issues in the assessment of difficult temperament: A reply to Thomas, Chess, and Korn. *Merrill Palmer Quarterly*, **29**, 89–97.

Bates, J. E. (2000). Temperament as an emotion construct. In M. Lewis and J. M. Haviland-Jones (eds), *Handbook of emotions*, (2nd edn), pp. 382–396. New York: Guilford Press.

Bates, J. E., Bennett-Freeland, C. A., & Lounsburg, M. L. (1979). Measurement of infant difficulties. *Child Development*, **50**, 794–803.

Bauer, P. J. & Hertsgaard, L. A. (1993). Increasing steps in recall of events: Factors facilitating immediate and long-term memory in 13.5-and-16.5-month old infants. *Child Development*, **64**, 1204–1223.

Bayley, N. (1969). *Manual for the Bayley Scales of infant development*. New York: Psychological Corporation.

Bayley, N. (1993). *Bayley scales of infant development*, (2nd edn). New York: Psychological Corporation.

Beck, A. T. (1979). *Cognitive therapy and the emotional disorders*. New York: Times Mirror.

Beckwith, L. (1971). Relationships between infants vocalizations and their mothers' behaviors. *Merrill Palmer Quarterly*, **17**, 211–226.

Bee, H. L., Van Egeren, L. F., Streissguth, A. P., Nyman, B. A., & Leckie, M. S. (1969). Social class differences in maternal teaching strategies and speech patterns. *Developmental Psychology*, **1**, 726–734.

Bendersky, M. & Lewis, M. (1986). The impact of birth order on mother–infant interactions in preterm and sick infants. *Journal of Development and Behavioral Pediatrics*, **7**, 242–246.

Bendersky, M. & Lewis, M. (1998). Prenatal cocaine exposure and impulse control at 2 years. *Annals of the New York Academy of Sciences*, **846**, 365–367.

Bendersky, M., Alessandri, S. M., Sullivan, M. W., & Lewis, M. (1995). Measuring the effects of prenatal cocaine exposure. In M. Lewis & M. Bendersky (eds), *Mothers, babies, and cocaine: The role of toxins in development*, pp. 163–178. Hillsdale, NJ: Erlbaum.

Bernstein, N. (1967). *The coordination and regulation of movements*. Oxford: Pergamon.

Berscheid, E. & Walster, E. (1974). Physical attractiveness. In L. Berkowitz (ed.), *Advances in experimental social psychology*, pp. 157–215. New York: Academic Press.

Bertalanffy, L. V. (1975). *Perspectives on general system theory*. New York: Braziller.

Bertenthal, B. I. & Clifton, R. K. (1998). Perception and action. In D. Kuhn & R. S. Siegler (eds), W. Damon (Series ed.), *Handbook of child psychology*: Vol. 2. *Cognition, perception, and language*, pp. 51–102. New York: Wiley.

Bertenthal, B. I. & Fischer, K. W. (1978). Development of self-recognition in the infant. *Developmental Psychology*, **14**, 44–50.

Bertenthal, B. I. & von Hofsten, C. (1998). Eye, head, and trunk control: The foundation for manual development. *Neuroscience and Biobehavioral Reviews*, **22**, 515–520.

Bertoncini, J., Bijeljac-Babic, R., Blumstein, S. E., & Mehler, J. (1987). Discrimination in neonates of very short CV's. *Journal of the Acoustical Society of America*, **82**, 31–37.

Besharov, D. & Germanis, P. (2000). Welfare reform—four years later. *The Public Interest*, Issue **140**, 17–35.

Best, C. T. (1995). Learning to perceive the sound patterns of English. In C. Rovee-Collier & L. P. Lipsitt (eds), *Advances in Infancy Research*, Vol. 9, pp. 217–304. Norwood, NJ: Ablex.

Best, C. T., McRoberts, G. W., & Sithole, N. M. (1988). Examination of the perceptual re-organization for nonnative speech contrasts: Zulu click discrimination by English-speaking adults and infants. *Journal of Experimental Psychology: Human Perception and Performance*, **14**, 345–360.

Best, C. T., Lafleur, R., & McRoberts, G. W. (1995). Divergent developmental patterns for infants' perception of two non-native contrasts. *Infant Behavior and Development*, **18**, 339–350.

Bigelow, A. E. (1998). Infants' sensitivity to familiar imperfect contingencies in social interaction. *Infant Behavior and Development*, **21**, 149–162.

Bigelow, A. E., Maclean, B. K., & MacDonald, D. (1996). Infants' response to live and replay interactions with self and mother. *Merril Palmer Quarterly*, **42**, 596–611.

Binet, A. & Simon, T. (1916). *The development of intelligence in children* (E. S. Kite, Trans.). Baltimore, MD: Williams & Wilkins.

Bischof-Kohler, D. (1991). The development of empathy in infants. In M. E. Lamb & H. Keller (eds), *Infant development: perspectives from German-speaking countries*, pp. 245–273. Hillsdale, NJ: Lawrence Erlbaum.

Blakemore, C. & Cooper, G. F. (1970). Development of the brain depends on the visual environment. *Nature*, **228**, 477–478.

Blass, E. M. & Shah, A. (1995). Pain-reducing properties of sucrose in human newborns. *Chemical Senses.* **20**, 29–35.

Bloom, L. (1973). *One word at a time: The use of single-word utterances before syntax.* The Hague: Mouton.

Bloom, P. (2000). *How children learn the meanings of words.* Cambridge, MA: MIT Press.

Blum, B. B. & Berrey, E. C. (1999). *Executive summary: Welfare research perspectives: Past, present, and future.* New York: National Center for Children in Poverty.

Bomba, P. C. & Siqueland, E. R. (1983). The nature and structure of infant form categories. *Journal of Experimental Child Psychology*, **35**, 294–328.

Bonvillian, J., Orlansky, M.D., & Novack, L. L. (1983). Developmental milestones: Sign language acquisition and motor development. *Child Development*, **54**, 1435–1445.

Bornstein, M. H. (1984). A descriptive taxonomy of psychological categories used by infants. In C. Sophian (ed.), *Origins of cognitive skills*, pp. 313–338. Hillsdale, NJ: Erlbaum.

Bornstein, M. H. (2001). Parenting infants. In M. H. Bornstein (ed.), *Handbook of parenting*, (2nd edn), Vol. 1, pp. 3–43. Mahwah, NJ: Lawrence Erlbaum.

Bornstein, M. H. & Sigman, M. D. (1986). Continuity in mental development from infancy. *Child Development*, **57**, 251–274.

Bornstein, M. H. & Suess, P. E. (2000). Physiological self-regulation and information processing in infancy: Cardiac vagal tone and habituation. *Child Development*, **71**, 273–287.

Bornstein, M. H. & Tamis-LeMonda, C. S. (1990). Activities and interactions of mothers and their firstborn infants in the first six months of life: stability, continuity, covariation, correspondance, and prediction. *Child Development*, **61**, 1206–1217.

Bornstein, M. H., Miyake, K., & Tamis-LeMonda, C. (1985–1986). A cross-national study of mother and infant activities and interactions: Some preliminary comparisons between Japan and the United States. *Annual Report of the Research and Clinical Center for Child Development*, 1–12. Sapporo, Japan: Hokkaido University.

Bornstein, M. H., Gaugran, J. M., & Homel, P. (1986). Infant temperament: Theory, tradition, critique, and new assessments. In C. Izard, & P. Read (eds), *Measuring emotions in infants and children*, Vol. 2: *Cambridge studies in social and emotional development*, pp. 172–199. New York: Cambridge University Press.

Bornstein, M. H., Toda, S., Azuma, H., Tamis-LeMonda, C. S., & Ogino, M. (1990). Mothers and infant activity and interaction in Japan and the United States: II. A comparative microanalysis of naturalistic interactions focused on the organization of infant attention. *International Journal of Behavioral Development*, **13**, 289–308.

Bornstein, M. H., Tamis-LeMonda, C. S., Tal, J., Ludemann, P., Toda, S., Rahn, C. W., Pecheux, M. G., Azuma, H., & Vardi, D. (1992). Maternal responsiveness to infants in three societies: the United States, France, and Japan. *Child Development*, **63**, 808–821.

Bornstein, M. H., Haynes, O. M., O'Reilly, A. W., & Painter, K. (1996). Solitary and collaborative pretense play in early childhood: Sources of individual variation in the development of representational competence. *Child Development*, **67**, 2910–2929.

Bornstein, M. H., Haynes, O. M., Pascual, L., Painter, K. M., & Galperín, C. (1999). Play in two societies: Pervasiveness of process, specificity of structure. *Child Development*, **70**, 317–331.

Bosch, L. & Sebastián-Gallés, N. (1997). Native-language recognition abilities in 4-month-old infants from monolingual and bilingual environments. *Cogniton*, **65**, 33–69.

Bott, E. (1957). *Family and social network*. London: Tavistock Institute of Human Relations.

Bower, T. G. R. (1966). The visual world of infants. *Scientific American*, **215**, 2–10.

Bower, T. G. R. (1982). *Development in infancy*, (2nd edn). San Francisco: WH Freeman.

Bower, T. G. R. & Paterson, J. G. (1972). Stages in the development of the object concept. *Cognition*, **1**, 47–55.

Bower, T. G. R. & Wishart, J. G. (1972). The effects of motor skill on object permanence. *Cognition*, **1**, 28–35.

Bower, T. G. R., Broughton, J. M., & Moore, M. K. (1970a). The coordination of vision and touch in infancy. *Perception and Psychophysics*, **8**, 51–53.

Bower, T. G. R., Broughton, J. M., & Moore, M. K. (1970b). Infant responses to approaching objects: an indicator of responses to distal variables. *Perception and Psychophysics*, **9**, 193–196.

Bowlby, J. (1951). *Maternal care and mental health*. Geneva: World Health Organisation.

Bowlby, J. (1969). *Attachment and loss*: Vol. 1. *Attachment*. New York: Basic Books.

Bowlby, J. (1973). *Attachment and loss*: Vol. 2: *Separation, anxiety, and anger*. New York: Basic.

Bowlby, J. (1982). *Attachment and loss*, Vol. 1. (2nd edn). New York: Basic

Boyle, C. A. Decoufle, P., & Yeargen-Allsopp. M. (1994). Prevalence and health impact of developmental disabilities in US children. *Pediatrics*, **93**, 399–403.

de Boysson-Bardies, B., Vihman, M. M., Rough-Hellichius, L., Duran, C., Landberg, I., & Arao, F. (1992). Material evidence of infant selection from the target language: A cross-linguistic phonetic study. In C. Ferguson, L. Menn, & C. Stoel-Gammon (eds), *Phonological development: Models, research, implications*, pp. 369–391. Timonium, MD: York Press.

Brandt, I. (1986). Patterns of early neurological development. In F. Falkner & J. M. Tanner (eds), *Human growth: A comprehensive treatise* (2nd edn), pp. 469–518.

Braungart, J. M. & Stifter, C. A. (1991). Regulation of negative reactivity during the strange situation: Temperament and attachment in 12-month-old infants. *Infant Behavior and Development*, **14**, 349–364.

Braungart-Riker, J., Garwood, M. M., Powers, B. P., & Notaro, P. C. (1998). Infant affect and affect regulation during the still-face paradigm with mothers and fathers: The role of infant characteristics and parental sensitivity. *Developmental Psychology*, **34**, 1428–1437.

Brazelton, T. B. (1984). *Neonatal behavioral assessment scale*. Philadelphia: Spastics International.

Bremner, J. G. (1994). *Infancy*. (2nd edn). Oxford: Blackwell Science.

Brent, M. R. (1997). Toward a unified model of lexical acquisition and lexical access. *Journal of Psycholinguistic Research*, **26**, 363–375.

Bresson, F., Maury, L., Le Bornie, G. P., & de Schonen, S. (1977). Reaching in infants. *Neuropsychologia*, **15**, 311–320.

Bridges, K. M. B. (1932). Emotional development in early infancy. *Child Development*, **3**, 324–334.

Bronfenbrenner, U. (1974). Developmental research, public policy, and the ecology of childhood. *Child Development*, **45**, 1–5.

Bronfenbrenner, U. (1979). *The ecology of human development: Experiments by nature and design*. Cambridge, MA: Harvard University Press.

Bronfenbrenner, U. & Morris, P.A. (1998). The ecology of developmental processes. In R. M. Lerner (ed.), *Theoretical models of human development. Volume 1* of the *Handbook of child psychology*, (5th edn), pp. 993–1028. Editor-in-chief: W. Damon. New York: Wiley.

Brooks-Gunn, J., Gross, R. T., Kraemer, H. C., Spiker, D., & Shapiro, S. (1992). Enhancing the cognitive outcomes of low birth weight, premature infants: For whom is the intervention most effective? *Pediatrics*, **89**, 1209–1215.

Brooks-Gunn, J., McCormick, M.C., Sharpiro, S., Benasich, A.A., and Black, G.W. (1994). The effects of early education intervention on maternal employment, public assistance, and health insurance: The infant health and development program. *American Journal of Public Health*, 84, 924–930.

Bruner, J. (1972). Nature and uses of immaturity. *American Psychologist*, **27**, 687–708.

Bruner, J. S. (1971). The growth and structure of skill. In K. J. Connolly (ed.), *Motor skills in infancy*. New York: Academic Press.

Bruner, J. & Ratner, N. (1978). Games, social exchange and the acquisition of language. *Journal of Child Language*, **5**, 391–401.

Bruner, J. S., Goodnow, J. J., & Austin, G. A. (1956). *A study of thinking*. New York: Wiley.

Bruner, J. S., Olver, R. R., & Greenfield, P. M. (1966). *Studies in cognitive growth*. New York: Wiley.

Bryant, D. & Maxwell, K. (1997). The effectiveness of early intervention for disadvantaged children. In M. Guralnick (ed.), *The effectiveness of early intervention*, pp. 23–46. Baltimore: Brookes Publishing.

Budwig, N., Strage, A., & Bamberg, M. (1986). The construction of joint activities with an age-mate: the transition from caregiver-child to peer play. In J. Cook-Gumperz, W. Corsaro, & J. Streeck (eds), *Children's worlds and children's language*, pp. 83–107. Berlin: Walter de Gruyter & Co.

Bullock, D. & Grossberg, S. (1988). Neural dynamics of planned arm movements: Emergent invariants and speed-accuracy properties during trajectory formation. *Psychological Review*, **95**, 49–90.

Burchinal, M.R., Campbell, F.A., Bryant, D.M., Wasik, B.H., & Ramey, C.T. (1997). Early intervention and mediating processes in cognitive performance of children of low-income African American families. *Child Development*, **68**, 935–954.

Burnham, D. (1993). Visual recognition of mother by young infants: Facilitation by speech. *Perception*, **22**, 1133–1153.

Bushnell, I. W. R. (2001). Mother's face recognition in newborn infants: Learning and memory. *Infant and Child Development*, **10**, 67–74.

Bushnell, E. W. & Boudreau, J. P. (1993). Motor development and the mind: The potential role of motor abilities as a determinant of aspects of perceptual development. *Child Development*, **64**, 1005–1021.

Bushnell, I. W. R., Sai, F., & Mullin, J. T. (1989). Neonatal recognition of the mother's face. *British Journal of Developmental Psychology*, **7**, 3–15.

Buss, A. H. (1980). *Self-consciousness and social anxiety*. San Francisco: W. H. Freeman.

Butterworth, G. (1981). Structure of the mind in human infancy. *Advances in Infancy Research*, **2**, 1–29.

Butterworth, G. & Grover, L. (1988). The origins of referential communication in human infancy. In L. Weiskrantz (ed.), *Thought without language*, pp. 5–24. Oxford: Clarendon Press.

Cairns, P., Shillcock, R., Chater, N., & Levy, J. (1997). Bootstrapping word boundaries: A bottom-up corpus-based approach to speech segmentation. *Cognitive Psychology*, **33**, 111–153.

Calkins, S. D., Fox, N. A., & Marshall, T. R. (1996). Behavioral and physiological antecedents of inhibited and uninhibited behavior. *Child Development*, **67**, 523–540.

Campbell, F.A. & Ramey, C.T. (1994). Effects of early intervention on intellectual and academic achievement: A follow-up study of children from low-income families. *Child Development*, **65**, 684–698.

Campbell, F.A., Pungello, E., Burchinal, M., & Ramey, C.T. (2001). The growth of competence: Intellectual and academic growth curves from an educational experiment. *Developmental Psychology*, **37**, 231–242.

Campos, J. J. & Stenberg, C. R. (1981). Perception, appraisal, and emotion: The onset of social referencing. In: M. E. Lamb, & L. R. Sherrod (eds.), *Infant social cognition: Empirical and theoretical considerations*, pp. 273–314. Hillsdale, NJ: Erlbaum.

Campos, J. J., Anderson, D. I., Barbu-Roth, M. A., Hubbard, E. M., Hertenstein, M. J., & Witherington, D. (2000). Travel broadens the mind. *Infancy*, **1**, 149–219.

Cantor, D., Kerwin, J., Levin, K., Heltemes, S., & Becher, D. (1995). *The impact of the family and medical leave act: A survey of employers*. Rockville, MD: Westat.

Carey, W. B. (1970). A simplified method for measuring infant temperament. *Journal of Pediatrics*, **77**, 188–194.

Carey, W. B. & McDevitt, S. C. (1978). The measurement of temperament in 3–7-year-old children. *Journal of Child Psychology and Psychiatry*, **19**, 245–253.

Carlson, B. M. (1994). *Human embryology and developmental biology*. St Louis: Mosby.

Carmichael, L. (1970). Onset and early development of behavior. In P. Mussen (ed.), *Carmichael's manual of child psychology*, pp. 447–563. New York: Wiley.

Carnegie Task Force on Meeting the Needs of Young Children. (1994). *Starting points: Meeting the needs of our youngest children*. New York: Carnegie Corporation.

Caron, R. F., Caron, A. T., & Myers, R. S. (1982). Abstraction of invariant face expressions in infancy. *Child Development*, 53, 1008–1015.

Caron, R. F., Caron, A. J., & Myers, R. S. (1985). Do infants see emotional expressions in static faces? *Child Development*, 56, 1552–1560.

Carpenter, M., Nagell, K., & Tomasello, M. (1998). Social cognition, joint attention, and communicative competence from 9 to 15 months of age. *Monographs of the Society for Research in Child Development*, 64 (4, No. 255).

Carter, A. S., Mayes, L. C., & Pajer, K. A. (1990). The role of dyadic affect in play and infant sex in predicting infant response to the still-face situation. *Child Development*, 61, 764–773.

Casselli, M., Bares, E., Casadio, P., & Fenson, J. (1995). A cross-linguistic study of early lexical development. *Cognitive Development*, 10, 159–199.

Casto, G. & Lewis, A. (1984). Parent involvement in infant and preschool programs. *Division of Early Childhood*, 9, 49–56.

Cattell, J. M. (1890). Mental tests and measurements. *Mind*, 15, 373–380.

Caviness, V. S., Kennedy, D. N., Bates, J. F., & Makris, N. (1996). The developing human brain: A morphometiric profile. In: R. W. Thatcher, G. R. Lyon, J. Rumsey, & N. Krasnegor (eds), *Developmental Neuroimaging*, pp. 3–14. San Diego: Academic Press.

Cernack, J. M. & Porter, R. H. (1985). Recognition of maternal axillary odors by infants. *Child Development*, 56, 1593–1598.

Chafel, J. A. (1992). Funding Head Start: What are the issues? *American Journal of Orthopsychiatry*, 62, 9–21.

Changeux, J. P. (1985). *Neuronal man: The biology of mind*. (Garey, Trans.). New York: Pantheon.

Charlesworth, W. R. (1969). The role of surprise in cognitive development. In D. Elkino & J. H. Flavell (eds), *Studies in cognitive development: Essays in honor of Jean Piaget*, pp. 257–314. London: Oxford University Press.

Cheney, D. L. & Seyfarth, R. M. (1990). *How monkeys see the world: Inside the mind of another species*. Chicago, IL: Chicago University Press.

Chibucos, T. & Lerner, R. M. (eds). (1999). *Serving children and families through community-university partnerships: Success stories*. Norwell, MA: Kluwer Academic Publishers.

Chick, G. & Barnett, L. A. (1995). Children's play and adult leisure. In A. D. Pellegrini (ed.), *The future of play theory*, pp. 45–69. Albany, NY: State University of New York Press.

Chiles, L. (1999). Foreword. In P. Ralston, R. M. Lerner, A. K. Mullis, C. Simerly, & J. Murray (eds), *Social change, public policy, and community collaboration: Training human development professionals for the twenty-first century*, pp. xi–xii). Norwell, MA: Kluwer.

Christophe, A. & Morton, J. (1998). Is Dutch native English? Linguistic analysis by 2-month-olds. *Developmental Science*, 1, 215–219.

Church, K. (1987). Phonological parsing and lexical retrieval. *Cognition*, **25**, 53–69.

Clifton, R. K., Morrongiello, B. A., Kulig, J. W., & Dowd, J. M. (1981). Newborns orientation towards sound: Possible implications for cortical development. *Child Development*, **53**, 833–838.

Coghill, G. E. (1929). *Anatomy and the problem of behavior*. Cambridge: Cambridge University Press.

Cohen, L. B. & Oakes, L. M. (1993). How infants perceive a simple causal event. *Developmental Psychology*, **29**, 421–433.

Cohn, J. F. & Tronick, E. Z. (1987). Mother–infant face-to-face interaction: The sequence of dyadic states at 3, 6, and 9 months. *Developmental Psychology*, **23**, 68–77.

Collis, G. M. & Schaffer, H. R. (1975). Synchronization of visual attention in mother-infant pairs. *Journal of Child Psychology and Psychiatry*, **16**, 315–320.

Commission on Family and Medical Leave (1996). *A workable balance: Report to Congress on family and medical leave policies*. Washington, DC: US Department of Labor, Women's Bureau.

Cooper, R. P. & Aslin, R. N. (1990). Preferences for infant-directed speech in the first month after birth. *Child Development*, **61**, 1584–1595.

Cornell, E. H. (1974). Infants' discrimination of photographs of faces following redundant presentations. *Journal of Experimental Child Psychology*, **18**, 98–106.

Cost, Quality, and Outcomes Study Team (1995). *Cost, quality, and child outcomes in child care centers, public report*, (2nd edn). Denver, CO: Economics Department, University of Colorado at Denver.

Cost, Quality, and Outcomes Study Team (1999). *The children of the Cost, Quality, and Outcomes Study Team go to school: Executive Summary*. Available HTTP: www.fpg.unc.edu/ ~NCEDL/PAGES/cqes.htm.

Courage, M. L. & Adams, R. J. (1990). Visual acuity assessment from birth to three years using the acuity card procedures: Cross-sectional and longitudinal samples. *Optometry and Vision Science*, **67**, 713–718.

Cowan, P. A., Cowan, C. P., Schulz, M. S., & Heming, G. (1994). Prebirth to preschool family factors in children's adaption to kindergarten. In R. D. Parke & S. G. Kellam (eds), *Exploring family relationships with other social contexts*, pp. 75–114. Hillsdale, NJ: Erlbaum.

Crook, C. K. (1978). Taste perception in the newborn infant. *Infant Behavior and Development*, **1**, 52–69.

Currie, J. (2000). *Early childhood intervention programs: What do we know?* JCPR working paper #169. Chicago: Joint Center for Poverty Research.

Currie, J. *Early childhood intervention programs: What do we know?* Commissioned paper for the Brookings Roundtable on Children [On-line]. Available: www.jcpr.org/conferences/childhoodbriefing.html

Cutler, A. & Carter, D. M. (1987). The predominance of strong initial syllables in the English vocabulary. *Computer Speech and Language*, **2**, 133–142.

Cutler, A. & Norris, D. G. (1988). The role of strong syllables in segmentation for lexical access. *Journal of Experimental Psychology: Human Perception and Performance*, **14**, 113–121.

Dalaker, J. & Proctor, B. D. (2000). *Poverty in the United States: 1999*. Current Population Reports, Series P60–210. Washington, DC: U.S. Government Printing Office.

Dale, N. (1989). Pretend play with mothers and siblings: relations between early performance and partners. *Journal of Child Psychiatry*, 30, 751–759.

Damast, A. M., Tamis-LeMonda, C. S., & Bornstein, M. H. (1996). Mother–child play: Sequential interactions and the relation between maternal beliefs and behaviors. *Child Development*, 67, 1752–1766.

Damon, W. (1983). *Social and personality development: infancy through adolescence*. New York: W.W. Norton & Company.

Dannemiller, J. L. & Stephens, B. R. (1988). A critical test of infant pattern preference models. *Child Development*, 59, 210–216.

Danziger, S. (2000). *Approaching the limit: Early lessons from welfare reform*. Paper prepared for the Conference 'Rural Dimensions of Welfare Reform,' Sponsored by the Joint Center for Poverty Research, Northwestern University/University of Chicago, May 2000.

Darlington, R. B., Royce, J. M., Snipper, A. S., Murray, H. W., & Lazar I. (1980). Preschool programs and later school competence of children from low-income families. *Science*, 208, 202–204.

Darwin, C. (1877). A biographical sketch of an infants. In A. Slater & D. Muir (eds.), *The Blackwell reader in developmental psychology*, pp. 17–26. Massachusetts and Oxford: Blackwell Publishers.

Darwin, C. R. (1965). *The expression of emotions in man and animals*. Chicago: University of Chicago Press. (Original edition, 1872.)

Davies, M. & Jacobs, F. (1994). Considering race, class, and gender in child and family policy. In F. Jacobs & M. Davies (eds), *More than kissing babies? Current child and family policy in the United States*, pp. 265–276. Westport, CT: Auburn House.

De Snoo, K. (1937). Das trinkende Kind im Uterus. *Monatsschr. Geburtsh. Gynaekol.*, 105, 88–97.

DeCasper, A. J. & Fifer, W. P. (1980). Of human bonding: Newborns prefer their mothers' voices. *Science*, 208, 1174–1176.

DeCasper, A. J. & Spence, M. J. (1986). Prenatal maternal speech influences newborns' perception of speech sounds. *Infant Behavior and Development*, 9, 133–150.

Dehaene-Lambertz, G. & Houston, D. M. (1998). Faster orientation latencies toward native language in two-month-olds. *Language and Speech*, 41, 21–43.

DeLoache, J. S., Pierroutsakos, S. L., Uttal, D. H., Rosengren, K. S., & Gottlieb, A. (1998). Grasping the nature of pictures. *Psychological Science*, 9, 205–210.

Dennis, W. (1973). *Children of the creche*. New York: Appleton-Century-Crofts.

Derbyshire, S. W. G. & Furedi, A. (1996). 'Fetal pain' is a misnomer. *British Medical Journal*, 313, 795.

Deruelle, C. & de Schonen, S. (1991). Hemispheric asymmetry in visual pattern processing in infancy. *Brain and Cognition*, 16, 151–179.

Deutsch, M. (1967). *The disadvantaged child*. New York: Basic Books.

DeWolf, M. S. & Ijzendoorn, M. H. (1997). Sensitivity and attachment: A meta-analysis on parental antecedents of infant attachment. *Child Development*, 64(4), 571–591.

Didow, S. M. & Eckerman, C. O. (1991). *Developments in toddlers' talk with unfamiliar peers*. Presented at Society for Research in Child Development, Seattle: Washington.

Diego, M. A., Jones, N. A., Field, T., & Hernandez-Reif, M. (1999). Aromatherapy reduces anxiety and enhances EEG patterns associated with positive mood and alertness. *International Journal of Neuroscience*, 96, 217–224.

Dion, K. K. (1973). Young children's stereotyping of facial attractiveness. *Developmental Psychology*, **9**, 183–188.

Dirks, J. & Gibson, E. (1977). Infants' perception of similarity between live people and their photographs. *Child Development*, **48**, 124–130.

Drachman, D. B. & Coulombre, A. J. (1962). Experimental clubfoot and arthrogyposis multiplex congenita. *Lancet*, **ii**, 523–526.

Drachman, D. B. & Sokoloff, L. (1966). The role of movement in embryonic joint development. *Developmental Biology*, **14**, 401–420.

Dunkeld, J. & Bower, T. G. R. (1980). Infant response to impending optical collision. *Perception*, **9**, 549–554.

Dunn, J. (1987). Understanding feelings: the early stages. In J. Bruner & H. Haste (eds), *Making sense: The child's construction of the world*, pp. 26–40. London: Methuen & Co. Ltd.

Dunn, J. & Dale, N. (1984). Collaboration in joint pretend. In I. Bretherton (ed.), *Symbolic play: the development of understanding*, pp. 131–158). New York: Academic Press.

Dunn, J. & Kendrick, C. (1979). Interaction between young siblings in the context of family relationships. In M. Lewis & L. Rosenblum (eds), *The child and its family: The genesis of behavior*, 2, pp. 143–168. New York: Plenum.

Dunn, J. & Wooding, C. (1977). Play in the home and its implications for learning. In B. Tizard & D. Harvey (eds), *Biology of play*, pp. 45–58. London: Heinemann.

Dweck, C. S. & Leggett, E. L. (1988). A social cognitive approach to motivation and personality. *Psychological Review*, **95**, 256–273.

Easterbrook, M. A., Kisilevsky, B. S., Hains, S. M. J., & Muir, D. W. (1999a). Faceness or complexity: Evidence from newborn visual tracking of facelike stimuli. *Infant Behavior and Development*, **22**, 17–35.

Easterbrook, M. A., Kisilevsky, B. S., Muir, D. W., & Laplante, D. P. (1999b). Newborns discriminate schematic faces from scrambled faces. *Canadian Journal of Experimental Psychology*, **53**, 231–241.

Echols, C. H., Crowhurst, M. J., & Childers, J. B. (1997). Perception of rhythmic units in speech by infants and adults. *Journal of Memory and Language*, **36**, 202–225.

Eckerman, C. O. & Didow, S. M. (1996). Nonverbal imitation and toddlers' mastery of verbal means of achieving coordinated action. *Developmental Psychology*, **32**, 141–152.

Eckerman, C. O., Whatley, J. L., & Kutz, S. L. (1975). Growth of social play with peers during the second year of life. *Developmental Psychology*, **11**, 42–49.

Edelman, P. (1997). The worst thing Bill Clinton has done. *The Atlantic Monthly*, **279**(3), 43–58.

Edelman, R. J. & Hampson, S. E. (1981). The recognition of embarrassment. *Personality and Social Psychology Bulletin*, 7, 109–116.

Edwards, C. P. & Lewis, M. (1979). Young children's concepts of social relations: Social functions and social objects. In M. Lewis & L. Rosenblum (eds), *The child and its family: The genesis of behavior*, 2, pp. 245–266. New York: Plenum.

Edwards, C. P. & Whiting, B. B. (1993). Mother, older sibling, and me: The overlapping roles of caregivers and companions in the social world of two- and three-year-olds in Ngeca, Kenya. In K. MacDonald (ed.), *Parent-child play: Descriptions and implications*, pp. 305–329.

Eimas, P. D. (1974). Auditory and linguistic processing of cues for place of articulation by infants. *Perception & Psychophysics*, **16**, 513–521.

Eimas, P. D. (1975). Auditory and phonetic coding of the cues for speech: Discrimination of the [r-l] distinction by young infants. *Perception & Psychophysics*, **18**, 341–347.

Eimas, P. D. (1991). Comment: Some effects of language acquisition on speech perception. In I. G. Mattingly & M. Studdert-Kennedy (eds), *Modularity and the motor theory of speech perception*, pp. 111–116. Hillsdale, NJ: Erlbaum.

Eimas, P. D. & Miller, J. L. (1980a). Contextual effects in infant speech perception. *Science*, **209**, 1140–1141.

Eimas, P. D. & Miller, J. L. (1980b). Discrimination of the information for manner of articulation. *Infant Behavior & Development*, **3**, 367–375.

Eimas, P. D., Siqueland, E. R., Jusczyk, P. W., & Vigorito, J. (1971). Speech perception in infants. *Science*, **171**, 303–306.

Ekman, P. & Friesen, W. V. (1978). *The Facial Action Coding System: A technique for the measurement of facial movement*. Palo Alto, CA: Consulting Psychologists Press.

Elicker, J., England, M., & Sroufe, L. A. (1992). Predicting peer competence and peer relationships in childhood from early parent-child relationships. In R. D. Parke & G. W. Ladd (eds), *Family-peer relationships: Modes of linkage*, pp. 77–106. Hillsdale, NJ: Erlbaum.

Engen, T. & Lipsitt, L. P. (1965). Decrement and recovery of responses to olfactory stimuli in the human neonate. *Journal of Comparative and Physiological Psychology*, **56**, 73–77.

Engler, J. & Binsfeld, C. (1998). The Governor's clergy summit in the City of Detroit. In R. M. Lerner & L. A. K. Simon (eds), *University-community collaborations for the twenty-first century: Outreach scholarship for youth and families*, pp. 451–459. New York: Garland Publishing.

Fagan, III, J. F. (1972). Infants' recognition memory for faces. *Journal of Experimental Child Psychology*, **14**, 453–476.

Fagan, III, J. F. (1976). Infants' recognition of invariant features of faces. *Child Development*, **47**, 627–638.

Fagan, J. W. & McGrath, S. K. (1981). Infant recognition memory and later intelligence. *Intelligence*, **5**, 121–130.

Fagan, J. F. & Singer, L. T. (1979). The role of simple feature differences in infants' recognition of faces. *Infant Behavior and Development*, **2**, 39–45.

Fagot, B. I. & Hagan, R. (1991). Observations of parent reactions to sex-stereotyped behaviors: Age and sex effects. *Child Development*, **62**, 258–271.

Fairbairn, W. R. D. (1952). *An object—relations theory of the personality*. New York. Basic Books.

Family Support America. (n.d.). *About family support*. Available HTTP: www.familysupportamerica.org/content/learning_dir/about_FS.htm.

Fantz, R. L. (1958). Pattern vision in young infants. *Psychological Record*, **8**, 43–47.

Fantz, R. L. (1964). Visual experience in infants: Decreased attention to familiar patterns relative to novel ones. *Science*, **146**, 668–670.

Farah, M. J., Wilson, K. D., Drain, M., & Tanaka, J. N. (1998). What is 'special' about face perception? *Psychological Review*, **105**, 482–498.

Farran, D. C. (1990). Effects of intervention with disadvantaged and disabled children: A decade review. In S. J. Meisels & J. P. Shonkoff (eds), *Handbook of early childhood intervention*, pp. 501–539. New York: Cambridge University Press.

Farver, J. M. & Howes, C. (1993). Cultural differences in American and Mexican mother–child pretend play. *Merrill-Palmer Quarterly*, **39**, 344–358.

Farver, J. M. & Wimbarti, S. (1995). Indonesian children's play with their mothers and older siblings. *Child Development*, **66**, 1493–1503.

Fein, G.G. (1981). Pretend play in childhood: an integrative review. *Child Development*, **52**, 1095–1118.

Feinman, S. (1982). Social referencing in infancy. *Merrill Palmer Quarterly*, **28**, 445–470.

Feinman, S. & Lewis, M. (1983). Social referencing and second order effects in ten-month-old infants. *Child Development*, **54**, 878–887.

Feinman, S., Roberts, D., Hsieh, K., Sawyer, D., & Swanson, D. (1992). A critical review of social referencing in infancy. In S. Feinman (ed.). *Social referencing and the social construction of reality in infancy*, pp. 15–54. New York: Plenum Press.

Feiring, C., Lewis, M., & Starr, M. D. (1984). Indirect effects and infants' reactions to strangers. *Developmental Psychology*, **20**, 485–491.

Feldman, S. & Zaller, J. (1992). The political culture of ambivalence: Ideological responses to the welfare state. *American Journal of Political Science*, **36**, 268–307.

Fenson, L., Dale, P. S., Reznick, J. S., Bates, E., Thal, D.J., & Pethicke, S.J. (1994). Variability in early communicative development. *Monographs of the Society for Research in Child Development*, **59**, **173**.

Ferguson, T. J., Stegge, H., & Damhuis, I. (1991). Children's understanding of guilt and shame. *Child Development*, **62**, 827–839.

Fernald, A. (1985). Four-month-old infants prefer to listen to motherese. *Infant Behavior and Development*, **8**, 181–195.

Fernald, A. (1992). Maternal vocalizations to infants as biologically relevant signals: An evolutionary perspective. In J. H. Barkow, L. Cosmides, & J. Tooby (eds), *The adapted mind: Evolutionary psychology and the generation of culture*, pp. 391–428. Oxford: Oxford University Press.

Fernald, A. (1993). Approval and disapproval: Infant responsiveness to vocal affect in familiar and unfamiliar languages. *Child Development*, **64**, 657–667.

Fernald, A., Taeschner, T., Dunn, J., Papousek, M., Boysson-Bardies, B., & Fukui, I. (1989). A cross-language study of prosodic modifications in mothers' and fathers' speech to preverbal infants. *Journal of Child Language*, **16**, 477–501.

Fernald, A., Pinto, J. P., Swingley, D., Weinberg, A., & McRoberts, G. W. (1998). Rapid gains in speed of verbal processing by infants in the second year. *Psychological Science*, **9**, 72–75.

Fernald, A., Swingley, D., & Pinto, J.P. (2001). When half a word is enough: Infants can recognize spoken words using partial phonetic information. *Child Development*, **72**, 1003–1015.

Field, T. (1984). Early interactions between infants and their postpartum depressed mothers. *Infant Behavior and Development*, **1**, 527–532.

Field, T. M. (1985). Neonatal perception of people: Maturational and individual differences. In T. M. Field & N. A. Fox (eds), *Social perception in young infants*, pp. 31–52. Norwood, NJ: Ablex.

Field, T. & Goldson, E. (1984). Pacifying effects of nonnutritive sucking on term and preterm neonates during heelstick procedures. *Pediatrics*, **74**, 1012–1015.

Field, T. M., Woodson, R., Greenberg, R., & Cohen, O. (1982). Discrimination and imitation of facial expressions by neonates. *Science*, **218**, 179–181.

Field, T. M., Woodson, R. W., Cohen, D., Greenberg, R., Garcia, R., & Collins, K. (1983). Discrimination and imitation of facial expressions by term and preterm neonates. *Infant Behavior and Development*, **6**, 485–489.

Field, T. M., Cohen, D., Garcia, R., & Greenberg, R. (1984). Mother-stranger face discrimination by the newborn. *Infant Behavior and Development*, **7**, 19–25.

Fiese, B. H. (1990). Playful relationships: A contextual analysis of mother-toddler interaction and symbolic play. *Child Development*, **61**, 1648–1656.

Fifer, W. P. & Moon, C. (1989). Psychobiology of newborn auditory preferences. *Seminars in Perinatology*, **13**, 430–433.

Fifer, W. P. & Moon, C. M. (1994). The role of mother's voice in the organization of brain function in the newborn. *Acta Paediatrics Supplement*, **397**, 86–93.

Fitzgerald, M. (1993). Development of pain pathways and mechanisms. In K. J. S. Anand & P. J. McGrath (eds). *Pain research and clinical management*, pp. 19–38, Amsterdam: Elsevier.

Fitzgerald, H. E. & Brackbill, Y. (1976). Classical conditioning in infancy: Development and constraints. *Psychological Bulletin*, **83**, 353–376.

Flavell, J. H. & Miller, P.H. (1998). Social Cognition. In D. Kuhn & R. S. Siegler (eds), *Handbook of child psychology*, Vol. 2: *Cognition, perception, and language* (5th edn), pp. 851–898. (Series ed., W. Damon). New York: Wiley.

Flege, J. E. (1995). Second language speech learning: Theory, findings, and problems. In W. Strange (ed.), *Speech perception and linguistic experience: Theoretical and methodological issues*, pp. 229–273. Timonium, MD: York Press.

Forssberg, H., Stokes, V., & Hirschfeld, H. (1992). Basic mechanisms of human locomotor development. In M. Gunnar & C. Nelson (eds), *Developmental behavioral neuroscience. Minnesota symposia on child psychology*, Vol. 24. Hillsdale, NJ: Erlbaum.

Fox, N. A. (1989). Psychophysiological correlates of emotional reactivity during the first year of life. *Developmental Psychology*, **25**, 364–372.

Fox, N. & Lewis, M. (1983). Cardiac response to speech sounds in pre-term infants. Effects of postnatal illness at three months. *Psychophysiology*, **20**, 481–488.

Fox, N. A. & Porges, S. W. (1985). The relation between neonatal heart period patterns and developmental outcome. *Child Development*, **56**, 28–37.

Fraiberg, S. (1974). Blind infants and their mothers: An examination of the sign system. In M. Lewis & L. A. Rosenblum (eds), *The effect of the infant on its caregiver*, pp. 215–232. New York: John Wiley & Sons.

Frank Porter Graham (2000). Early learning, later success: The Abecedarian study. Executive Summary [On line]. Available: www.fpg.unc.edu/~abc

Frank, M. & Zigler, E.F. (1996). Family leave: A developmental perspective. In E. F. Zigler, S. L. Kagan, & N. W. Hall (eds), *Children, families, and government: Preparing for the twenty-first century*, pp. 117–131. New York: Cambridge University Press.

Frazer, J. (1915). *The golden bough*. New York: Macmillan.

Freud, S. (1948). *The psychopathology of everyday life* (2nd ed). London:Benn.

Freud, S. (1959). Creative writers and daydreaming. In J. Strachey (ed.), *The standard edition of the complete works of Sigmund Freud*, Vol. IX, pp. 143–153.

Freud, A. & Dann, S. (1951). An experiment in group upbringing. In R. Eissler. A. Freud, H. Hartmann, & E. Kris (eds), *The psychoanalytic study of the child*, Vol. 6. New York: International Universities Press.

Friedman, P. (2000). The Earned Income Tax Credit. *Welfare Information Network Issue Note*, 4(4).

Frodi, A., Bridges, L. J., & Grolnick, W. S. (1985). Correlates of mastery-related behavior: a short-term longitudinal study of infants in their second year. *Child Development*, 56, 1291–1298.

Fullard, W., McDevitt, S. C., & Carey, W. B. (1984). Toddler Temperament Scale: For 1–3 year-old children. *Journal of Pediatric Research*, 9, 205–217.

Furstenberg, F., Brooks-Gunn, J., & Morgran, S. P. (1987). *Adolescent mothers in later life*. New York: Cambridge.

Galinsky, E., Howes, C., Kontos, S., & Shinn, M. (1994). *The study of children in family child care and relative child care*. New York: Families and Work Institute.

Gallup, G. G., Jr. (1977). Self-recognition in primates: A comparative approach to the bidirectional properties of consciousness. *American Psychologist*, 32, 329–338.

Galton, F. (1883). *Inquiry into human faculty and its development*. London: Macmillan.

Garber, H. L. (1988). *The Milwaukee Project: Preventing mental retardation in children at risk*. Washington, DC: American Association on Mental Retardation.

Garcia-Coll, C., Kagan, J., & Reznick, J. S. (1984). Behavioral inhibition in young children. *Child Development*, 55, 1005–1019.

Garvey, C. (1990). *Play*. Cambridge, MA: Harvard University Press.

Gaze, R. (1971). Behavioural neural consequences of compound eye formation. *Centre National de Recherche Scientifique Bulletin*, 141, 1–31.

Geldart, S., Maurer, D., & Carney, K. (1999a). Effects of eye size on adults' aesthetic ratings of faces and 5-month-olds' looking times. *Perception*, 28, 361–374.

Geldart, S., Maurer, D., & Henderson, H. (1999b). Effects of the height of the internal features of faces on adults' aesthetic ratings and 5-month-olds' looking times. *Perception*, 28, 839–850.

Gesell, A. (1934). *An atlas of infant behavior*. New Haven, CT: Yale University Press.

Gesell, A. & Ames, L. (1940). The ontogenetic organization of prone behavior in human infancy. *Journal of Genetic Psychology*, 56, 247–263.

Gesell, A. & Thompson, H. (1941). Twins T and C from infancy to adolescence:A biogenetic study of individual differences by the method of co-twin control. *Genetic Psychology Monographys*, 24, 1–99.

Giannakoulopoulos, X., Sepulveda, W., Kourtis, P., Glover, V., & Fisk, N. M. (1994). Fetal plasma cortisol and b-endorphin response to intrauterine needling. *Lancet*, 344, 77–81.

Gibson, E. J. (1988). Exploratory behavior in the development of perceiving, acting, and the acquiring of knowledge. *Annual Review of Psychology*, 39, 1–41.

Gibson, J. G. (1950). *Perception of the visual world*. Boston: Houghton & Mifflin.

Glover, V. & Fisk, N. M. (1996). We don't know; better to err on the safe side from mid-gestation. *British Medical Journal*, 313, 796.

Gogate, L. J., Bahrick, L. E., & Watson, J. D. (2000). A study of multimodal motherese: The role of temporal synchrony between verbal labels and gestures. *Child Development*, 71, 878–894.

Goldfield, E. C. (1995). *Emergent forms: Origins and early development of human action and perception.* New York: Oxford University Press.

Goldfield, E. C., Wolff, P. H., & Schmidt, R. C. (1999a). Dynamics of oral-respiratory coordination in full-term and preterm infants: I. Comparisons at 38–40 weeks postconceptional age. *Developmental Science*, 2, 363–373.

Goldfield, E. C., Wolff, P. H., & Schmidt, R. C. (1999b). Dynamics of oral-respiratory coordination in full-term and preterm infants: II. Continuing effects at 3 months post term. *Developmental Science*, 2, 374–384.

Goldsmith, H. H. (1996). Studying temperament via construction of the Toddler Behavior Assessment Questionnaire. *Child Development*, 67, 218–235.

Gomez, R. L. & Gerken, L. A. (1999). Artificial grammar learning by one-year-olds leads to specific and abstract knowledge. *Cognition*, 70, 109–135.

Göncü, A. (1993). Development of intersubjectivity in social pretend play. *Human Development*, 36, 185–198.

Göncü, A., Mistry, R., & Mosier, C. (1991). *Cultural variations in the play of toddlers.* Paper presented at the Socitey for Research in Child Development, Seattle.

Goodall, Jane. (1988). *In the shadow of man.* San Diego, CA: San Diego State University Press.

Goodman, C. S & Shatz, C. J. (1993). Developmental mechanisms that generate precise patterns of neuronal connectivity. *Cell*, 72, 77–98.

Goodwyn, S. W. & Acredolo, L. P. (1993). Symbolic gesture versus word: Is there a modality advantage for onset of symbol use? *Child Development*, 64, 688–701.

Gordon, D. E. (1993). The inhibitions of pretend play and its implications for development. *Human Development*, 36, 215–234.

Gordon, I. J. Guinagh, B., & Jester, R. E. (1977). The Florida Parent Education Infant and Toddler Programs. In M. C. Day & R. K. Parker (eds.), *The preschool in action: Exploring early childhood programs.* Boston: Allyn & Bacon.

Goren, C. C., Sarty, M., & Wu, P. Y. K. (1975). Visual following and pattern discrimination of face-like stimuli by newborn infants. *Pediatrics*, 56, 544–549.

Gottlieb, G. (1991). Experiential canalization of behavioral development: Theory. *Developmental Psychology*, 27, 4–13.

Gould, S. J. (1992). Heterochrony. In E. F. Keller & E. A. Lloyd (eds). *Keywords in evolutionary biology* pp. 158–165. Cambridge MA: Harvard University Press.

Gould, J. L. & Marler, P. (1987). Learning by instinct. *Scientific American*, 256, 62–73.

Grammar, K. & Thornhill, R. (1994). Human (*Homo sapiens*) facial attractiveness and sexual selection: The role of symmetry and averageness. *Journal of Comparative Psychology*, 108, 233–242.

Grecco, C., Hayne, H., & Rovee-Collier, C. (1990). Roles of function, reminding, and variability in categorization by 3-month-old infants. *Journal of Experimental Psychology : Learning, Memory, and Cognition*, 16, 617–633.

Greenbaum, C. W. & Landau, R. (1977). In P. H. Leiderman. S. R. Tulkin, & A. Rosenfeld (eds), *Culture and infancy: Variations In the human experience.* New York: Academic.

Greenberg, M. T. & Crnic, K. A. (1988). Longitudinal predictors of development status and social interaction in premature and full-term infants at age two. *Child Development*, **59**, 554–570.

Greene, J., Fox, N., & Lewis, M. (1983). The relationship between neonatal characteristics and three month mother–infant interaction in high risk infants. *Child Development*, **54**, 1286–1296.

Gregg, N. M. (1942). Congenital cataracts following German measles in the mother. *Transactions of the Ophthalmological Society of Australia*, **3**, 35.

Grieser, D.I. & Kuhl, P.K. (1988). Maternal speech to infants in a tonal language: Support for universal prosodic features in motherese. *Developmental Psychology*, **24**, 14–20.

Grillner, S. (1985). Neurobiological bases of rhythmic motor acts in vertebrates. *Science*, **228**, 143–149.

Grillner, S., Georgopoulos, A. P., & Jordan, L. M. (1999). Selection and initiation of motor behavior. In P. Stein, S. Grillner, A. Selverston, & D. Stuart (eds), *Neurons, networks, and motor behavior* (pp. 3–19). Cambridge, MA:MIT Press.

Grolnick, W. S., Frodi, A., & Bridges, L. J. (1984). Maternal control style and the mastery motivation of one-year-olds. *Infant Mental Health Journal*, **5**, 72–82.

Groos, K. (1898). *The play of animals*. New York: Appleton.

Gunnar, M. R. (1986). Human developmental psychoneuroendicronology: A review of research on neuroendocrine responses to challenge and threat in infancy and childhood. In M. E. Lamb, A. L. Brown, & B. Rogoff (eds), *Advances in developmental psychology*, Vol. 4, pp. 51–103. Hillsdale, NJ: Erlbaum.

Gunnar, M. R. (1989). Studies of the human infants' adrenocortical response to potentially stressful events. In M. Lewis & J. Worobey (eds), *Infant stress and coping: New directions for child development*, **45**, pp. 3–18. San Francisco: Jossey Bass.

Gunnar, M. R., Tout, K., De Haan, M., Pierce, S., & Stansbury, K. (1997). Temperament, social competence, and adrenocortical activity in preschoolers. *Developmental Psychobiology*, **31**, 65–85.

Guralnick, M. J. (ed.). (1997). *The effectiveness of early intervention*. Baltimore: Brookes Publishing.

Gutelius, M.F., Kirsch, A. D., MacDonald, S., Brooks, M.R., & McErleand, T. (1977). Controlled study of child health supervision: Behavioral results. *Pediatrics*, **60**, 294–304.

Gyomrai-Ludowyk, E. (1963). The analysis of a young concentration camp victim. *Psychoanalytic Study of the Child*, **18**, 484–510.

de Haan, M. & Nelson, C. A. (1997). Recognition of the mother's face by six-month-old infants: A neurobehavioral study. *Child Development*, **68**, 187–210.

de Haan, M. & Nelson, C. A. (1999). Brain activity differentiates face and object processing in 6-month-old infants. *Developmental Psychology*, **35**, 1113–1121.

Haight, W. & Miller, P. J. (1992). The development of everyday pretend play: a longitudinal study of mothers' participation. *Merrill-Palmer Quarterly*, **38**, 331–349.

Hains, S. M. J. & Muir, D. W. (1996a). Infant sensitivity to adult eye direction. *Child Development*, **67**, 1940–1951.

Hains, S. M. J. & Muir, D. W. (1996b). Effects of stimulus contingency in infant-adult interactions. *Infant Behavior and Development*, **19**, 49–61.

Haith, M. M. & Benson, J. B. (1998). Infant cognition. In W. Damon (series ed.) and D. Kuhn & R. Siegler (vol. eds), *Handbook of child psychology*: Vol. 2. *Cognition, perception, and language development*, (5th edn), pp. 199–254. New York: Wiley.

Haith, M. M., Bergman, T., & Moore, M. J. (1977). Eye contact and face scanning in early infancy. *Science*, **198**, 853–855.

Haith, H. M., Hazan, C., & Goodman, G. S. (1988). Expectation and anticipation of dynamic visual events by 3. 5-month-old babies. *Child Development*, **59**, 467–479.

Hall, W. G. & Williams, C. L. (1983). Sucking isn't feeding, or is it? A search for developmental continuities. *Advances in the study of behavior*, Vol. 13, pp. 219–254. New York: Academic Press.

Hanna, E. & Meltzoff, A. N. (1991). *Learning from others in infant daycare: remembering and imitating the actions of another*. Paper presented at the Meeting of the Society for Research in Child Development, Seattle: Washington.

Harlow, H. F. (1958). The nature of love. *American Psychologist*, **13**, 673–685.

Harlow, H. F. (1969). Age-mate or peer affectional system. In D. S. Lehrman, R. A. Hinde, & E. Shaw (eds), *Advances in the study of behavior*, Vol. 2, pp. 333–383. New York: Academic Press.

Harlow, H. & Harlow, M. K. (1965). The affectional systems. In A. M. Schrier, H. F. Harlow, & F. Stollnitz (eds), *Behavior of nonhuman primates*, Vol. 2, pp. 287–334. New York: Academic Press.

Harris, G. (1997). Development of taste perception and appetite regulation. In G. Bremner, A. Slater & G. Butterworth (eds), *Infant development: Recent advances*, pp. 9–30. Hove: Psychology Press.

Harris, P. L. (1987). The development of search. In P. Salapatek & L. Cohen (eds), *Handbook of infant perception*: Vol. 2. Orlando, FL: Academic Press.

Haskins, R. (1989). Beyond metaphor: The efficacy of early childhood education. *American Psychologist*, **44**, 274–282.

Hauser, M. D. (1996). *The evolution of communication*. Cambridge, MA: MIT Press.

Hauser, M.D., Newport, E.L., & Aslin, R.N. (2001). Segmentation of the speech stream in a non-human primate: statistical learning in cotton-top tamarins. *Cognition*, **78**, 53–64.

Hauser-Cram, P., Peirson, D. E., Walker, D. K., & Tivnan, T. (1991). *Early education in the public schools*. San Francisco: Jossey-Bass.

Hayes, B. K. & Taplin, J. E. (1993). Developmental differences in the use of prototype and exemplar-specific information. *Journal of Experimental Child Psychology*, **55**, 329–352.

Hayes, R. A., Slater, A., & Brown, E. (2000). Infants' ability to categorise on the basis of rhyme. *Cognitive Development*, **15**, 405–419.

Head Start (2000). *2000 Statistical Fact Sheet* [On-line]. Available: http://www.acf.dhhs.gov/program/hsb

Hebb, D. O. (1949). *Organization of behavior*. New York: Wiley.

Hebbeler, K. & Wagner, M. (1998). *The National Early Intervention Longitudinal Study (NEILS): Design overview*. Menlo Park: CA: SRI International.

Heckhausen, H. (1984). Emergent achievement behavior: Some early developments. In J. Nicholl (ed.), *The development of achievement motivation*, pp. 1–32. Greenwich, CT: JAI Press.

Heckhausen, H. (1987). Emotional components of action: Their ontogeny as reflected in achievement behavior. In D. Görlitz & J.F. Wohlwill (eds), *Curiosity, imagination, and play: On the development of spontaneous cognitive and motivational processes*, pp. 326–348. Hillsdale, NJ: Erlbaum .

Heckman, J. J. (1999). Doing it right: Job training and education. *Public Interest*, 86–106.

Hemandez-Reif, M., Field, T., del Pino, N., & Diego, M. (2000). Less exploring by mouth occurs in newborns of depressed mothers. *Infant Mental Health Journal*, **21**, 204–210.

Hepper, P. G. (1991). An examination of fetal learning before and after birth. *Irish Journal of Psychology*, **12**, 95–107.

Hepper, P. G. (1992). Fetal psychology. An embryonic science. In J. G. Nijhuis (ed.), *Fetal behaviour. Developmental and perinatal aspects*, pp. 129–156, Oxford: Oxford University Press.

Hepper, P. G. (1994). The beginnings of mind—evidence from the behaviour of the fetus. *Journal of Reproductive and Infant Psychology*, **12**, 143–154.

Hepper, P. G. (1996). Fetal memory: Does it exist? What does it do? *Acta Paediatr Suppl* **416**, 16–20.

Hepper, P. G. & Leader, L. R. (1996). Fetal habituation. *Fetal and Maternal Medicine Review*, **8**, 109–123.

Hepper, P. G. & Shahidullah, S. (1994a). The development of fetal hearing. *Fetal and Maternal Medicine Review*, **6**, 167–179.

Hepper, P. G. & Shahidullah, S. (1994b). Development of fetal hearing. *Archives of Disease in Childhood*, **71**, F81–F87.

Hernandez-Reif, Field, T., Diego, M., & Largie, S. (2001). Haptic habituation to temperature is slower in newborns of depressed mothers (in press).

Hertsgaard, L., Gunnar, M., Erickson, M. F., & Nachmias, M. (1995). Adrenocortical responses to the Strange Situation with disorganized/disoriented attachment relationships. *Child Development*, **66**, 1100–1106.

Hess, R. D. & Shipman, V. (1965). Early experiences and socialization of cognitive modes in children. *Child Development*, **36**, 869–886.

Heyes, C. M. (1998). Theory of mind in nonhuman primates. *Behavioral and Brain Sciences*, **21**, 101–134.

Hildebrand, M. (1985). Walking and running. In M. Hildebrand, D. M. Bramble, K. F. Liem, & D. B. Wake (eds), *Functional vertebrate morphology*, pp. 38–57. Cambridge MA: Harvard/Belknap.

Hilgard, E. R. (1977). *Divided consciousness: Multiple controls in human thought and action*. New York: Wiley.

Hill, R., Foote N., Aldous, J., Carlson, R., & MacDonald, R. (1970). *Family development in three generations: A longitudinal study of changing family patterns of planning and achievement*. Cambridge. MA: Schenkman.

Hill, L. M., Platt, L. D. & Manning, F. A. (1979). Immediate effect of amniocentesis on fetal breathing and gross body movements. *American Journal of Obstetrics and Gynecology*, **135**, 689–690.

Hinde R. A. (1976). Interactions, relationships, and social structure. *Man*, **II**, 1–17.

Hirsch, H. V. B. & Spinelli, D. N. (1970). Visual experience modifies distribution of horizontally and vertically oriented receptive fields in cats. *Science*, **168**, 869–871.

Hochberg, J. & Brooks, V. (1962). Pictorial recognition as an unlearned ability: A study of one child's performance. *American Journal of Psychology*, **75**, 624–628.

Hoffman, M. L. (1988). Moral development. In M. Lamb & M. Bornstein (eds), *Developmental psychology: An advanced textbook* (2nd edn), pp. 497–548. Hillsdale, NJ: Lawrence Erlbaum.

von Holst, E. (1937/1973). On the nature of order in the central nervous system. In R. Martin (ed. and trans.), *The collected papers of Erich von Holst*, Vol. 1: *The behavioral physiology of animals and man*, pp. 3–32. Coral Gables, FL: University of Miami Press (work originally published in 1937).

Holt, K. (1998). Constraints in the emergence of preferred locomotory patterns. In D. A. Rosenbaum & C. E. Collyer (eds), *Timing of behavior: Neural, psychological, and computational perspectives*, pp. 261–291. Cambridge, MA: MIT Press.

Hood, B. M. (1995). Gravity rules for 2- to 4-year-olds? *Cognitive Development*, 10, 577–598.

Hood, B., Carey, S., & Prasada, S. (2000). Predicting the outcome of physical events: Two-year-olds fail to reveal knowledge of solidity and support. *Child Development*, 71, 1540–1554.

Hooker, D. (1952). *The prenatal origin of behavior*. Kansas: University of Kansas Press.

Horney, K. (1939). *New ways in psychoanalysis*. New York: Norton.

Howes, C. (1992). Mastery of the communication of meaning in social pretend play. In A. Pellegrini (ed.), *The collaborative construction of pretend*, pp. 13–24. Albany, NY: State University of New York Press.

Howes, C. (1997). Teacher sensitivity, children's attachment and play with peers. *Early Education and Development*, 8, 41–49.

Howes, C. & Farver, J. (1987). Social pretend play in 2-year-olds: Effects of age of partner. *Early Childhood Research Quarterly*, 2, 305–314.

Howes, C. & Tonyan, H. (1999). Peer relations. In L. Balter & C. S. Tamis-LeMonda (eds), *Child psychology: A handbook of contemporary issues*, pp. 143–157. Philadelphia: Psychology Press.

Howes, C. & Unger, O. (1992). Collaborative construction of social pretend play between toddler-age partners: Illustrative Study #2. In A. Pellegrini (ed.), *The collaborative construction of pretend*, pp. 45–54. Albany, NY: State University of New York Press.

Howes, C., Hamilton, C. E., & Phillipsen, L. (1998). Stability and continuity of child-caregiver and child-peer relationships. *Child Development*, 69, 418–426.

Hull, C. L. (1920). Quantitative aspects of the evolution of concepts. *Psychological Monographs*, No. 123.

Hunter, M. A. & Ames, E. W. (1988). A multifactor model of infant preferences for novel and familiar stimuli. In C. Rovee-Collier & L. Lipsitt (eds), *Advances in Infancy Research*, 5, Norwood, NJ: Ablex.

Huston, A. C., McLoyd, V., & Garcia Coll, C. (1994). Children and poverty: Issues in contemporary research. *Child Development*, 65, 275–282.

Illingworth, R. S. (1983). *The development of the infant and young child*. Edinburgh: Churchill Livingstone.

Individuals with Disabilities Education Act, Amendments of 1997, PL 105–17.

Internal Revenue Service (1999). *IRS Publication 596: Earned Income Credit*. Washington, DC: US Government Printing Office.

Isabella, R. A. (1993). Origins of attachment: Maternal interactive behavior across the first year. *Child Development*, 64, 373–384.

Iverson, P. & Kuhl, P. K. (1995). Mapping the perceptual magnet effect for speech using signal detection theory and multidimensional scaling. *Journal of the Acoustical Society of America*, 97, 553–562.

Ivkovich, D., Collins, K. L., Eckerman, C. O., Krasneger, N. A., & Stanton, M. E. (1999). Classical delay eyeblink conditioning in 4- and 5-month-old human infants. *Psychological Science*, **10**, 4–8.

Izard, C. E. (1978). Emotions and emotion-cognition relationships. In M. Lewis & L. A. Rosenblum (eds), *The development of affect*, pp. 389–413. New York: Plenum.

Izard, C. E. (1982). (ed.). *Measuring emotions in infants and children*. London: Cambridge University Press.

Izard, C. E. (1983). *The maximally discriminate facial coding system (MAX)(Revised)*. Newark, DE: University of Delaware, Instructional Resources Center.

Izard, C. E. (1995). The maximally discriminative facial movement coding system, (3rd edn). Newark, DE: Instructional Resources Center.

Jacklin, C. N. Snow, M. E., & Maccoby, E. E. (1981). Tactile sensitivity and muscle strength in newborn boys and girls. *Infant Behavior and Development*,. **4**, 261–268.

Jacobs, F. (1994). Child and family policy: Framing the issues. In F. Jacobs & M. Davies (eds), *More than kissing babies? Current child and family policy in the United States*, pp. 9–35. Westport, CT: Auburn House.

Jacobson, J. L. (1981). The role of inanimate objects in early peer interaction. *Child Development*, **52**, 618–626.

Jakobson, R. (1941/1968). *Child language, aphasia and phonological universals*. The Hague: Mouton.

James, W. (1890). *The principles of psychology*. New York: Holt.

James, D., Pillai, M., & Smoleniec, J. (1995). Neurobehavioural development in the human fetus. In J.-P. Lecanuet, W. P. Fifer, N. A. Krasnegor, & W. P. Smotherman (eds), *Fetal development. A psychobiological perspective*, pp. 101–128. Hillsdale, NJ: LEA.

Janoff-Bulman, R. (1979). Characterological versus behavioral self-blame: Inquiries into depression and rape. *Journal of Personality and Social Psychology*, **37**, 1798–1809.

Johnson, D. L. (1988). Primary prevention of behavior problems in young children: The Houston Parent-Child Development Center. In R. H. Price, E. L. Cowen, R. P. Lorion, & J. Ramos-McKay (eds), *14 Ounces of prevention: A casebook for practitioners*. Washington, DC: American Psychological Association.

Johnson, E. K. & Jusczyk, P. W. (2001). Word segmentation by 8-month-olds: When speech cues count more than statistics. *Journal of Memory and Language*.

Johnson, S., Slaughter, V., & Carey, S. (1998). Whose gaze will infants follow? The elicitation of gaze-following in 12-month-olds. *Developmental Science*, **1**, 233–238.

Johnson, M. H., Dziurawiec, S., Ellis, H., & Morton, J. (1991). Newborns' preferential tracking of face-like stimuli and its subsequent decline. *Cognition*, **40**, 1–19.

Jusczyk, P. W. (1977). Perception of syllable-final stops by two-month-old infants. *Perception and Psychophysics*, **21**, 450–454.

Jusczyk, P. W. (1993). From general to language specific capacities: The WRAPSA Model of how speech perception develops. *Journal of Phonetics*, **21**, 3–28.

Jusczyk, P. W. (1997). *The discovery of spoken language*. Cambridge, MA: MIT Press.

Jusczyk, P. W. & Aslin, R. N. (1995). Infants' detection of sound patterns of words in fluent speech. *Cognitive Psychology*, **29**, 1–23.

Jusczyk, P. W. & Hohne, E. A. (1997). Infants' memory for spoken words. *Science*, **277**, 1984–1986.

Jusczyk, P. W. & Thompson, E. J. (1978). Perception of a phonetic contrast in multisyllabic utterances by two-month-old infants. *Perception & Psychophysics*, **23**, 105–109.

Jusczyk, P. W., Copan, H., & Thompson, E. (1978). Perception by two-month-olds of glide contrasts in multisyllabic utterances. *Perception & Psychophysics*, **24**, 515–520.

Jusczyk, P. W., Pisoni, D. B., & Mullennix, J. (1992). Some consequences of stimulus variability on speech processing by 2-month old infants. *Cognition*, **43**, 253–291.

Jusczyk, P. W., Cutler, A., & Redanz, N. (1993a). Preference for the predominant stress patterns of English words. *Child Development*, **64**, 675–687.

Jusczyk, P. W., Friederici, A. D., Wessels, J., Svenkerud, V. Y., & Jusczyk, A. M. (1993b). Infants' sensitivity to the sound patterns of native language words. *Journal of Memory and Language*, **32**, 402–420.

Jusczyk, P. W., Luce, P. A., & Charles Luce, J. (1994). Infants' sensitivity to phonotactic patterns in the native language. *Journal of Memory and Language*, **33**, 630–645.

Jusczyk, P. W., Hohne, E. A., & Bauman, A. (1999a). Infants' sensitivity to allophonic cues for word segmentation. *Perception & Psychophysics*, **61**, 1465–1476.

Jusczyk, P. W., Houston, D., & Newsome, M. (1999b). The beginnings of word segmentation in English-learning infants. *Cognitive Psychology*, **39**, 159–207.

Kagan, J. & Lewis, M. (1965). Studies of attention in the human infant. *Merrill-Palmer Quarterly*, **11**, 95–127.

Kagan, S. L. & Weissbourd, B. (1994). Toward a new normative system of family support. In S.L. Kagan & B. Weissbourd, *Putting families first: America's family support movement and the challenge of change*, pp. 473–490. San Francisco: Jossey-Bass.

Kagan, J., Reznick, S., & Snidman, N. (1987). The physiology and psychology of behavioral inhibition in young children. *Child Development*, **58**, 1459–1473.

Kalakanis, L. & Langlois, J. H. (2000). Do newborn infants prefer attractive faces? Unpublished manuscript, University of Texas, Austin, Texas.

Karr-Kaitin, K. (1994). Congressional responses to families in the workplace: The Family and Medical Leave Act of 1987–1988. In F. Jacobs & M. Davies (eds.), *More than kissing babies? Current child and family policy in the United States*, pp. 91–120. Westport, CT: Auburn House.

Karweit, N. L. (1989). Effective preschool programs for students at risk. In R. E. Slavin, N. L. Karweit, & N. A. Madden (eds), *Effective programs for students at risk*, pp. 75–102. Needham, MA: Allyn & Bacon.

Kaslow, N. J., Ream, L. P., Pollack, S. L., & Siegel, A. W. (1988). Attributional style and self-control behavior in depressed and nondepressed children and their parents. *Journal of Abnormal Child Psychology*, **16**(2), 163–175.

Katz, M. (1989). *The undeserving poor*. New York: Pantheon Books.

Kawakami, K., Takai, K. K., Okazaki, Y., Kurihara, H., Shimizu, Y., & Yanaihara, T. (1997). The effect of odors on human newborn infants under stress. *Infant Behavior and Development*, **20**, 531–535.

Kaye, K. L. & Bower, T. G. R. (1994). Learning and intermodal transfer of information in newborns. *Psychological Science*, **5**, 286–288.

Kelso, J. A. S. (1995). *Dynamic patterns: The self-organization of brain and behavior*. Cambridge, MA: MIT Press.

Kennedy, E. M. (1999). University-community partnerships: A mutually beneficial effort to aid community development and improve academic learning opportunities. *Applied Developmental Science*, **3**, 197–198.

Kent, R. D. & Bauer, H. R. (1985). Vocalizations of one year olds. *Journal of Child Language*, **12**, 491–526.

Kestenbaum, R. & Nelson, C. A. (1990). The recognition and categorization of upright and inverted emotional expressions by 7-month-old infants. *Infant Behavior and Development*, **13**, 497–511.

Kimura, T., Okada, M., & Ishida, H. (1979). Kinesiological characteristics of primate walking: Its significance in human walking. In M. Morbeck, H. Preuschoft, & N. Gomberg (eds), *Environment, behavior, and morphology: Dynamic interactions in primates*, pp. 297–311. New York: Gustav Fischer.

Kisker, E. E. & Love, J. M. (1999). *Leading the way: Characteristics of early experiences of selected Early Head Start program, Executive Summary*, Vols I and II. Washington, DC: Commissioner's Office of Research and Evaluation and the Head Start Bureau, Administration on Children, Youth and Families, US Department of Health and Human Services.

Klaus, R. A. & Gray, S. W. (1968). The Early Training Project for disadvantaged children: A report after five years. *Monographs of the Society for Research in Child Development*, **33** (4, Serial No. 120).

Klein, M. (1930). The importance of symbol-formation in the development of the ego. In M. Klein (ed.), *Contributions to psychoanalysis, 1921–1945*. New York: McGraw-Hill.

Kleiner, K. A. (1993). Specific vs. non-specific face recognition device. In B. de Boysson-Bardies, S. de Schonen, P. Jusczyk, P. McNeilage, & J. Morton (eds), *Developmental neurocognition: speech and face processing in the first year of life*, pp. 103–108. Dordrecht, The Netherlands: Kluwer Academic Publishers.

Klinnert, M. (1984). The regulation of infant behavior by maternal facial expression. *Infant Behavior and Development*, **7**, 447–465.

Kochanska, G. (1993). Toward a synthesis of parental socialization and child development in the early development of conscience. *Child Development*, **64**, 325–347.

Kochanska, G. (1997). Mutually responsive orientation between mothers and their young children; Implications for early socialization. *Child Development*, **68**, 94–112.

Kochanska, G. & Murray, K. T. (2000). Mutually responsive orientation between mothers and their young children: Implications for early socialization. *Child Development*, **68**, 94–112.

Kohut, H. (1977). *The restoration of the self*. New York: International Universities Press.

Konner, M. (1975). Relations among infants and juveniles in comparative perspective. In M. Lewis & L. Rosenblum (eds), *Friendship and peer relations: The origins of behavior*, **4**, pp. 99–129. New York: Wiley.

Kuhl, P. K. (1979). Speech perception in early infancy: Perceptual constancy for spectrally dissimilar vowel categories. *Journal of the Acoustical Society of America*, **66**, 1668–1679.

Kuhl, P. K. (1985). Methods in the study of infant speech perception. In G. Gottlieb, & N. A. Krasnegor (eds), *Measurement of audition and vision in the first year of post natal life: A methodological overview*, pp. 223–251. Norwood, NJ: Ablex.

Kuhl, P. K. (1991). Human adults and human infants show a 'perceptual magnet effect' for the prototypes of speech categories, monkeys do not. *Perception & Psychophysics*, **50**, 93–107.

Kuhl, P. K. (1993). Innate predispositions and the effects of experience in speech perception: The native language magnet theory. In B. de Boysson-Bardies, S. de Schonen, P. Jusczyk, P. McNeilage, & J. Morton (eds), *Developmental neurocognition: Speech and face processing in the first year of life*, pp. 259–274. Dordrecht: Kluwer.

Kuhl, P. K. & Miller, J. D. (1982). Discrimination of auditory target dimensions in the presence or absence of variation in a second dimension by infants. *Perception & Psychophysics*, **31**, 279–292.

Kuhl, P. K., Williams, K. A., Lacerda, F., Stevens, K. N., & Lindblom, B. (1992). Linguistic experiences alter phonetic perception in infants by 6 months of age. *Science*, **255**, 606–608.

Kuo, Z.-Y. (1976). *The dynamics of behavior development: An epigenetic view*. New York: Plenum.

Laing, R. D. (1970). *Knots*. New York: Pantheon.

Lamb, M. E. (1976). The role of the father: An overview. In M. E. Lamb (ed.), *The role of the father in child development*. New York: Wiley.

Lamb, M. E. & Easterbrooks, M. A. (1981). Individual differences in parental sensitivity: Origins, components, and consequences. In M. E. Lamb & L. R. Sherrod (eds), *Infant social cognition*: Empincal and theoretical considerations, pp. 127–155. Hillsdale, NJ: Lawrence Erlbaum.

Landesman, S. & Butterfield, E.C. (1987). Normalization and deinstitutionalization of mentally retarded individuals: Controversy and facts. *American Psychologist*, **42**, 809–816.

Landesman, S. & Ramey, C. T. (1989). Developmental psychology and mental retardation: Integrating scientific principles with treatment practices. *American Psychologist*, **44**, 409–415.

Landesman-Dwyer, S. & Butterfield, E. C. (1983). Mental retardation: Developmental issues in cognitive and social adaptation. In M. Lewis (ed.), *Origins of intelligence: Infancy and early childhood*, (2nd edn), pp. 479–519. New York: Plenum Press.

Langlois, J. H. & Roggman, L. A. (1990). Attractive faces are only average. *Psychological Science*, **1**, 115–121.

Langlois, J. H. & Stephan, C. (1977). The effects of physical attractiveness and ethnicity on children's behavioral attributions and peer preferences. *Child Development*, **48**, 1694–1698.

Langlois, J. H., Roggman, L. A., Casey, R. J., Ritter, J. M., Rieser-Danner, L. A., & Jenkins, V. Y. (1987). Infant preferences for attractive faces: Rudiments of a stereotype? *Developmental Psychology*, **23**, 363–369.

Langlois, J. H., Roggman, L. A., & Rieser-Danner, L. A. (1990). Infants' differential social responses to attractive and unattractive faces. *Developmental Psychology*, **26**, 153–159.

Langlois, J. H., Ritter, J. M., Roggman, L. A., & Vaughn, L. S. (1991). Facial diversity and infant preferences for attractive faces. *Developmental Psychology*, **27**, 79–84.

Langlois, J. H., Roggman, L. A., & Musselman, L. (1994). What is average and what is not average about attractive faces? *Psychological Science*, **5**, 214–220.

Lazar, I., Darlington, R., Murray, H., Royce, J., & Snipper, A. (1982). Lasting effects of early education: A report from the Consortium of Longitudinal Studies. *Monographs of the Society for Research in Child Development*, **47**, (2–3, Serial No. 195).

Leach, E. (1964). Anthropological aspects of language: Animal categories and verbal abuse. In E. H. Lenneberg (ed.), *New directions in the study of language*, pp. 23–63. Cambridge, MA: MIT Press.

Leader, L. R., Baillie, P., Martin, B., Molteno, C., & Wynchank, S. (1984). Foetal responses to vibrotactile stimulation. A possible predictor of foetal and neonatal outcome. *Australian and New Zealand Journal of Obstetrics and Gynaecology*, **24**, 251–256.

Lecanuet, J-P., Granier-Deferre, C., DeCasper, A. J., Maugeais, R., Andrieu, A-J., & Busnel, M-C. (1987). Perception et discrimination foetale de stimuli langagiers, mise en evidence a partir de la reactivite cardiaque. Resultats preliminaires. *Compte-Rendus de l'Academie des Sciences de Paris*. Serie III, **305**, 161–164

Legerstee, M., Anderson, D., & Schaffer, A. (1998). Five- and eight-month-old infants recognize their faces and voices as familiar and social stimuli. *Child Development*, **69**, 37–50.

Leinbach, M. D. & Fagot, B. I. (1993). Categorical habituation to male and female faces: Gender schematic processing in infancy. *Infant Behavior and Development*, **16**, 317–332.

Lenz, W. & Knapp, K. (1962). Foetal malformations due to thalidomide. *German Medical Monthly*, **7**, 253.

Lerner, R. M. (1998). Theories of human development: Contemporary perspectives. In R. M. Lerner (ed.), *Theoretical models of human development*. Vol. 1 of the *Handbook of child psychology*, (5th edn), pp. 1–24. Editor-in-chief: W. Damon. New York: Wiley.

Lerner, R. M., Sparks, E. S., & McCubbin, L. (1999). *Family diversity and family policy: Strengthening families for America's children*. Norwell, MA: Kluwer.

Lester, B. M., Hoffman, J., & Brazelton, T. B. (1985). The rhythmic structure of mother–infant interaction in term, & pre-term infants. *Child Development*, **56**, 15–27.

Lewin, K. (1943). Psychology and the process of group living. *Journal of Social Psychology*, **17**, 113–131.

Lewis, H. B. (1971). *Shame and guilt in neurosis*. New York: International Universities Press.

Lewis, H. B. (1987). Shame: The 'sleeper' in psychopathology. In H. B. Lewis (ed.), *The role of shame in symptom formation*, pp. 1–28. Hillsdale, NJ: Lawrence Erlbaum.

Lewis, J. M. (1993). Childhood play in normality, pathology, and therapy. *American Journal of Orthopsychiatry*, **63**, 6–15.

Lewis, M. (1969). Infants' response to facial stimuli during the first year of life. *Developmental Psychology*, **1**, 75–86.

Lewis, M. (1971). Individual differences in measurement of early cognitive growth. In J. Hellmuth (ed.), *Exceptional Infant, 2, Studies in abnormalities*. New York: Wiley.

Lewis, M. (1978). The infant and its caregiver: The role of contingency. *Allied Health and Behavioral Sciences*, **4**, 469–474.

Lewis, M. (1980). Issues in the development of fear. In I. L. Kutash & L. B. Schlesinger (eds), *Pressure point: perspectives on stress and anxiety*, pp. 48–62. San Francisco: Jossey-Bass.

Lewis, M. (1987). Social development in infancy and early childhood. In J. D. Osofsky (ed.), *Handbook of Infant Development*, (2nd edn), pp. 419–493.

Lewis, M. (1991). Self-knowledge and social development in early life. In L. Pervin (ed.), *Handbook of personality: Theory and research*, pp. 277–300. New York: Guilford Publications, Inc.

Lewis, M. (1991). Ways of knowing: Objective self-awareness or consciousness. *Developmental Review (Special Issue)*, **11**, 231–243.

Lewis, M. (1992). *Shame, the exposed self*. New York: The Free Press.

Lewis, M. (1992a). The self in self-conscious emotions. A commentary in D. Stipek, S. Recchia, & S. McClintic. Self-evaluation in young children. *Monographs of the Society for Research in Child Development*, **57**, (1, Serial No.226), pp. 85–95.

Lewis, M. (1992b). *Shame, The exposed self*. New York: The Free Press.

Lewis, M. (1997). *Altering fate: Why the past does not predict the future*. New York: Guilford Press.

Lewis, M. (1998). The development and structure of emotions. In M. Mascolo, & S. Griffin (eds), *What develops in emotional development?* pp. 29–50. New York: Plenum Press.

Lewis, M. (1999). Social cognition and the self. In P. Rochat (ed.), *Early social cognition* (pp. 81–98). Mahwah, NJ: Lawrence Erlbaum.

Lewis, M. & Brooks, J. (1974). Self, other and fear: Infants' reactions to people. In M. Lewis & L. Rosenblum (eds), *The origins of fear: The origins of behavior*, 2, pp. 195–227. New York: Wiley.

Lewis, M. & Brooks-Gunn, J. (1978). Self knowledge and emotional development. In M. Lewis & L. Rosenblum (eds), *The development of affect: The genesis of behavior*, 1, pp. 205–226. New York: Plenum.

Lewis, M. & Brooks-Gunn, J. (1979). *Social cognition and the acquisition of self*. New York: Plenum.

Lewis, M. & Brooks-Gunn, J. (1982). The self as social knowledge. In M. D. Lynch, A. Norem-Hebeisen, & J. Gergen (eds), *Self-concept: Advances in theory and research*, pp. 101–118. Cambridge, MA: Ballinger.

Lewis, M. & Coates, D. L. (1980). Mother–infant interactions and cognitive development in 12-week-old infants. *Infant Behavior and Development*, 3, 95–105.

Lewis, M. & Feiring, C. (1979). The child's social network: Social object, social functions and their relationship. In M. Lewis & L. Rosenblum (eds), *The child and its family: The genesis of behavior*, Vol. 2, pp. 9–27. New York: Plenum.

Lewis, M. & Feiring, C. (1989). Infant, mother, and mother–infant interaction behavior and subsequent attachment. *Child Development*, 60, 831–837.

Lewis, M. & Freedle, R. (1973). Mother–infant dyad. The cradle of meaning. In P. Pilner, L. Krames, & T. Alloway (eds), *Communication and affect: Language and thought*, pp. 127–155. New York: Academic Press.

Lewis, M. & Goldberg, S. (1969). Perceptual cognitive development in infancy: A generalized expectancy model as a function of the mother–infant interaction. *Merrill Palmer Quarterly*, 15, 81–100.

Lewis, M. & Lee-Painter, S. (1974). An interactional approach to the mother infant dyad. In M. Lewis & L. Rosenblum (eds). *The effect of the infant on its caregiver: The origins of behavior*, 1, pp. 21–48. New York: Wiley

Lewis, M. & Michalson, L. (1983). *Children's emotions and moods: Developmental theory and measurement*. New York: Plenum.

Lewis, M. & Ramsay, D. (1995a). Developmental change in infants' response to stress. *Child Development*, 66, 657–670.

Lewis, M. & Ramsay, D. (1995b). Stability and change in cortisol and behavioral responses to stress during the first 18 months of life. *Developmental Psychobiology*, 28(8), 419–428.

Lewis, M. & Ramsay, D. (1997). Stress reactivity and self-recognition. *Child Development*, 68, 621–629.

Lewis, M. & Ramsay, D. (1999). Effect of maternal soothing on infant stress reactivity. *Child Development*, 70, 11–20.

Lewis, M. & Rosenblum, L. (eds). (1974). *The origins of fear: The origins of behavior*, Vol. 2. New York: Wiley.

Lewis, M. & Rosenblum, L. (1975). Introduction. In M. Lewis & L. Rosenblum (eds), *Friendship and peer relations: The origins of behavior*, **4**, pp. 1–9. New York: Wiley.

Lewis, M. & Schaeffer, S. (1981). Peer behavior and mother-infant interaction in maltreated children. In M. Lewis & L. Rosenblum (eds), *The uncommon child: The genesis of behavior*, **3**, pp. 193–223. New York: Plenum.

Lewis, M. & Sullivan, M. W. (1985). Imitation in the first six months of life: Phenomenon in the eye of the beholder. *Merrill Palmer Quarterly*, **31**, 315–333.

Lewis, M. & Sullivan, M. W. (1994). Developmental intervention in the lives of infants and parents. In C. B. Fisher & R. M. Lerner (eds). *Applied developmental psychology*, pp. 375–406. New York: McGraw-Hill.

Lewis, M. & Thomas, D. (1990). Cortisol release in infants in response to inoculation. *Child Development*, **61**, 50–59.

Lewis, M., Meyers, W. J., Kagan, J., & Grossberg, R. (1963). Attention to visual patterns in infants. Paper presented at Symposium on Studies of attention in infants: Methodological problems and preliminary results, at *Meeting of the American Psychological Association*, Philadelphia, PA.

Lewis, M., Kagan, J., & Kalafat, J. (1966a). Patterns of fixation in infants. *Child Development*, **37**, 331–341.

Lewis, M., Kagan, J., Kalafat, J., & Campbell, H. (1966b). The cardiac response as a correlate of attention in infants. *Child Development*, **37**, 63–71.

Lewis, M., Goldberg, S., & Campbell, H. (1969). A developmental study of information processing within the first three years of life: Response decrement to a redundant signal. *Monographs of the Society for Research in Child Development*, **34** (9, Serial No. 133).

Lewis, M., Sullivan, M. W., & Michalson, L. (1984). The cognitive-emotional fugue. In C. E. Izard, J. Kagan & R. Zajonc (eds), *Emotion, cognition, and behavior*, pp. 264–288. New York: Cambridge University Press.

Lewis, M., Sullivan, M. W., Stanger, C., & Weiss, M. (1989). Self-development and self-concious emotions. *Child Development*, **60**, 146–156.

Lewis, M., Alessandri, S., & Sullivan, M. W. (1990). Violation of expectancy, loss of control, and anger in young infants. *Developmental Psychology*, **26**, 745–751.

Lewis, M., Ramsay, D. S., & Kawakami, K. (1993). Differences between Japanese infants and Caucasian American infants in behavioral and cortisol response to innoculation. *Child Development*, **64**, 1722–1731.

Light, P. (1987). Taking roles. In J. Bruner & H. Haste (eds), *Making sense: The child's construction of the world*, pp. 41–61. London: Methuen.

Liley, A. W. (1972). The foetus as a personality. *Australian and New Zealand Journal of Psychiatry*, **6**, 99–105.

Lillard, A. S. (1993). Pretend play skills and the child's theory of mind. *Child Development*, **64**, 348–371.

Lillard, A. S. (1998). Playing with a theory of mind. In O. N. Saracho & B. Spodek (eds), *Multiple perspectives on play in early childhood education*, pp. 11–33. New York: State University Press.

Little, J. F. (1999). *Alcohol and smoking. Effects on fetal behaviour*. PhD thesis. Queen's University Belfast, UK.

Lively, S. E. & Pisoni, D. B. (1997). On prototypes and phonetic categories: A critical magnet effect in speech perception. *Journal of Experimental Psychology: Human Perception and Performance*, **23**, 1665–1679.

Lloyd, B. (1987). Social representations of gender. In J. Bruner & H. Haste (eds), *Making sense: the child's construction of the world*, pp. 147–162. London: Methuen.

Lloyd-Thomas, A. R. & Fitzgerald, M. (1996). Reflex responses do not necessarily signify pain. *British Medical Journal*, **313**, 797–798.

Locke, J. L. (1993). *The child's path to spoken language*. Cambridge, MA: Harvard UP.

Long, S.K., Kirby, G.G., Kurka, R., & Waters, S. (1998). *Child care assistance under welfare reform: Early response by the states*. (Occasional Paper 15; Assessing the New Federalism Project). Washington, DC: The Urban Institute.

Ludemann, P. M. (1991). Generalized discrimination of positive facial expressions by seven- and ten-month-old infants. *Child Development*, **62**, 55–67.

Ludemann, P.M. & Nelson, C.A. (1988). Categorical representation of facial expressions by 7-month-old infants. *Developmental Psychology*, **24**, 492–501.

Lynn, D. B. (1974). *The father: His role in child development*. Monterey: Brooks/Cole.

McCall, R. B. & Carriger, M. S. (1993). A meta-analysis of infant habituation and recognition memory performance as predictors of later IQ. *Child Development*, **64**, 57–79.

McCall, R. B., Appelbaum, M. I., & Hogarty. P. S. (1973). Developmental changes in mental performance. *Monographs of the Society for Research in Child Development*, **38** (Serial No. 150).

McCarton, C. M., Brooks-Gunn, J., Wallace, I. F., Bauer, C. R., Bennett, F. C., Bernbaum, J. C., Broyles, R. S., Casey, P. H., McCormick, M. C., Scott, D. T., Tyson, J., Tonascia, J., & Meinert, C. L. (1997). Results at age 8 years of early intervention for low-birth-weight premature infants: The Infant Health and Development Program. *JAMA*, **277**, 126–132.

Maccoby, E. & Martin, J. (1983). Socialization in the context of the family: Parent-child interaction. In P. H. Mussen (Series ed.) & E. M. Hetherington (Vol. ed.), *Handbook of child psychology*: Vol. 4. *Socialization, personality, and social development*, pp. 1–101. New York: Wiley.

McDonough, L. & Mandler, J. M. (1998). Inductive generalization in 9- and 11-month-olds. *Developmental Science*, **1**, 227–232.

Macfarlane, A. J. (1975). Olfaction in the development of social preferences in the human neonate. *Ciba Foundation Symposium*, **33**, 103–117.

McGraw, M. (1945). *Neuromuscular maturation of the human infant*. New York: Hafner.

McGurk, H. & Lewis, M. (1974). Space perception in early infancy: Perception within a common auditory-visual space? *Science*, **186**(4164), 649–650.

McKey, R. H., Condelli, L., Ganson, H., Barrett, B. J., McConkey, C., & Plantz, M. C. (1985). *The impact of Head Start on children, families, and communities*. Washington, DC: CSR, Inc.

MacFarlane, A. (1978). *The psychology of childbirth*. London: Open Books.

Mackey, W. C. (1985). *Fathering behaviors: The dynamics of the man-child bond*. New York: Plenum.

McVicker Hunt, J. (1961). *Intelligence and experience*. New York: Ronald Press.

McVicker Hunt, J. (1964). The psychological basis for using preschool enrichment as an antidote for cultural deprivation. *Merrill-Palmer Quaterly*, **10**, 209–248.

Madden, J., Levenstein, P., & Levenstein, S. (1976). Longitudinal IQ outcomes of the mother-child home program. *Child Development*, **46**, 1015–1025.

Magnusson, D. & Stattin, H. (1998). Person-context interaction theories. In R. M. Lerner (ed.), *Theoretical models of human development*, Vol. 1 of the *Handbook of child psychology*, (5th edn), pp. 685–759. Editor-in-chief: W. Damon. New York: Wiley.

Main, M. & Solomon, J. (1990). Procedures for identifying infants as disorganized/disoriented during the Ainsworth strange situation. In M. T. Greenberg, D. Cicchetti, & E. M. Cummings (eds), *Attachment in the preschool years*, pp. 121–160. Chicago: University of Chicago Press.

Mandler, J. M. (1992). How to build a baby: II. Conceptual primitives. *Psychological Review*, **99**, 587–604.

Mandler, J. M. (1999). Seeing is not the same as thinking: Commentary on 'Making sense of infant categorization'. *Developmental Review*, **19**, 297–306.

Mandler, J. M. & Bauer, P. J. (1988). The cradle of categorization: Is the basic level basic? *Cognitive Development*, **3**, 247–264.

Mandler, J. M. & McDonough, L. (1993). Concept formation in infancy. *Cognitive Development*, **8**, 291–318.

Mandler, J. M. & McDonough, L. (1996). Drinking and driving don't mix: Inductive generalization in infancy. *Cognition*, **59**, 307–335.

Mandler, J. M., Fivush, R., & Reznick, J. S. (1987). The development of contextual categories. *Cognitive Development*, **2**, 339–354.

Mandler, J. M., Bauer, P. J., & McDonough, L. (1991). Separating the sheep from the goats: Differentiating global categories. *Cognitive Psychology*, **23**, 263–298.

Mandel, D. R., Jusczyk, P. W., & Pisoni, D. B. (1995). Infants' recognition of the sound patterns of their own names. *Psychological Science*, **6**, 315–318.

Maratos, O. (1998). Neonatal, early and later imitation: Same order phenomena? In F. Simion & G. Butterworth (eds), *The development of sensory, motor and cognitive capacities in early infancy*, pp. 145–60. Hove: Psychology Press.

Marcus, G. F. (2001). *The algebraic mind*. Cambridge, MA: MIT Press.

Marcus, G. F., Vijayan, S., Rao, S. B., & Vishton, P. M. (1999). Rule learning by seven-month-old infants. *Science*, **283**, 434–435.

Mareschal, D., French, R. M., & Quinn, P. C. (2000). A connectionist account of asymmetric category learning in early infancy. *Developmental Psychology*, **36**, 635–645.

Markman, E. (1989). *Categorization and naming in children*. Cambridge, MA: MIT Press.

Marler, P. (1990). Innate learning preferences: Signals for communication. *Developmental Psychobiology*, **23**, 557–569.

Martin, R. M. (1975). Effects of familiar and complex stimuli on infant attention. *Developmental Psychology*, **11**, 178–185.

Martin, S. L., Ramey, C. T., & Ramey, S. L. (1990). The prevention of intellectual impairment in children of impoverished families: Findings of a randomized trial of educational day care. *American Journal of Public Health*, **80**, 844–847.

Martlew, M., Connolly, K., & McCleod, C. (1976). Language use, role and context in a five-year-old. *Journal of Child Language*, **5**, 81–99.

Maslin, C. A., Bretherton, I., & Morgan, G. A. (1987). *Toddlers' independent mastery motivation as related to attachment security and quality of maternal scaffolding.* Paper presented at the MacArthur foundation Research Network Summer Institute, Durango, Co.

Mastropieri, D. & Turkewicz, G. (1999). Prenatal experience and neonatal responsiveness to vocal expressions of emotion. *Developmental Psychobiology*, **35**, 204–214.

Masur-Frank, E. & Ritz, E. G. (1983). Patterns of gestural, vocal, and verbal imitation performance in infancy. *Merrill Palmer Quarterly*, **83**, 1–47.

Mattys, S. L. & Jusczyk, P. W. (2001). Phonotactic cues for segmentation of fluent speech by infants. *Cognition*, **78**, 91–121.

Mattys, S. L., Jusczyk, P. W., Luce, P. A., & Morgan, J. L. (1999). Word segmentation in infants: How phonotactics and prosody combine. *Cognitive Psychology*, **38**, 465–494.

Maurer, D. (1985). Infants' perception of facedness. In T. M. Field & N. A. Fox (eds), *Social Perception in Infants*, pp. 73–100. Norwood, NJ: Ablex.

Maurer, D. & Salapatek, P. (1976). Developmental changes in the scanning of faces by young infants. *Child Development*, **47**, 523–527.

Mayes, L. C. & Carter, A. S. (1990). Emerging social regulatory capacities as seen in the still-face situation. *Child Development*, **61**, 754–763.

Mehler, J., Bertoncini, J., Barriere, M., & Jassik-Gerschenfeld, D. (1978). Infant recognition of mother's voice. *Perception*, **7**, 491–497.

Mehler, J., Jusczyk, P. W., Lambertz, G., Halsted, N., Bertoncini, J., & Amiel-Tison, C. (1988). A precursor of language acquisition in young infants. *Cognition*, **29**, 144–178.

Meier, R. P. & Newport, E. L. (1990). Out of the hands of babes: On a possible sign advantage in language acquisition. *Language*, **66**, 1–23.

Meisels, S.J. & Shonkoff, J. (2000). Early childhood intervention: A continuing evolution. In J.P. Shonkoff & S.J. Meisels (eds), *Handbook of early childhood intervention*, (2nd edn), pp. 3–31. New York: Cambridge University Press.

Mellor, D. H. (1990). *Ways of communicating.* Cambridge, UK: Cambridge University Press.

Meltzoff, A. N. (1988). Infant imitation after a 1-week delay: Long-term memory for novel acts and multiple stimuli. *Developmental Psychology*, **24**, 470–476.

Meltzoff, A. N. & Borton, R. W. (1979). Intermodal matching by human neonates. *Nature*, **282**, 403–404.

Meltzoff, A. N. & Moore, M. K. (1977). Imitation of facial and manual gestures by human neonates. *Science*, **198**, 75–78.

Meltzoff, A. N. & Moore, M. K. (1983). Newborn infants imitate adult facial gestures. *Child Development*, **54**, 702–709.

Meltzoff, A. N. & Moore, M. K. (2000). Resolving the debate about early imitation. In D. Muir & A. Slater (eds), *Infant development: The essential readings*, pp. 176–181. Boston, MA: Blackwell Science.

Melzack, R. & Scott, T. H. (1957). The effects of early experience on the response to pain. *Journal of Comparative and Physiological Psychology*, **50**, 155–161.

Mennella, J. A. & Beauchamp, G. K. (1991). Maternal diet alters the sensory qualities of human milk and the nursling's behavior. *Pediatrics*, **88**, 737–744.

Michotte, A. (1962). *Causalité, permanence et réalité phénoménales*. Louvain: Publications Universitaires Belgium.

Miller, J. L. & Eimas, P. D. (1983). Studies on the categorization of speech by infants. *Cognition*, **13**, 135–165.

Miller, & Garvey, C. (1984). Mother-baby role play: its origins in social support. In I. Bretherton (ed.), *Symbolic play: the development of understanding*, pp. 101–130. New York: Aademic Press.

Miller, J. L. & Liberman, A. M. (1979). Some effects of later-occurring information on the perception of stop consonant and semivowel. *Perception & Psychophysics*, **25**, 457–465.

Miller, C. L., Younger, B. A., & Morse, P. A. (1982). Categorization of male and female voices in infancy. *Infant Behavior and Development*, **5**, 143–159.

Misulis, K. E. (1994). General description of evoked potentials. In *Spehlmann's evoked potential primer: visual, auditory, and somatosensory evoked potentials in clinical diagnosis*, (2nd edn), pp. 5–9. Boston, MA: Butterworth-Heinemann.

Moessinger, A. C. (1988). Morphological consequences of depressed or impaired fetal activity. In W. P. Smotherman & S. R. Robinson (eds), *Behavior of the fetus*, pp. 163–173. Caldwell NJ: Telford.

Mondloch, C. J., Lewis, T. L., Budreau, D. R., Maurer, D., Dannemiller, J. L., Stephens, B. R., & Kleiner-Gathercoal, K. A. (1999). Face perception during early infancy. *Psychological Science*, **10**, 419–422.

Moon, C., Cooper, R. P., & Fifer, W. P. (1993). Two-day old infants prefer their native language. *Infant Behavior and Development*, **16**, 495–500.

Moore, K. L. (1988). *The developing human*. Philadelphia: W. B Saunders.

Morgan, J. L. (1994). Converging measures of speech segmentation in prelingual infants. *Infant Behavior & Development*, **17**, 387–400.

Morgan, J. L. & Saffran, J. R. (1995). Emerging integration of sequential and suprasegmental information in preverbal speech segmentation. *Child Development*, **66**, 911–936.

Morgan, G. A., Maslin, C. A., Ridgeway, D., & Kang-Park, J. (1988). Toddler mastery motivation and aspects of mother–child affect communication (Summary). *Program and proceedings of the developmental psychobiology research group fifth biennial retreat*, **5**, 15–16.

Morgan, G. A., Maslin-Cole, C. A., Biringen, Z., & Harmon, R. J. (1991). Play assessment of mastery motivation in infants and young children. In. C. E. Schaefer, K. Gitlin, & A. Sandgrund (eds), *Play diagnosis and assessment*, pp. 65–86. New York: John Wiley & Sons.

Morrison, A. P. (1986). The eye turned inward: Shame and the self. In O. L. Nathanson (ed.), *The many faces of shame*, pp. 271–291. New York: Guilford Press.

Morrison, A. P. (1989). *Shame: The underside of narcissism*. Hillsdale, NJ: Analytic Press.

Morrongiello, B. A., Fenwick, K. D., & Chance, G. (1998). Crossmodal learning in newborn infants: Inferences about properties of auditory-visual events. *Infant Behavior and Development*, **21**, 543–553.

Morse, P. A. (1972). The discrimination of speech and nonspeech stimuli in early infancy. *Journal of Experimental Child Psychology*, **13**, 477–492.

Morton, J. & Johnson, M. H. (1991). CONSPEC and CONLERN: A two-process theory of infant face recognition. *Psychological Review*, **98**, 164–181.

Muir, D. W. & Hains, S. M. J. (1993). Infant sensitivity to perturbations in adult facial, vocal, tactile, and contingent stimulation during face-to-face interactions. In B. de Boysson-Bardies, S. de Schonen, P. Jusczyk, P. McNeilage, & J. Morton (eds), *Developmental neurocognition: speech and face processing in the first year of life*, pp. 171–185. Dordrecht, The Netherlands: Kluwer Academic Publishers.

Muir, D. W., Humphrey, D. E., & Humphrey, G. K. (1994). Pattern and space perception in young infants. *Spatial Vision*, 8, 141–165.

Muir, D. W., Humphrey, D. E., & Humphrey, G. K. (1999). Pattern and space perception in young infants. In A. Slater & D. Muir, *The Blackwell reader in developmental psychology*, pp. 116–142. Boston, MA: Blackwell Science.

Mullen, K. (1994). Earliest recollections of childhood: a demographic analysis. *Cognition*, 52, 55–79.

Mumme, D. L., Fernald, A., & Herrera, C. (1996). Infants' responses to facial and vocal emotional signals in a social referencing paradigm. *Child Development*, 67, 3219–3237.

Murphy, C. M. & Messer, D. J. (1977). Mothers, infants and pointing: A study of a gesture. In H. R. Schaffer (ed.), *Studies of mother-infant interaction*. London: Academic Press.

Murray, L. & Trevarthan, C. (1985). Emotional regulation of interactions between 2-month-olds and their mothers. In T. M. Field, & N. A. Fox (eds), *Social perception in infants*, pp. 177–197. Norwood, NJ: Ablex.

Nachmias, M., Gunnar, M., Mangelsdorf, S., Parritz, R. H., & Buss, K. (1996). Behavioral inhibition and stress reactivity: The moderating role of attachment security. *Child Development*, 67, 508–522.

Nathanielsz, P. W. (1999). *Life in the womb. The origin of health and disease*. New York: Promethean Press.

National Research Council (1998). *Preventing reading difficulties in young children*. Committee on the Prevention of Reading Difficulties in Young Children, C. E. Snow, M. S. Burns, & P. Griffin (eds). Commission on Behavioral and Social Sciences and Education. Washington, DC: National Academy Press.

National Research Council and Institute of Medicine (2000). *From neurons to neighborhoods: The science of early childhood development*. Committee on Integrating the Science of Early Childhood Development. J. P. Shonkoff & D. A. Phillips, (eds). Board on Children, Youth, and Families, Commission on Behavioral and Social Sciences and Education. Washington, DC: National Academy Press.

Nazzi, T., Bertoncini, J., & Mehler, J. (1998). Language discrimination by newborns: Towards an understanding of the role of rhythm. *Journal of Experimental Psychology: Human Perception & Performance*, 24, 756–766.

Nazzi, T., Jusczyk, P. W., & Johnson, E. K. (2000). Language discrimination by English-learning 5-month-olds: Effects of rhythm and familiarity. *Journal of Memory and Language*, 43, 1–19.

Neldam, S. (1986). Fetal movements as an indicator of fetal well-being. *Danish Medical Bulletin*, 33, 212–220.

Nelson, C. A. (1987). The recognition of facial expressions in the first two years of life: Mechanisms of development. *Child Development*, 58, 889–909.

Nelson, C. A. (1993). The recognition of facial expressions in infancy: Behavioral and electrophysiological evidence. In B. de Boysson-Bardies, S. de Schonen, P. Jusczyk, P. McNeilage, & J. Morton (eds), *Developmental neurocognition: speech and face processing in the first year of life*, pp. 187–198. Dordrecht, The Netherlands: Kluwer Academic Publishers.

Nelson, C. A. (1999). How important are the first 3 years of life? *Applied Developmental Science*, 3, 235–238.

Nelson, C. A. & Collins, P. F. (1992). Neural and behavioral correlates of visual recognition memory in 4- and 8-month-old infants. *Brain and Cognition*, 19, 105–121.

Nelson, C. A. & de Haan, M. (1996). Neural correlates of infants' visual responsiveness to facial expressions of emotion. *Developmental Psychology*, 29, 577–595.

Nelson, C. A. & Dolgin, K. G. (1985). The generalized discrimination of facial expressions by seven-month-old infants. *Child Development*, 56, 58–61.

New, R. S. (1994). Child's play—*una cosa naturale*: An Italian perspective. In J. L. Roopnarine, J. E. Johnson, & F. H. Hooper (eds), *Children's play in diverse cultures*, pp. 123–147. Albany, NY: State University of New York Press.

Newport, E. L. & Aslin, R. N. (2000). Innately constrained learning: Blending old and new approaches to language acquisition. In S. C. Howell, S. A. Fish, & T. K. Lucas (eds), *Proceedings of the 24th Annual Boston University Conference on Language Development*, Vol. 1, pp. 1–21. Somerville, MA: Cascadilla Press.

Nicely, P., Tamis-LeMonda, C. S., & Bornstein, M. H. (1999). Mothers' attuned responses to infant affect expressivity promote earlier achievement of language milestones. *Infant Behavior and Development*, 22, 557–568.

NICHD Early Child Care Research Network (1994). Child care and child development: The NICHD Study of Early Child Care. In S. L. Friedman & H. C. Haywood (eds), *Developmental follow-up: Concepts, domains, and methods*, pp. 377–396. New York: Academic.

NICHD Early Child Care Research Network (1996). Characteristics of infant child care: Factors contributing to positive caregiving. *Early Childhood Research Quarterly*, 11(3), 269–306.

NICHD Early Child Care Research Network (1997). Child care in the first year of life. *Merrill-Palmer Quarterly*, 43, 340–360.

NICHD Early Child Care Research Network (1997). The effects of infant child care on infant-mother attachment security: Results of the NICHD Study of Early Child Care. *Child Development*, 68(5), 860–879.

NICHD Early Child Care Research Network (1998). Early child care and self-control, compliance and problem behavior at twenty-four and thirty-six months. *Child Development*, 69(3), 1145–1170.

NICHD Early Child Care Research Network (1999). Child care and mother–child interaction in the first three years of life. *Developmental Psychology*, 35(6), 1399–1413.

NICHD Early Child Care Research Network (1999a). Child care and mother-child interaction in the first three years of life. *Developmental Psychology*, 35, 1399–1413.

NICHD Early Child Care Research Network (1999b). Child outcomes when child care center classes meet recommended standards for quality. *American Journal of Public Health*, 89, 1072–1077.

Nijhuis, J. G., Prechtl, H. F. R., Martin, C. B., & Bots, R. S. G. M. (1982). Are there behavioural states in the human fetus? *Early Human Development*, 6, 177–195.

Nilsson, L., Furuhjelm, M., Ingelman-Sundberg, A., Wirsén, C., & Forsblad, B. (1977). *A child is born*. London:Faber & Faber.

Noirot, E. & Algeria, J. (1983). Neonate orientation towards human voice differs with type of feeding. *Behavior Processes*, 8, 65–71.

O'Connell, B. & Bretherton, I. (1984). Toddlers' play, alone and with mother. In I. Bretherton (ed.), *Symbolic play: The development of understanding*, pp. 101–130. New York: Academic Press.

Oller, D. K. (1980). The emergence of speech sounds in infancy. In G. H. Yeni-Komshian, C. A. Ferguson, & J. Kavanagh (eds), *Child phonology: production*, Vol. 1, pp. 93–112. New York: Academic Press.

Oppenheim, R. (1981). Ontogenetic adaptations and retrogressive processes in development of the nervous system and behavior: a neuroembryologic perspective. In K. J. Connolly & H. F. R. Prechtl (eds), *Maturation and development: Biological and psychological perspectives*, pp. 73–109. London: Heinemann.

Oppenheim, R. W. (1984). Ontogenetic adaptations in neural development; Toward a more 'ecological' developmental psychobiology. In H. F. R. Prechtl (ed.), *Continuity of neural functions from prenatal to postnatal life*, pp. 16–30. London: Spastics International.

Oppenheim, R. W. (1991). Cell death during development of the nervous system. *Annual Review of Neuroscience*, **14**, 453–501.

Osofsky, J. D. (1979). *Handbook of infant development*. New York: Wiley.

Oster, H. (1978). Facial expression and affect development. In M. Lewis, & L. A. Rosenblum (eds), *The development of affect*, pp. 43–75. New York: Plenum Press.

Pascalis, O., de Haan, M., Nelson, C. A., & de Schonen, S. (1998). Long-term recognition memory for faces assessed by visual paired comparison in 3- and 6-month-old infants. *Journal of Experimental Psychology: Learning, Memory, and Cognition*, **24**, 249–260.

Pascalis, O., de Schonen, S., Morton, J., Deruelle, C., & Fabre-Grenet, M. (1995). Mother's face recognition by neonates: A replication and an extension. *Infant Behavior and Development*, **18**, 79–85.

Patrick, J., Campbell, K., Carmichael, L., Natale, R., & Richardson, B. (1980). Patterns of human fetal breathing during the last 10 weeks of pregnancy. *Obstetrics and Gynecology*, **56**, 24–30.

Peiper, A. (1963). *Cerebral functions in infancy and childhood*. New York: Consultants Bureau.

Peleg, D. & Goldman, J. A. (1980). Fetal heart rate acceleration in response to light stimulation as a clinical measure of fetal well-being. A preliminary report. *Journal of Perinatal Medicine*, **8**, 38–41.

Perez-Granados, D. R. & Callanan, M. A. (1997). Conversations with mothers and siblings: young children's semantic and conceptual development. *Developmental Psychology*, **33**, 120–134.

Petitto, L. A. & Marentette, P. F. (1991). Babbling in the manual mode: Evidence for the ontogeny of language. *Science*, **251**, 1493–1496.

Phillips, R. D., Wagner, S. H., Fells, C. A., & Lynch, M. (1990). Do infants recognize emotion in facial expressions?: Categorical and 'metaphorical' evidence. *Infant Behavior and Development*, **13**, 71–84.

Piaget, J. (1937). *The construction of reality in the child*. London: Routledge and Kegan Paul, 1955.

Piaget, J. (1952). *The origins of intelligence in children*. New York: Norton.

Piaget, J. (1953). *The origins of intelligence in the child*. London: Routledge and Kegan Paul.

Piaget, J. (1954). *The construction of reality in the child*. New York: Basic Books.

Piaget, J. (1962). *Play, dreams, and imagination in childhood*. New York: Norton.

Piaget, J. (1972). *The psychology of intelligence*. Totowa, NJ: Littlefield, Adams.

Piven, F.F. & Cloward, R.A. (1993). *Regulating the poor: The functions of public welfare* (revised edn). New York: Vintage.

Polishuk, W. Z., Laufer, N., & Sadovsky, E. (1975). Fetal reaction to external light. *Harefuah*, **89**, 395–397.

Polka, L. & Bohn, O.-S. (1996). Cross-language comparison of vowel perception in English-learning and German-learning infants. *Journal of the Acoustical Society of America*, **100**, 577–592.

Polka, L. & Werker, J. F. (1994). Developmental changes in perception of nonnative vowel contrasts. *Journal of Experimental Psychology: Human Perception & Performance*, **20**, 421–435.

Pollack, I. (1952). The information in elementary auditory displays. *Journal of the Acoustical Society of America*, **24**, 745–749.

Porges, S. W. (1985). Spontaneous oscillations in heart rate. Potential index of stress. In P. G. Mogberg (ed.), *Animal stress: New directions in defining and evaluating the effects of stress*, pp. 97–111. Bethesda, MD: APS.

Porges, S. W. (1996). Physiological regulation in high-risk infants: A model for assessment and potential intervention. *Development and Psychopathology*, **8**, 29–42.

Porges, S. W. & Doussard-Roosevelt, J. (1997). Early physiological patterns and later behavior. In H. W. Reese & M. Frazen *et al.* (eds), *Biological and neuropsychological mechanisms: Lifespan developmental psychology*, pp. 163–179. Mahwah, NJ: Erlbaum.

Porges, S. W., Doussard-Roosevelt, J., Portales, A., & Greenspan, S. (1996). Infant regulation of the vagal 'brake' predicts child behavior problems: A psychobiological model of social behavior. *Developmental Psychology*, **29**, 691–712.

Porter, R. H. (1991). Mutual mother-infant recognition in humans. In P. G. Hepper (ed.), *Kin recognition*, pp. 413–432. Cambridge: Cambridge University Press.

Porter, R. H. & Winberg, J. (1999). Unique salience of maternal breast odors for newborn infants. *Neuroscience and Biobehavioural Reviews*, **23**, 439–449.

des Portes, V., Pinard, J. M., Billuart, P., Vinet, M. C., Koulakoff, A., Carrie, A., Gelot, A., Dupuis, E., Motte, J., Berwald-Netter, Y., Catala, M., Kahn, A., Beldjord, C., & Chelly, J. (1998). A novel CNS gene required for neuronal migration and involved in X-linked subcortical laminar heterotopia and lissencephaly syndrome. *Cell*, **92**, 51–61.

Poulson, C. L., Kymissis, E., Reeve, K. F., & Andreatos, M. (1991). Generalized vocal imitation in infants. *Journal of Experimental Child Psychology*, **51**, 267–279.

Povinelli, D. J. & Giambrone, S. (2001). Reasoning about beliefs: A human specialization? *Child Development*, **72**, 691–695.

Powell, C. & Grantham-McGregor, S. (1989). Home visiting of varying frequency and child development. *Pediatrics*, **84**, 157–164.

Power, T. G. (2000). *Play and exploration in children and animals*. NJ: Lawrence Erlbaum.

Power, T. G., Chapieski, M. L., & McGrath, M. P. (1985). Assessment of individual differences in infant exploration and play. *Developmental Psychology*, **21**, 974–981.

Prechtl, H. F. R. (1974). The behavioural states of the newborn infant (a review). *Brain Research*, **76**, 1304–1311.

Prechtl, H. F. R. (1988). Developmental neurology of the fetus. *Clinical Obstetrics & Gynaecology*, 2, 21–36.

Prechtl, H. F. & O'Brien (1982). Behavioral states of the full term newborn: The emergence of a concept. In P. Stratton (ed.), *Psychobiology of the human newborn*, pp. 53–73. New York: Wiley.

Premack, D. & Woodruff, G. (1978). Does the chimpanzee have a theory of mind? *Behavioral and Brain Sciences*, 4, 515–526.

Preyer, W. (1885). *Specielle Physiologie des Embryo*. Leipzig:Grieben.

Primus, W., Rawlings, L., Larin, K., & Porter, K. (1999). *The initial impacts of welfare reform on the incomes of single-mother families*. Washington, DC: Center on Budget and Policy Priorities.

Provence, S. & Lipton, R. C. (1962). *Infants in institutions*. London: Bailey & Swinfer.

Querleu, D., Renard, X., Versyp, F., Paris-Delrue, L., & Crepin, G. (1988). Fetal hearing. *European Journal of Obstetrics, Gynecology and Reproductive Biology*, 29, 191–212.

Querleu, D., Renard, X., Boutteville, C., & Crepin, G. (1989). Hearing by the human fetus? *Seminars in Perinatology*, 13, 409–420.

Quinn, P. C. (2001a). Concepts are not just for objects:Categorization of spatial relation information by infants. In D. H. Rakison & L. M. Oakes (eds), *Early category and concept development:Making sense of the blooming, buzzing confusion*. Oxford, UK: Oxford University Press (in press).

Quinn, P. C. (2001b). Early categorization: A new synthesis. In U. Goswami (ed.), *Blackwell handbook of childhood cognitive development*. Oxford, UK: Blackwell (in press).

Quinn, P. C. & Bomba, P. C. (1986). Evidence for a general category of oblique orientations in 4-month-old infants. *Journal of Experimental Child Psychology*, 42, 345–354.

Quinn, P. C. & Eimas, P. D. (1986). On categorization in early infancy. *Merrill-Palmer Quarterly*, 32, 331–363.

Quinn, P. C. & Eimas, P. D. (1996a). Perceptual cues that permit categorical differentiation of animal species by infants. *Journal of Experimental Child Psychology*, 63, 189–211.

Quinn, P. C. & Eimas, P. D. (1996b). Perceptual organization and categorization in young infants. In C. Rovee-Collier & L. P. Lipsitt (eds), *Advances in infancy research*, Vol. 10, pp. 1–36. Norwood, NJ: Ablex.

Quinn, P. C. & Eimas, P. D. (1997). A reexamination of the perceptual-to-conceptual shift in mental representations. *Review of General Psychology*, 1, 271–287.

Quinn, P. C. & Eimas, P. D. (1998). Evidence for a global categorical representation for humans by young infants. *Journal of Experimental Child Psychology*, 69, 151–174.

Quinn, P. C. & Eimas, P. D. (2000). The emergence of category representations during infancy: Are separate perceptual and conceptual processes required? *Journal of Cognition and Development*, 1, 55–61.

Quinn, P. C. & Johnson, M. H. (1997). The emergence of perceptual category representations in young infants: A connectionist analysis. *Journal of Experimental Child Psychology*, 66, 236–263.

Quinn, P. C. & Johnson, M. H. (2000). Global-before-basic object categorization in connectionist networks and 2-month-old infants. *Infancy*, 1, 31–46.

Quinn, P. C., Eimas, P. D., & Rosenkrantz, S. L. (1993). Evidence for representations of perceptually similar natural categories by 3-month-old and 4-month-old infants. *Perception*, **22**, 463–475.

Quinn, P. C., Eimas, P. D., & Tarr, M. J. (2001a). Perceptual categorization of cat and dog silhouettes by 3-to-4-month-old infants. *Journal of Experimental Child Psychology*, **79**, 78–94.

Quinn, P. C., Slater, A. M., Brown, E., & Hayes, R. A. (2001b). Developmental change in form categorization in early infancy. *British Journal of Developmental Psychology*, **19**, 207–18.

Rakic, P. (1972). Model of cell migration to the superficial layers of the fetal monkey neocortex. *Journal of Comparative Neurology*, **145**, 61–84.

Rakison, D. & Butterworth, G. (1998). Infants' use of object parts in early categorization. *Developmental Psychology*, **34**, 49–62.

Ralston, P., Lerner, R. M., Mullis, A. K., Simerly, C., & Murray, J. (eds) (1999). *Social change, public policy, and community collaboration: Training human development professionals for the twenty-first century*. Norwell, MA: Kluwer.

Ramey, C. T. & Campbell, F. A. (1984). Preventive education for high-risk children: Cognitive consequences of the Carolina Abecedarian Project. *American Journal of Mental Deficiency*, **88**, 515–523.

Ramey, C. T. & Campbell, F. A. (1992). Poverty, early childhood education, and academic competence: The abecedarian experiment. In A. Huston (ed.), *Children in poverty*, pp. 190–221. New York: Cambridge University Press.

Ramey, C. T. & Finklestein, N. W. (1981). Psychosocial mental retardation: A biological and social coalescence. In M. Begab, H. Garber, & H. C. Haywood (eds), *Psychological influences in retarded performance*, pp. 65–92. Baltimore: University Park Press.

Ramey, C. T. & Ramey, S. L. (1996). Early intervention: Optimizing development for children with disabilities and risk conditions. In M. Wolraich (ed.), *Disorders of development and learning: A practical guide to assessment and management*, (2nd edn), pp. 141–158. Philadelphia: Mosby.

Ramey, C. T. & Ramey, S. L. (1998). Early intervention and early experience. *American Psychologist*, **53**, 109–120.

Ramey, C. T. & Ramey, S. L. (1999). *Right from birth: Building your child's foundation for life*. New York: Goddard Press.

Ramey, C. T. & Ramey, S. L. (2000). Intelligence and public policy. In R. J. Sternberg (ed.), *Handbook of intelligence*, pp. 534–548. New York: Cambridge University Press.

Ramey, C. T. & Ramey, S. L. (2001). Early educational interventions and intelligence. In E. Zigler & S. Styfco (eds), *The Head Start debates*. Connecticut: Yale University Press (in press).

Ramey, C. T. & Smith, B. (1977). Assessing the intellectual consequences of early intervention with high-risk infants. *American Journal of Mental Deficiency*, **81**, 318–324.

Ramey, S. L. & Ramey, C. T. (1994). Early educational intervention with disadvantaged children: To what effect? *Journal of Applied and Preventative Psychology*, **1**(3), 131–140.

Ramey, S. L. & Ramey, C. T. (1999). Early experience and early intervention for children 'at risk' for developmental delay and mental retardation. *Mental Retardation and Developmental Disabilities Research Reviews*, **5**, 1–10.

Ramey, S. L. & Ramey, C. T. (2000). Early childhood experiences and developmental competence. In S. Danziger & J. Waldfogel (eds), *Securing the future: Investing in children from birth to college*, pp. 122–152. New York: Russell Sage Foundation.

Ramey, S. L. & Sackett, G. P. (2000). The early caregiving environment: Expanding views on non-parental care and cumulative life experiences. In A. Sameroff, M. Lewis, & S. Miller (eds), *Handbook of developmental psychopathology*, (2nd ed), pp. 365–380. New York: Plenum Publishing.

Ramey, C. T., McGinness, G., Cross, L., Collier, A., & Barrie-Blackley, S. (1981). The abecedarian approach to social competence. Cognitive and liguistic intervention for disadvantaged preschoolers. In K. Borman (ed.), *The social life of children in a changing society*, pp. 145–174. Hillsdale, NJ: Erlbaum.

Ramey, C. T., Bryant, D. M, Wasik, B. H., Sparling, J. J., Fendt, K. H., & LaVange, L. M. (1992). Infant Health and Development Program for low birth weight, premature infants: Program elements, family participation, and child intelligence. *Pediatrics*, 3, 454–465.

Ramey, C. T., Ramey, S. L., Gaines, R., & Blair, C. (1995). Two-generation early intervention programs: A child development perspective. In I. Sigel (Series ed.) and S. Smith (Vol. ed.), *Two-generation programs for families in poverty: a new intervention strategy*. Vol. 9 *Advances in Applied Developmental Psychology*, pp.199–228. Norwood, NJ: Ablex Publishing Corporation.

Ramey, S. L., Sparling, J., Dragomir, C., Ramey, C., Echols, K., & Soroceanu, L. (1995). Recovery by children under 3 years old from depriving orphanage experiences, Symposium Presentation. Indianapolis, IN: Society for Research in Child Development.

Ramey, C. T., Campbell, F. A., Burchinal, M., Skinner, M. L., Gardner, D. M., & Ramey, S. L. (2000). Persistent effects of early childhood education on high-risk children and their mothers. *Applied Developmental Science*, 4, 2–14.

Ramey, C. T., Ramey, S. L., Lanzi, R. G., & Cotton, J. N. (2001). Early educational interventions for high risk children: How center-based treatment can augment and improve parenting effectiveness. In J. Borowski and S. Ramey (eds), *Parenting and the child's world: Influences on academics, intellectual, and social-emotional development. social-emotional development*, pp. 125–140. Mahwah, NJ: Lawrence Erlbaum Associates, Inc.

Ramsay, D. & Lewis, M. (1999). Adrenocortical reactivity to stress at six months related to behavioral inhibition in the second year. Poster presented at the biennial meeting of the Society for Research in Child Development. Alburquerque, NM.

Ramsey, J. L., Langlois, J. H., Hoss, R., & Rubenstein, A. J. (2000, July). *Origins of a stereotype: Cognitive categorization of attractive and unattractive faces by young infants*. Poster presented at the biennial meeting of the International Conference of Infant Studies, Brighton, England.

Raver, C. C. (1996). Relations between social contingency in mother–child interaction and 2-year-olds' social competence. *Developmental Psychology*, 32, 850–859.

Reaux, J. E., Theall, L. A., & Povinelli, D. J. (1999). A longitudinal investigation of chimpanzees' understanding of visual perception. *Child Development*, 70, 275–290.

Reed, E. S. (1988). Changing theories of postural development. In M. Woollacott & A. Shumway-Cook (eds), *The development of posture and gait across the life span*, pp. 3–24. Columbia SC: University of South Carolina Press.

Reissland, N. (1988). Neonatal imitation in the first year of life: observations in Rural Nepal. *Developmental Psychology*, 24, 464–469.

Reynolds, A. J. (2000). *Success in early intervention: The Chicago Child-Parent Centers.* Lincoln, NB: University of Nebraska Press.

Richards, J. (1987). Infant visual attention and respiratory sinus arrhythmia. *Child Development,* 58, 488–496.

Robertson, J. & Robertson, J. (1971). Young children in brief separation: A fresh look. *Psychoanalytic Study of the Child,* 26, 264–315.

Roggman, L. A. (1991). Assessing social interactions of mothers and infants through play. In. C. E. Schaefer, K. Gitlin, & A. Sandgrund (eds), *Play diagnosis and assessment,* pp. 427–462. New York: John Wiley & Sons.

Rogoff, B. (1998). Cognition as a collaborative process. In D. Kuhn & R. S. Siegler (eds), *Cognition, perception, and language,* Vol. 2 of the *Handbook of child psychology,* (5th edn), pp. 679–744. Editor-in-chief: W. Damon. New York: Wiley.

Rogoff, B., Mistry, J., Göncü, A., & Mosier, C. (1993). Guided participation in cultural activity by toddlers and caregivers. *Monographs of the Society for Research in Child Development,* 58, 1–179 (7, Serial No. 236).

Ron, M., Yaffe, H., & Polishuk, W. Z. (1976). Fetal heart rate response to amniocentesis in cases of decreased fetal movements. *Obstetrics and Gynecology,* 48, 456–459.

Rosch, E. (1978). Principles of categorization. In E. Rosch & B. B. Lloyd (eds), *Cognition and categorization,* pp. 27–48. Hillsdale, NJ: Erlbaum.

Rosch, E., Mervis, C. B., Gray, W. D., Johnson, D. M., & Boyes-Braem, P. (1976). Basic objects in natural categories. *Cognitive Psychology,* 8, 382–439.

Rosenblum, L. & Kaufman, I. C. (1968). Variations in infant development and response to maternal loss in monkeys. *American Journal of Orthopsychiatry,* 38, 418–426.

Rosenstein, D. & Oster, H. (1988). Differential facial responses to four basic tastes in newborns. *Child Development,* 59, 1555–1568.

Rosenstein, D. & Oster, H. (1997). Differential facial responses to four basic tastes in newborns. In P. Ekman, E. L. Rosenberg, *et al.* (eds) (1997). *What the face reveals: Basic and applied studies of spontaneous expression using the Facial Action Coding System (FACS),* pp. 302–327. *Series in affective science.* New York, NY: Oxford University Press.

Ross, C. A. (1989). *Multiple personality disorder: Diagnosis, clinical features, and treatment.* New York: Wiley.

Rothbart, M. K. (1981). Measurement of temperament in infancy. *Child Development,* 52, 569–578.

Rothbart, M. K. & Bates, J. E. (1998). Temperament. In N. Eisenberg and W. Damon (Eds.), *The handbook of child psychology,* (5th edn), Vol. 3: *Social, emotional, and personality development,* pp. 105–176. New York, NY: Wiley.

Rothbart, M. K. & Derryberry, D. (1981). Development of individual differences in temperament. In M. Lamb & A. Brown (eds), *Advances in developmental psychology,* 1, pp. 37–77. Hillsdale, NJ: Erlbaum.

Rovee-Collier, C. (1986). The rise and fall of infant classical conditioning research: Its promise for the study of early development. *Advances in Infancy Research,* 4, 139–159.

Rovee-Collier, C. (1987). Learning and memory in children. In J. D. Osofsky (ed.), *Handbook of infant development* (2nd edn). New York: Wiley.

Rovee-Collier, C. (1999). The development of infant memory. *Current Directions in Psychological Science,* 8, 80–85.

Rovee-Collier, C. & Fagan, J. W. (1976). Extended conditioning and 24-hour retention in infants. *Journal of Experimental Child Psychology*, **21**, 1.

Rubenstein, J. & Howes, C. (1976). The effects of peers on toddler interaction with mother and toys. *Child Development*, **47**, 597–605.

Rubenstein, A. J. & Langlois, J. H. (2000). *The ability to form stereotypic associations during infancy: A look at the basis of the 'beauty is good' stereotype*. Poster presented at the biennial meeting of the International Conference of Infant Studies, Brighton, England.

Rubenstein, A. J., Kalakanis, L., & Langlois, J. H (1999). Infant preferences for attractive faces: A cognitive explanation. *Developmental Psychology*, **35**, 848–855.

Rubin, K. H. & Howe, N. (1986). Social play and perspective-taking. In G. Fein & M. Rivkin (eds), *The young child at play*, pp. 113–125. Washington, DC: National Association for the Education of Young Children.

Rubin, K. H., Fein, G. G., & Vandenberg, B. (1983). Play. In P. H. Mussen (ed.), *Handbook of Child Psychology: Socialization, Personality, and Social Development*, pp. 716–757.

Ruff, H. A. (1982). An ecological approach to infant memory. In M. Moscovitch (ed.), *Infant memory*. New York: Plenum.

Ruff, H. A. & Lawson, K. R. (1991). Assessment of infants' attention during play with objects. In. C. E. Schaefer, K. Gitlin, & A. Sandgrund (eds), *Play diagnosis and assessment*, pp. 115–129. New York: John Wiley & Sons.

Rutter, M. (1979). Maternal deprivation, 1972–1978: New findings, new concepts, new approaches. *Child Development*, **10**, 283–305.

Rutter, M. (1996). Profound Early Deprivation and Later Social Relationship in Earl Adoptees from Romanian Orphanages Followed at Age 4. Paper presented at the 10th Biennial International Conference on Infant Studies, Providence, R. I. (April).

Saarni, C., Mumme, D. L., & Campos, J. J. (1998). Emotional development: Action, communication, and understanding. In W. Damon & N. Eisenberg (eds), *Handbook of child psychology: Social, emotional, and personality development*, (5th ed), Vol. 3, pp. 237–309. New York: John Wiley, & Sons, Inc.

Sackett, G. P., Novak, M. F. S. X., & Kroeker, R. (1999). Early experience effects on adaptive behavior: Theory revisited. *Mental Retardation and Developmental Disabilities Research Reviews*. New York: Wiley.

Saffran, J. R., Aslin, R. N., & Newport, E. L. (1996). Statistical learning by 8-month-old infants. *Science*, **274**, 1926–1928.

Saffran, J. R., Johnson, E. K., Aslin, R. N., & Newport, E. L. (1999). Statistical learning of tone sequences by human adults and infants. *Cognition*, **70**, 27–52.

Sameroff, A. J. (1983). Developmental systems: Contexts and evolution. In W. Kessen (ed.), *Handbook of Child Psychology*: Vol. 1. *History, theory, and methods*, **1**, pp. 237–294. New York: Wiley.

Sameroff, A. J., Seifer, R., & Elias, P. K. (1982). Sociocultural variability in infant temperament ratings. *Child Development*, **53**, 164–173.

Sampaio, E. (1989). Is there a critical age for using the Sonicguide with blind infants? *Journal of Visual Impairment & Blindness*, **83**, 105–108.

Samuels, C. A. & Ewy, R. (1985). Aesthetic perception of faces during infancy. *British Journal of Developmental Psychology*, **3**, 221–228.

Samuels, C. A., Butterworth, G., Roberts, T., Graupner, L., & Hole, G. (1994). Facial aesthetics: Babies prefer attractiveness to symmetry. *Perception*, **23**, 823–831.

Sants, J. & Barnes, P. (1985). *Personality, development and learning: Unit 2, Childhood.* Milton Keynes: The Open University Press.

Scarr, S. & McCartney, K. (1988). Far from home: An experimental evaluation of the mother-child home program in Bermuda. *Child Development*, **59**, 531–543.

Schaal, B., Orgeur, P., Lecanuet, J-P., Locatelli, A., Granier-Deferre, C., & Poindron, P. (1991). Chémoreception nasale in utero:Expériences préliminaires chez le foetus ovin. *Comptes Rendus de l'Académie des Sciences (Paris), Série III*, **113**, 319–325.

Schaal, B., Orgeur, P., & Rognon, C. (1995). Odor sensing in the human fetus: anatomical, functional, and chemoecological bases. In J-P. Lecanuet, W. P. Fifer, N. A. Krasnegor, & W. P. Smotherman (eds), *Fetal development. A psychobiological perspective*, pp. 205–237, Hillsdale, NJ: LEA.

Schaffer, H. R. (1974). Cognitive components of the infant's response to strangeness. In M. Lewis & L. A. Rosenblum (eds), *The origins of fear*, pp. 11–24. New York: Wiley.

Schaffer, H. R. (1984). *The child's entry into a social world.* London: Academic Press.

Schiff, W. (1965). Perception of impending collision. *Psychological Monographs*, **79**.

Schmidt, L. A., Fox, N. A., Rubin, K. H., Sternberg, E. M., Gold, P. W., Smith, C. C., & Schulkin, J. (1997). Behavioral and neuroendocrine responses in shy children. *Developmental Psychobiology*, **30**, 127–140.

de Schonen, S. & Deruelle, C. (1994). Pattern and face recognition in infancy: Do both hemispheres perceive objects in the same way? In A. Vyt, H. Bloch, & M. H. Bornstein (eds), *Early child development in the French tradition: Contributions from current research*, pp. 35–53. Hillsdale, NJ: Lawrence Erlbaum Associates.

de Schonen, S. & Mathivet, E. (1989). First come, first served: A scenario about the development of hemispheric specialization in face recognition during infancy. *Cahiers de Psychologie Cognitive European Bulletin of Cognitive Psychology*, **9**, 3–44.

de Schonen, S. & Mathivet, E. (1990). Hemispheric asymmetry in a face discrimination task in infants. *Child Development*, **61**, 1192–1205.

Schneider-Rosen, K. (1990). The development of reorganization of attachment relationships. In M. T. Greenberg, D. Cicchetti, & E. M. Cummings (eds), *Attachment in the preschool years*, pp. 185–220. Chicago: University of Chicago Press.

Schorr, L. B. & Schorr, D. (1988). *Within our reach: Breaking the cycle of disadvantage.* New York: Anchor Press.

Schweinhart, L. J., Barnes, H. V., & Weikart, D. P. (1993a). Significant benefits: The High/Scope Perry Preschool Study through age 27. *Monographs of the High/Scope Educational Research Foundation* (No. 10). Ypsilanti, MI: High/Scope Press.

Schweinhart, L. J., Berrueta-Clement, J. R., Barnett, W. S., Epstein, A. S., & Weikart, D. P. (1985). Effects of the Perry Preschool Program on youths through age 19: A summary. *Topics in Early Childhood Special Education*, **5**, 26–35.

Sereno, M. I., Dale, A. M., Reppas, J. B., Kwong, K. K., Belliveau, J. W., Brady, T. J., Rosen, B. R., & Tootell, R. B. H. (1995). Borders of multiple visual areas in humans revealed by functional magnetic resonance imaging. *Science*, **268**, 889–893.

Serrano, J. M., Iglesias, J., & Loeches, A. (1992). Visual discrimination and recognition of facial expressions of anger, fear, and surprise in 4- to 6-month-old infants. *Developmental Psychobiology*, **25**, 411–425.

Serrano, J. M., Iglesias, J., & Loeches, A. (1995). Infants' responses to adult static facial expressions. *Infant Behavior and Development*, **18**, 477–482.

Shahidullah, S. & Hepper, P. G. (1993). The developmental origins of fetal responsiveness to an acoustic stimulus. *Journal of Reproductive and Infant Psychology*, **11**, 135–142.

Shahidullah, S. & Hepper, P. G. (1994). Frequency discrimination by the fetus. *Early Human Development*, **36**, 13–26.

Sherrington, C. S. (1947). *The integrative action of the nervous system*. New Haven: Yale University Press (1st edition 1906).

Shik, M. L., Severin, F. V., & Orlovsky, G. N. (1966). Control of walking and running by means of electrical stimulation of the mid-brain. *Biophysics*, **11**, 756–765.

Shore, R. (1997). *Rethinking the brain: New insights into early development*. New York: Families and Work Institute.

Singer, J. L. (1995). Imaginative play in childhood: precursor of subjunctive thought, daydreaming, and adult pretending games. In A. D. Pellegrini (ed.), *The future of play theory*, pp. 187–219. Albany, NY: State University of New York Press.

Skeels, H. M. & Dye, H. A. (1939). A study of the effects of differential stimulation in mentally retarded children. *Proceedings of the American Association of Mental Deficiency*, **44**, 114–136.

Slade, A. (1987). A longitudinal study of maternal involvement and symbolic play during the toddler period. *Child Development*, **58**, 367–375.

Slater, A. (1989). Visual memory and perception in early infancy. In A. Slater & G. Bremner (eds). *Infant development*. London: Lawrence Erlbaum, pp. 43–71.

Slater, A. M. & Morison, V. (1985). Shape constancy and slant perception at birth. *Perception*, **14**, 337–344.

Slater, A., Mattock, A., & Brown, E. (1990). Size constancy at birth: Newborn infants' responses to retinal and real size. *Journal of Experimental Child Psychology*, **49**, 314–322.

Slater, A., Von der Schulenburg, C., Brown, E., Badenoch, M., Butterworth, G., Parsons, S., & Samuels, C. (1998). Newborn infants prefer attractive faces. *Infant Behavior and Development*, **21**, 345–354.

Slater, A., Quinn, P., Brown, E., & Hayes, R. (1999). Intermodal perception at birth: Intersensory redundancy guides newborn infants' learning of arbitrary auditory-visual pairings. *Developmental Science*, **2**, 333–338.

Slater, A., Bremner, G., Johnson, S. P., Sherwood, P., Hayes, R., & Brown, E. (2000). Newborn infants' preference for attractive faces: The role of internal and external facial features. *Infancy*, **2**, 265–274.

Smith, E. E. & Medin, D. L. (1981). *Categories and concepts*. Cambridge, MA: Harvard University Press.

Soken, N. H. & Pick, A. D. (1999). Infants' perception of dynamic affective expressions: Do infants distinguish specific expressions? *Child Development*, **70**, 1275–1282.

Sokolov, E. N. (1963). *Perception and the conditioned reflex*. New York: Macmillan.

Sorce, J. F., Emde, R. N., Campos, J., & Klinnert, M. D. (1985). Maternal emotional signaling: Its effect on the visual cliff behavior of one-year olds. *Developmental Psychology*, **21**, 195–200.

Spangler, G. & Grossman, K. E. (1993). Behavioral organization in the securely and insecurely attached infants. *Child Development*, **64**, 1439–1450.

Sparling, J. J. & Lewis, I. (1979). *Learning games for the first three years: A guide to parent-child play*. New York: Walker.

Sparling, J. J. & Lewis, I. (1984). *Partners for learning*. Lewisville, NC: Kaplan Press.

Sparling, J. J., Lewis, I., & Neuwirth, S. (1992). *Early partners*. Lewisville, NC: Kaplan Press.

Spencer, J., Quinn, P. C., Johnson, M. H., & Karmiloff-Smith, A. (1997). Heads you win, tails you lose: Evidence for young infants categorizing mammals by head and facial attributes (Special Issue: Perceptual Development). *Early Development and Parenting*, 6, 113–126.

Sperry, R. W. (1951). Mechanisms of neural maturation. In S. S. Stevens (ed.). *Handbook of experimental psychology*. New York: Wiley.

Spiker, C. C. (1956). Experiments with children on the hypothesis of acquired distinctiveness and equivalence of cues. *Child Development*, 27, 253–263.

Spring, D. R. & Dale, P. S. (1977). Discrimination of linguistic stress in early infancy. *Journal of Speech and Hearing Research*, 20, 224–232.

Stansbury, K. & Gunnar, M. R. (1994). Adrenocortical activity and emotion regulation. In N. A. Fox (ed.), *The development of emotion regulation: Biological and behavioral considerations*. Monographs of the Society for Research in Child Development.

Stark, R. E., Bernstein, L. E., & Demorest, M. E. (1993). Vocal communication in the first 18 months of life. *Journal of Speech and Hearing Research*, 36, 548–558.

Staveteig, S. & Wigton, A. (2000). *Key findings by race and ethnicity: Snapshots of America's families II: A view of the nation and 13 states from the National Survey of America's families*. Washington, DC: Urban Institute.

Steiner, J. E. (1979). Human facial expressions in response to taste and smell stimulation. In H. W. Reese and L. P. Lipsitt (eds), *Advances in child development and behavior,* 13, pp. 257–293, New York: Academic Press.

Stenberg, C. R. & Campos, J. J. (1990). The development of anger expressions in infancy. In N. L. Stein, B. Leventhal, & T. Trabasso (eds), *Psychological and biological approaches to emotion*, pp. 247–256. Hillsdale, NJ: LEA.

Stenberg, C. R., Campos, J. J., & Emde, R. N. (1983). The facial expression of anger in seven-month-old infants. *Child Development*, 54, 178–184.

Stern, D. N. (1985). *The interpersonal world of the infant*. New York: Basic Books, Inc.

Stern, D. N. (1993). The role of feelings for an interpersonal self. In U. Neisser (ed.), *The perceived self*, pp. 205–215. New York: Cambridge University Press.

Sternberg, R. J. & Grigorenko, E. L. (eds) (1997a). *Intelligence, heredity, and environment*. New York: Cambridge University Press.

Sternberg, R. J. & Grigorenko, E. L. (1997b). Interventions for cognitive development in children 0–3 years old. In M. E. Young (ed.), *Early child development: Investing in our children's future*, pp. 127–156. New York: Elsevier.

Stipek, D., Recchia, S., & McClintic, S. (1992). *Self-evaluation in young children*. Monographs of the Society for Research in Child Development, 57 (1, Serial no. 226).

Stockinger-Forys, S. K. & McCune-Nicolich, L. (1984). Sociodramatic play at 3 years of age. In I. Bretherton (ed.), *Symbolic play: the development of understanding*, pp. 159–191. New York: Academic Press.

Stoel-Gammon, C. (1998). Role of babbling and phonology in early linguistic development. In A. M. Wetherby, S. F. Warren, & J. Reichle (eds), *Transitions in prelinguistic communication*, pp. 87–110. Baltimore: Paul Brookes Publishing Co.

Streeter, L. A. (1976). Language perception of 2-month old infants shows effects of both innate mechanisms and experience. *Nature*, 259, 39–41.

Stucki, M., Kaufmann-Hayoz, R., & Kaufmann, F. (1987). Infants' recognition of a face revealed through motion: Contribution of internal facial movement and head movement. *Canadian Journal of Experimental Child Psychology*, 44, 80–91.

Sullivan, M. W., Lewis, M., & Alessandri, S. (1992). Cross-age stability in emotional expressions during learning and extinction. *Developmental Psychology*, **28**, 58–63.

Sussman, J. E. & Lauckner-Morano, V. J. (1995). Further tests of the 'perceptual magnet effect' in the perception of [i]: Identification and change/no change discrimination. *Journal of the Acoustical Society of America*, **97**, 539–552.

Swaiman, K. F. & Ashwal, S. (1999). *Pediatric neurology: Principles and practice* (3rd edn). St Louis: Mosby.

Swain, I. U., Zelazo, P. R., & Clifton, R. K. (1993). Newborn infants' memory for speech sounds retained over 24 hours. *Developmental Psychology*, **29**, 312–323.

Swoboda, P., Morse, P. A., & Leavitt, L. A. (1976). Continuous vowel discrimination in normal and at-risk infants. *Child Development*, **47**, 459–465.

Swoboda, P., Kass, J., Morse, P. A., & Leavitt, L. A. (1978). Memory factors in infant vowel discrimination of normal and at-risk infants. *Child Development*, **49**, 332–339.

Symons, L. A., Hains, S. M. J., & Muir, D. W. (1998). Look at me: Five-month-old infants' sensitivity to very small deviations in eye-gaze during social interactions. *Infant Behavior and Development*, **21**, 531–536.

Szawarski, Z. (1996). Probably no pain in the absence of 'self'. *British Medical Journal*, **313**, 796–797.

Taine, H. (1877). Acquisition of language by children. *Mind*, **2**, 252–259.

Tamis-LeMonda, C. S. & Bornstein, M. H. (1990). Language, play, and attention at one year. *Infant Behavior and Development*, **13**, 85–98.

Tamis-LeMonda, C. S. & Bornstein, M. H. (1991). Individual variation, correspondence, stability, and change in mother-toddler play. *Infant Behavior and Development*, **14**, 143–162.

Tamis-LeMonda, C. S. & Bornstein, M. H. (1994). Specificity in mother-toddler language-play relations across the second year. *Developmental Psychology*, **30**, 283–292.

Tamis-LeMonda, C. S. & Bornstein, M. H. (1996). Variation in children's exploratory, nonsymbolic, and symbolic play: an explanatory multidimensional framework. In C. Rovee-Collier & L. Lipsitt (eds), *Advances in infancy research*, pp. 37–78. Norwood, NJ: Ablex.

Tamis-LeMonda, C. S., Bornstein, M. H., Cyphers, L., & Toda, S. (1992). Language and play at one year: A comparison between Japan and the United States. *International Journal of Behavioral Development*, **15**, 19–42.

Tamis-LeMonda, C. S., Bornstein, M. H., Baumwell, L., & Damast, A. M. (1996). Sensitivity in parenting interactions across the first two years: Influences on children's language and play, In C. S. Tamis-LeMonda (Guest ed.), *Parenting sensitivity: individual, contextual and cultural factors in recent conceptualizations*: Thematic Issue of *Early Development and Parenting*, **5**, 173–183.

Tamis-LeMonda, C. S., Bornstein, M. H., Kahana-Kalman, R., Baumwell, L., & Cyphers, L. (1998). Predicting variation in the timing of linguistic milestones in the second year: An events-history approach. *Journal of Child Language*, **25**, 675–700.

Tamis-LeMonda, C. S., Bornstein, M. H., & Baumwell, L. (2001). Maternal responsiveness and infant activity as predictors of the timing of first-to-second year language milestones. *Child Development*, **72**(3), 748–767.

Tangney, J. P. (1990). Assessing individual differences in proneness to shame and guilt: Development of the Self-Conscious Affect and Attribution Inventory. *Journal of Personality and Social Psychology*, **59**, 102–111.

Tangney, J. P. (1995). Shame-proneness, guilt proneness and interpersonal processes. In J. P. Tangney & K. W. Fischer (eds), *Self-conscious emotions: Shame, guilt and pride*, pp. 114–139. New York: Guilford.

Teller, D. Y. (1979). The forced-choice preferential looking procedure: A psychophysical technique for use with human infants. *Infant Behavior and Development*, **2**, 135–153.

Terr, L. C. (1981). Forbidden games: Post-traumatic children's play. *Journal of the American Academy of Child Psychiatry*, **20**, 741–760.

The Infant Health and Development Program (1990). Enhancing the outcomes of low-birth-weight, premature infants. *Journal of the American Medical Association*, **263**, 3035–3042.

Thelen, E. (1989). Self-organization in developmental processes: Can systems approaches work? In M. Gunnar & E. Thelen (eds), *Systems in development: The Minnesota symposia in child psychology*, Vol. 22, pp. 77–117. Hillsdale, NJ: Erlbaum.

Thelen, E. & Smith, L. (1994). *A dynamic systems approach to the development of cognition and action*. Cambridge, MA: MIT Press.

Thelen, E. & Smith, L. B. (1998). Dynamic systems theories. In R. M. Lerner (ed.), *Theoretical models of human development*, Vol. 1 of the *Handbook of child psychology*, (5th edn), pp. 563–633. Editor-in-chief: W. Damon. New York: Wiley.

Thelen, E. & Spencer, J. P. (1998). Postural control during reaching in young infants: A dynamic systems approach. *Neuroscience and Biobehavioral Reviews*, **22**, 507–514.

Thomas, A., Birch, H. G., Chess, S., Hertzig, M., & Korn, S. (1963). *Behavior individuality in early childhood*. New York: New York University Press.

Thompson, L. S. (1999). Creating partnerships with government, communities, and universities to achieve results for children. *Applied Developmental Science*, **3**, 213–216.

Thompson, L. A., Fagan, J. F., & Fulker, D. W. (1991). Longitudinal prediction of specific cognitive abilities from infant novelty preference. *Child Development*, **62**, 530–538.

Thyer, N., Hickson, L., & Dodd, B. (2000). The perceptual magnet effect in Australian English vowels. *Perception & Psychophysics*, **62**, 1–20.

Tiedemann. (1927). Observations on the development of the mental faculties of children (C. Murchison & S. Langer, Trans.). *The Pedagogical Seminary and Journal of Genetic Psychology*, **34**, 205–230. (Original work published 1787)

Tincoff, R. & Jusczyk, P. W. (1999). Some beginnings of word comprehension in 6-month-olds. *Psychological Science*, **10**, 172–175.

Tizard, J. & Tizard, B. (1971). The social development of two-year-old children in residential nurseries. In H. R. Schaffer (ed.), *The origins of human social relations*. New York: Academic Press.

Tomasello, M. (1999). *The cultural origins of human cognition*. Cambridge, MA: Harvard UP.

Tomkins, S. D. (1962). *Affect, imagery, consciousness*, Vol. 1: *The positive affects*. New York: Springer.

Tomkins, S. S. (1962). *Affect, imagery, consciousness*: Vol. 1, *The positive affects*. New York: Springer.

Tomkins, S. S. (1963). *Affect, imagery, consciousness*: Vol. 2, *The negative affects*. New York: Springer.

Trehub, S. E. (1973). Infants' sensitivity to vowel and tonal contrasts. *Developmental Psychology*, **9**, 91–96.

Trehub, S. E. (1976). The discrimination of foreign speech contrasts by infants and adults. *Child Development*, **47**, 466–472.

Trevarthen, C. (1993). The self born in intersubjectivity: the psychology of an infant communicating. In U. Neisser (ed.), *The perceived self*, pp. 121–173. New York: Cambridge University Press.

Trivers, R. L. (1974). Parent-offspring conflict. *American Zoologist*, **14**, 249–264.

Tronick, E., Als, H., Adamson, L., Wise, S., & Brazelton, T. B. (1978). The infants' response to entrapment between contradictory messages in face-to-face interaction. *Journal of the American Academy of Child Psychiatry*, **17**, 1–13.

Tsushima, T., Takizawa, O., Sasaki, M., Siraki, S., Nishi, K., Kohno, M., Menyuk, P., & Best, C. (1994). Discrimination of English /r-l/ and /w-y/ by Japanese infants at 6–12 months: Language specific developmental changes in speech perception abilities. Paper presented at the International Conference on Spoken Language Processing, Yokohama, Japan.

Turvey, M. T. (1990). Coordination. *American Psychologist*, **45**, 938–953.

US Department of Education (1999). *Twenty-first annual report to Congress on the implementation of the Individuals with Disabilities Education Act*. Washington, DC: US Government Printing Office.

US Department of Health and Human Services (1999a). *Head Start, administration for children and families fact sheet*. Available HTTP: www.acf.dhhs.gov/programs/opa/facts/headstpr.htm.

US Department of Health and Human Services (1999b). *1999 Head Start fact sheet*, Available HTTP: www2.acf.dhhs.gov/programs/hsb/about/99_hsfs.htm.

US Department of Health and Human Services (2000a). *Child Health USA 2000*. Washington, DC: United States Government Printing Office.

US Department of Health and Human Services (2000b). *Fact sheet: Child care and development fund*. Available HTTP: www.acf.dhhs.gov/programs/opa/facts/ccfund.htm.

US Department of Health and Human Services (2000c). *Temporary Assistance for Needy Families (TANF) Program: Third annual report to Congress*. Washington, DC: US Government Printing Office.

US Department of Health and Human Services (2000d), *Trends in the well-being of America's children and youth, 1999*. Washington, DC: United States Government Printing Office.

Vandell, D. L. & Wilson, K. S. (1987). Infants' interactions with mother, sibling, and peer: contrasts and relations between interaction systems. *Child Development*, **58**, 176–186.

Vandenberg, B. (1986). Play theory. In G. Fein & M. Rivkin (eds), *The young child at play*, pp. 17–27. Washington, DC: National Association for the Education of Young Children.

Vandivere, S., Moore, K. A., & Zaslow, M. (2000). Children's family environments: Findings from the National Survey of America's Families. *Snapshots of America's families II: A view of the nation and 13 states from the National Survey of America's families*. Washington, DC: Urban Institute.

Verba, M. (1994). The beginnings of collaboration in peer interaction. *Human Development*, 37, 125–139.

Vihman, M. M. (1992). Early syllables and the construction of phonology. In C. A. Ferguson, L. Menn, & C. Stoel-Gammon (eds), *Phonological development: Models, research, implications*, pp. 393–422. Timonium, MD: York Press.

Vihman, M. M., Macken, M. A., Miller, R., Simmons, H., & Miller, J. (1985). From babbling to speech: A re-assessment of the continuity issue. *Language*, **61**, 397–445.

de Vries, J. P. P., Visser, G. H. A., & Prechtl, H. F. R. (1985). The emergence of fetal behaviour. II. Quantitative aspects. *Early Human Development*, **12**, 99–120.

Vygotsky, L. S. (1962). *Thought and language* (E. Hanfmann & G. Vacar, Trans.). Cambridge, MA: MIT Press.

Vygotsky, L. S. (1962). *Thought and language*. (E. Hanfmann & G. Vakar, Trans.). Cambridge: MIT Press.

Vygotsky, L. S. (1962). *Thought and language*. Cambridge, MA: Massachusetts Institute of Technology Press.

Vygotsky, L. S. (1967). Play and its role in the mental development of the child. *Soviet Psychology*, **12**, 62–76.

Vygotsky, L. (1978). *Mind in society*. Cambridge, MA: Harvard University Press.

Waddington, C. H. (1971). Concepts of development. In E. Tobach, L. Aronson & E. Shaw (eds), *The biopsychology of development*, pp. 17–23. San Diego, CA: Academic Press.

Walden, T. & Baxter, A. (1989). The effect of context and age on social referencing. *Child Development*, **60**, 1511–1518.

Walker-Andrews, A. S. (1986). Intermodal perception of expressive behaviors: Relation of eye and voice? *Developmental Psychology*, **22**, 373–377.

Wallace, D. B., Franklin, M. B., & Keegan, R. T. (1994). *The observing eye: a century of baby diaries.*

Wallach, M. A. & Wallach, L. (1976). *Teaching all children to read*. Chicago: University of Chicago Press.

Walton, G. E. & Bower, T. G. (1993). Newborns form 'prototypes' in less than 1 minute. *Psychological Science*, **4**, 203–205.

Walton, G. E., Bower, N. J. A., & Bower, T. G. R. (1992). Recognition of familiar faces by newborns. *Infant Behavior and Development*, **15**, 265–269.

Walton, G. E., Armstrong, E., & Bower, T. G. R. (1997). Faces as forms in the world of the newborn. *Infant Behavior and Development*, **20**, 537–543.

Walton, G. E., Armstrong, E., & Bower, T. G. R. (1998). Newborns learn to identify a face in eight-tenths of a second. *Developmental Science*, **1**, 79–84.

Ward, C. D., Phillips, P. M., & Cooper, R. P. (1998). *Lack of preference for the paternal face in four-month-olds*. Poster presented at the biennial meeting of the International Conference of Infant Studies, Atlanta, GA.

Wasik, B. H., Ramey, C. T., Bryant, D. M., & Sparling, J. J. (1990). A longitudinal study of two early intervention strategies. Project CARE. *Child Development*, **61**, 1682–1696.

Waxman, S. R. & Markow, D. B. (1995). Words as invitations to form categories: Evidence from 12- to 13-month-old infants. *Cognitive Psychology*, **29**, 257–302.

van de Weijer, J. (1998). *Language input for word discovery*. Unpublished PhD, University of Nijmegen, Nijmegen.

Weikart, D. P., Bond, J. T., & McNeil, J. T. (1978). The Ypsilanti Perry Preschool Project: Preschool years and longitudinal results through fourth grade. *Monographs of the High/Scope.*

Weinberg, M. K. & Tronick, E. Z. (1996). Infant affective reactions to the resumption of maternal interaction after the still-face. *Child Development*, **67**, 905–914.

Weiss, H. (1988). Family support and education programs: Working through ecological theories of human development. In H. Weiss & F. Jacobs (eds), *Evaluating family programs*, pp. 33–36. Hawthorne, NY: Aldine de Gruyter.

Weiss, P. (1939). *Principles of development*. New York: Henry Holt.

Wellman, H. M. (1990). *The child's theory of mind*. Cambridge, MA: MIT Press.

Wellman, H. M., Cross, D., & Watson, J. (2001). Meta-analysis of theory-of-mind development: The truth about false belief. *Child Development*, 72(3), 655–684.

Werker, J. F. (1989). Becoming a native listener. *American Scientist, 77*, 54–59.

Werker, J. F. (1991). The ontogeny of speech perception. In I. G. Mattingly & M. Studdert-Kennedy (eds), *Modularity and the motor theory of speech perception*, pp. 91–109. Hillsdale, NJ: Erlbaum.

Werker, J. F. & McLeod, P. J. (1990). Infant preference for both male and female infant-directed-talk: A developmental study of attentional and affective responsiveness. *Canadian Journal of Psychology*, **43**, 230–246.

Werker, J. F. & Tees, R. C. (1984). Cross-language speech perception: Evidence for perceptual reorganization during the first year of life. *Infant Behavior and Development*, 7, 49–63.

Wertheimer, M. (1961). Psychomotor coordination of auditory and visual space at birth. *Science*, **134**, 1692.

White, K. R. & Boyce, G. C. (eds). (1993). Comparative evaluations of early intervention alternatives [Special issue]. *Early Educational Development*, **4**.

Whiting, B. B. & Whiting, J. W. M. (1975). *Children of six cultures: A psychocultural analysis*. Cambridge, MA: Harvard University Press.

Williams, L. (1977). *The effects of phonetic environment and stress placement on infant discrimination of place of stop consonant articulation*. Paper presented at the Second Boston University Conference on Language Development, Boston, MA.

Wilson, N. & Tolson, S. H. (1983). An analysis of adult-child interaction patterns in three generational black families. Paper presented at the Society for Research in Child Development Symposium on Grandparents and Very Young Children.

Wimmer, H. & Perner, J. (1983). Beliefs about beliefs: Representation and constraining function of wrong beliefs in young children's understanding of deception. *Cognition*, **13**, 103–128.

Winnicott, D. W. (1959). Classification: Is there a psycho-analytic contribution to psychiatric classification. *The maturational process and the facilitating environment*. New York: International University Press.

Winnicott, D. W. (1977). *The piggle*. New York: International Universities Press, Inc.

Wishart, J. G. & Bower, T. G. R. (1984). A normative study of the development of the object concept. In C. Rovee-Collier & L. Lipsitt (eds), *Advances in Infancy Research*, **3**, pp. 57–123. Norwood, NJ: Ablex.

Wittgenstein, L. (1953). *Philosophical investigations* (G. E. M. Anscombe, Trans.). Oxford: Blackwell.

Wolf, C. M. (1996). The development of behavioral response to pain in the human newborn. *Dissertation-Abstracts-International: Section B: The Sciences and Engineering*, **57**, 1472.

Wolf, S. & Wolff, H. G. (1947). *Human gastric function*. New York: Oxford University Press.

Wolff, P. H. (1987). *The development of behavioral states and the expression of emotions in early infancy.* Chicago: University of Chicago Press.

Woodward, A. L. (1998). Infants selectively encode the goal of an actor's reach. *Cognition,* **69**, 1–34.

Wynn, K. (1992). Evidence against empiricist accounts of the origins of numerical knowledge. *Mind and Language,* **7**, 315–332.

Wynn, K. (1995). Infants possess a system of numerical knowledge. *Current Directions in Psychological Science,* **4**, 172–177.

Yarrow, L. J. (1961). Maternal deprivation: Toward an empirical and conceptual re-evaluation. *Psychological Bulletin,* **58**, 459–490.

Yarrow, L. J., MacTurk, R. H., Vietze, P. M., McCarthy, M. E., Klein, R. P., & McQuiston, S. (1984). Developmental course of parental stimulation and its relationship to mastery motivation during infancy. *Developmental Psychology,* **20**, 492–503.

Yonas, A., Pettersen, L., & Lockman, J. J. (1979). Young infants' sensitivity to optical information for collision. *Canadian Journal of Psychology,* **33**, 268–276.

Youngblade, L. M. & Dunn, J. (1995). Individual differences in young children's pretend play with mother and sibling: links to relationships and understanding of other people's feelings and beliefs. *Child Development,* **66**, 1472–1492.

Younger, B. A., & Fearing, D. D. (1999). Parsing items into separate categories: Developmental change in infant categorization. *Child Development,* **70**, 291–303.

Zaslow, M., Tout, K., Smith, S., & Moore, K. (1998). Implications of the 1996 welfare legislation for children: A research perspective. *Social Policy Report, Society for Research in Child Development,* **12**(3).

Zebrowitz-McArthur, L. (1982). Judging a book by its cover: A cognitive analysis of the relationship between physical appearance and stereotyping. In A. H. Hastorf & A. M. Isen (eds), *Cognitive social psychology,* pp. 149–209. New York: Elsevier.

Zedlewski, S. R. (2000). Family economic well-being: Findings from the National Survey of America's Families. *Snapshots of America's families II: A view of the nation and 13 states from the National Survey of America's families.* Washington, DC: Urban Institute.

Zigler, E. F. (1967). Familial mental retardation: A continuing dilemma. *Science,* **155**, 292–298.

Zuckerman, B. & Kahn, R. (2000). Pathways to early child health and development. In S. Danziger & J. Waldfogel (eds), *Securing the future: Investing in children from birth to college,* pp. 87–121. New York: Russell Sage Foundation.

Index